QUANTITATIVE METHODS FOR BUSINESS AND ECONOMICS

QUANTITATIVE METHODS FOR BUSINESS AND ECONOMICS

ADIL H. MOUHAMMED
UNIVERSITY OF ILLINOIS
At SPRINGFIELD

M.E.Sharpe
Armonk, New York
London, England

Library of Congress Cataloging-in-Publication Data

Mouhammed, Adil Hasan.
    Quantitative methods for business and economics / Adil Mouhammed.
    p.   cm.
    Includes bibliographical references and index.
    ISBN 0-7656-0458-2 (alk. paper)
    1. Economics, Mathematical.   I. Title.
HD 135.M68   1999
330'.01'51—dc21   99-28683
                                                          CIP

Printed in the United States of America

Contents

Preface

The basic objective behind the writing of this book is to provide both students and individuals with a simple and rigorous introduction to various quantitative methods used in business and economics. It is a simple text because it does not need prerequisites other than high school algebra; it is rigorous because it is built on mathematical sophistication. In addition, the length of the text is relatively short so it can be used over one semester.

The book starts with matrix algebra. Chapter 1 describes the three methods for solving a system of equations and linear independence of vectors. Applications to macroeconomics and market models are provided, and the models are solved by the three methods of solution. In chapter 2 derivatives and their applications to economic theory are provided. For example, derivatives are applied to various economic models such as profit maximization, cost minimization, elasticities, derivation of demand and supply curves, derivation of compensated demand curve, producer and consumer equilibrium, and so forth. In chapter 3, using the matrix theory of chapter 1, the input-output model is outlined. Types I and II employment and income multipliers as well as sectoral prices are derived from the input-output model. The effects of incoming and outgoing industries are explained, and the total backward and forward linkages are measured.

In Chapter 4 the topic of optimization theory is introduced. Students will be able to maximize and minimize functions of one variable and several variables. Economic applications of cost and profit maximization are also provided. Constrained optimization is also furnished in this chapter. Economic and business applications of this type of optimization are provided to problems such as the derivation of demand curves from utility function, the derivation of factor demand curves from the production function and cost function, and the derivation of compensated demand curves from expenditure function. Chapter 5 introduces the inventory model, which is an application of optimization theory to business decision. Economic order quantity, optimal quantity, and planned shortage problems are provided, along with various examples. Chapter 6 is devoted to the dynamic techniques used in business and economics. Integration, definite and indefinite, is introduced along with its application to various economic and business problems such as consumer and producer surplus and the present value of a financial sum. In addition, first- and second-order linear difference equations are introduced, with several economic applications such as the Domar and Harrod models of economic growth and the Cobweb price model. Similarly, the first- and second-order differential equations are introduced with various economic applications.

Chapters 7 and 8 introduce the topic of linear programming. In chapter 7 the formulation of linear programming problems and the graphical solution are provided. Also, the simplex method is described and used for solving maximization and minimization problems. Various problems with the simplex method are analyzed in the chapter. Chapter 8 is devoted to sensitivity analysis, range analysis, and duality. An appendix in this chapter tackles issues such as free variable, dual-simplex method, two-phase method of solution, and other issues.

In chapter 9 decision theory is analyzed in depth. Decision making under both certainty and risk is explained by using various criteria. Also, decision making under prior and posterior information is determined by using prior and Bayesian probabilities. Decision making under conflict is explained in chapter 10, which is devoted to game theory. Zero- and nonzero-sum games are analyzed, and methods of solution are provided. Also, the prisoner's dilemma is explained in this chapter. Chapter 11 is devoted to the analysis of Markov chains. States, stages, and transitional probabilities are presented. Once these concepts are understood, the chapter explains the steady-state probabilities and the absorbing and nonabsorbing states. In addition, the fundamental matrix and some business applications are provided.

Chapter 12 introduces the general linear model. This chapter can be considered as an introductory foundation to econometrics. The general linear model is used to measure economic relationships and test economic propositions. Estimation and hypothesis testing are provided as well as the coefficient of determination, R^2, and the adjusted R^{-2}. In addition, forecasting and confidence intervals for the predicted values are furnished. Various business and economic applications are provided at the end of the chapter.

As can be seen, this text will not only provide users with knowledge in mathematical analysis and its application to business and economics, but students will also understand several quantitative models such as inventory analysis, input-output model, decision theory, Markov chains, and so forth. Put differently, I have attempted to provide readers with the basic techniques they can utilize in solving real-world problems. Also, my aim is to have readers interested in quantitative methods establish an excellent background to go further in acquiring more knowledge in this field.

This book can be used as an introductory text in quantitative methods for junior and senior students, and can also serve as a reference book—do it your own way—for MBA students who lack a solid background in quantitative techniques. In addition, the text is very helpful for a course in managerial economics, where students need to know topics such as differentiation with applications to business and economics, optimization, linear programming, regression analysis, and decision theory.

Springfield, Illinois
Fall 1999

Acknowledgments

In writing *Quantitative Methods for Business and Economics*, I am indebted to various individuals. First, I thank the previous dean of the School of Business and Management, Sangamon State University, John Nosari, for giving me release time necessary to finish the writing of the text. Given the various courses I teach each academic year, that release time was important, for without it I could not have completed the book. Also, I have been using some chapters of this book in a course entitled "Quantitative Methods for Business and Economics" since 1990. I have received very important feedback from the students who took that course. In addition, my children, Mouhammed and Hayder, have helped me in shaping the book into its final form. Moreover, I received some typing support from Marilynn Mooney secretary in the Department of Economics at the University of Illinois at Springfield. Finally, I appreciate the help and encouragement I received from my wife, Majda Salman, and some of my colleagues at the University of Illinois at Springfield, in particular David Olson, Leonard Branson, and Bonnie Moe of the Department of Accountancy. Any errors are mine.

CHAPTER ONE

Vectors and Matrices

Vectors and matrices are very important tools in economic analysis. This chapter outlines the algebra of vectors. Students will not only be able to add and subtract vectors but also to multiply vectors. For economic modeling, linear independence is indispensable in that economic models must have unique solutions, and linear independence provides these solutions. Similarly, linear and convex combinations are also important for economics.

An extension of vector analysis is matrix algebra. The types of matrices and matrix operations are outlined in this chapter. A system of equations is solved by using matrix methods such as the inverse method, Cramer's rule and the Gauss-Jordan method. Eigenvalues and vectors are explained and used for diagonalizing matrices. Finally, various economic applications of matrices are provided.

Vectors

A vector is a symbol used to refer to a set of variables or coefficients. For example,

$$\mathbf{Y} = (y_1, y_2, y_3, ..., y_n),$$

where $\mathbf{Y}$ is used to represent n-variables. Vector $\mathbf{A}$ can be represented by

$$\mathbf{A} = (a_1, a_2, a_3, ..., a_n),$$

where $\mathbf{A}$ contains a set of coefficients denoted by a's. Also, vector $\mathbf{Y}$ can also be a set of real integer numbers such as $\mathbf{Y} = (3, 4, 6, 8)$.

Vector $\mathbf{Y}$ has a dimension as well. The dimension of a vector is the total number of elements (components) in that vector. For example, the above vector, $\mathbf{Y}$, has four components and hence it is said to be of dimension four. Very compactly, a vector such as $\mathbf{Y}$, where $\mathbf{Y} = (5, 6, 7)$, has one row and three columns. Accordingly, it is said to be a vector of dimension 1 by 3 or $\mathbf{Y}_{1 \times 3}$ or $\mathbf{Y}_{1\,3}$, where 1 and 3 indicate number of rows and columns, respectively. In general, $\mathbf{Y}_{m \times n}$ is said to be a vector of dimension m x n: with m rows and n columns.

Example:

$$\mathbf{A} = (3 \quad 3), \quad \mathbf{B} = (5 \quad 6 \quad 7), \quad \mathbf{C} = \begin{bmatrix} 4 \\ 6 \\ 7 \end{bmatrix}$$

All these vectors have different dimensions: **A** is 1 x 2, **B** is 1 x 3, and **A** is 3 x 1. Vectors **A** and **B** are called row vectors, whereas vector **C** is a column vector.

The Transpose of a Vector

The transpose of a vector is a process by which a row vector is converted into a column vector or vice versa (Hadley 1973). The transposition of a vector is denoted by t.

Example: $\mathbf{A}^t$ for $\mathbf{A} = (3 \quad 4 \quad 5)$ and $\mathbf{B}^t$ for $\mathbf{B} = \begin{bmatrix} 4 \\ 5 \\ 7 \end{bmatrix}$ are

$$\mathbf{A}^t = \begin{bmatrix} 3 \\ 4 \\ 5 \end{bmatrix} \text{ and } \mathbf{B}^t = (4 \quad 5 \quad 7).$$

Algebra of Vectors

In vector analysis there are some algebraic operations such as vector addition, subtraction, and multiplication (Hadley 1973; Chiang 1984; Kolman 1980).

Addition and Subtraction of Vectors

Vectors can be added or subtracted if they have the same dimensions. In these operations the corresponding elements are added or subtracted.

Example 1: Find $\mathbf{C} = \mathbf{A} - \mathbf{B}$ and $\mathbf{C} = \mathbf{A} + \mathbf{B}$ for $\mathbf{A} = (4 \quad 7 \quad 8)$ and $\mathbf{B} = (6 \quad 9 \quad 3)$.
Solution $\mathbf{C} = \mathbf{A} - \mathbf{B} = (4\text{-}6 \quad 7\text{-}9 \quad 8\text{-}3) = (\text{-}2 \quad \text{-}2 \quad 5).$
$\mathbf{C} = \mathbf{A} + \mathbf{B} = (4\text{+}6 \quad 7\text{+}9 \quad 8\text{+}3) = (10 \quad 16 \quad 11).$

Example 2: Find $\mathbf{C} = \mathbf{A} + \mathbf{B}$ and $\mathbf{C} = \mathbf{B} + \mathbf{A}$ for $\mathbf{A} = \begin{bmatrix} 11 \\ 7 \\ 13 \end{bmatrix}$ and $\mathbf{B} = \begin{bmatrix} 14 \\ 10 \\ 81 \end{bmatrix}$.

Solution: $C = A + B = \begin{bmatrix} 11 \\ 7 \\ 13 \end{bmatrix} + \begin{bmatrix} 14 \\ 10 \\ 81 \end{bmatrix} = \begin{bmatrix} 25 \\ 17 \\ 94 \end{bmatrix}$ and $C = B + A = \begin{bmatrix} 25 \\ 17 \\ 94 \end{bmatrix}$.

Example 3: Find $C = A - B$ for $A = (3\ 5\ 7)$, $B = \begin{bmatrix} 3 \\ 0 \\ 9 \end{bmatrix}$. These vectors cannot be

added or subtracted because they have different dimensions. But one can find

$C = A - B^t$ and $C = A^t - B$. That is, $C = A - B^t = (3\text{-}3\ \ 5\text{-}0\ \ 7\text{-}9) = (0\ \ \ 5\ \ \text{-}2)$,

and

$$C = A^t - B = \begin{bmatrix} 3 \\ 5 \\ 7 \end{bmatrix} - \begin{bmatrix} 3 \\ 0 \\ 9 \end{bmatrix} = \begin{bmatrix} 0 \\ 5 \\ -2 \end{bmatrix}.$$

Multiplication of Vectors

Multiplication by Scalar. A scalar is a constant or a coefficient. If a scalar is multiplied by a column or a row vector, the scalar must be multiplied by each component of that vector. For example, if a is a scalar equal to 5 and B is a row vector equal to (3 5 9), then aB is equal to 5 (3 5 9) = (15 25 45).

Example 1: Let b be a scalar equal to -2 and X be a vector equal to $X = \begin{bmatrix} -2 \\ 3 \\ 4 \end{bmatrix}$,

then $bX = (-2)X = (-2) \begin{bmatrix} -2 \\ 3 \\ 4 \end{bmatrix} = \begin{bmatrix} 4 \\ -6 \\ -8 \end{bmatrix}$.

Multiplication by Vectors. Vectors can be multiplied if the number of columns in the first vector (n) is equal to the number of rows in the second vector (m). In other words, $A_{m \times n} B_{n \times k} = C_{m \times k}$. That is, the dimension of the new vector C is equal to m x k, where m and k are number of rows of the first vector and number of columns of the second vector, respectively.

Example 1: Given $A_{1 \times 2} = (3\ \ 2)$ and $B_{2 \times 1} = \begin{bmatrix} 4 \\ 5 \end{bmatrix}$, find **AB** (or **A x B**) and **BA**.

Solution: To implement this operation we multiply the first row of vector **A** by the first column of vector **B** and sum the multiplication. That is,

$$\mathbf{AB} = 3 \times 4 + 2 \times 5 = 12 + 10 = 22.$$

This type of multiplication **AB** is usually called scalar or dot product. For **BA**,

$$\mathbf{BA} = \begin{bmatrix} 4 \\ 5 \end{bmatrix} (3 \quad 2) = \begin{bmatrix} 12 & 8 \\ 15 & 10 \end{bmatrix},\text{ which is a matrix of dimension 2 x 2.}$$

Example 2: Given $\mathbf{A}_{3 \times 1} = \begin{bmatrix} 4 \\ 3 \\ 6 \end{bmatrix}$ and $\mathbf{B}_{1 \times 3} = (2 \quad 5 \quad 8)$, find **AB** and **BA**

Solution:

$$\mathbf{A}_{3 \times 1}\,\mathbf{B}_{1 \times 3} = \mathbf{C}_{3 \times 3} = \begin{bmatrix} 4\times 2 & 4\times 5 & 4\times 8 \\ 3\times 2 & 3\times 5 & 3\times 8 \\ 6\times 2 & 6\times 5 & 6\times 8 \end{bmatrix} = \begin{bmatrix} 8 & 20 & 32 \\ 6 & 15 & 24 \\ 12 & 30 & 48 \end{bmatrix}.$$

C is a 3 x 3 matrix. For **BA**,

$$\mathbf{BA} = (2 \quad 5 \quad 8) \begin{bmatrix} 4 \\ 3 \\ 6 \end{bmatrix} = 71.$$

Example 3: Find $\mathbf{AB} = \mathbf{C}$ for $\mathbf{A}_{1 \times 2} = (3 \quad 5)$ and $\mathbf{B}_{1 \times 2} = (0 \quad 4)$. This multiplication cannot be performed because the number of columns in the first vector is two, which is not equal to the number of rows in the second vector, which is one.

Geometric Representation of Vectors

Vectors of two and three dimensions can be graphed. For example, vectors **A** = (3 4) and **B** = (2 -5) can be graphed by taking **X** equals 3 and 2 (the first elements of vectors **A** and **B**, respectively) and **Y** equals 4 and -5 (the second elements of vectors **A** and **B**, respectively). This can be shown as follows:

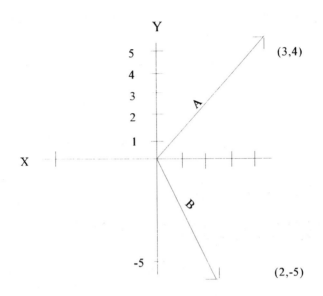

Some Types of Vectors

1. A Zero Vector: This is a row or a column vector whose elements are zero. For example,

$$A = (0 \ 0 \ 0).$$

2. A Sum Vector: This is a row or a column vector whose elements are ones. For example,

$$A = (1 \ 1 \ 1 \ 1).$$

3. A Unit Vector: This is a row or a column vector whose first element is one and the remainders are zeros, or the second element is one and the rest are zeros and so on. For example, $A = (1 \ 0 \ 0 \ 0)$, $B = (0 \ 1 \ 0 \ 0)$, $C = (0 \ 0 \ 1 \ 0)$, and $Y = (0 \ 0 \ 0 \ 1)$.

4. An Orthogonal Vector: Vectors **A** and **B** are said to be orthogonal if $\mathbf{A'B} = 0$.

Example 1: $\mathbf{A'} = (3 \quad 2 \quad 1)$ and $\mathbf{B} = \begin{bmatrix} 1 \\ -1 \\ -1 \end{bmatrix}$, $\mathbf{A'B} = [(3 \times 1 + 2 \times (-1) + 1(-1)] = 0$

Example 2: $\mathbf{A'} = (4 \quad -1)$ and $\mathbf{B} = \begin{bmatrix} 1 \\ 4 \end{bmatrix}$, then $\mathbf{A'B} = (4 \quad -1)\begin{bmatrix} 1 \\ 4 \end{bmatrix} = 0$.

Length (Magnitude) of Vectors

The length of vector **A**, written as I**A**I, is the distance from the origin to **A**. The length can be calculated as follows:

$$IAI = (A^tA)^{1/2}$$

Example 1. Find the length of $\mathbf{A'} = (3 \quad 2 \quad 1)$.

Solution: $\mathbf{A'A} = (3 \quad 2 \quad 1)\begin{bmatrix} 3 \\ 2 \\ 1 \end{bmatrix} = (9 + 4 + 1) = 14$ and $(14)^{1/2}$ is 3.74.

Distance

The distance between vectors **A** and **B**, written as I**A** - **B**I, can be found by using the formula

$$IA - BI = [(A-B)^t (A-B)]^{1/2}.$$

Example 1: Find the distance between $\mathbf{A} = \begin{bmatrix} 6 \\ 4 \end{bmatrix}$ and $\mathbf{B} = \begin{bmatrix} 3 \\ 2 \end{bmatrix}$.

Solution: $(\mathbf{A} - \mathbf{B}) = \begin{bmatrix} 6 - 3 \\ 4 - 2 \end{bmatrix} = \begin{bmatrix} 3 \\ 2 \end{bmatrix}$ and $(\mathbf{A} - \mathbf{B})^t = (3 \quad 2)$. Therefore,

$$(A - B)^t (A - B) = (3 \quad 2) \begin{bmatrix} 3 \\ 2 \end{bmatrix} = 13, \text{ and } |A - B| = [13]^{1/2} = 3.61.$$

Linear Combination of Vectors

Vector B can be written as a linear combination of vectors A_i, where $i = 1, 2, ..., n$. That is,

$$B = \sum_{i}^{n} a_i A_i, \text{ where } i = 1, 2, ..., n.$$

Example 1: Write vector $B = \begin{bmatrix} 9 \\ 16 \end{bmatrix}$ as a linear combination of A_1 and A_2, where

$A_1 = \begin{bmatrix} 1 \\ 3 \end{bmatrix}$ and $A_2 = \begin{bmatrix} 2 \\ 5 \end{bmatrix}$. This can be done by using the formula

$$B = a_1 A_1 + a_2 A_2, \text{ or}$$

$$\begin{bmatrix} 9 \\ 16 \end{bmatrix} = a_1 \begin{bmatrix} 1 \\ 3 \end{bmatrix} + a_2 \begin{bmatrix} 2 \\ 5 \end{bmatrix}.$$

These are two equations that can be written as,

$$9 = 1a_1 + 2a_2$$

$$16 = 3a_1 + 5a_2.$$

Solving these equations for a_1 and a_2 yields $a_1 = -13$ and $a_2 = 11$. Inserting these values in the formula, we obtain

$$B = -13A_1 + 11A_2,$$

which is the required linear combination.

Example 2: Write the vector $B = (1 \ -2 \ 5)$ as a linear combination of vectors A_1,

A_2, and A_3, where $A_1 = (1 \ \ 1 \ \ 1)$, $A_2 = (1 \ \ 2 \ \ 3)$ and $A_3 = (2 \ \ -1 \ \ 1)$.

Solution: This combination can be written as

$$B = a_1 A_1 + a_2 A_2 + a_3 A_3.$$

This equation represents a system of three equations:

$$1 = a_1 + a_2 + 2a_3$$

$$-2 = a_1 + 2a_2 - a_3$$

$$5 = a_1 + 3a_2 + a_3.$$

Solving for a's yields $a_1 = -6$, $a_2 = 3$, and $a_3 = 2$, thus

$$B = -6A_1 + 3A_2 + 2A_3.$$

Finally, if the sum of the coefficients a_i, where $i = 1, ..., n$, is equal to one, the combination is called a *convex linear combination of vectors*.

For example, if $a_1 = 0.5$, then $a_2 = 1 - 0.5 = 0.5$. If $A_1 = \begin{bmatrix} 3 \\ 5 \end{bmatrix}$ and $A_2 = \begin{bmatrix} 4 \\ 2 \end{bmatrix}$,

then $A_3 = a_1 A_1 + a_2 A_2$, which is equal to

$$A_3 = (0.5) \begin{bmatrix} 3 \\ 5 \end{bmatrix} + (0.5) \begin{bmatrix} 4 \\ 2 \end{bmatrix} = \begin{bmatrix} 1.5 \\ 2.5 \end{bmatrix} + \begin{bmatrix} 2 \\ 1 \end{bmatrix} = \begin{bmatrix} 3.5 \\ 3.5 \end{bmatrix}.$$

And students can graph vector A_3 to see what this combination means.

Linear Independence of Vectors

A set of vectors $a_i A_i$ ($i = 1, 2, ..., n$), where a_i is a set of coefficients, is said to be linearly independent if ($a_i A_i = 0$) for all a_i equal to zero; otherwise, the set of vectors A_i is said to be linearly dependent (Lipschutz 1968).
Example 1: Suppose vectors A_1 and A_2 are equal to

$$A_1 = (2 \ \ 1)$$

$$A_2 = (3 \ \ 5).$$

Show whether A_1 and A_2 are linearly independent vectors. To do so, write the two vectors as a system of two equations:

$$a_1 A_1 + a_2 A_2 = 0, \text{ or}$$

$$2a_1 + 3a_2 = 0 \tag{1}$$

$$1a_1 + 5a_2 = 0. \tag{2}$$

From equation (1) we obtain $2a_1 = -3a_2$ or $a_1 = 1.5a_2$. Using this solution in equation (2) yields $1.5\ a_2 + 5\ a_2 = 0$ or $a_2 = 0$ and thus $a_1 = 0$. Therefore, the two vectors are linearly independent.

Example 2: Show whether $A_1 = (5\ 2)$ and $A_2 = (10\ 4)$ are linearly independent vectors. To do so, write the two vectors as a system of two equations:

$$a_1\ A_1 + a_2\ A_2 = 0, \text{ or}$$

$$5a_1 + 10a_2 = 0 \tag{3}$$

$$2a_1 + 4\ a_2 = 0 \tag{4}$$

From equation (3) we obtain $a_1 = -2a_2$. Using this solution in equation (4) yields,

$$-4a_2 + 4a_2 = 0;$$

thus, $a_1 = -2a_2$ and hence the two vectors are linearly dependent, because a_1 is not equal to zero.

The Concept of a Basis

A set S of vectors can be a basis if it is linearly independent and can generate the space (i.e., any other vector can be written as a linear combination of the set S).

Example 1: Show whether the set of vectors $S = (A_1, A_2)$, where $A_1 = (2\ 3)$ and $A_2 = (1\ 5)$, is a basis for R^2.

First, vectors A_1 and A_2 are linearly independent, as was shown previously, because $a_1 = a_2 = 0$. Second, to show that A_1 and A_2 span (generate) the space, we let $A_3 = (2\ 9)$ be any vector in R^2. We now seek constants b_1 and b_2 such that

$$b_1 A_1 + b_2 A_2 = A_3, \text{ or}$$

$$2b_1 + 1b_2 = 2$$

$$3b_1 + 5b_2 = 9.$$

Solving for b_1 and b_2 yields, $b_1 = 1/7$ and $b_2 = 12/7$, and

$$\mathbf{A}_3 = 1/7\mathbf{A}_1 + 12/7\mathbf{A}_2.$$

Hence, the set of vectors generates the space and is a basis for $\mathbf{R}^2$.

Example 2: Show that the set of vectors $\mathbf{S} = [\mathbf{A}_1, \mathbf{A}_2, \mathbf{A}_3]$, where $\mathbf{A}_1 = (1 \ 0 \ 1)$, $\mathbf{A}_2 = (0 \ 1 \ -1)$, $\mathbf{A}_3 = (0 \ 2 \ 2)$, is a basis for $\mathbf{R}^3$.
  First, to show that $\mathbf{S}$ is linearly independent, we form the equation

$$a_1\mathbf{A}_1 + a_2\mathbf{A}_2 + a_3\mathbf{A}_3 = \mathbf{0}.$$

Substituting for $\mathbf{A}_1$, $\mathbf{A}_2$, and $\mathbf{A}_3$ in the equation, we obtain
$$a_1 = 0$$
$$a_2 + 2a_3 = 0$$
$$-a_2 + 2a_3 = 0.$$

Solving for a's we obtain the solution $a_1 = a_2 = a_3 = 0$, a solution showing that $\mathbf{S}$ is a linearly independent set.
  Second, to show that $\mathbf{S}$ spans the space, we let $\mathbf{A}_4 = (3 \ 5 \ 7)$ be any vector in $\mathbf{R}^3$. We now seek constants b_1, b_2, and b_3, such that $\mathbf{A}_4$ can be written as a linear combination of $\mathbf{S}$. This is shown as

$$b_1\mathbf{A}_1 + b_2\mathbf{A}_2 + b_3\mathbf{A}_3 = \mathbf{A}_4,$$

substituting for the vectors $\mathbf{A}_1$, $\mathbf{A}_2$, $\mathbf{A}_3$, and $\mathbf{A}_4$, and solving for b's. Because there is a solution for b's, the set of vectors $\mathbf{S}$ does span the space; consequently, it is a basis.

Matrices

A matrix is defined as a collection of rows and columns, and is denoted by $\mathbf{A}$ or $\mathbf{B}$ or any convenient letter (Perlis 1952). For example,

$$\mathbf{A} = \begin{bmatrix} a_{11} & a_{21} & \cdots & a_{1n} \\ a_{21} & a_{22} & \cdots & a_{2n} \\ \cdots & \cdots & \cdots & \cdots \\ a_{m1} & a_{m2} & \cdots & a_{mn} \end{bmatrix}$$

Matrix **A** has m rows and n columns (i.e., it is of dimension m x n). Another example of a matrix is matrix **B**, which can be written as

$$\mathbf{B} = \begin{bmatrix} 3 & 5 & 6 & 9 \\ 0 & 11 & 13 & 8 \\ 6 & 8 & 3 & 4 \end{bmatrix}.$$

Matrix **B** has three rows and four columns. In general, matrix $\mathbf{A}_{m \times n}$ is a matrix having m rows and n columns. And the numbers of rows and columns in any matrix indicate the dimension of that matrix. For example, matrix **B** is of dimension 3 x 4.

Algebra of Matrices

The operations of addition, subtraction, and multiplication of matrices can be performed if some conditions are met (Aitken 1948).

Addition and Subtraction of Matrices

Two matrices **A** and **B** can be added or subtracted if the two matrices have the same dimension. This can be done by adding or subtracting the corresponding elements. For example, if **A** and **B** are

$$\mathbf{A} = \begin{bmatrix} 5 & 3 & 4 \\ 3 & -2 & 3 \\ 2 & 3 & 2 \end{bmatrix} \text{ and } \mathbf{B} = \begin{bmatrix} 10 & 4 & 3 \\ 11 & 6 & 2 \\ 9 & 7 & 0 \end{bmatrix},$$

then **A** + **B** and **A** - **B** would be

$$\mathbf{A} + \mathbf{B} = \begin{bmatrix} 5+10 & 0+4 & 4+3 \\ 3+11 & -2+6 & 3+2 \\ 2+9 & 3+7 & 2+0 \end{bmatrix} = \begin{bmatrix} 15 & 4 & 7 \\ 14 & 4 & 5 \\ 11 & 10 & 2 \end{bmatrix}$$

$$\mathbf{A} - \mathbf{B} = \begin{bmatrix} 5-10 & 0-4 & 4-3 \\ 3-11 & -2-6 & 3-2 \\ 2-9 & 3-7 & 2-0 \end{bmatrix}. \text{ And } \mathbf{B} + \mathbf{A} = \mathbf{A} + \mathbf{B}$$

Example 1: Find **A** + **B** and **A** - **B** for

$$\mathbf{A} = \begin{vmatrix} 3 & 2 \\ 4 & 6 \\ 4 & 8 \end{vmatrix} \text{ and } \mathbf{B} = \begin{vmatrix} 3 & 5 & 6 \\ 2 & 0 & 7 \\ 5 & 3 & 2 \end{vmatrix}.$$

These matrices cannot be added or subtracted because they have different dimensions: **A** is 3 x 2 and **B** is 3 x 3.

Matrix Multiplications

There are two types of matrix multiplication: multiplication by a scalar and multiplication by a matrix.

Scalar Multiplication. In this type of multiplication we multiply the scalar by each element of the given matrix.

Example 1: Find a**B**, where (a) is (5) and **B** is equal to

$$\mathbf{B} = \begin{vmatrix} 3 & 4 & 0 \\ 1 & 2 & 5 \\ 3 & 4 & 1 \end{vmatrix}. \text{ Hence, a}\mathbf{B} = (5)\begin{vmatrix} 3 & 4 & 0 \\ 1 & 2 & 5 \\ 3 & 4 & 1 \end{vmatrix} = \begin{vmatrix} 15 & 20 & 0 \\ 5 & 10 & 25 \\ 15 & 20 & 5 \end{vmatrix}.$$

Example 2: Find a**A** where (a) is a scalar and

$$\mathbf{A} = \begin{vmatrix} 3 & 8 & 7 \\ 0 & 4 & 9 \\ 1 & 1 & 2 \end{vmatrix}. \text{ Hence , a}\mathbf{A} = \begin{vmatrix} 3a & 8a & 7a \\ 0 & 4a & 9a \\ a & a & 2a \end{vmatrix}.$$

Multiplication by a Matrix. Multiplication by a matrix can be performed if the number of columns in the first matrix is equal to the number of rows in the second matrix. In this type of multiplication, we always multiply each row of the first matrix by each column of the second matrix and sum the resulting outcome.

Example 1: Find **C** = **AB** and **C** = **BA** for **A** = (2 3) and **B** = $\begin{vmatrix} 4 & 6 \\ 5 & 7 \end{vmatrix}$.

AB = **C** = (2 x 4 + 3 x 5   2 x 6 + 3 x 7) = (23 33), but **C** = **BA** is not defined (why?).

Example 2: Find $C = AB$ for $A = \begin{bmatrix} 3 & 0 \\ 4 & 1 \end{bmatrix}$ and $B = \begin{bmatrix} 3 & 3 & 1 \\ 0 & 5 & 6 \end{bmatrix}$.

Since A is 2 x 2 and B is 2 x 3, C must be 2 x 3. That is,

$$C = AB = \begin{bmatrix} 3 & 0 \\ 4 & 1 \end{bmatrix} \times \begin{bmatrix} 3 & 3 & 1 \\ 0 & 5 & 6 \end{bmatrix} = \begin{bmatrix} 3x3+0x0 & 3x3+0x5 & 3x1+0x6 \\ 4x3+1x0 & 4x3+1x5 & 4x1+1x6 \end{bmatrix} = \begin{bmatrix} 9 & 9 & 3 \\ 12 & 17 & 10 \end{bmatrix}.$$

Example 3: Find $C = AB$ for $A = \begin{bmatrix} 4 \\ 6 \\ 3 \end{bmatrix}$ and $B = (3 \quad 2 \quad 5)$.

$$C = AB = \begin{bmatrix} 4x3 & 4x2 & 4x5 \\ 6x3 & 6x2 & 6x5 \\ 3x3 & 3x2 & 3x5 \end{bmatrix} = \begin{bmatrix} 12 & 8 & 20 \\ 18 & 12 & 30 \\ 9 & 6 & 15 \end{bmatrix}.$$

Properties of Matrix Multiplications. There are several properties for matrix multiplications.

Property 1: The distributive law is valid in matrix multiplications.

$$A (B + C) = AB + AC$$

$$(B + C) A = BA + CA$$

Property 2: The associative law is valid in matrix multiplication.

$$(AB)C = A(BC) = ABC$$

Property 3: If I is an identity matrix, then

$$AI = IA = A.$$

The Transpose of a Matrix

Transposition means interchanging the rows or columns of a given matrix. That is, the rows become columns and the columns become rows. Transposition is denoted by the letter t. For example, the transpose of matrix **B**, where

$$B = \begin{bmatrix} 3 & 5 & 6 & 9 \\ 0 & 11 & 13 & 8 \\ 6 & 8 & 3 & 4 \end{bmatrix} \quad \text{is} \quad B^t = \begin{bmatrix} 3 & 0 & 6 \\ 5 & 11 & 8 \\ 6 & 13 & 3 \\ 9 & 8 & 4 \end{bmatrix}$$

Thus, the dimension of **B** is changed from 3 x 4 to 4 x 3.

Properties of the Transpose

The following properties are held for the transpose of a matrix:

Property 1: $(A^t)^t = A$

Property 2: $(aA)^t = aA^t$, where (a) is a scalar $(a^t = a)$.

Property 3: $(A + B)^t = A^t + B^t$

Property 4: $(AB)^t = B^t A^t$

Types of Matrices

The following types of matrices are the ones students usually encounter in business and economic literature:

1. *A Zero Matrix*: All elements of this matrix are zeros. For example,

$$A = \begin{bmatrix} 0 & 0 & 0 \\ 0 & 0 & 0 \\ 0 & 0 & 0 \end{bmatrix}.$$

2. *Identity Matrix*: This matrix has column vectors called *unit vectors*, such as,

$$A = \begin{bmatrix} 1 & 0 \\ 0 & 1 \end{bmatrix}, \quad A = \begin{bmatrix} 1 & 0 & 0 \\ 0 & 1 & 0 \\ 0 & 0 & 1 \end{bmatrix}, \quad A = \begin{bmatrix} 1 & 0 & 0 & 0 & 0 \\ 0 & 1 & 0 & 0 & 0 \\ 0 & 0 & 1 & 0 & 0 \\ 0 & 0 & 0 & 1 & 0 \\ 0 & 0 & 0 & 0 & 1 \end{bmatrix}, \text{ and so on.}$$

3. *A Diagonal Matrix*: All elements off the diagonal of this matrix are zeros.

$$A = \begin{bmatrix} 1 & 0 \\ 0 & 1 \end{bmatrix}, A = \begin{bmatrix} 2 & 0 & 0 \\ 0 & 3 & 0 \\ 0 & 0 & 4 \end{bmatrix}, \text{ and so on.}$$

4. *A Scalar Matrix*: This is a matrix whose elements on the diagonal are equal.

$$A = \begin{bmatrix} 1 & 0 \\ 0 & 1 \end{bmatrix}, A = \begin{bmatrix} 3 & 0 & 0 \\ 0 & 3 & 0 \\ 0 & 0 & 3 \end{bmatrix}, \text{ and so on.}$$

5. *A Triangular Matrix*: A matrix whose lower and upper elements are arranged in such a way that they resemble a triangle.

$$A = \begin{bmatrix} 3 & 1 \\ 0 & 2 \end{bmatrix}, A = \begin{bmatrix} 2 & 6 & 7 \\ 0 & 5 & 9 \\ 0 & 0 & 3 \end{bmatrix}, A = \begin{bmatrix} 4 & 0 & 0 \\ 3 & 2 & 0 \\ 6 & 5 & 7 \end{bmatrix}, \text{ and so on.}$$

6. *Idempotent Matrix*: This is a matrix having the property that $A^2 = A$. For example,

$$A^2 = A, \text{ if } A = \begin{bmatrix} 2/3 & 1/3 \\ 2/3 & 1/3 \end{bmatrix}, \text{ then } AA = A^2 = \begin{bmatrix} 2/3 & 1/3 \\ 2/3 & 1/3 \end{bmatrix}.$$

Another example would be the identity matrix I. If $I = \begin{bmatrix} 1 & 0 \\ 0 & 1 \end{bmatrix}$, then $I^2 = \begin{bmatrix} 1 & 0 \\ 0 & 1 \end{bmatrix}$.

7. *A Symmetric Matrix*: A matrix is said to be symmetric if $A = A^t$.

$$A = \begin{bmatrix} 8 & 2 & 1 \\ 2 & 3 & 4 \\ 1 & 4 & 5 \end{bmatrix} \text{ and } A^t = \begin{bmatrix} 8 & 2 & 1 \\ 2 & 3 & 4 \\ 1 & 4 & 5 \end{bmatrix}.$$

8. *A Skew-Symmetric Matrix:* This is a matrix whose **A** is equal to -**A**^{t}.

$$\mathbf{A} = \begin{bmatrix} 0 & 4 \\ -4 & 0 \end{bmatrix} \text{ and } - \mathbf{A}^t = \begin{bmatrix} 0 & 4 \\ -4 & 0 \end{bmatrix}.$$

9. *An Orthogonal Matrix:* This is a matrix having the property that $\mathbf{AA}^t = \mathbf{A}^t\mathbf{A} = \mathbf{I}$.

The Determinants

The determinant of matrix **A** is denoted by IAI. To obtain IAI one should understand the following concepts.

Minor: The minor IM$_{ij}$I of an element in a matrix is obtained by deleting the ith row and the jth column of that matrix.

Example 1: Find IM$_{ij}$I for $\mathbf{A} = \begin{bmatrix} 3 & 7 \\ 4 & 8 \end{bmatrix}$, where ij represents the ith row and the jth column

respectively.

$$\left| M_{11} \right| = 8, \left| M_{12} \right| = 4, \left| M_{21} \right| = 7, \text{ and } \left| M_{22} \right| = 3.$$

Example 2: Find $\left| M_{ij} \right|$ for $\mathbf{A} = \begin{bmatrix} a_{11} & a_{12} & a_{13} \\ a_{21} & a_{22} & a_{23} \\ a_{31} & a_{32} & a_{23} \end{bmatrix}$.

Solution:

$$|M_{11}| = \begin{vmatrix} a_{22} & a_{23} \\ a_{32} & a_{33} \end{vmatrix}, \ |M_{12}| = \begin{vmatrix} a_{21} & a_{23} \\ a_{31} & a_{33} \end{vmatrix}, \ |M_{13}| = \begin{vmatrix} a_{21} & a_{22} \\ a_{31} & a_{32} \end{vmatrix},$$

$$|M_{21}| = \begin{vmatrix} a_{12} & a_{13} \\ a_{32} & a_{33} \end{vmatrix}, \ |M_{22}| = \begin{vmatrix} a_{11} & a_{13} \\ a_{31} & a_{33} \end{vmatrix}, \ |M_{23}| = \begin{vmatrix} a_{11} & a_{12} \\ a_{31} & a_{32} \end{vmatrix},$$

$$|M_{31}| = \begin{vmatrix} a_{12} & a_{13} \\ a_{22} & a_{23} \end{vmatrix}, \ |M_{32}| = \begin{vmatrix} a_{11} & a_{13} \\ a_{21} & a_{23} \end{vmatrix}, \ |M_{33}| = \begin{vmatrix} a_{11} & a_{13} \\ a_{21} & a_{22} \end{vmatrix}.$$

The values of $|M_{ij}|$ would be,

$$|M_{11}| = a_{22}a_{33} - a_{23}a_{32}, |M_{12}| = a_{21}a_{33} - a_{23}a_{31} , |M_{13}| = a_{21}a_{32} - a_{31}a_{22},$$

$$|M_{21}| = a_{12}a_{33} - a_{32}a_{13}, |M_{22}| = a_{11}a_{13} - a_{31}a_{13} , |M_{23}| = a_{11}a_{32} - a_{31}a_{12},$$

$$|M_{31}| = a_{12}a_{23} - a_{22}a_{13}, |M_{32}| = a_{11}a_{23} - a_{21}a_{13} , |M_{33}| = a_{11}a_{22} - a_{21}a_{12}.$$

Example 3: Find $|M_{ij}|$ for $\mathbf{A} = \begin{bmatrix} 3 & 0 & 9 \\ 1 & 3 & 0 \\ 5 & 7 & 8 \end{bmatrix}$.

$$|M_{11}| = \begin{vmatrix} 3 & 0 \\ 7 & 8 \end{vmatrix}, |M_{12}| = \begin{vmatrix} 1 & 0 \\ 5 & 8 \end{vmatrix}, |M_{13}| = \begin{vmatrix} 1 & 3 \\ 5 & 7 \end{vmatrix}, |M_{21}| = \begin{vmatrix} 0 & 9 \\ 7 & 8 \end{vmatrix},$$

$$|M_{22}| = \begin{vmatrix} 3 & 9 \\ 5 & 8 \end{vmatrix}, |M_{23}| = \begin{vmatrix} 3 & 0 \\ 5 & 7 \end{vmatrix}, |M_{31}| = \begin{vmatrix} 0 & 9 \\ 3 & 0 \end{vmatrix}, |M_{32}| = \begin{vmatrix} 3 & 9 \\ 1 & 0 \end{vmatrix},$$

$$|M_{23}| = \begin{vmatrix} 3 & 0 \\ 1 & 3 \end{vmatrix}.$$

Thus, $|M_{11}| = 3 \times 8 - 0 = 24, |M_{12}| = 1 \times 8 - 5 \times 0 = 8, |M_{13}| = 7 - 15 = -8,$
$|M_{21}| = 24, |M_{22}| = 24 - 45 = -21, |M_{23}| = 21, |M_{31}| = -27, |M_{32}| = -9,$ and $|M_{33}| = 9.$

Cofactor: The cofactor $|C_{ij}|$ of an element in matrix A is a signed minor. The following formula is used to find $|C_{ij}|$,

$$|c_{ij}| = (-1)^{i+j} |M_{ij}|$$

where i and j refer to the ith row and j^{th} column, respectively, and $|M_{ij}|$ are the minors of the elements of that matrix.

Example 1: Find $|C_{ij}|$ for $\mathbf{A} = \begin{bmatrix} 2 & 3 \\ 7 & 9 \end{bmatrix}$.

To use the cofactor formula we need to find $|M_{ij}|$. These are, $|M_{11}| = 9$, $|M_{12}| = 7$, $|M_{21}| = 3$, and $|M_{22}| = 2$. Using these elements in the $|C_{ij}|$ formula yields

$$|C_{11}| = (-1)^{1+1} \, |M_{11}| = (-1)^2 \, (9) = 9$$

$$|C_{12}| = (-1)^{1+2} \, |M_{12}| = (-1)^3 \, (7) = -7$$

$$|C_{21}| = (-1)^{2+1} \, |M_{21}| = (-1)^3 \, (3) = -3$$

$$|C_{22}| = (-1)^{2+2} \, |M_{22}| = (-1)^4 \, (2) = 2.$$

If the matrix of cofactors is called **C**, where

$$\mathbf{C} = \begin{bmatrix} C_{11} & C_{12} \\ C_{21} & C_{22} \end{bmatrix}, \text{ then } \mathbf{C} \text{ for this example would be}$$

$$\mathbf{C} = \begin{bmatrix} 9 & -7 \\ -3 & 2 \end{bmatrix} \text{ and } \mathbf{C}^t = \begin{bmatrix} 9 & -3 \\ -7 & 2 \end{bmatrix}. \quad \mathbf{C}^t \text{ is called the adjoint matrix.}$$

Example 2: Find the cofactors for matrix **A**, where

$$\mathbf{A} = \begin{bmatrix} 2 & 0 & 1 \\ 3 & 5 & 7 \\ 0 & 0 & 3 \end{bmatrix}.$$

Before applying the cofactor formula we need to find the minors for the elements of matrix **A**.

$$|M_{11}| = \begin{vmatrix} 5 & 7 \\ 0 & 3 \end{vmatrix}, \, |M_{12}| = \begin{vmatrix} 3 & 7 \\ 0 & 3 \end{vmatrix}, \, |M_{13}| = \begin{vmatrix} 3 & 5 \\ 0 & 0 \end{vmatrix}, \, |M_{21}| = \begin{vmatrix} 0 & 1 \\ 0 & 3 \end{vmatrix},$$

$$|M_{22}| = \begin{vmatrix} 2 & 1 \\ 0 & 3 \end{vmatrix}, \, |M_{23}| = \begin{vmatrix} 2 & 0 \\ 0 & 0 \end{vmatrix}, \, |M_{31}| = \begin{vmatrix} 0 & 1 \\ 5 & 7 \end{vmatrix}, \, |M_{32}| = \begin{vmatrix} 2 & 1 \\ 3 & 7 \end{vmatrix},$$

$$|M_{23}| = \begin{vmatrix} 2 & 0 \\ 3 & 5 \end{vmatrix}.$$

And the values of these minors are, 15, 9, 0, 0, 6, 0, -5, 11, and 10.
The cofactors are

$$IC_{11}I = (-1)^{1+1} IM_{11}I = (-1)^2 (15) = 15$$

$$IC_{12}I = (-1)^{1+2} IM_{12}I = (-1)^3 (9) = -9$$

$$IC_{13}I = (-1)^{1+3} IM_{13}I = 1 (0) = 0$$

$$IC_{21}I = (-1)^{2+1} IM_{21}I = -1 (0) = 0$$

$$IC_{22}I = (-1)^{2+2} IM_{22}I = 1 (6) = 6$$

$$IC_{23}I = (-1)^{2+3} IM_{23}I = -1 (0) = 0$$

$$IC_{31}I = (-1)^{3+1} IM_{31}I = 1 (-5) = -5$$

$$IC_{32}I = (-1)^{3+2} IM_{32}I = -1 (11) = -11$$

$$IC_{33}I = (-1)^{3+3} IM_{33}I = 1 (10) = 10$$

$$\text{Thus, } \mathbf{C} = \begin{vmatrix} 15 & -9 & 0 \\ 0 & 6 & 0 \\ -5 & -11 & 10 \end{vmatrix} \text{ and } \mathbf{C}^t = \begin{bmatrix} 15 & 0 & -5 \\ -9 & 6 & -11 \\ 0 & 0 & 10 \end{bmatrix}.$$

Determinant. The determinant of matrix $\mathbf{A}_{2 \times 2}$, which is denoted by IAI, is obtained by using the formula

$$IAI = a_{11} IC_{11}I + a_{12} IC_{12}I,$$

where $\mathbf{A} = \begin{bmatrix} a_{11} & a_{12} \\ a_{21} & a_{22} \end{bmatrix}$ and $IC_{11}I$ and $IC_{12}I$ are the cofactors of a_{11} and a_{12}

obtained by using the cofactor formula. This formula says that $IC_{11}I = a_{22}$ and $IC_{12}I = -a_{21}$. Hence, $IAI = a_{11} a_{22} - a_{12}a_{22}$.

Example 1: Find IAI for $\mathbf{A} = \begin{bmatrix} 3 & 4 \\ 2 & 9 \end{bmatrix}$.

We know that $a_{11} = 3$ and $a_{12} = 4$, and $IC_{11}I$ and $IC_{12}I$ are obtained by

$$IC_{11}I = (-1)^{1+1} IM_{11}I = 1 (9) = 9$$

$$IC_{12}I = (-1)^{1+2} IM_{12}I = -1 (2) = -2.$$

Using the determinant formula we obtain,

$$IAI = 3 (9) + 4 (-2) = 27 - 8 = 19.$$

Example 2: Find IAI for $\mathbf{A} = \begin{bmatrix} a_{11} & a_{12} & a_{13} \\ a_{21} & a_{22} & a_{23} \\ a_{31} & a_{32} & a_{33} \end{bmatrix}$.

For this example our formula of the determinant becomes

$$IAI = a_{11} IC_{11}I + a_{12} IC_{12}I + a_{13} IC_{13}I$$

where $IC_{11}I$, $IC_{12}I$, and $IC_{13}I$ are the cofactors of a_{11}, a_{12}, and a_{13}, respectively.

Example 3: Find IAI for $\mathbf{A} = \begin{bmatrix} 3 & 4 & 5 \\ 1 & 0 & 3 \\ 0 & 3 & 6 \end{bmatrix}$.

Solution : $IM_{11}I = \begin{vmatrix} 0 & 3 \\ 3 & 6 \end{vmatrix} = -9, IM_{12}I = \begin{vmatrix} 1 & 3 \\ 0 & 6 \end{vmatrix} = 6, \text{ and } IM_{13}I = \begin{vmatrix} 1 & 0 \\ 0 & 3 \end{vmatrix} = 3.$

Accordingly, $IC_{11}I = (-1)^{1+1} IM_{11}I = (1) (-9) = -9,$

$$IC_{12}I = (-1)^{1+2} IM_{12}I = -1 (6) = -6$$

$$\text{and } IC_{13}I = (-1)^{1+3} IM_{13}I = 1 (3) = 3$$

Hence, $IAI = 3 (-9) + 4(-6) + 5(3) = -27 - 24 + 15 = -51 + 15 = -36.$

One should note that IAI can be found by expanding along any column or row of a square matrix, a matrix whose number of rows equals the number of columns. For our example, because the first column has a zero element, one can use it. In this regard the determinant formula becomes

$$|A| = a_{11} \ |C_{11}| + a_{21} \ |C_{21}| + a_{31} \ |C_{31}|$$

where

$$|C_{11}| = -9, \ |C_{21}| = (-1)^{2+1} \ |M_{21}| = (-1)$$

$$|A| = (3)(-9) + (-9)(1) = -27 - 9 = -36.$$

Matrix Inversion

If the determinant of matrix **A** exists, the matrix is said to be nonsingular. Should this be the case, the inverse of the matrix does exist and is denoted by A^{-1}. In contrast, if the determinant of matrix A does not exist, the matrix is said to be singular and the inverse does not exist.

To find the inverse of a matrix we follow these steps. First, the cofactor of each element of the given matrix must be found. Second, the cofactor matrix must be transposed, and this matrix is called the adjoint matrix. Third, we find the determinant of that matrix. Fourth, the reciprocal of the determinant, a scalar, must be multiplied by the adjoint matrix.

Example 1: Find the inverse for $A = \begin{bmatrix} 3 & 4 \\ 2 & 1 \end{bmatrix}$.

First, the cofactor of each element is

$$|C_{11}| = (-1)^{1+1} \ |M_{11}| = 1$$

$$|C_{12}| = (-1)^{1+2} \ |M_{12}| = -2$$

$$|C_{21}| = (-1)^{2+1} \ |M_{21}| = -4$$

$$|C_{22}| = (-1)^{2+2} \ |M_{22}| = 3.$$

Thus,

$$C = \begin{bmatrix} 1 & -2 \\ -4 & 3 \end{bmatrix} \text{ and second, } C^t = \begin{bmatrix} 1 & -4 \\ -2 & 3 \end{bmatrix}.$$

Third, $|A| = a_{11} \ |C_{11}| + a_{12} \ |C_{12}| = 3(1) + 4(-2) = -5$, and fourth,

$$\mathbf{A}^{-1} = [1 \,/\, \text{IAI}] \; \mathbf{C}^t = (1/\text{-}5) \begin{bmatrix} 1 & -4 \\ -2 & 3 \end{bmatrix} = \begin{bmatrix} -1/5 & 4/5 \\ 2/5 & -3/5 \end{bmatrix}.$$

To check whether the right inverse has been found, find $\mathbf{A}^{-1}\mathbf{A} = \mathbf{I}$.
If $\mathbf{A}^{-1}\mathbf{A} = \mathbf{I}$ or $\mathbf{A}\mathbf{A}^{-1} = \mathbf{I}$, then the inverse is correct. For example, for the above matrix, $\mathbf{A}^{-1}\mathbf{A}$ is equal to

$$\begin{bmatrix} -1/5 & 4/5 \\ 2/5 & -3/5 \end{bmatrix} \; \text{x} \; \begin{bmatrix} 3 & 4 \\ 2 & 1 \end{bmatrix} = \begin{bmatrix} 1 & 0 \\ 0 & 1 \end{bmatrix}$$

Example 2: Find $\mathbf{A}^{-1}$ for

$$\mathbf{A} = \begin{bmatrix} 1 & 3 & 1 \\ 2 & 5 & 0 \\ 4 & 0 & 7 \end{bmatrix}.$$

The minors of this matrix are
$|M_{11}| = 35, \; |M_{12}| = 14, \; |M_{13}| = -20, |M_{21}| = 21, |M_{22}| = 3, |M_{23}| = -12, |M_{31}| = -5,$
$|M_{32}| = -2,$ and $|M_{33}| = -1.$ The cofactors are calculated as follows:

$IC_{11}I = (-1)^{1+1} M_{11} = 1(35) = 35, \; IC_{12}I = (-1)\,(14) = -14, \; IC_{13}I = 1(-20) = -20,$

$IC_{21}I = (-1)(21) = -21, \; IC_{22}I = 1\,(3) = 3, \; IC_{23}I = (-1)\,(-12) = 12,$

$IC_{31}I = (1)(-5) = -5, \; IC_{32}I = (-1)(-2) = 2, \; IC_{33}I = (1)(-1) = -1.$

$$\text{Thus, } \mathbf{C} = \begin{bmatrix} 35 & -14 & -20 \\ -21 & 3 & 12 \\ -5 & 2 & -1 \end{bmatrix} \text{ and } \mathbf{C}^t = \begin{bmatrix} 35 & -21 & -5 \\ -14 & 3 & 2 \\ -20 & 12 & -1 \end{bmatrix}.$$

As IAI= $1 (35) + 3 (-14) + 1 (-20) = 35 - 42 - 20 = 35 - 62 = -27,$

$$\mathbf{A}^{-1} = (1/\text{-}27) \begin{bmatrix} 35 & -21 & -5 \\ -14 & 3 & 2 \\ -20 & 12 & -1 \end{bmatrix}.$$

Check $AA^{-1} = A^{-1}A = I$.

Solving Systems of Simultaneous Equations

A system of equations is called a *simultaneous system,* because the unknown variables must be solved at the same time: You cannot solve for one variable unless you solve for the others.

For example, the following system is called a *system of two equations*:

$$a_{11}X_1 + a_{12}X_2 = b_1$$

$$a_{21}X_1 + a_{22}X_2 = b_2$$

where X_1 and X_2 are the two unknown variables to be solved, and we cannot solve for X_1 unless we solve for X_2. Also, a_{11}, a_{12}, a_{21}, and a_{22} are the coefficients of X_1 and X_2.

In matrix form, the above two equations can be written as

$$AX = b,$$

where X is a column vector consisting of $\begin{bmatrix} X_1 \\ X_2 \end{bmatrix}$, b is the vector of the right-hand side

$\begin{bmatrix} b_1 \\ b_2 \end{bmatrix}$, and A is a coefficient matrix of dimension 2 x 2, which consists of

$$A = \begin{bmatrix} a_{11} & a_{12} \\ a_{21} & a_{22} \end{bmatrix}.$$

Methods of Solution

A system of equations can be solved by three methods: the Inverse Method, Cramer's Rule, and the Gauss-Jordan method.

The Inverse Method

In a matrix form the above system was written as

$$AX = b.$$

If we multiply the above equation by A^{-1}, we get

$$A^{-1}AX = A^{-1}b$$

but $A^{-1}A = I$; therefore,

$$IX = A^{-1}b$$

and $IX = X$, thus

$$X = A^{-1}b.$$

Because we know b, we need to find A^{-1}, which we know how to obtain. If we find the inverse we multiply it by vector **b**, and the outcome will be the solution.

Example 1: Solve the system

$$3X_1 + 2X_2 = 6$$

$$X_1 + 3X_2 = 5$$

The **A** matrix of this system is

$$A = \begin{bmatrix} 3 & 2 \\ 1 & 3 \end{bmatrix}.$$

First, the cofactors are

$$IC_{ij}I = (-1)^{i+j} IM_{ij}I$$

$$IC_{11}I = (-1)^2 IM_{11}I = 1(3) = 3$$

$$IC_{12}I = (-1)^{1+2} IM_{12}I = (-1)(1) = -1$$

$$IC_{21}I = (-1)^{2+1} IM_{21}I = -1 (2) = -2$$

$$IC_{22}I = (-1)^{2+2} IM_{22}I = 1 (3) = 3.$$

Second,

$$C = \begin{bmatrix} 3 & -1 \\ -2 & 3 \end{bmatrix} \text{ and } C' = \begin{bmatrix} 3 & -2 \\ -1 & 3 \end{bmatrix}. \text{ Third, } IAI = (3)\,3 + (-1)\,(2) = 7;$$

hence,

$$A^{-1} = (1/7) \begin{bmatrix} 3 & -2 \\ -1 & 3 \end{bmatrix} = \begin{bmatrix} 3/7 & -2/7 \\ -1/7 & 3/7 \end{bmatrix}. \text{ Using } X = A^{-1}b \text{ yields}$$

$$\begin{bmatrix} X_1 \\ X_2 \end{bmatrix} = \begin{bmatrix} 3/7 & -2/7 \\ 1/7 & 3/7 \end{bmatrix} \begin{bmatrix} 6 \\ 5 \end{bmatrix} = \begin{bmatrix} 8/7 \\ 9/7 \end{bmatrix}, \text{ which is the required solution.}$$

Example 2: Solve the system of equations:

$$2X + Z = 3$$

$$3X + 5Y + 7Z = 1$$

$$3Z = 7.$$

We have already found the minors and the cofactors of this system. The cofactor matrix **C** was

$$C = \begin{bmatrix} 15 & -9 & 0 \\ 0 & 6 & 0 \\ -5 & -11 & 10 \end{bmatrix} \text{ and. } C' = \begin{bmatrix} 15 & 0 & -5 \\ -9 & 6 & -11 \\ 0 & 0 & 10 \end{bmatrix}.$$

$IAI = 2\,(15) + 0\,(-9) + 1\,(0) = 30$, and the inverse would be

$$A^{-1} = (1/30) \begin{bmatrix} 15 & 0 & -5 \\ -9 & 6 & -11 \\ -5 & 0 & 10 \end{bmatrix} = \begin{bmatrix} 15/30 & 0 & -5/30 \\ -9/30 & 6/30 & -11/30 \\ 0 & 0 & 10/30 \end{bmatrix}.$$

The solution is

$$\begin{vmatrix} X \\ Y \\ Z \end{vmatrix} = \begin{vmatrix} 15/30 & 0 & -5/30 \\ -9/30 & 6/30 & -11/30 \\ 0 & 0 & 10/30 \end{vmatrix} \begin{bmatrix} 3 \\ 1 \\ 7 \end{bmatrix} = \begin{bmatrix} 10/30 \\ -98/30 \\ 70/30 \end{bmatrix}.$$

The Gauss-Jordan Method

This method works through several operations to reduce a given matrix of coefficients of a system of equations into an identity matrix. Let us provide this example for an illustration of this method.

Example 1: Solve the following system of two equations:

$$2X_1 + 3X_2 = 5$$

$$1X_1 + 1X_2 = 3.$$

Solution: Form the augmented matrix **A** consisting of the coefficients of X_1 and X_2 and the column of the right-hand side of the above system. That is,

$$\mathbf{A} = \begin{bmatrix} 2 & 3 & 5 \\ 1 & 1 & 3 \end{bmatrix}.$$

As mentioned, we want to reduce the coefficient matrix (the first two columns of **A**) into an identity matrix of dimension 2x2; this can be done through the following operations:

Multiplying the first row by (1/2), keeping the second row intact, yields:

$$\begin{vmatrix} 1 & 3/2 & 5/2 \\ 1 & 1 & 3 \end{vmatrix}.$$

The first element of the first row is (1); accordingly, the first row is the pivotal row to perform the operations with. We need now to make the first element of the second row (0). To do so, we keep the first row intact, multiply it by (-1), and add the result to the second row, which yields

$$\begin{vmatrix} 1 & 3/2 & 5/2 \\ 0 & -1/2 & 1/2 \end{vmatrix}.$$

Now, we need to convert the (-1/2) into (1) to create a pivotal row. This can be done by multiplying the second row by (-2); keeping the first row intact yields,

$$\begin{vmatrix} 1 & 3/2 & 5/2 \\ 0 & 1 & -1 \end{vmatrix}.$$

Again, we want to convert the (3/2) into (0). To do so, we keep the second row intact (the pivot), multiply it by (-3/2), and add the result to the first row, which yields

$$\begin{vmatrix} 1 & 0 & 4 \\ 0 & 1 & -1 \end{vmatrix}.$$

As can be seen through several operations, we reduce the coefficient matrix into an identity matrix of dimension 2 x 2. The last column of the above matrix is the solution for X_1 and X_2, respectively.

Example 2: Solve the system of equations:

$$3X_1 + 2X_2 = 6$$

$$X_1 + X_2 = 4.$$

Solution:

$$\mathbf{A} = \begin{vmatrix} 3 & 2 & 6 \\ 1 & 1 & 4 \end{vmatrix}$$

Multiply the first element of the first row by (1/3) to convert it into (1) and keep the second row intact; this yields

$$\begin{vmatrix} 1 & 2/3 & 2 \\ 1 & 1 & 4 \end{vmatrix}.$$

Multiply the first row by (-1); the result is added to the second row, which yields

$$\begin{vmatrix} 1 & 2/3 & 2 \\ 0 & 1/3 & 2 \end{vmatrix}.$$

Multiplying the second row by (3) in order to convert the element (1/3) into (1) and keeping the first row intact yields

$$\begin{vmatrix} 1 & 2/3 & 2 \\ 0 & 1 & 6 \end{vmatrix}.$$

Finally, keeping the second row intact, multiplying it by (-2/3), and adding the result to the first row in order to convert the (2/3) into (0) yields

$$\begin{vmatrix} 1 & 0 & -2 \\ 0 & 1 & 6 \end{vmatrix}.$$

Thus, the solution for X_1 and X_2 is (-2) and (6), respectively.

Example 3: Solve the system of equations:

$$X_1 + X_2 + 3X_3 = 3$$

$$X_1 + 2X_2 + X_3 = 2$$

$$4X_1 + 2X_2 + 3X_3 = 5.$$

Solution: Form the augmented matrix

$$\begin{vmatrix} 1 & 1 & 3 & 3 \\ 1 & 2 & 1 & 2 \\ 4 & 2 & 3 & 5 \end{vmatrix}.$$

The first element of the first row is already (1), so the first row is a pivot. Multiply the first row by (-1) and add the result to the second row to make the first element of the second row (0); then multiply the first row by (-4), and add the result to the third row to convert the (4) into (0), which yields

$$\begin{vmatrix} 1 & 1 & 3 & 3 \\ 0 & 1 & -2 & -1 \\ 0 & -2 & -9 & -7 \end{vmatrix}.$$

We need to convert the second element of the second row into (1), but it is already (1), so it is the pivotal row. Now, multiply the second row by (-1), and add the result to the first row to convert the element from (1) to (0), and also multiply the second row by (2) and add the result to the third row, which yields

$$\begin{vmatrix} 1 & 0 & 5 & 4 \\ 0 & 1 & -2 & -1 \\ 0 & 0 & -13 & -9 \end{vmatrix}.$$

Now, multiplying the third row by (-1/13) yields

$$\begin{vmatrix} 1 & 0 & 5 & | & 4 \\ 0 & 1 & -2 & | & -1 \\ 0 & 0 & 1 & | & 9/13 \end{vmatrix}.$$

Finally, multiply the third row by (2), add the result to the second row, and multiply the third row by (-5); the result is added to the first row, which yields

$$\begin{vmatrix} 1 & 0 & 0 & | & 7/13 \\ 0 & 1 & 0 & | & 5/13 \\ 0 & 0 & 1 & | & 9/13 \end{vmatrix},$$

which is the required solution.

Example 4: Solve the system of equations:

$$2X_2 = 4$$

$$X_1 + 3X_2 = 5.$$

Solution: Form the augmented matrix

$$\begin{vmatrix} 0 & 2 & 4 \\ 1 & 3 & 5 \end{vmatrix}.$$

Because the first element of the first row is (0), we interchange the rows by making the second row the first row, which yields

$$\begin{vmatrix} 1 & 3 & 5 \\ 0 & 2 & 4 \end{vmatrix}.$$

We need to change the element (2) into (1). Multiplying the second row by (1/2) yields

$$\begin{vmatrix} 1 & 3 & 5 \\ 0 & 1 & 2 \end{vmatrix}.$$

Multiply the second row by (-3); the result is added to the first row, which yields

$$\begin{vmatrix} 1 & 0 & | & -1 \\ 0 & 1 & | & 2 \end{vmatrix}.$$

Thus, the solution for X_1 and X_2 is (-1) and (2), respectively.

Cramer's Rule

This method, sometimes called the *determinant method*, works according to this formula:

$$X_i = IA_iI / IAI,$$

where X_i indicates the variables we want to solve for, and IA_iI is the determinant obtained by putting the right–hand side of the system in place of the column of coefficients of the variable whose solution is needed, and IAI is the determinant of the system.

Example 1: Solve the system

$$3X_1 + 2X_2 = 5$$

$$X_1 + 3X_2 = 7$$

Solution: $IAI = \begin{vmatrix} 3 & 2 \\ 1 & 3 \end{vmatrix} = 7, IA_1I = \begin{vmatrix} 5 & 2 \\ 7 & 3 \end{vmatrix} = -1, IA_2I = \begin{vmatrix} 3 & 5 \\ 1 & 7 \end{vmatrix} = 16$

Therefore, the solution would be

$$X_1 = IA_1I/IAI = -1/7 \quad \text{and} \quad X_2 = IA_2I/IAI = 16/7.$$

Example 2: Solve the system

$$5X_1 + 3X_2 = 13$$

$$4X_2 = 11.$$

Solution:

$IAI = \begin{vmatrix} 5 & 3 \\ 0 & 4 \end{vmatrix} = 20. IA_1I = \begin{vmatrix} 13 & 3 \\ 11 & 4 \end{vmatrix} = 9, IA_2I = \begin{vmatrix} 5 & 13 \\ 0 & 11 \end{vmatrix} = 55, \text{thus}$

$$X_1 = IA_1I / IAI = 9/20 \quad \text{and} \quad X_2 = IA_2I / IAI = 55/20.$$

Example 3: Solve the system

$$X_1 + X_2 + 3X_3 = 3$$

$$X_1 + X_3 = 2$$

$$4X_1 + 2X_2 + 3X_3 = 5.$$

Solution:

$$IAI = \begin{vmatrix} 1 & 1 & 3 \\ 1 & 0 & 1 \\ 4 & 2 & 3 \end{vmatrix} = 5$$

$$IA_1I = \begin{vmatrix} 3 & 1 & 3 \\ 2 & 0 & 1 \\ 5 & 2 & 3 \end{vmatrix} = 5$$

$$IA_2I = \begin{vmatrix} 1 & 3 & 3 \\ 1 & 2 & 1 \\ 4 & 5 & 3 \end{vmatrix} = -5$$

$$IA_3I = \begin{vmatrix} 1 & 1 & 3 \\ 1 & 0 & 2 \\ 4 & 2 & 5 \end{vmatrix} = 5$$

Therefore, $X_1 = 1$, $X_2 = -1$, and $X_3 = 1$.

Example 4: The following system of equations represents a beef market:

$$Q_d = 4 - 1.0 P_d$$

$$Q_s = -2 + 1.0 P_d$$

$$Q_s = Q_d$$

The first equation reflects the demand for beef, showing a negative relation between the price of beef and the quantity demanded for beef. The second equation represents the supply of beef, indicating that the quantity supplied of beef is related positively to the price of beef. The third equation indicates the equilibrium between the quantity supplied and the quantity demanded for beef. The third equation is used to find the equilibrium price and quantity (Bressler 1975).

Solution: We like to find the equilibrium price and quantity of beef. This can be done by rewriting the equations as follows:

$$0Q_s + Q_d + 1.0\,P_d = 4$$

$$Q_s + 0Q_d - 1.0\,P_d = -2$$

$$Q_s - Q_d = 0.$$

Hence,

$$IAI = \begin{vmatrix} 0 & 1 & 1 \\ 1 & 0 & -1 \\ 1 & -1 & 0 \end{vmatrix} = -2$$

$$IA_1I = \begin{vmatrix} 4 & 1 & 1 \\ -2 & 0 & -1 \\ 0 & -1 & 0 \end{vmatrix} = -2$$

$$IA_2I = \begin{vmatrix} 0 & 4 & 1 \\ 1 & -2 & -1 \\ 1 & 0 & 0 \end{vmatrix} = -2$$

$$IA_3I = \begin{vmatrix} 0 & 1 & 4 \\ 1 & 0 & -2 \\ 1 & -1 & 0 \end{vmatrix} = -6$$

Therefore, $Q_s = -2/-2 = 1$, $Q_d = -2/-2 = 1$, and $P = -6/-2 = 3$.

Example 5: Given this simple Keynesian model of income determination,

$$I = 12$$

$$C = 5 + 0.90\,Y$$

$$Y = C + I$$

where I , C, and Y are investment, consumption, and income, respectively.
This model says that investment is given from sources outside of the model.
Consumption is related positively to income, that is, if income increases by a dollar,
consumption will increase by 90 cents. This relation is called the *Keynesian
consumption function*. The third identity indicates that income is made of
investment and consumption (Allen 1956).
Solution: Rewrite the above system as follows:

$$I = 12$$

$$- 0.90 \, Y + C = 5$$

$$Y - C - I = 0$$

hence,

$$|A| = \begin{vmatrix} 0 & 0 & 1 \\ -0.9 & 1 & 0 \\ 1 & -1 & -1 \end{vmatrix} = -0.10$$

$$|A_1| = \begin{vmatrix} 12 & 0 & 1 \\ 5 & 1 & 0 \\ 0 & -1 & -1 \end{vmatrix} = -17$$

$$|A_2| = \begin{vmatrix} 0 & 12 & 1 \\ -0.90 & 5 & 0 \\ 1 & 0 & -1 \end{vmatrix} = -15.8$$

$$|A_3| = \begin{vmatrix} 0 & 0 & 12 \\ -0.90 & 1 & 5 \\ 1 & -1 & 0 \end{vmatrix} = -1.2$$

The solution would be, Y = -17 / -0.10 = 170, C = - 15.8 / -0.10 = 158, and
I = -1.2 / -0.10 = 12.

Eigenvalues, Eigenvectors, and Diagonalization of Matrices

To obtain the eigenvalues or the characteristic roots of a given matrix, say matrix **A**, we use the formula

$$I (A - sI) I = 0 \tag{5}$$

where (s) is the eigenvalues, **I** is an identity matrix of same dimension as **A**, and the two bars (**I** and **I**) are the sign of the determinant of matrix (**A** - s**I**). Having done so, one can obtain the eigenvectors by using the formula

$$I (A - sI) I X = 0. \tag{6}$$

As the second equation usually has a determinant of zero, a unique solution for vector **X** cannot be found. In other words, we have an infinite number of solutions. Example 1: Find the eigenvalues and vectors for

$$A = \begin{bmatrix} 4 & 2 \\ 1 & 3 \end{bmatrix}.$$

Solution: Using equation (5) we obtain,

$$\left| \begin{bmatrix} 4 & 2 \\ 1 & 3 \end{bmatrix} -(s) \begin{bmatrix} 1 & 0 \\ 0 & 1 \end{bmatrix} \right| = 0,$$

which can be simplified to

$$\begin{vmatrix} 4 - s & 2 \\ 1 & 3 - s \end{vmatrix} = 0$$

and the value of the determinant would be

$$(4 - s)(3 - s) - 2 = 0.$$

This equation is a quadratic equation whose roots (solutions) are $s = 2$ and $s = 5$. These roots are the eigenvalues or the characteristic roots of matrix **A**.

To find the eigenvectors associated with these roots, we take each root one at a time and substitute it in equation (6). Mathematically, for $s = 2$, equation (6) becomes

$$\begin{bmatrix} 2 & 2 \\ 1 & 1 \end{bmatrix} \begin{bmatrix} X_1 \\ X_2 \end{bmatrix} = \begin{bmatrix} 0 \\ 0 \end{bmatrix},$$

that is,

$$2X_1 + 2X_2 = 0,$$

or

$$X_1 = -X_2.$$

Let X_2 be any real value such as $X_2 = 1$; hence, $X_1 = -1$. In other words, the first eigenvector $\mathbf{Z}_1$ is equal to

$$\mathbf{Z}_1 = \begin{bmatrix} -1 \\ 1 \end{bmatrix}.$$

For the second eigenvalue, i.e., $s = 5$, equation (6) becomes

$$\begin{bmatrix} -1 & 2 \\ 1 & -2 \end{bmatrix} \begin{bmatrix} X_1 \\ X_1 \end{bmatrix} = \begin{bmatrix} 0 \\ 0 \end{bmatrix},$$

which can be written as

$$-X_1 + 2X_2 = 0$$

or

$$X_1 = 2X_2.$$

For a real value of X_2 such as $X_2 = 2$, X_1 becomes $X_1 = 4$. Hence, the second eigenvector $\mathbf{Z}_2$ is equal to

$$\mathbf{Z}_2 = \begin{bmatrix} 4 \\ 2 \end{bmatrix}.$$

If vectors $\mathbf{Z}_1$ and $\mathbf{Z}_2$ are used to form a matrix, say matrix $\mathbf{Z}$, then this matrix will have two linearly independent columns. That is,

$$\mathbf{Z} = \begin{bmatrix} -1 & 4 \\ 1 & 2 \end{bmatrix}$$

and $I\mathbf{Z}I = -6$. Also, $\mathbf{Z}^{-1} = \begin{bmatrix} -2/6 & 4/6 \\ 1/6 & 1/6 \end{bmatrix}$.

Now, as we know matrix $\mathbf{A}$ and matrix $\mathbf{Z}$ we can diagonalize matrix $\mathbf{A}$ by using the multiplication

$$\mathbf{Z}^{-1}\mathbf{A}\mathbf{Z} = \mathbf{D},$$

where $\mathbf{D}$ is a diagonal matrix whose diagonal consists of the eigenvalues of matrix $\mathbf{A}$. Using this multiplication, we find

$$\mathbf{D} = \begin{bmatrix} -2/6 & 4/6 \\ 1/6 & 1/6 \end{bmatrix} \begin{bmatrix} 4 & 2 \\ 1 & 3 \end{bmatrix} \begin{bmatrix} -1 & 4 \\ 1 & 2 \end{bmatrix} = \begin{bmatrix} 2 & 0 \\ 0 & 5 \end{bmatrix},$$

and $\mathbf{D}$ is said to be similar to $\mathbf{A}$.

Example 2: Find the eigenvalues and vectors for $\mathbf{A} = \begin{bmatrix} 6 & 10 \\ -2 & -3 \end{bmatrix}$.

Solution: Using equation (5), we obtain

$$\left| \begin{bmatrix} 6 & 10 \\ -2 & -3 \end{bmatrix} - (s) \begin{bmatrix} 1 & 0 \\ 0 & 1 \end{bmatrix} \right| = \begin{vmatrix} 6-s & 10 \\ -2 & -3-s \end{vmatrix} = 0$$

and the determinant $I\mathbf{A} - s\mathbf{I}\ I = 0$ is $I\mathbf{A} - s\mathbf{I}\ I = (6-s)(-3-s) + 20 = 0$ or

$$s^2 - 3s + 2 = 0.$$

Solving for (s) by using the quadratic formula yields

$$s = 1 \text{ and } s = 2,$$

which are the required eigenvalues for matrix **A**.

To find the eigenvectors, we use one at a time the values of the characteristic roots in equation (6). For s = 1, equation (6) becomes

$$| \mathbf{A} - \mathbf{1I} | X = \begin{vmatrix} 5 & 10 \\ -2 & -4 \end{vmatrix} \begin{vmatrix} X_1 \\ X_2 \end{vmatrix} = \begin{vmatrix} 0 \\ 0 \end{vmatrix}.$$

This is, $5X_1 + 10X_2 = 0$ and $-2X_1 - 4X_2 = 0$

or

$$X_1 = -2X_2.$$

For $X_2 = 1$ (any other real value can be used), $X_1 = -2$. Hence, the first eigenvector is

$$\mathbf{Z}_1 = \begin{vmatrix} -2 \\ 1 \end{vmatrix}.$$

For the second eigenvalue, i.e., s = 2, equation (6) gives

$$| \mathbf{A} - s\mathbf{I} | X = \begin{vmatrix} 6 & 10 \\ -2 & -3 \end{vmatrix} - 2 \begin{vmatrix} 1 & 0 \\ 0 & 1 \end{vmatrix} \begin{vmatrix} X_1 \\ X_2 \end{vmatrix} = \begin{vmatrix} 0 \\ 0 \end{vmatrix}$$

or

$$4X_1 + 10X_2 = 0 \text{ and } -2X_1 - 5X_2 = 0,$$

which gives the solution $X_1 = -(5/2)X_2$, a solution that yields infinite values for X_1 for various values of X_2. Let us assume that $X_2 = 2$, then $X_1 = -5$. Hence, the second eigenvector is equal to

$$Z_2 = \begin{bmatrix} -5 \\ 2 \end{bmatrix}.$$

Therefore, the **Z** matrix would be,

$$Z = \begin{bmatrix} -2 & -5 \\ 1 & 2 \end{bmatrix}$$

and **Z** has two linearly independent columns, because $|Z| = 1$. Also,

$$Z^{-1} = \begin{bmatrix} 2 & 5 \\ -1 & -2 \end{bmatrix}.$$

To diagonalize matrix **A**, use $Z^{-1}AZ = D$. Performing this multiplication, one can obtain

$$D = Z^{-1}AZ = \begin{bmatrix} 1 & 0 \\ 0 & 2 \end{bmatrix}.$$

Problems

1.   For $B = (7 \ -5 \ \ 3)$ and $C = (-5 \ \ 0 \ \ -4)$, find $A = B - C$, $A = B + C$, and $A = B^t - C^t$.

2.   For $A = (5 \ 6 \ 7 \ \ 8)$, $D = (-6 \ 0 \ 0 \ 5)$, and $F = (0 \ 0 \ 0 \ 5)$, find $C^t = A^t + D$ and $D^t = A^t + F^t$.

3.   For $A = (5 \ 7 \ 0)$ and $B = (3 \ 2 \ 1)$, find $C = AB^t$, $C = A^tB$, and $C = AB$.

4.   Graph $A = (3 \ -5)$ and $B = (8 \ \ 3)$. If $a = 2$, graph aA and aB. Find the distance between **A** and **B**.

5.   Show whether $A = (2 \ \ 5)$ and $B = (4 \ \ 6)$ are linearly independent vectors. Can they form a basis? Are the two vectors $A = (2 \ \ 4)$ and $B =$

(4   8) linearly independent? Can they form a basis?

6.   If vector **P** represents the prices of three commodities, where **P** = (2   6   8), and vector **Q** represents units of the three commodities, where **Q** = (13   34   40), find total expenditures **E** = **PQ**^{t}.

7.   For matrix **A** = $\begin{bmatrix} 3 & 4 \\ 2 & 1 \end{bmatrix}$ and **B**= $\begin{bmatrix} 5 & -2 \\ 6 & 4 \end{bmatrix}$ find **C** = **A** + **B**, **C** = **A**^{t} - **B**,

C = **B** + **A**, **C** = **AB**, and **C** = **BA**.

8.   For matrix **A** and matrix **B** in problem 7, find **A**$^{-1}$ and **B**$^{-1}$. Also, find **A**$^{-1}$**A**, **AA**$^{-1}$, **BB**$^{-1}$, and **B**$^{-1}$**B**.

9.   For matrix **B**= $\begin{bmatrix} 3 & 2 & 0 \\ 5 & -1 & 3 \\ 4 & 3 & 7 \end{bmatrix}$ find **B**$^{-1}$ and **B**$^{-1}$**B**.

10.   Given the following system of equations:

(a) $3x + 2y = 10$ (b) $2x + 2y + 1z = 9$

$1x + 4y = 15$ $1y + 2z = 12$

$3x + 4z = 15$

find the solutions for both systems by using Cramer's rule, the inverse method, and the Gauss-Jordan method.

11.   Assume a simple macroeconomic model consisting of investment Io, consumption c, and income y. The model is formed as follows:

$$Io = 25$$

$$c = 10 + 0.90y$$

$$y = c + Io$$

Find the equilibrium values for y and c by using Cramer's rule and the inverse method.

12.   For the following two market models,

(a) $Qs = 3 + 2P$ and $Qd = 13 - 2P$

(b) $Qs = 3P$ and $Qd = 15 - 5P + yo$, where $yo = 9$,

find the equilibrium quantities and prices by using Cramer's rule.

13.   Diagonalize the following matrices:

$$A = \begin{bmatrix} 4 & 1 \\ 1 & 3 \end{bmatrix}, \ B = \begin{bmatrix} -2 & 1 \\ 1 & -2 \end{bmatrix}, \ \text{and } C = \begin{bmatrix} 3 & 2 \\ 1 & 4 \end{bmatrix}.$$

CHAPTER TWO

Derivatives and Applications

Economic decisions are based on marginal analysis. For example, the monopolist's best level of output is determined by equating marginal cost and marginal revenue. To find the marginal cost and revenue, total cost and revenue functions must be differentiated with respect to the output level. Similarly, derivatives can be used in many applications in business and economics. For this reason, the rules of differentiation are outlined in this chapter, and many applications are provided.

The Concept of Derivative

The derivative of a function measures the rate of change of the dependent variable y with respect to the independent variable x--the slope of the function. That is, the derivative indicates the impact of a small change in x on y. For example, suppose the dependent variable y is the quantity supplied by a producer, and x is the price of that product. Mathematically, the function is written as

$$y = f(x).$$

Now, if the price x changes by a very small amount (dx), the quantity supplied will change by a very small amount (dy) as well. These small changes, dx and dy, are called the differential of x and y, respectively. After these changes, the new magnitude of the two variables becomes $(y + dy)$ and $(x + dx)$. And dy/dx is called the derivative of y with respect to x. In other words, dy/dx shows the changes in y per unit change in x. The process of finding the derivative is called the *differentiation process*.

If a given function is a univariate function, such as the above, the following rules of differentiation (Glaister 1984; Chiang 1984; Ostrosky and Koch 1986) are applied:

Rule 1: Derivative of a Constant Function

If $y = f(x) = k$, where k is a constant, then $dy/dx = 0$

Example 1: Differentiate $y = f(x) = 30$.

Solution: $dy/dx = 0$

Example 2: If the fixed cost of a product q is FC = 20, then the derivative of the fixed cost with respect to q is $d(FC)/dq = 0$. That is, if q changes, the fixed cost will not change.

Rule 2: Derivative of a Power Function

If $y = f(x) = x^n$, then $dy/dx = nx^{n-1}$.

Example 1: Differentiate $y = x^{10}$.
Solution: $dy/dx = 10x^9$

Example 2: Differentiate $y = x^4$.
Solution: $dy/dx = 4x^3$

Example 3: If the variable cost (VC) of a product q is $VC = q^3$, then the marginal cost MC is $d(VC)/dq = 3q^2$.

Rule 3: Derivative of a Constant Times a Power Function

If $y = kx^n$, where k is a constant, then $dy/dx = nkx^{n-1}$.

Example 1: Differentiate $y = 6x$.

Solution: $dy/dx = 6$
Example 2: Differentiate $y = 6x^2$.

Solution: $dy/dx = 12x$.

Example 3: Differentiate $y = 3x^3$.
Solution: $dy/dx = 9x^2$

Example 4: The total cost TC consists of fixed and variable costs. If TC = 40 + $2Q^2$, where the fixed cost is 40 and the variable cost is $2q^2$, find the marginal cost MC.

Solution: $MC = d(TC)dq = 4q$

Rule 4: Derivative of a Sum or a Difference of Functions

If $y = f(x) + g(x)$ and $y = f(x) - g(x)$, then $dy/dx = f'(x) + g'(x)$ and $dy/dx = f'(x) - g'(x)$, where $f'(x) = df/dx$ and $g'(x) = dg/dx$.

Example 1: Differentiate $y = 3x + 5x^2$.
Solution: $dy/dx = 3 + 10x$

Example 2: Differentiate $y = 7x^3 - 3x^4$.
Solution: $dy/dx = 21x^2 - 12x^3$

Example 3: Differentiate $y = 40 + 3x^2 - 5x$.
Solution: $dy/dx = 6x - 5$

Example 4: If the total revenue $(TR) = 12x + x^2$, where x is the output level, then the marginal revenue (MR) is

$$MR = d(TR)/dx = 12 + 2x.$$

Example 5: If the total cost $(TC) = 12 + x^2 + x^3$, where x is the output level, the marginal cost (MC) is

$$MC = d(TC)/dx = 2x + 3x^2.$$

Example 6: If the total utility obtained from commodity X is $(TU) = 3x^2 + 4x^4$, the marginal utility (MU) would be

$$MU = d(TU)/dx = 6x + 16x^3.$$

Example 7: If the demand function for corn is $y = 3 - 0.4x$, the elasticity (e) is

$$e = (dy/dx)(x/y).$$

But

$$dy/dx = -0.4.$$

Thus,

$$e = -0.4\ x/y.$$

If x is $1.00 and y is 10 units, the elasticity would be

$$e = -0.4 \, (1/10) = -0.04.$$

Example 8: Suppose a monopolist faces a demand curve of a form $p = 42 - q$ and a total cost equation $TC = 3q^2 + 2q + 5$. Find the best level of output that can be produced by this monopolist as well as the profit.
Solution: We need to obtain the total revenue TR.

$$TR = pq \tag{1}$$

But,

$$p = 42 - q. \tag{2}$$

Inserting equation (2) in (1) yields,

$$TR = (42 - q)q = 42q - q^2. \tag{3}$$

Hence, the marginal revenue (MR) would be

$$MR = d(TR)/dq = 42 - 2q. \tag{4}$$

Similarly, from the total cost one can obtain the marginal cost (MC) by

$$MC = d(TC)/dq = 6q + 2. \tag{5}$$

According to the theory of monopoly, a monopolist produces the best level of output maximizing profit when the marginal cost is equal to the marginal revenue. Thus, equating equations (4) and (5) yields,

$$6q + 2 = 42 - 2q. \tag{6}$$

Solving for q we obtain 5 units. If q is 5, the total revenue is $175.00 and total cost is $90.00. The difference between total revenue and total cost is $85.00, which is the required profit.

Rule 5: Derivative of a Product of Functions

Given $y = f(x)g(x)$, where $f(x)$ and $g(x)$ are differentiable functions, then $dy/dx = f'(x) \, g(x) + g'(x) \, f(x)$.

Example 1: Differentiate y = 2x (3x+3).
Solution: Let f(x)= 2x and g(x) = 3x + 3, then dy/dx= 2(3x + 3) + 3(2x).

Example 2: Differentiate y = (2x + 1) (3x² - 2x).
Solution: Let f(x)= (2x + 1) and g(x)= (3x² -2x), then

dy/dx= (2)(3x² - 2x) + (6x- 2)(2x + 1).

Example 3: Differentiate y = 3x(2 - 2x).
Solution: dy/dx= 3(2 -2x) + (-2)(3x).

Example 4: If p = f(q), where p and q are the price and output, respectively, find the marginal revenue (MR).
Solution: Because

$$p = f(q), \text{ then } f'(q) = dp/dq \qquad (7)$$

but the total revenue TR is equal to

$$TR = pq \qquad (8)$$

Using equation (7) in (8) yields,

$$TR = f(q)q \qquad (9)$$

Differentiating (9) with respect to q by using Rule 5 yields,

$$d(TR)/dq = MR = f'(q)q + f(q). \qquad (10)$$

Using equation (7) in (10) yields,

$$MR = (dp/dq)q + p. \qquad (11)$$

Equation (11) can be rewritten as

$$MR = [1 + (q/p)(dp/dq)]. \qquad (12)$$

Because the elasticity of demand is e = (dq/dp)(p/q), then 1/e = (dp/dq)(q/p). Using this fact in equation (12), we obtain:

$$MR = p[1 + 1/e],$$

which is the required solution.

Rule 6: Derivative of a Quotient of Functions

Given y = f(X) / g(X), where f(X) and g(X) are differentiable functions, then

dy/dx = [f '(x) g(x) - g'(x) f(x)] / [g(x)]^2.

Example 1: Differentiate y = (3x - 2) / x^2.

Solution: dy/dx = 3 (x^2) - 2x(3x -2) / [(x^2)]^2

Example 2: Differentiate y = 1/x^3.

Solution: dy/dx = - 3x^2 / [(x^3)]^2

Example 3: Differentiate y = (4x^2 - 2x) / 3x.

Solution: dy/dx = [(8x - 2)(3x) - 3 (4x^2 - 2x)] / [(3x)]^2

Rule 7: Derivative of a Function of a Function (the Chain Rule)

Given y = f(u), where u = g(x), then dy/dx = dy/du · du/dx

Example 1: Differentiate y = 2u, where u = 2x.

Solution: dy/du = 2 and du/dx = 2. Thus, dy/dx = (2) (2).

Example 2: Differentiate y = u^5, where u = 2x^4 - 4x + 3.

Solution: dy/dx = 5u^4 (8x^3 - 4) or dy/dx = 5 (2x^4 - 4x + 3)^4 (8x^3 - 4).

Example 3: Differentiate y = u^3 + 7, where u = x^2 + 1.

Solution: dy/dx = 3u^2 · 2x = 3 (x^2 + 1)^2 · 2x

Example 4: Differentiate y = u - 2 and u = (1/x) - 5.

Solution: dy/dx = 1 (-1 / x^2)

Rule 8: Derivative of a Power of a Function of a Function

Given y = [u(x)]^n , where n is an integer and u is a function of x, then dy/dx = n [u(x)]$^{n-1}$ · du/dx.

Example 1: Differentiate y = $(x^2 + 3)^3$.
Solution: Let u = $x^2 + 3$, then du/dx = 2x. Thus, dy/dx = $3(x^2 + 3)^2$ · 2x.

Example 2: Differentiate y = $(2x^4 - 3x + 16)^5$.
Solution: Let u = $2x^4 - 3x + 16$, then du/dx = $8x^3 - 3$. Therefore,

$$dy/dx = 5 (2x^4 - 3x + 16)^4 · (8x^3 - 3).$$

Example 3: Differentiate y = $(3x^2 - x / 5x)^3$.
Solution: Let u = $(3x^2 - x) / 5x$, then du/dx = $(6x - 1) (5x) - 5 (3x^2 - x) / [5x]^2$,

thus dy/dx = $3(3x^2 - x / 5x)^2$· $(6x - 1)(5x) - (5)(3x^2 - x) / [(5x)]^2$.

Example 4: Differentiate y = (x - 1).
Solution: dy/dx = $1(x - 1)^0 (1) = 1$

Rule 9: Derivative of a Logarithmic Function of Base b

Given y = $\log_b$ u, where u = f(x) and b > 1, then by the chain rule
dy/dx = [1/ u] $\log_b$e · du/dx.

Example 1: Differentiate y = $\log_b x^2$.
Solution: Let u = x^2, then du/dx = 2x. Hence, dy/dx = $[1/x^2] \log_b$e · 2x.

Example 2: Differentiate y = $\log_b$ x.
Solution: Let u = x, then du/dx = 1. Hence, dy/dx = [1/x] $\log_b$ e.

Example 3: Differentiate y = $\log_b (4x^3 + 3x)$.
Solution: Let u = $4x^3 + 3x$, then du/dx = $12x^2 + 3$. Hence,

$$dy/dx = [1/4x^3 + 3x)] \log_b e (12x^2 + 3).$$

Example 4: Differentiate y = $\log_b$ (3/x).
Solution: Let u = 3/x, then du/dx = $-3/x^2$. Hence, dy/dx = 1/[3/x] $\log_b$ e $(-3/x^2)$.

Rule 10: Derivative of a Logarithmic Function of Base e

Given y = $\log_b$ u, if the base b is equal to e, then y = $\log_e$ u = ln u, where ln is the natural logarithm. Thus, dy/dx = 1/u · du/dx, which is a special case of rule 9.

Example 1: Differentiate y = lnx.
Solution: Let u = x, then du/dx = 1. Hence, dy/dx = [1/x] · 1.

Example 2: Differentiate y = ln $3x^2$.
Solution: Let u = $3x^2$, then du/dx = 6x. Hence, dy/dx = [$1/3x^2$] · 6x.

Example 3: Differentiate y = ln (x^2 - 2x).
Solution: Let u = x^2 - 2x, then du/dx = 2x - 2. Hence,

$$dy/dx = [1/(x^2 - 2x)] · (2x - 2).$$

Rule 11: Derivative of a General Exponential Function

Give y = $(a)^U$, where a > 0 but is not equal to 1, and u = f(x), then
dy/dx = $(a)^U$ ln (a) du/dx.

Example 1: Differentiate y = $(2)^X$.
Solution: Let u = x, then du/dx = 1. Hence, dy/dx = $(2)^X$ ln (2) (1).

Example 2: Differentiate y = $(8)^{2X}$.
Solution: Let u = 2x, then du/dx = 2. Hence, dy/dx = $(8)^{2X}$ ln (8) (2).

Rule 12: Derivative of an Exponential Function of Base e

Given y = $(a)^U$, and if a = e, then y = e^U. Hence, dy/dx = e^U du/dx.

Example 1: Differentiate y = e^X.
Solution: Let u = x, then du/dx = 1. Hence, dy/dx = e^X (1).

Example 2: Differentiate y = e^{3X-2}.
Solution: Let u = 3x - 2, then du/dx = 3. Hence, dy/dx = e^{3X-2} (3).

Rule 13: Derivative of an Inverse Function

Instead of obtaining dy/dx we want to obtain dx/dy. Thus, all the above rules of differentiation are applied without changes.

Example 1: Differentiate y = x^3 + 2x.
Solution: dy/dx = $3x^2$ + 2. Hence, dx/dy = 1/[$3x^2$ + 2].

Example 2: Differentiate x = y + y^2 + $5y^3$.
Solution: dx/dy = 1 + 2y + $15y^2$.

Rule 14: Implicit Differentiation

The function $y = f(x)$ is said to be an *explicit function*, because y is expressed in terms of x. But if the function is written as $g(x,y) = 0$, then the function is said to be an *implicit function*. And the differentiation of such a function is called *implicit differentiation*. Here, we treat dy/dx as unknown and differentiate the function with respect to x. Having done so, we solve for dy/dx.

Example 1: Differentiate $xy = 9$ implicitly. To differentiate this function implicitly with respect to x, we do the following. Rewrite the function as $xy - 9 = 0$, and differentiate with respect to x: the derivative of x with respect to x (which is one) times the second variable y, then the derivative of y with respect to x (which is dy/dx) times the first variable x. This gives

$$dy/dx = y + [dy/dx] x = 0.$$

Solving for dy/dx, we obtain

$$dy/dx = - y/x.$$

Example 2: Differentiate $x^2 + y^2 - 20 = 0$ implicitly with respect to x.
Solution: $2x + 2y \, dy/dx = 0$. Thus, $dy/dx = - x/y$.

Example 3: Differentiate $xy - y + 4x = 0$ implicitly with respect to x.
Solution: $y + (dy/dx) x - (dy/dx) + 4 = 0$. Solving for dy/dx yields

$$dy/dx = - (y + 4) / (x - 1).$$

Example 4: Consumer Equilibrium. A consumer can achieve equilibrium if the indifference curve is tangent to the budget line, that is, if the slope of the indifference curve is equal to the slope of the budget line. This tangency point gives the number of units of commodities x and y that our consumer should buy to maximize his or her utility subject to the amount of income (budget).

Suppose the indifference curve equation is $X^{0.5} Y^{0.5} = 15$. Let the budget equation be $2x + 3y = M$, where x and y are two commodities, and the prices of x and y are $2 and $3, respectively; and M is the total income the consumer has. Given this information, we want to find how many units of x and y our consumer should buy. Solution: Obtain dy/dx, the marginal rate of substitution of x for y, from the indifference equation as well as from the budget equation, then equate the results and solve for x and y. Mathematically,

$$0.5x^{-0.5} y^{0.5} + 0.5y^{-0.5} \, dy/dx \, x^{0.5} = 0$$

$$dy/dx = - 0.5x^{-0.5} y^{0.5} / 0.5y^{-0.5} x^{0.5}$$

$$dy/dx = - y/x. \tag{13}$$

Rewrite the budget equation as

$$3y = M - 2x \quad \text{or}$$

$$y = [1/3] M - [2/3]x, \text{ then}$$

$$dy/dx = - 2/3. \tag{14}$$

(Or the budget line equation can be differentiated implicitly to find dy/dx.)
Equating equations (13) and (14) yields

$$2/3 = y/x.$$

Hence,

$$2x = 3y \text{ or } x = 1.5 \, y. \tag{15}$$

Inserting equation (15), which shows the income-consumption curve, in the indifference curve equation yields

$$(1.5 \, y)^{0.5} y^{0.5} = 15$$

$$(1.5)^{0.5} y = 15.$$

Thus, $y = 15/(1.5)^{0.5} = 12.3$. And we can solve for x from equation (15) as well.
Example 5: Producer Equilibrium. A producer will be in equilibrium if the isoquant is a tangent to the isocost curve. This tangency point will determine the units of inputs (capital and labor) the producer should purchase in order to maximize profits or to minimize cost.

Assume the isoquant equation (which is the production function when the output q is equal to 12) is

$$L^{0.4} K^{0.6} = 12$$

and the isocost equation is

$$5L + 3K = T,$$

where T is the total cost. The prices of the factors of production, labor and capital, are $5.00 and $3.00, respectively. The question is how many units of labor (L) and capital (K) should our producer buy?

Solution: Differentiating the isoquant equation implicitly with respect to L, we obtain

$$0.4L^{-0.6} K^{0.6} + 0.6K^{-0.4} (dK/dL) L^{0.4} = 0.$$

Solving for dK/dL, whose absolute value is the marginal rate of technical substitution of L for K, yields

$$dK/dL = (-2/3) K/L. \qquad (16)$$

Now, differentiating the isocost equation with respect to L yields,

$$dK/dL = -3/5. \qquad (17)$$

Equating equations (16) and (17) yields

$$-3/5 = -2/3 \ (K/L) \qquad (18)$$

$$9/10 = K/L \ \text{ or}$$

$$9L = 10K$$

$$L = 10/9 \ K. \qquad (19)$$

Inserting equation (19), which shows the expansion path, in the isoquant, one can solve for K, and the outcome is inserted in equation (19) again to obtain L.

Higher-Order Derivatives

Differentiating the function y = f(x) gives the rate of change in y with respect to x. By using the same rules of differentiation, one can differentiate the first derivative again. The second derivative measures the rate of change of the rate of change of y with respect to x and is denoted by f''(x) or d^2y/dx^2. Actually, we can differentiate the function to a higher order if the function allows us to do so.

Example 1: Find the second and third derivatives for y = $3x^2$.
Solution: dy/dx = 6x, d^2y/dx^2 = 6, and d^3y/dx^3 = 0.

Example 2: Find the second, third, and fourth derivatives for y = e^x.

Solution: $dy/dx = e^x$, $d^2y/dx^2 = e^x$, $d^3y/dx^3 = e^x$, and $d^4y/dx^4 = e^x$

Example 3: Find the second derivative for $y = 1/x$.
Solution: $dy/dx = -1/x^2$ and $d^2y/dx^2 = 1/x^4$.

Example 4: Find the second derivative for $y = \ln(2x + 1)$.
Solution: $dy/dx = (1/2x + 1) \cdot (2) = 2/(2x + 1)$, and

$$d^2y/dx^2 = -2(2) / [(2x + 1)]^2$$

Partial Differentiation

This differentiation is used to measure the impact of a change in an independent variable, holding all other independent variables constant, on the dependent variable. In other words, the function we deal with is a function of several variables, such as $y = f(x_1, x_2, x_3,..., x_n)$, whose independent variables x_i, where $i = (1,..., n)$, are independent of each other (Allen 1956, 1938). For the partial derivatives, the notations f_{x1}, f_{x2}, and f_{xn} will be used in this text. For example, f_{x1} means the partial derivative of the function with respect to x_1 holding other independent variables constant. Other notations such as $\partial f / \partial x_1$ are also used. One should note also that f_{x1} is still a function of the same independent variables. That is, $f_{x1}(x_1, x_2, x_3,...x_n)$.

Example 1: Differentiate $y = 3x_1x_2$ partially with respect to x_1 and x_2.
Solution: This function can be expressed as $y = 3x_1x_2 = f(x_1, x_2)$; hence,

$$\partial f/\partial x_1 = f_{x1} = 3x_2 \quad \text{and} \quad \partial f/\partial x_2 = f_{x2} = 3x_1,$$

where f_{x1} means the partial derivative of the function with respect to x_1 holding x_2 constant, and f_{x2} indicates the partial derivative of the function with respect to x_2 holding x_1 constant. As one can see, the same rules of differentiation are used.

Example 2: Differentiate $y = 4x_1^2 x_2^3$ partially with respect to x_1 and x_2.
Solution: $\partial f/\partial x_1 = f_{x1} = 8x_1x_2^3$ and $\partial f/\partial x_2 = f_{x2} = 12x_1^2x_2^2$.

Example 3: Differentiate the function $y = x_1^2 + x_2^2$ partially with respect to x_1 and x_2.
Solution: $\partial f/\partial x_1 = f_{x1} = 2x_1$ and $\partial f/\partial x_2 = f_{x2} = 2x_2$.

Example 4: Differentiate the function $Z = 3xy^2 + y^3 - 3x^2$ partially with respect to x and y.
Solution: $\partial Z/\partial x = Z_x = 3y^2 - 6x$ and $\partial Z/\partial y = Z_y = 6xy + 3y^2$.

Example 5: The Production Function. Production function shows the relationship between factors of production and output level. One form of the production functions is called *Cobb-Douglas* production function. Suppose this function takes the following form:

$$Q = 4L^{0.3}K^{0.7}$$

where Q, L, and K are the output level, units of labor, and units of capital, respectively. For such a function, researchers are interested in finding the marginal products of labor and capital as well as the elasticities. The marginal products are the partial derivatives of output with respect to labor (Q_l) and capital (Q_k). Hence,

$$\partial Q/\partial L = Q_l = 1.2L^{-0.7}K^{0.7}$$

$$\partial Q/\partial K = Q_k = 2.8L^{0.3}K^{-0.3}.$$

Moreover, one can find the elasticity of output with respect to K as follows:

$$e_k = Q_l\, K/Q = 2.8L^{0.3}K^{-0.3}\, K/Q$$

$$= 4\,(0.7L^{0.3}K^{0.7})\,/\,Q$$

$$= 0.7.$$

Similarly, one can find $e_l = (Q_l L/Q)$, which is equal to 0.3.

Example 6: Euler's Theorem. For a function Z = f(x,y), this theorem says that Z = $f_x\, x + f_y\, y$. This theorem is very important in the neoclassical theory of income distribution. It suggests that the output level is distributed according to the marginal productivities of labor and capital. For example, let us use the production function introduced in example 5. According to this theorem, we have

$$Q = Q_l\, L + Q_k\, K.$$

Substitute the partial derivatives of Q with respect to L and K in the above equation to obtain

$$Q = (1.2L^{-0.7}K^{0.7})L + (2.8L^{0.3}K^{-0.3})K.$$

After simple manipulation, one can obtain

$$Q = 4\, L^{0.3}\, K^{0.7},$$

which is the production function. In other words, output is distributed to L and K according to their productivities.

Example 7: The Jacobian Determinant

$$IJI = \begin{vmatrix} Z_x & Z_y \\ G_x & G_y \end{vmatrix}$$

For two functions $Z = z(x,y)$ and $G = g(x,y)$, the Jacobian determinant would be where Z_x, Z_y, G_x, and G_y are the first partial derivatives of Z and G with respect to x and y, respectively. If $IJI = 0$, the two functions are dependent (related); otherwise, they are independent. For example, suppose the following functions are given

$$Z = 3xy \text{ and } G = 5x + 3y;$$

the Jacobian determinant IJI would be

$$IJI = \begin{vmatrix} 3y & 3x \\ 5 & 3 \end{vmatrix}$$

and the functions are independent unless $x = y = 0$.

One should note that the same procedure is used for three functions. In this case, however, the Jacobian determinant will be of dimension 3 by 3. For example, for the functions $Z = z(x, y, t)$, $G = g(x, y, t)$, and $L = l(x, y, t)$, the Jacobian determinant IJI would be:

$$IJI = \begin{vmatrix} Z_x & Z_y & Z_t \\ G_x & G_y & G_t \\ L_x & L_y & L_t \end{vmatrix} .$$

Implicit Differentiation

To differentiate the function $f(x_1, x_2,...x_n) = 0$ implicitly, one can use this formula:

$$\partial x_1 / \partial x_j = - f_{xj} / f_{x1} \text{ for } j = 2,3,...n \text{ and } f_{x1} \neq 0.$$

Example 1: Differentiate the function $f(x_1, x_2, x_3) = 3x_1x_2x_3 - 10 = 0$ implicitly.

Solution: $\partial x_1 / \partial x_2 = - f_{x2} / f_{x1}$, $\partial f/\partial x_2 = f_{x2} = 3x_1x_3$, and $\partial f/\partial x_1 = f_{x1} = 3x_2x_3$,

hence $\partial x_1 / \partial x_2 = - 3x_1x_3 / 3x_2x_3 = - x_1 / x_2$.

Also, we can find $\partial X_1 / \partial X_3 = - f_{x3} / f_{x1}$. $\partial f/\partial x_3 = f_{x3} = 3x_1 x_2$ and we know f_{x1}. Thus,

$\partial x_1 / \partial x_3 = - x_1 / x_3$.

Example 2: Differentiate the function $f(x, y , z) = 3x^2 y^2z - 3xy - 3 = 0$ implicitly.
Solution:
$$\partial Y/ \partial X = - f_x / f_y = - (6xy^2z - 3y) / (6x^2yz - 3x)$$

$$\partial Y / \partial Z = - f_z / f_y = - 3x^2y^2 / (6x^2yz - 3x)$$

$$\partial Z / \partial X = - f_x / f_z = - (6xy^2z - 3y) / 3x^2y^2$$

Example 3: Find $- f_x / f_y$ and $- f_z / f_y$ by differentiating the function $f(x, y , z) =$

$3e^{XYZ} + 2\ln (x + y) - 4 = 0$ implicitly.
Solution:

$$\partial y / \partial x = - f_x / f_y = - [3yze^{XYZ} + (2/x + y)] / [3xze^{XYZ} + (2/ x + y)], \text{ and}$$

$$\partial y / \partial z = - fz / fy = - [3xye^{XYZ}] / [3xze^{XYZ} + (2/x + y)].$$

Higher-Order Partial Derivatives

Similar to a higher-order differentiation of functions of one variable, the multivariate functions can be differentiated to higher orders such as first, second, third, and so on as long as the given function permits that. Literally, for example, the second-order partial differentiation measures the rate of change of the rate of change of the dependent variable with respect to a change in an independent variable, holding all other independent variables constant.

Suppose we have the function $Y = f(X_1, X_2, X_3,..., X_n)$ the following notations are used to indicate the second-order partial derivatives: f_{x1x1}, f_{x1x2}, f_{x1x3}, f_{x1xn}, f_{x2x2}, f_{x3x3}, and f_{xnxn}. One should note that the notations f_{x1x1}, f_{x2x2}, f_{x3x3}, and f_{xnxn} indicate the direct second order partial derivatives, whereas f_{x1x2}, f_{x1x3},, f_{x1xn}, f_{x2xn} and so on indicate the cross-partial higher-order derivatives. In addition, and according to Young's theorem, the second-order cross-partial derivatives such as f_{x1x2} and f_{x2x1} are equal. Similarly, f_{x3x1} and f_{x1x3} are equal as well.

Example 1: Find all second-order partial derivatives for $Y = 4x_1x_2$.
Solution: The first partial derivatives are

$$f_{x1} = 4x_2 \text{ and } f_{x2} = 4x_1,$$

the second direct partial derivatives are

$$f_{x1x1} = 0 \text{ and } f_{x2x2} = 0,$$

and the second cross-partial derivatives are

$$f_{x1x2} = 4 \text{ and } f_{x2x1} = 4.$$

Example 2: Find all second-order partial derivatives for $Y = 5x_1^2x_2^2 + x_1 + 3x_2$.
Solution:

$$f_{x1} = 10x_1x_2^2 + 1 \text{ and } f_{x2} = 10x_1^2x_2 + 6x_2. \ f_{x1x1} = 10x_2^2 \text{ and } f_{x2x2} = 10x_1^2 + 6.$$

And $f_{x1x2} = 20x_1x_2$ and $f_{x2x1} = 20x_1x_2$.

Example 3: Find all partial derivatives for $Z = e^{xy}$.
Solution: $Z_x = ye^{xy}$ and $Z_y = xe^{xy}$, $Z_{xx} = y^2e^{xy}$ and $Z_{yy} = x^2e^{xy}$, $Z_{xy} = e^{xy} + xye^{xy}$ and $Z_{yx} = e^{xy} + xye^{xy}$.

Example 4: The Hessian Determinant. For the function $Z = f(x,y)$, the second-order direct and cross-partial derivatives form the Hessian determinant IHI, which is used, as we shall see, to determine whether a given function has optimum values or not. For example, for a function such as

$$Z = 4x^2y^2,$$

the Hessian determinant would be

$$|H| = \begin{vmatrix} Z_{xx} & Z_{xy} \\ Z_{yx} & Z_{yy} \end{vmatrix}.$$

The second-order partial derivatives are obtained as follows:

$$Z_x = 8xy^2 \quad \text{and } Z_y = 8x^2y$$

$$Z_{xx} = 8y^2 \quad \text{and } Z_{yy} = 8x^2$$

$$Z_{xy} = 16xy \quad \text{and } Z_{yx} = 16xy.$$

Thus, the Hessian determinant is

$$|H| = \begin{vmatrix} 8Y^2 & 16Y \\ 16XY & 8X^2 \end{vmatrix}.$$

Accordingly, $|H| = 64x^2y^2 - 256x^2y^2 = -192x^2y^2$.

Example 5: Find the Hessian determinant for $Z = 2xy$.
Solution:

$$Z_x = 2_y \quad \text{and} \quad Z_y = 2_x$$

$$Z_{xx} = 0 \quad \text{and} \quad Z_{yy} = 0$$

$$Z_{xy} = 2 \quad \text{and} \quad Z_{yx} = 2.$$

Therefore, the Hessian determinant would be

$$|H| = \begin{vmatrix} 0 & 2 \\ 2 & 0 \end{vmatrix}.$$

Total Differentials

For a function such as, $Z = f(X,Y)$, the total differential dZ of the function measures the small change in Z, (dZ), caused by the changes in both X, (dX), and

Y, (dY). In other words, the total differential is used if both X and Y change simultaneously--no independent variable is constant. Therefore, the total differential (dZ) of the function $Z = f(x,y)$ is

$$dZ = f_x dx + f_y dy,$$

where f_x (or Z_x) and f_y (or Z_y) are the partial derivatives of the function with respect to x and y, respectively. Generally, for a function of n variables such as

$$Z = f(x_1, x_2, x_3, ..., x_n)$$

the total differential would be

$$dZ = f_{x1} dx_1 + f_{x2} dx_2 + f_{x3} dx_3 + ... + f_{xn} dx_n.$$

Example 1: Differentiate the function $Z = 5XY$ totally.
Solution:

$$Z_x = 5y \text{ and } Z_y = 5x;$$

thus, the total differential is

$$dZ = 5ydx + 5xdy.$$

Example 2: Differentiate the function $Z = 8x^2y^2$ totally.
Solution:

$$Z_x = 16xy^2 \text{ and } Z_y = 16x^2y,$$

and the total differential is

$$dZ = (16xy^2)dx + (16x^{2y})dy.$$

Example 3: The Utility function $U = 2x^{0.4}y^{0.6}$, where x and y are two commodities, shows that a consumer obtains certain utils from the consumption of x and y.
Solution: Differentiate the utility function totally to obtain

$$U_x = 0.8x^{-0.6}y^{0.6} \text{ and } U_y = 1.2x^{0.4}y^{-0.4}$$

or

$$U_x = 0.8(y/x)^{0.6} \text{ and } U_y = 1.2 (x/y)^{0.4}.$$

thus,

$$du = 0.8(y/x)^{0.6} dx + 1.2 (x/y)^{0.4} dy.$$

If $x = 5$ units of commodity x and $y = 10$ units of commodity y, then the increase (du) in the utility for $dx = dy = 1$ would be

$$du = 0.8(10/5)^{0.6} (1) + 1.2(5/10)^{0.4} (1) = 2.12 \text{ utils.}$$

Example 4: Suppose the corn market is modeled as follows:

$$Q_d = 4 - (1/2)P + 2y + P_b \tag{20}$$

$$Q_s = -2 + (2/3) P \tag{21}$$

$$Q_d = Q_s = Q. \tag{22}$$

The question is to express the above model implicitly and to differentiate the implicit form of the model totally in order to find $\partial Q/\partial y$ and $\partial P/\partial y$, assuming P_b is a constant, where y and P_b are income and price of beef, respectively (Chiang 1984).
Solution: Using equation (22) in equations (20) and (21) yields

$$Q = 4 - (1/2)P + 2y + P_b \tag{23}$$

$$Q = -2 + (2/3)P. \tag{24}$$

Writing equations (23) and (24) implicitly yields

$$f^1(.) = Q - 4 + (1/2) P - 2y - Pb = 0 \tag{25}$$

$$f^2(.) = Q + 2 - (2/3) P = 0. \tag{26}$$

Taking the total differential of $f^1(.)$ and $f^2(.)$, ignoring the signs, and keeping in mind that dZ is equal to zero yields

$$(\partial f^1/\partial Q) dQ + (\partial f^1/\partial P) dP + (\partial f^1/\partial y) dy + (\partial f^1/\partial P_b) dP_b = 0 \tag{27}$$

$$(\partial f^2/\partial Q) dQ + (\partial f^2/\partial P) dP \qquad\qquad = 0. \tag{28}$$

To find the impact of the change in y (i.e., ∂y) on the entire model,
equations (27) and (28) must be divided by ∂y, where y is the exogenous variable.

That is,

$$(\partial f^1 / \partial Q)\ \partial Q/\partial y + (\partial f^1/\partial P)\ \partial P/\partial y = -\partial f^1 /\partial y \qquad (29)$$

$$(\partial f^2 / \partial Q)\ \partial Q/\partial y + (\partial f^2/\partial P)\ \partial P/\partial y = 0. \qquad (30)$$

From the implicit form of the model (equations [25] and [26]) we can find the following partial derivatives:

$$\partial f^1 / \partial Q = 1,\quad \partial f^1/\partial P = 1/2,\quad \partial f^1/\partial y = -2,$$

$$\partial f^2 / \partial Q = 1,\quad \partial f^2/\partial P = -2/3.$$

Using these values in equations (29) and (30) yields,

$$1\ \partial Q/\partial y + 1/2\ \partial P/\partial y = 2 \qquad (31)$$

$$1\ \partial Q/\partial y - 2/3\ \partial P/\partial y = 0 \qquad (32)$$

Using Cramer's rule, we can solve for $\partial Q/\partial Y$ and $\partial P/\partial y$. That is,

$$IAI = \begin{vmatrix} 1 & 1/2 \\ 1 & -2/3 \end{vmatrix} = -2/3 -1/2 = -7/6$$

$$IA_1I = \begin{vmatrix} 2 & 1/2 \\ 0 & -2/3 \end{vmatrix} = -2/3$$

$$IA_2I = \begin{vmatrix} 1 & 2 \\ 1 & 0 \end{vmatrix} = -2.$$

Therefore, $\partial Q/\partial y = -2/3 / -7/6 = 12/21$ and $\partial P/\partial y = -2/ -7/6 = 14/6$, which is the required solution, indicating that if y increases, both Q and P will increase.

Second-Order Total Differentials

Similar to the second-order differentiation, one can find a second-order total differential for the function $Z = f(x,y)$. The first-order total differential (Tintner and Milham 1970) was

$$dZ = f_x dx + f_y dy. \tag{33}$$

As mentioned previously, the partial derivatives f_x (or Z_x) and f_y (or Z_y) are functions of x and y, respectively. That is,

$$dZ = f_x(x,y) + f_y(x,y). \tag{34}$$

Now, the second-order total differential of equation (34) can be obtained by using equation (33). That is,

$$dZ (dZ) = (f_{xx}dx)dx + (f_{xy}dy)dx + (f_{yx}dx)dy + (f_{yy}dy)dy,$$

which is equal to

$$d^2Z = f_{xx}d^2x + 2f_{xy}dydx + f_{yy}d^2y. \tag{35}$$

The second-order total differentials say that the change of the original change in Z, dZ is the sum of the change of the change in x, the change of the change in y, and double the change in f_x (or f_y) caused by a small change in y, f_{xy}, or in x, f_{yx}.

Example 1: Find the first- and second-order total differentials for $Z = 12x^2y$.
Solution:

$$Z_x = 24xy \quad \text{and} \quad Z_y = 12x^2$$

$$Z_{xx} = 24y \quad \text{and} \quad Z_{yy} = 0,$$

$$Z_{xy} = 24x \quad \text{and} \quad Z_{yx} = 24x$$

thus,

$$dZ = (24xy)dx + (12x^2)dy, \text{ and}$$

$$d^2Z = (24xy)d^2x + (48x)dxdy.$$

Example 2: Find the first- and second-order total differentials for $Z = \ln(x^2 + y^2)$.
Solution:

$$Z_x = 2x / (x^2 + y^2)$$

$$Z_y = 2y / (x^2 + y^2)$$

$$Z_{xx} = [2(x^2 + y^2) - 4x^2] / (x^2 + y^2)^2$$

$$Z_{yy} = [2(x^2 + y^2) - 4y^2] / (x^2 + y^2)^2$$

$$Z_{xy} = -4xy / (x^2 + y^2)^2,$$

thus,

$$dZ = (2x / x^2 + y^2)dx + (2y / x^2 + y^2)dy$$

and

$$d^2Z = [2(x^2 + y^2) - 4x^2 / (x^2 + y^2)^2]d^2x - [8xy / (x^2 + y^2)^2]dxdy +$$

$$[2(x^2 + y^2 - 4y^2 / (x^2 + y^2)^2] d^2.$$

Total Derivatives

Given a function of the form $Z = f(x,y)$, we are interested in finding the rate of change of the function with respect to x when x and y are related (Draper and Klingman 1972). That is to say, in this kind of differentiation the independent variables are actually dependent on other variables. Three cases are available:

Case 1: Given the function $Z = f(x,y)$, where $y = g(x)$, the total derivative of Z with respect to x is

$$dZ/dx = f_x dx/dx + f_y dy/dx,$$

but dx/dx is equal to one, hence

$$dZ/dx = f_x + f_y dy/dx,$$

where f_x and f_y are the partial derivatives of the function with respect to x and y, respectively. One should note that f_x is the direct effect of the change in x on Z, and $f_y dy/dx$ measures the indirect effect of the change in y on Z --change runs from y to x, then to Z.

Example 1: Find the total derivative for $Z = 3xy$ where $y = 3x^2$.
Solution:

$$Z_x = f_x = 3y, \ Z_y = f_y = 3x, \text{ and } dy/dx = 6x.$$

Hence,

$$dZ/dx = 3y + 3x\,(6x) = 3y + 18x^2.$$

The answer means that the total differential of the function is divided by dx.

Example 2: Find the total derivative for $Z = e^{XY}$, where $y = 2x$.
Solution:

$$Z_x = ye^{XY},\ Z_y = xe^{XY},\ \text{and}\ dy/dx = 2.$$

Hence,

$$dZ/dx = ye^{XY} + 2xe^{XY}.$$

Example 3: For a general function of the form $Z = f(x, y_1, y_2, ..., y_n)$ where $y_1 = g(x)$, $y_2 = s(x)$, and $y_n = i(x)$, the total derivative would be,

$$dZ/dx = f_x + f_{y1}dy_1/dx + f_{y2}dy_2/dx + ... + f_{yn}dy_n/dx.$$

Example 4: Find the total derivative for $Z = 3xy_1y_2$, where $y_1 = 2x^2$ and $y_2 = x$.
Solution:

$$Z_x = f_x = 3y_1y_2,\ dy_1/dx = 4x,\ dy_2/dx = 1,$$

$$Z_{y1} = f_{y1} = 3xy_2,\ \text{and}\ Z_{y2} = f_{y2} = 3xy_1.$$

Hence,

$$dZ/dx = 3y_1y_2 + 12x^2y_2 + 3xy_1$$

Case 2: Given the function $Z = f(x,y)$, where x and y are functions of another variable t, that is, $x = g(t)$ and $y = u(t)$, the total derivative would be

$$dZ/dt = Z_x dx/dt + Z_y dy/dt$$

where

$$Z_x = f_x\ \text{and}\ Z_y = f_y.$$

Example 1: Find the total derivative for $Z = 3xy$, where $x = 3t$ and $y = 5t^2$.
Solution:

$$Z_x = 3y, Z_y = 3x, dx/dt = 3, \text{ and } dy/dt = 10t.$$

Hence,

$$dZ/dt = 3y \, (3) + 3x \, (10t) = 9y + 30xt.$$

Example 2: Find the total derivative for $Z = \ln(x + y)$, where $x = \ln t$, and $y = 3t$.
Solution:

$$Zx = (1/x + y), \quad Zy = (1/x + y), dx/dt = 1/t, dy/dt = 3.$$

Hence,

$$dZ/dt = [1/(x + y)] \, (1/t) + [1/x + y](3) = [1/(x + y)]/t + 3/(x + y).$$

Example 3: Find the total derivative for the general function $Z = f(x_1, x_2, ..., x_n)$, where $x_1 = g(t)$, $x_2 = s(t)$, and $x_n = u(t)$.

Solution: $dZ/dt = Z_{x1} \, g'(t) + Z_{x2} \, s'(t) + ... + Z_{xn} \, u'(t)$

where Z_{xi}, i=1...n, are the partial derivatives of the function with respect to x_i, and $g'(t)$, $s'(t)$, and $u'(t)$ are the derivatives of the functions g, s, and u with respect to t.

Example 4: Find the total derivative for $Z = 3x_1x_2x_3$, where $x_1 = 4t^2$, $x_2 = \ln 2t$, and $x_3 = e^t$.
Solution: $Z_{x1} = 3x_2x_3$, $Z_{x2} = 3x_1x_3$, $Z_{x3} = 3x_1x_2$, $dx_1/dt = 8t$, $dx_2/dt = 2/t$, and $dx_3/dt = e^t$. Hence,

$$dZ/dt = 3x_2x_3 \, (8t) + 3x_1x_3 \, (2/t) + 3x_1x_2 \, (e^t).$$

Case 3: Given $Z = f(x, y)$ where $x = S(t_1,t_2)$ and $y = U(t_1,t_2)$, the total derivative (Chiang 1984; Bressler 1975) would be

$$Z_{t1} = Z_x \, S_{t1} + Z_y \, U_{t1}$$

and

$$Z_{t2} = Z_x \, S_{t2} + Z_y \, U_{t2},$$

where Z_{t1} and Z_{t2} are the partial derivatives of Z with respect to t_1 and t_2. S_{t1}, S_{t2}, U_{t1}, and U_{t2} are the partial derivatives of the functions S and U with respect to t_1

and t_2, respectively. As can be seen, each independent variable of the function Z is a function of the two variables t_1 and t_2.

Example 1: Find the total derivatives for $Z = 3xy$, where $x = 3t_1t_2$ and $y = t_1t_2^2$.
Solution:

$$Z_x = 3y, \ Z_y = 3x, \ X_{t1} = 3t_2, \ X_{t2} = 3t_1, \ Y_{t1} = t_2^2, \ Y_{t2} = 2t_1t_2.$$

Hence,

$$Z_{t1} = 3y \ (3t_2) + 3x \ (t_2^2)$$

$$Z_{t2} = 3y \ (3t_1) + 3x \ (2t_1t_2)$$

Example 2: Find the total derivatives for $Z = f(x_1, x_2, ..., x_n)$, where $X_1 = G(t_1,t_2)$, $X_2 = S(t_1,t_2)$, and $X_n = U(t_1,t_2)$.
Solution:

$$Z_{t1} = Z_{x1} \ G_{t1} + Z_{x2} \ S_{t1} + ... + Z_{xn} \ U_{t1} \text{ and } Z_{t2} = Z_{x1} \ G_{t2} + Z_{x2} \ S_{t2} + ... + Z_{xn} U_{t2}$$

Example 3: Find the total derivatives for $Z = WXY$, where, $W = t_1 + t_2$, $X = 3t_1 - t_2$, and $Y = t_1t_2$.

Solution: $Z_w = XY, \ Z_x = WY, \ Z_y = WX, \ W_{t1} = 1, \ W_{t2} = 1, \ X_{t1} = 3, \ X_{t2} = -1$, $Y_{t1} = t_2$, and $Y_{t2} = t_1$.

Hence,

$$Z_{t1} = XY \ (1) + WY \ (3) + WX \ (t_2)$$

$$Z_{t2} = XY \ (1) + WY \ (-1) + WX \ (t_1).$$

Problems

1.   Find dy/dx for the following functions:

$y = 15 + 3x + 2x^2$ $y = e^{3x}$

$y = 7x^3$ $y = (1/x^2)e^x$

$y = (x^3 - 4)^4$ $y = x^3 \ln(2x)$

$$y = x^2/(x^3 + 2x)$$

$$y = [(x - 2)/x]^3$$

$$y = \ln (x + x^2 + 5)$$

$$y = xy^2 - 2x^2 + 5y = 0$$

$$y = 5x^2 / (3x^2 + 2x)$$

$$y = x^3 + y^3 + 3xy = 0$$

$$y = (3)^u, \text{ where } u = 6x + 3.$$

$$y = (5)^{4u}, \text{ where } u = x^3.$$

$$y = \log_b (3x^2 + x)$$

$$y = x^{2x}$$

2.   Given the following utility function and budget line equation:

$$u = x^{1/3}y^{2/3} \quad \text{and } 3x + 4y = 120$$

find the units of x and y the consumer has to purchase in order to maximize the utility function.

3.   Given the following production function and cost equation

$$Q = L^{1/4}K^{3/4} \quad \text{and } 5L + 3K = 150,$$

find the units of L and K the producer has to employ in order to minimize production cost.

4.   Differentiate the following functions partially:

$$z = 2x_1 + 3x_1x_2 - 8x_2^2$$

$$z = x_1x_2 + \ln (x_1)$$

$$z = (x_1^3 + x_2^2) + x_1x2$$

$$z = x_1e^{x1/ \ x2}$$

$$z = (x_1^2x_2)^{1/2}$$

$$z = 3x_1/x_2$$

$$z = \ln (x_1 + 4x_1x_2)$$

$$z = 5x_1x_2 + 3x_2 = 0$$

$$z = 3x^2 + 6y^2$$

$$z = 5xy$$

$$z = 5x/y$$

$$z = (5x + 3)^3 / y$$

$$z = (3x + 2y)^2 (5x + y)^3$$

$$z = ye^{5xy}$$

5.   Find the first- and second-order total differentials for the following functions:

$$z = 3x_1x_2 + x_2^2 + x_1^2 \qquad\qquad z = L^{1/3}K^{2/3}$$

$$z = xy/(5x + y) \qquad\qquad z = e^{xy}$$

$$z = 5\ln(xy) \qquad\qquad z = (3x + 2y)(x^2 + y^2)$$

6.   Find the total derivative for the following functions:

$$z = 4x^2 + 6y^3, \text{ where } x = 5y^3$$

$$z = (x + 3y)(2x + 6), \text{ where } x = 5y + 3y^3$$

$$Q = L^{4/5}K^{1/5}, \text{ where } L = 3t + 2 \text{ and } K = 5t$$

$$u = x^{1/3}y^{2/3}, \text{ where } x = 2t^2 \text{ and } y = 3t^2$$

$$z = 4x^3 + xy + y^2, \text{ where } x = t_1 + 2t_2 \text{ and } y = 3t_1 + 4t_2^4.$$

7.   Given the following macroeconomic model:

$$Y = C + Io$$

$$C = 3 + 0.5(Y - T)$$

$$T = 2 + 0.01$$

where Y is income, Io is investment, C is consumption expenditures, and T is the tax level, find the impact of investment Io on Y, C, and T.

8.   For the first two functions of problem 4, find the Jacobian and the Hessian determinants.

9.   For the production function $Q = 2L^{1/2}K^{1/2}$, find the marginal products of labor and capital. Also, find the elasticity of output with respect to Labor L and capital K.

10.   A firm has a revenue function $R(Q) = 20Q - 2Q^2$ and a cost function $C(Q) = Q^3 - 15Q^2 + 20Q$. Find the marginal revenue, the marginal cost, and the best level of output.

CHAPTER THREE

The Input-Output Model

The economic impacts of one sector (or a new firm) on an economy is usually measured by an analytical tool (or model) called "input-output." This model has been utilized to study the economic impact not only on the national level for the United States economy and others, but also on the regional level. As the input-output model has become very well-known among economists and policy analysts, there is no actual need to review all the technical elements of this model. However, some basic elements are explained to familiarize students with this valuable technique and to show how this model explains and predicts economic reality.

The input-output model is not only a theory of production but is also an effective application of the Walrasian general equilibrium analysis. It is a theory of production because this model outlines a production function, a linear relation between input and output, for each sector in the economy. And it is an application of the general equilibrium analysis, because it consists of a system of simultaneous equations describing demand for and supply of each sectoral output. Stated somewhat differently, the input-output model describes the structural interdependence among the various economic sectors of a region or a nation.

The fundamental idea of the input-output model is that an economy can be divided into various economic sectors called "industries" or "activities" producing different products. Each activity (or industry), say X_1, requires a certain number of inputs, produced by other industries, in order to produce its own production. By the same token, the other industries X_i, i = 2, ..., n, require a certain number of inputs produced by industry X_1 and others to produce their own production. In other words, the input-output model shows the interdependence among the various economic sectors of an economy by describing the interindustry flows (the transaction matrix) of inputs and outputs that make up the economy.

The Input-Output Table

In Table 3.1, the structure of a typical input-output table (Leontief 1986; Emerson and Lampheer 1975) is presented. As shown, the table consists of four quadrants, and the first two quadrants are very important for measuring the economic impacts.

Table 3.1. **Quadrants of Input-Output**

PS*	IG&S*					TID*	FD*					TD*	TO*
	S_1	S_2	S_3	S_4 ...S_n			I	H	C	G	E		
S_1	X_{11}	X_{12}	X_{13}	$X_{14}...X_{1n}$		SX_{1n}	I_1	H_1	C_1	G_1	E_1	Y_1	X_1
S_2	X_{21}	X_{22}	X_{23}	$X_{24}...X_{2n}$		SX_{2n}	I_2	H_2	C_2	G_2	E_2	Y_2	X_2
S_3	X_{31}	X_{32}	X_{33}	$X_{34}...X_{3n}$		SX_{3n}	I_3	H_3	C_3	G_3	E_3	Y_3	X_3
.	.		(Quadrant I)			. .		(Quadrant II)		.		. .	...
S_n	X_{n1}	X_{n2}	X_{n3}	$X_{n4}...X_{nn}$		SX_{nn}	I_n	H_n	C_n	G_n	E_n	Y_n	X_n

Total Purchases

M	M_1	M_2	M_3	$M_4...M_n$	M		S_{MI}	S_{MH}	S_{MC}	S_{MG}	S_{ME}		M
I	I_1	I_2	I_3	$I_4... I_n$	I		S_{II}	S_{IH}	S_{IC}	S_{IG}	S_{IE}		I
H	H_1	H_2	H_3	$H_4...H_n$	H		S_{HI}	S_{HH}	S_{HC}	S_{HG}	S_{HE}		H
			(Quadrant IV)						(Quadrant III)				
D	D_1	D_2	D_3	$D_4...D_n$	D		S_{DI}	S_{DH}	S_{DC}	S_{DG}	S_{DE}		D
G	G_1	G_2	G_3	$G_4...G_n$	G		S_{GI}	S_{GH}	S_{GC}	S_{GG}	S_{GE}		G

Value Added V_1 V_2 V_3 $V_4... V_n$	V

Total Inputs X_1 X_2 X_3 $X_4.. .X_n$	X

*PS = producing sector; IG&S = intermediate goods and services; TID = total intermediate demand; FD = final demand; TD = total final demand; TO = total output.

Quadrant (I) in Table 3.1 shows the interindustry transactions (flows) among the various economic sectors (S_1, S_2, ..., S_n). The economy's producing sectors are rows S_1 through S_n. For example, row (S_1) indicates that industry 1 sells (X_{11}) units of its production to itself, sells (X_{12}) units of its production to industry (S_2), and sells (X_{1n}) units of its production to industry (S_n). The sum of (S_1) industry's production sold to the column industries represents the total intermediate supply of industry (S_1).

By the same token, one can describe the flow of production from row industry (S_n) to the column industries. For example, row (S_n) industry sells the amount (X_{n1}) of its own production to column (S_1) industry, sells the amount (X_{n2}) of its production to column (S_2) industry, and sells (X_{nn}) of its output to itself. The sum of these sales is called the "intermediate supply" of row (S_n) industry or the "total intermediate demand" of the column industries on the production of row (S_n) industry.

Similarly, each column in Table 3.1 indicates the purchasing industry of the production (inputs) produced by the row industries S_1 through S_n; each purchasing industry buys these inputs in order to produce its own production. For example, column (S_3) industry purchases (X_{13}) units of production from row (S_1) industry, purchases (X_{23}) amount of production from row (S_2) industry, and purchases (X_{n3}) units of production from row (S_n) industry. These quantities of production, purchased by column (S_3) industry, are used to produce the output of column (S_3) industry, (X_3). One should note that the sum of the purchases is actually the sum of each column industry, a sum representing the total intermediate demand of each industry (S_1 through S_n) or the production of column (S_1) industry.

Quadrant (II) in Table 3.1 shows the users of the products produced by row S_1 through row S_n industries. Those users represent the various components of final demands. The symbol (I) represents the accumulation of inventory by the row industries; (H) shows the final sales made by the row industries to the households; (C) illustrates the sales made by the row industries to buyers who use the production for the purpose of capital formation; (G) indicates governments' purchases from the row industries; and (E) represents exports made by the producing sectors. For example, (H_1) indicates that a part of the production of row (S_1) industry is bought by the households for their consumption. Also, (H_1) indicates that row (S_1) industry sells the mount (H_1) of its production to the households. By the same token, row (S_n) industry sells the amount (H_n) of its production to the households for final consumption, or the households' purchase (H_n) of output from row (S_n) industry to satisfy their consumption demands.

Similarly, the various levels of government (G) purchase (G_1) amount of production produced by row (S_1) industry, or the latter industry sells (G_1) amount of its production to the governments. By the same token, the governments purchase (G_n) amount of production, produced by row (S_n) industry, for its final consumption.

The other component of final demand is exports (E). For example, (E_1) in Table 3.1 indicates that foreign countries purchase this amount of production from row (S_1) industry, or the latter industry exports (E_1) amount of its production to foreign countries. By the same token, (E_n) represents the amount of exports, which is produced by row (S_n) industry, purchased (imported) by the foreign countries.

By the same procedure one can interpret (I) and (C). For example, (I_1) represents the accumulation of inventory made by row (S_1) industry. Similarly, (C_3) records the sales of row (S_3) industry to purchasers who use the production of (S_3) industry for capital formation rather than consumption.

Quadrant (III) in Table 3.1 shows the values of sales to the various components of final demand users, and the sold items are the primary factors such as land, capital, and so on. For example, (S_{HH}) indicates the households' purchases of domestic services, which are sold by the households' (row H). Similarly, (S_{HG}) indicates the households' sales of labor inputs to the governments (G). In addition, (S_{GH}) indicates the sales of government output and services to the households (column H), or it represents the households purchases (column H) from the governments (row G). One should also note that (S_{MH}) represents the households purchases of imports from the foreign countries. Also, (S_{MG}) represents government imports form the foreign countries, and all other symbols are interpreted according to this procedure.

Quadrant (IV) in Table 3.1 shows payments made by the column industries to (M), (I), (H), (D), and (G). These payments are paid to the primary inputs such as capital, labor, land, and natural resources, and to the governments in the form of taxes (the source of funds). The symbols are defined as follows. (I) represents inventory depletions during the period covered by the study. (H) shows payments received by the households because they provide their input (labor power) to the column industries. For example, (H_1) represents payments to the households that are made by column (S_1) industry. (D) reflects depreciation of the capital stock used in the production process. For instance, (D_2) represents payments made by column (S_2) industry to the depreciation of means of production used to produce the output (X_2) of industry (S_2). That is, (D_2) represents the amount of fund set aside (capital account) by column (S_2) industry to purchase the input of capital. One should note that (D_2) may not equal the investment expenditures of column (S_2) industry. It should be mentioned that the sum of (I), (H), (D), and (G) gives the value added for each industry. For example, the sum of (H_3), (I_3), (D_3), and (G_3) gives the value added (V_3) for column (S_3) industry.

Finally, quadrant (IV) contains imports (M) made by the column industries to produce their products. For example, (M_1) shows the imports made by column (S_1) industry to produce its output, (X_1). Thus, for industry (S_1) the total intermediate purchases used to produce the output (X_1) are the sum of column (S_1) of quadrant (I) plus the imports (M_1) of quadrant (IV).

Example 1: A hypothetical input-output table for a five-sector economy is shown below.

Table 3.2. **The Four Quadrants of the Input-Output Model***

S	S_1	S_2	S_3	S_4	S_5	TID	HOU	INV	EXP	TFD	TO
S_1	20	10	30	5	25	90	40	5	30	75	165
S_2	10	0	15	0	8	33	5	0	20	25	58
S_3	35	7	4	3	11	60	0	10	10	20	80
S_4	5	8	1	14	12	40	0	15	5	20	60
S_5	20	8	10	18	0	56	15	15	5	35	91

TP	90	33	60	40	56	279	60	45	70	175
IMP	20	10	0	5	14	49	5	5	0	(10)	49(59)
T	20	5	10	5	4	44	(20)	(0)	(10)	(30)	44(74)
HOU	15	3	5	3	4	30	2	0	0	2	32
CAP	10	2	5	0	10	27	0	0	0	0	27
NR	10	5	0	7	3	25	0	0	0	0	25
VA	55	15	20	15	21	126	2	0	0	2	128
TI	165	58	80	60	91	454	67	50	70	177	631

*TID = total intermediate demand; HOU = households; INV = investment; EXP = exports; TFD = total final demand; TO = total output; TP = total purchases; IMP = imports; T = taxes (government); CAP = capital; NR = natural resources; VA = value added; TI = total input.

The meaning of these transactions has already been explained; as a reminder, some of the interpretations are given. In Table 3.2, the output of industry (S_1) is the sum of (TID) and (TFD), where TID = 20 + 10 + 30 + 5 + 25 = \$90 and TFD = 40 + 5 + 30 = \$75—the sum of row 1. Hence, the total production of industry (S_1) is \$165. The transaction of \$10 in row (S_1) and column (S_2) indicates that industry (S_2) purchases \$10 worth of output from industry (S_1) to produce its output. The value added (VA) of column (S_1), which is equal to \$55, is obtained by summing 20, 15, 10, and 10: the sum of T, HOU, CAP, and NR (TI) of column (S_1) is equal to the sum of TP, IMP, and VA (i.e., 90 + 20 + 55 = \$165). The transaction of (\$20) in row (T) and column (HOU) indicates that households pay \$20 to the governments as taxes. The other transactions can be interpreted similarly.

The Assumptions of the Input-Output Model

Without exception all economic models are based on vital assumptions, and the input-output model is one of them (Chenery and Clark 1959). As Table 3.2 indicates, the input-output model assumes that there is a single process production function for every industry (sector). For example, the single production function for column (S_3) industry is

$$X_3 = X_{i3}/a_{i3} \tag{1}$$

for i = 1, 2, ..., n. In general, for industry (j) one can write the single production function as

$$X_j = X_{1j}/a_{1j} = X_{2j}/a_{2j} = ... = X_{nj}/a_{nj} \qquad (2)$$

and

$$X_j = \min (X_{1j}/a_{1j}, X_{2j}/a_{2j}, ..., X_{nj}/a_{nj}) \qquad (3)$$

This production function is a simple linear function showing the proportional relationship between the output level (X_j) and the input level (X_{ij}), and the coefficient of proportionality is $(1/a_{ij})$, i and j = 1,2, ..., n.

In fact, the above assumption can be broken into two assumptions. The first assumption is that of constant return to scale. That is, if input increases by 10 percent, output will also increase by 10 percent. For example, if

$$X_3 = (1/0.5)X_{i3}, \qquad (4)$$

where $0.5 = a_{i3}$ and X_{i3} is equal to two units, then X_3 will be equal to four units. If we assume that input increases by two units (i.e., from two to four units), the output level will be eight units. Hence, if the input increases by 100 percent, output will have to increase by 100 percent as well.

The second assumption is that of zero substitution among inputs. This assumption, which is brought about by the existence of a single method of production in each industry, indicates that the isoquant of the production function is of L-shape. Because one method of production exists, the planned output level determines the required level of inputs, as the technical coefficients (a_{ij}) are constant. For example, Table 3.1 indicates that to produce (X_3) units of production, column (S_3) industry needs to purchase (X_{23}) units of intermediate inputs from row (S_2) industry: $X_{23} = a_{23}X_3$. Thus, the proportionality assumption suggests that for every unit of output produced by column (S_3) industry, (a_{23}) units of input are always needed from row (S_2) industry as long as the production process of industry (S_3) remains technologically unchanged.

Normally, the technological coefficients are determined by dividing the required intermediate inputs by the total production of that column industry. In other words, each column of input coefficients represents a single process of technical coefficients. In general, the technical coefficients for the whole economy can be obtained as follows:

$$a_{ij} = X_{ij} / X_j \qquad (5)$$

where i and j = 1, 2, ..., n, or by using matrix multiplication such that

$$a_{ij} = A = TX_r \qquad (6)$$

where (T) and (X_r) are the transaction matrix and a diagonal matrix whose elements are the reciprocal of total sectoral production, respectively.

The third assumption of the input-output model is the "additivity assumption." This assumption is used to rule out external economies and diseconomies. Once these economies and diseconomies are excluded, the remaining condition under which output is produced is the constant return to scale.

Example 2: The following is a two-sector economy whose input-output table is,

	S_1	S_2	HOU	EXP	Total Output
			Final Demand		
S_1	85	260	25	150	520
S_2	110	55	200	650	1015
HOU	150	250	25	75	500
NR	175	450	250	200	1075
Total Input	520	1015	500	1075	

Find matrix (A) for the open input-output model and interpret its elements.
Solution: To find matrix A we have to use equation (5) or (6) as follows.
Using equation (5) gives

$$a_{11} = X_{11}/X_1 = 85/520 \ \ = 0.16346$$

$$a_{21} = X_{21}/X_1 = 110/520 = 0.21154$$

$$a_{12} = X_{12}/X_2 = 260/1015 = 0.25616$$

$$a_{22} = X_{22}/X_2 = 55/1015 \ \ = 0.05419$$

Thus,

$$A = \begin{bmatrix} 0.16346 & 0.25616 \\ 0.21154 & 0.05419 \end{bmatrix}.$$

Or using equation (6) gives

$$A = \begin{bmatrix} 85 & 260 \\ 110 & 55 \end{bmatrix} \begin{bmatrix} 1/520 & 0 \\ 0 & 1/1015 \end{bmatrix} = \begin{bmatrix} 85/520 & 260/1015 \\ 110/520 & 55/1015 \end{bmatrix}.$$

As can be seen, the sum of each column of matrix (A) does not exceed unity (why?).

The interpretation of matrix (A) is very simple. The first element of (0.163461) says that to produce a dollar's worth of output, the first sector has to purchase inputs worth ($0.163461) from itself. The second element of (0.211538) suggests that the first sector has to purchase input worth ($0.211538) from the second sector in order to produce a dollar's worth of output. The third element indicates that the second sector has to buy input worth ($0.256157) from the first sector in order to produce a dollar's worth of output. Similarly, the second sector has to buy ($0.054187) worth of output from the second sector in order to produce a dollar's worth of output.

Example 3: For the same input-output table, find matrix (A*), the closed technological matrix, and interpret its elements.
Solution: To find (A*), we must initially incorporate the household's row and column into matrix (A). This can be done by using equation (5) or (6). Using equation 6, (A*) is shown below.

$$
A^* = \begin{bmatrix} 85 & 260 & 25 \\ 110 & 55 & 200 \\ 150 & 250 & 25 \end{bmatrix} \bullet \begin{bmatrix} 1/520 & 0 & 0 \\ 0 & 1/1015 & 0 \\ 0 & 0 & 1/500 \end{bmatrix} =
$$

$$
\begin{bmatrix} 0.163461 & 0.256157 & 0.05 \\ 0.211538 & 0.054187 & 0.40 \\ 0.288461 & 0.246305 & 0.05 \end{bmatrix}.
$$

The interpretation is similar to the one given in example 2, with one qualification: Each element of A* represents the direct, indirect, and induced effect of a dollar increase in final demand.

The Mathematical Structure of the Input-Output Model

The most important quadrants of the input-output table (Table 3.1) for the mathematical representation are quadrants (I) and (II). From the transactions table (Quadrant I of Table 3.1), the interindustry flows, measured by constant prices, can be represented by X_{ij}, where i represents the amount of product (input) produced by row i industry and purchased by column j industry to produce its output, X_j.

For n industries the interindustry flows are represented by

$$\sum_{i}^{n} X_{ij} \tag{7}$$

where $j = 1, 2, ..., n$.

From quadrant (II) the total final demand, which absorbs the output of industries (i) through (n), can be denoted by (Y_i), where $i = 1, 2, ..., n$. For example, for $i = 2$, (Y_2) represents the final demand on the production of row (S_2) industry.

The last variable we need is the last column of Table 3.1, the value of the total sectoral output (X_j). For example, for $j = 3$, (X_3) represents the production of row (S_3) industry. Given these notations, one can represent each row of quadrants (I) and (II) of Table 3.1 as follows:

$$X_{11} + X_{12} + X_{13} + ... + X_{1n} + Y_1 = X_1$$

$$X_{21} + X_{22} + X_{23} + ... + X_{2n} + Y_2 = X_2$$

$$X_{31} + X_{32} + X_{33} + ... + X_{3n} + Y_3 = X_3 \tag{8}$$

$$\dots\dots\dots\dots\dots\dots\dots\dots\dots$$

$$X_{n1} + X_{n2} + X_{n3} + ... + X_{nn} + Y_n = X_n$$

Because the input-output model assumes the interindustry flows, X_{ij}, are linear and proportional functions of the level of output X_j, then $(a_{ij}s)$ are the proportionality coefficients, which represent the number of units of the i*th* product (produced by row i industry) required to produce one unit of output of the j*th* column industry. That is,

$$X_{ij} = a_{ij} X_j \tag{9}$$

for i and $j = 1, 2, 3, ..., n$. Using equation (9) in system (8) yields

$$a_{11} X_1 + a_{12} X_2 + a_{13} X_3 + ... + a_{1n} X_n + Y_1 = X_1$$

$$a_{21} X_1 + a_{22} X_2 + a_{23} X_3 + ... + a_{2n} X_n + Y_2 = X_2$$

$$a_{31} X_1 + a_{32} X_2 + a_{33} X_3 + ... + a_{3n} X_n + Y_3 = X_3 \tag{10}$$

$$\dots\dots\dots\dots\dots\dots\dots\dots\dots\dots\dots\dots\dots$$

$$a_{n1} X_1 + a_{n2} X_2 + a_{n3} X_3 + ... + a_{nn} X_n + Y_n = X_n$$

System (10) can be written in matrix notations as

$$AX + Y = X \tag{11}$$

That is,

$$A = \begin{bmatrix} a_{11} & a_{12} & a_{13} \cdots a_{1n} \\ a_{21} & a_{22} & a_{23} \cdots a_{2n} \\ a_{31} & a_{32} & a_{33} \cdots a_{3n} \\ \cdots\cdots\cdots\cdots\cdots\cdots \\ a_{n1} & a_{n2} & a_{n3} \cdots a_{nn} \end{bmatrix}, \quad X = \begin{bmatrix} X_1 \\ X_2 \\ X_3 \\ \cdot \\ \cdot \\ X_n \end{bmatrix}, \quad Y = \begin{bmatrix} Y_1 \\ Y_2 \\ Y_3 \\ \cdot \\ \cdot \\ Y_n \end{bmatrix}.$$

where matrix (A) is called the "technological matrix" (or the "direct requirements matrix") because it contains the technological fixed coefficients of the input-output model; (X) represents the column vector of total output for each industry; and (Y) represents the column vector of final demands for each industry's output. Equation (11) can be rewritten as

$$Y = X - AX = (I - A)X \tag{12}$$

where (I) is an identity matrix of dimension nxn, i.e.,

$$I = \begin{bmatrix} 1 & 0 & \cdots & 0 & 0 \\ 0 & 1 & & 0 & 0 \\ 0 & 0 & & 0 & 0 \\ \cdot & \cdot & & \cdot & \cdot \\ \cdot & \cdot & & 1 & \cdot \\ 0 & 0 & & 0 & 1 \end{bmatrix}$$

and $(I - A)$ is called the Leontief matrix, named after the Nobel laureate who developed the input-output model. If equation (12) is multiplied by the inverse of $(I - A)$, we obtain

$$X = (I - A)^{-1}Y. \qquad (13)$$

Equation (13) suggests that if we know the technological matrix, **(A)**, and the column vector of final demand, **(Y)**, we can determine the output level **(X)** of each industry (Miernyk 1965).

It should be noted that if matrix **(A)** is used, as in equation (13), the input-output model is called "open model," but if **(A*)** is used, equation (13) becomes

$$X = (I - A^*)^{-1}Y \qquad (14)$$

and equation (14) is called the "closed input-output model" (Richardson 1972, 1979). In other words, it is a closed model since an exogenous sector such as the household sector is incorporated into the technological matrix A.

Example 4: Find **(I - A)** and **(I - A)**$^{-1}$ for the two-sector economy of example 2.

$$(I - A) = \begin{bmatrix} 1 & 0 \\ 0 & 1 \end{bmatrix} - \begin{bmatrix} 0.16346 & 0.25616 \\ 0.21154 & 0.05419 \end{bmatrix} = \begin{bmatrix} 0.83654 & -0.25616 \\ -0.21154 & 0.94581 \end{bmatrix}.$$

Using the materials of chapter 1, the inverse of **(I - A)** would be

$$(I - A)^{-1} = \begin{bmatrix} 1.283296 & 0.347563 \\ 0.287041 & 1.135036 \end{bmatrix}.$$

Matrix **(I - A)**$^{-1}$ is called the "direct and indirect requirements matrix" whose elements indicate the direct and indirect effects of a dollar increase (decrease) in final demand.

Example 5: Find **(I - A*)** and **(I - A*)**$^{-1}$ for the two-sector economy of example 2.

$$(I - A^*) = \begin{bmatrix} 1 & 0 & 0 \\ 0 & 1 & 0 \\ 0 & 0 & 1 \end{bmatrix} - \begin{bmatrix} 0.163461 & 0.256157 & 0.05 \\ -0.211538 & 0.54187 & 0.40 \\ -0.288461 & 0.246305 & 0.05 \end{bmatrix} =$$

$$
\begin{bmatrix}
0.836538 & -0.255615 & -0.05 \\
-0.21153 & 0.945812 & -0.40 \\
-0.288461 & -0.24630 & 0.95
\end{bmatrix} .
$$

Accordingly, the inverse of $(I - A^*)$ would be

$$
(I - A^*)^{-1} =
\begin{bmatrix}
1.398724 & 0.447006 & 0.261830 \\
0.553101 & 1.364260 & 0.603536 \\
0.568115 & 0.489440 & 1.288612
\end{bmatrix} .
$$

Matrix $(I - A^*)^{-1}$ is called the "direct, indirect, and induced requirements matrix" whose elements indicate the direct, indirect, and induced effects per a dollar increase (decrease) in final demand.

Given the $(I - A^*)^{-1}$ and suppose the final demand of sector (2) increases by \$100, what will the level of output be? To determine the sectoral levels of production, equation (14) is used, and the results are

$$
X =
\begin{bmatrix}
X_1 \\
X_2 \\
X_3
\end{bmatrix}
=
\begin{bmatrix}
1.398724 & 0.447006 & 0.261830 \\
0.553101 & 1.364260 & 0.603536 \\
0.568115 & 0.489440 & 1.288612
\end{bmatrix}
\begin{bmatrix}
0 \\
100 \\
0
\end{bmatrix}
=
\begin{bmatrix}
44.7 \\
136.43 \\
48.94
\end{bmatrix} .
$$

Multipliers in the Input-Output Model

One of the significant applications of the input-output model is the measurement of the economic impacts of one industry on other activities (Pleeter 1980; Miernyk 1967). Measuring the impacts of such activities is accomplished by obtaining various multipliers for each economic activity, and the starting point for measuring such impacts is $(I - A)^{-1}$ and $(I - A^*)^{-1}$.

If we take the open input-output model

$$
X = (I - A)^{-1} Y
$$

and let

$$(I - A)^{-1} = B \qquad (15)$$

the model can be rewritten in full as

$$
\begin{bmatrix} X_1 \\ X_2 \\ X_3 \\ \cdot \\ \cdot \\ \cdot \\ X_n \end{bmatrix}
=
\begin{bmatrix}
b_{11} & b_{12} & b_{13} & \cdots & b_{1n} \\
b_{21} & b_{22} & b_{23} & \cdots & b_{2n} \\
b_{31} & b_{32} & b_{33} & \cdots & b_{3n} \\
\multicolumn{5}{c}{\cdots\cdots\cdots\cdots\cdots} \\
b_{n1} & b_{n2} & b_{n3} & \cdots & b_{nn}
\end{bmatrix}
\begin{bmatrix} Y_1 \\ Y_2 \\ Y_3 \\ \cdot \\ \cdot \\ \cdot \\ Y_n \end{bmatrix}
\qquad (16)
$$

Using matrix multiplication, system (16) becomes:

$$X_1 = b_{11}Y_1 + b_{12}Y_2 + b_{13}Y_3 + \ldots + b_{1n}Y_n$$

$$X_2 = b_{21}Y_1 + b_{22}Y_2 + b_{23}Y_3 + \ldots + b_{2n}Y_n$$

$$X_3 = b_{31}Y_1 + b_{32}Y_2 + b_{33}Y_3 + \ldots + b_{3n}Y_n \qquad (17)$$

$$\cdots\cdots\cdots\cdots\cdots$$

$$X_n = b_{n1}Y_1 + b_{n2}Y_2 + b_{n3}Y_3 + \ldots + b_{nn}Y_n$$

If we take the partial derivatives of X_i, where i = 1,2,..n, with respect to Y_j, j = 1, 2, ..., n, we obtain

$$\partial X_i / \partial Y_j = b_{ij} \qquad (18)$$

These partial derivatives indicate the economic impacts of a dollar change in the final demand of sector (j) on the output level of each sector. For example, if the final demand of sector (1), Y_1, increases by a dollar, the direct impact on the production of sector (1) is (b_{11}), and the indirect impact on the production levels of sector (2) and (n) are (b_{21}) and (b_{n1}), respectively. That is, the sum of column (1) of $B = (I - A)^{-1}$ measures the total output multiplier (direct and indirect impacts) of a dollar change in final demand of sector (1) on the output levels of all economic sectors (activities). For this basic reason the matrix $(\mathbf{I} - \mathbf{A})^{-1}$ is called the "direct and indirect requirements matrix," whereas $(\mathbf{I} - \mathbf{A}^*)^{-1}$ is called the "direct, indirect and induced matrix"; it is induced because $(\mathbf{A}^*)$ contains the row and column of the household sector, indicating that when the household receives a dollar, a part of it, say (a), where (a) is the marginal propensity to consume, will be spent again; and this process will continue until the induced impact of the dollar dies out.

Example 6: Find the total output multipliers for the two-sector economy of example 2 (or 4).
Solution: The output multipliers of sector (1) and (2) are 1.283296 + 0.287041 = $1.570337 and 0.347563 + 1.135036 = $1.482599, respectively. These multipliers suggest that if the final demand of sector (1) increases by a dollar, the output level of sectors (1) and (2) will increase by ($1.570337). Similarly, if the final demand of sector (2) increases by a dollar, the output level of sector (2) will increase by ($1.482599).

The second types of multipliers that can be obtained from the input-output model are the Type (I) and (II) income multipliers. The Type (I) income multiplier is obtained from the open input-output model. If the household row in matrix (A) becomes vector (H), the reciprocal of each element of vector (H) can be used to construct a diagonal matrix, say $\mathbf{H}_r$. For example, for

$$\mathbf{H} = [h_1 \quad h_2],$$

matrix $\mathbf{H}_r$ is equal to

$$\mathbf{H}_1 = \begin{bmatrix} 1/h_1 & 0 \\ 0 & 1/h_2 \end{bmatrix}.$$

The Type (I) income multiplier would be

$$\mathbf{K} = \mathbf{H} (\mathbf{I} - \mathbf{A})^{-1} \mathbf{H}_r \tag{19}$$

where $\mathbf{K}$ is a vector of the form

$$\mathbf{K} = [k_1 \quad k_2 \quad k_3, \quad ..., \quad k_n]$$

containing the Type (I) income multiplier for each industry. Each multiplier is the ratio of direct and indirect income change to the direct income change. In other words, a dollar increase in sector (1)'s spending will generate a magnified increase of ($1)(h1)(k1) in the household's income.

Example 7: Find the Type (I) income multiplier for the two-sector economy of example 2.
Solution: To find these multipliers, equation (19) is used, and the results are

$$\mathbf{K} = [0.288461 \quad 0.246305] \begin{bmatrix} 1.283296 & 0.347563 \\ 0.287041 & 1.135036 \end{bmatrix} \begin{bmatrix} 3.466673 & 0 \\ 0 & 4.060006 \end{bmatrix} =$$

$$[1.528388 \quad 1.542085].$$

These multipliers suggest that if spending of sector (1) increases by ($1000), the community's income will increase by $(1000)(1.528388)(0.287041) = 438.7$. Similarly, if spending of sector (2) increases by ($1000), the community's income will increase by $(1000)(1.542085)(0.246305) = 379.8$.

   As far as the Type (II) income multipliers are concerned, these multipliers are obtained from the closed input-output model. If the household's row vector, obtained from the (**A***) matrix, is denoted by

$$\mathbf{H}^* = [h^*1 \quad h^*2 \dots h^*n]$$

and the diagonal matrix (**H***r) is constructed, as in the Type (I) income multipliers, then **K***, the Type (II) income multipliers, would be

$$\mathbf{K}^* = \mathbf{H}^* (\mathbf{I} - \mathbf{A}^*)^{-1} \mathbf{H}^* r \qquad (20)$$

where

$$\mathbf{K}^* = [k^*1 \quad k^*2 \dots k^*n]$$

which is a row vector containing the Type (II) multipliers of all industries. These multipliers are the ratios of the direct, indirect, and induced income changes to the direct income change. For example, (k*1) indicates that if spending of sector (1) increases by $1000, the household income will increase by ($1000)(H*1)(k*1).
Example 8: Find the Type (II) income multipliers for the two-sector economy of example 2. To find these multipliers, equation (20) is used, and the results are

$$K^* = [0.288461 \quad 0.246305 \quad 0.08] \begin{bmatrix} 1.398724 & 0.447006 & 0.261830 \\ 0.553101 & 1.364260 & 0.603538 \\ 0.568115 & 0.489440 & 1.288612 \end{bmatrix}.$$

$$\begin{bmatrix} 1/0.288461 & 0 & 0 \\ 0 & 1/0.246305 & 0 \\ 0 & 0 & 1/0.05 \end{bmatrix} = [1.969472 \quad 1.987133 \quad 5.772256].$$

These multipliers suggest that if spending of sector (1) increases by ($1000), the community's income will increase by (1000)(1.9969472)(0.288461) = 576.04. The other multipliers are interpreted similarly. As can be readily seen, the difference between the Type (I) and Type (II) income multipliers is that the latter contains the induced effects, whereas the former does not; this explains why the Type (II) multipliers are larger than the Type (I).

The third type of multiplier that can be obtained from the input-output model is called the "employment multiplier." This type of multiplier consists of two types: the Type (I) and Type (II) employment multipliers. The Type (I) employment multipliers are obtained from the open input-output model. Let (L) be a vector of the form,

$$L = [l_1, l_2, ... l_n],$$

where the components $(l_1, l_2, ..., l_n)$ are the labor-output ratios or the marginal labor (employment)-output ratios. Let (Lr) be a diagonal matrix whose diagonal elements are the reciprocal of the various components of (L) vector. For a two-sector model, (Lr) would be

$$L_r = \begin{bmatrix} 1/l_1 & 0 \\ 0 & 1/l_2 \end{bmatrix}.$$

Therefore, the Type (I) employment multiplier (E) is

$$E = L (I - A)^{-1} L_r \qquad (21)$$

where (E) is a row vector of the form

$$E = [e_1 \ e_2 \ ... \ e_n]$$

containing the Type (I) employment multiplier for each industry. These multipliers indicate the estimated direct and indirect changes, resulting from a dollar increase in sales to final demand, to the direct (initial) employment change. That is, if the final demand of sector (1) increases by \$1000, the economy's employment will increase by $(\$1000)(l_1)(e_1)$.

Example 9: If the employment coefficients are (0.009) and (0.005) for sectors (1) and (2), respectively, find the Type (I) employment multipliers.
Solution: To find such multipliers, equation (21) is used, and the results are

$$E = [0.009 \quad 0.005] \begin{bmatrix} 1.283296 & 0.347563 \\ \\ 0.287041 & 1.135036 \end{bmatrix} \begin{bmatrix} 1/0.009 & 0 \\ \\ 0 & 1/0.005 \end{bmatrix} =$$

$$[1.442763 \quad 1.760649].$$

These multipliers suggest that if spending of sector (1) increases by (\$1000), the community's employment will increase by $(1000)(1.442763)(0.009) = 12.98$ jobs. For sector (2), if its spending increases by (\$1000), the community's employment will increase by $(1000)(1.760649)(0.005) = 8.8$ jobs.

For the Type (II) employment multiplier, this multiplier is obtained from the closed input-output model. That is,

$$E^* = L (I - A^*)^{-1} Lr. \qquad (22)$$

By the same token, (E^*) is a row vector of the form

$$E^* = [e^*_1 \ e^*_2 \ ... \ e^*_n].$$

These multipliers indicate the estimated direct, indirect, and induced changes in employment, resulting from a dollar increase in sales to final demand, to the initial (direct) employment change. In other words, if the final demand of sector (1) increases by (\$1000), the economy's employment will eventually increase by

($1000)($e^*_i$)($l_i$).

Example 10: If the employment coefficients of sectors 1, 2, and 3 (households) are (0.009), (0.005), and (0.04), respectively, find the Type (II) employment multipliers.

Solution: To find these multipliers, equation (22) is used, and the results are

$$E^* = [0.009 \quad 0.005 \quad 0.04] \begin{vmatrix} 1.398724 & 0.447006 & 0.261830 \\ 0.553101 & 1.364260 & 0.603536 \\ 0.568115 & 0.489440 & 1.288612 \end{vmatrix} \cdot$$

$$\begin{vmatrix} 1/0.009 & 0 & 0 \\ 0 & 1/0.005 & 0 \\ 0 & 0 & 1/0.04 \end{vmatrix} = [4.2320962 \quad 6.0844 \quad 1.4229661].$$

These multipliers suggest that if spending of sector (1) increases by ($1000), the community's employment will increase by (1000)(4.230962)(0.009) = 38.08 jobs. Similarly, if spending of sector (2) increases by ($1000), the community employment will increase by (1000)(6.0844)(0.005) = 30.4 jobs. Usually, the household multiplier is not used, because this sector is not a processing sector.

The Economic Impacts of a New Industry

The input-output model provides an essential tool for measuring the economic impacts of a new industry entering a region or an existing industry leaving the region. Generally, these impacts can be quantified by two approaches: the final-demand and the inclusion of the new industry in the (**A**) matrix (Miller and Blair 1985).

The final-demand approach analyzes the new industry by measuring the new increase in final demand as a result of introducing this industry. For example, if an economy consists of two sectors, the new industry may have some linkages with these sectors, such as the new industry requires (a_{13}) and (a_{23}) inputs obtained from sectors (1) and (2) to produce one unit of its output. If the expected production of the new industry, say X_3, is ($10,000), the increase in final demand (ΔY) placed upon the two sectors will be

$$\Delta Y = \begin{bmatrix} a_{13}X_3 \\ \\ a_{23}X_3 \end{bmatrix} = \begin{bmatrix} a_{13}\,(10000) \\ \\ a_{23}\,(10000) \end{bmatrix}.$$

If a_{13} and a_{23} are 0.02 and 0.005 , then

$$\Delta Y = \begin{bmatrix} 200 \\ \\ 50 \end{bmatrix}.$$

The inclusion of the new industry in the (**A**) matrix suggests that the economic impacts of the new industry can be measured by considering the new industry as a new sector in the economy, purchasing inputs and selling output to the other sectors of the economy. For instance, take the two-sector economy given above and consider the new industry as a third sector. The (**A**) matrix will have a new column showing the input requirements to produce a dollar's worth of output of the new industry (the third sector). In addition, the (**A**) matrix will have a new row showing the inputs required to produce a dollar's worth of output in sectors (1), (2), and (3).

Example 11: An economy consists of two sectors whose technological matrix (**A**) is given below. A new industry enters the economy, whose linkages with sectors (1), (2), and itself are shown in matrix (**A$_1$**), the new technological matrix. Compare the economic performance of the economy with and without the inclusion of the new industry if the final demand of sector (2) increases by ($1000). That is, $\Delta y = [0 \quad 1000]^t$.

Solution: The two technological matrices are

$$\mathbf{A} = \begin{array}{c} \\ S_1 \\ \\ S_2 \end{array} \begin{array}{cc} S_1 & S_2 \\ \left[\begin{array}{cc} 0.09 & 0.006 \\ \\ 0.10 & 0.070 \end{array}\right] \end{array} \text{ and } \mathbf{A_1} = \begin{array}{c} \\ S_1 \\ S_2 \\ S_3 \end{array} \begin{array}{ccc} S_1 & S_2 & S_3 \\ \left[\begin{array}{ccc} 0.090 & 0.060 & 0.050 \\ 0.100 & 0.070 & 0.110 \\ 0.002 & 0.032 & 0.070 \end{array}\right] \end{array}.$$

Hence,

$$(\mathbf{I} - \mathbf{A})^{-1} = \begin{bmatrix} 1.099680 & 0.007094 \\ 0.118245 & 1.076031 \end{bmatrix}$$

and $\Delta \mathbf{X} = (\mathbf{I} - \mathbf{A})^{-1} \Delta \mathbf{Y}$

$$(\mathbf{I} - \mathbf{A})^{-1} \begin{bmatrix} 0 \\ 1000 \end{bmatrix} = \begin{bmatrix} 7.094714 \\ 1076.031 \end{bmatrix}$$

Using matrix $\mathbf{A}_1$, one can obtain

$$(\mathbf{I} - \mathbf{A}_1)^{-1} = \begin{bmatrix} 1.100041 & 0.009169 & 0.060226 \\ 0.119048 & 1.080655 & 0.134219 \\ 0.006461 & 0.037203 & 1.080016 \end{bmatrix}$$

and

$$(\mathbf{I} - \mathbf{A})^{-1} \begin{bmatrix} 0 \\ 1000 \\ 0 \end{bmatrix} = \begin{bmatrix} 9.169350 \\ 1080.655 \\ 37.20355 \end{bmatrix} \cdot$$

As can be seen there is a difference between the two previous outcomes. In fact, if we include the new industry into matrix $(\mathbf{A})$, larger economic impacts on the economy will be realized.

Backward and Forward Linkages

The matrices $(\mathbf{A})$ and $(\mathbf{I} - \mathbf{A})^{-1}$ can be used to measure the backward linkages among economic sectors (Miller and Blair 1985). The direct backward linkage is calculated from the $(\mathbf{A})$ matrix by summing its jth column. That is,

$$\sum_{i}^{n} aij.$$

For example, if $j = 1$ and $i = 1$ and 2, the backward linkage of sector 1 would be

$$\sum ai_1 = a_{11} + a_{21}.$$

The total backward linkage is obtained from $(I - A)^{-1}$. If this matrix is denoted by (B), the total backward linkage would be

$$\sum_{i}^{n} bij.$$

For example, if $j = 1$ and $i = 1$ and 2, the above formula becomes

$$\sum_{i}^{2} bi_1 = b_{11} + b_{21}.$$

With respect to the forward linkages, these linkages are obtained from the direct output coefficients matrix and output matrix. If the first matrix is (L), the second matrix will be $(I - L)^{-1} = F$. Accordingly, the direct forward linkage of sector (i) is the sum of the i*th* row of (L). Mathematically, for a two-sector economy if $i = 1$ and $j = 1$ and 2, the direct forward linkage of sector (1) would be

$$\sum_{j}^{2} L_{1_j} = L_{11} + L_{12}$$

or

$$\sum_{j}^{n} Lij.$$

Finally, the direct and indirect forward linkage of sector (i) is

$$\sum_{i}^{n} Fij.$$

For example, if $i = 1$ and $j = 1$ and 2, the above formula becomes

$$\sum_{j}^{2} F_{1_j} = F_{11} + F_{12}.$$

Example 12: Find the direct and total backward linkages for the following two-sector economy whose interindustry flow matrix and total output are

$$T = \begin{bmatrix} 400 & 800 \\ 300 & 700 \end{bmatrix} \qquad X = \begin{bmatrix} 2000 \\ 3000 \end{bmatrix}.$$

Solution:

$$A = T\, Xr = \begin{bmatrix} 0.20 & 0.267 \\ 0.15 & 0.233 \end{bmatrix}$$

and direct backward linkage is (0.35) and (0.50), the sum of columns (1) and (2), respectively. Accordingly, $(I - A)^{-1}$ would be

$$(I - A)^{-1} = \begin{bmatrix} 1.337285 & 0.465521 \\ 0.261529 & 1.394821 \end{bmatrix}$$

and the total backward linkages of sectors (1) and (2) are the sum of columns (1) and (2) of $(I - A)^{-1}$, which are 1.598814 and 1.860342, respectively.

The forward direct linkages are calculated by finding matrix (L). For our example, matrix (L) is

$$L = \begin{bmatrix} 400/200 & 800/2000 \\ 300/3000 & 700/3000 \end{bmatrix} = \begin{bmatrix} 0.20 & 0.40 \\ 0.10 & 0.233 \end{bmatrix}$$

and the forward linkages of sectors (1) and (2) are (0.60) and (0.334), respectively—the sum of rows (1) and (2). The total forward linkages are obtained by summing each row of $(I - L)^{-1}$, that is,

$$(I - L)^{-1} = \begin{bmatrix} 1.337168 & 0.697350 \\ 0.174337 & 1.394700 \end{bmatrix}$$

and the linkages of sectors (1) and (2) are (2.034518) and (1.569037), respectively.

Prices in the Open Input-Output Model

The transaction table (Table 3.1) of the input-output model is measured by constant prices. If these interindustry flows are measured by physical units, rather than monetary units, one can derive the output prices for each economic sector (Leontief 1986). For example, for a two-sector economy, the technological matrix, which is measured in physical units, is

$$A = \begin{bmatrix} a_{11} & a_{12} \\ a_{21} & a_{22} \end{bmatrix}.$$

Let the prices of these two sectors be represented by vector (**P**), which has the following form:

$$P = \begin{bmatrix} p_1 \\ p_2 \end{bmatrix}.$$

If the transpose of (**I** - **A**) is multiplied by the price vector (**P**), and if the outcomes are subtracted from P_1 and P_2, and if the final result is equal to vector (**V**), where

$$V = \begin{bmatrix} v_1 \\ v_2 \end{bmatrix},$$

we obtain,

$$p_1 - a_{11}p_1 - a_{21}p_2 = V_1$$

$$p_2 - a_{12}p_1 - a_{22}p_2 = V_2.$$

These equations indicate that the prices of the two products minus the costs of the intermediate products paid by the two sectors must be equal to the value added (V_1 and V_2) per unit of output. And the per unit value added consists of wages, interest on capital, taxes, and so on.

In matrix notations the preceding arguments can be rewritten as

$$(I - A)^t\, P = V$$

and therefore,

$$P = (I - A^t)^{-1}V.$$

But as it has been just mentioned, vector (**V**) consists of several payments to various exogenous sectors, and one can aggregate these payments into two components: wage (**W**) and return on capital (r**B**), where (r) and (**B**) are the price of capital (rate of return) and the quantity of capital, respectively. One should note that (**B**) is actually a matrix of capital stock coefficients, whose columns indicate the physical capital requirements per unit of output. Consequently, the above equations can be rewritten as

$$(I - A)^t\, P = V = W + rB$$

or

$$(I - A^t - rB^t)\, P = W.$$

Solving for (**P**), we obtain the price vector

$$(I - A^t - rB^t)^{-1}(I - A^t - rB^t)\, P = (I - A^t - rB^t)^{-1}W$$

or

$$P = (I - A^t - rB^t)^{-1}W \tag{23}$$

Example 13: For the following two-sector economy, the physical technological and capital coefficient matrices are

$$A = \begin{bmatrix} 0.20 & 0.25 \\ 0.32 & 0.35 \end{bmatrix} \quad \text{and} \quad B = \begin{bmatrix} 0.05 & 0.08 \\ 0.11 & 0.13 \end{bmatrix}.$$

Find the sectoral prices if the rate of return is (15%), and (**W**) is equal to

$$W = \begin{bmatrix} \$30.00 \\ \$25.00 \end{bmatrix}.$$

Solution: Using equation (32) yields

$$P = \left(\begin{bmatrix} 1 & 0 \\ 0 & 1 \end{bmatrix} - \begin{bmatrix} 0.20 & 0.32 \\ 0.25 & 0.35 \end{bmatrix} - 0.15 \begin{bmatrix} 0.05 & 0.11 \\ 0.08 & 0.13 \end{bmatrix} \right)^{-1} \begin{bmatrix} 30 \\ 25 \end{bmatrix} =$$

$$\left(\begin{bmatrix} 0.80 & -0.32 \\ -0.25 & 0.65 \end{bmatrix} - \begin{bmatrix} 0.0075 & 0.0165 \\ 0.012 & 0.0195 \end{bmatrix} \right)^{-1} \begin{bmatrix} 30 \\ 25 \end{bmatrix} = \begin{bmatrix} 0.7925 & -0.3365 \\ -0.262 & 0.6305 \end{bmatrix}^{-1} \begin{bmatrix} 30 \\ 25 \end{bmatrix}$$

$$= \begin{bmatrix} 1.532168 & 0.817723 \\ 0.636682 & 1.925842 \end{bmatrix} \begin{bmatrix} 30 \\ 25 \end{bmatrix} = \begin{bmatrix} 66.40814 \\ 67.24652 \end{bmatrix}$$

which are the required sectoral prices.

Example 14: Suppose that the rate of return on capital increases from (15) to (25) percent; assuming everything else is constant, what will the prices be?
Solution: To find the prices we multiply matrix (**B^t**) by (0.25) and repeat the same

procedure, which yields

$$P = \begin{bmatrix} 1.573423 & 0.885449 \\ \\ 0.687974 & 2.006593 \end{bmatrix} \begin{bmatrix} 30 \\ \\ 25 \end{bmatrix} = \begin{bmatrix} 69.33893 \\ \\ 70.80407 \end{bmatrix}.$$

As can be seen, the prices are increased to higher levels when the rate of return on capital increases from (15) to (25) percent. If capital and its rate of return are associated with the capitalists, the owners of means of production, one can argue that this class will be better off economically when the rate of return increases. In fact, as the rate of return increases one can expect a higher rate of inflation (profit inflation).

But price increases, after the increase in the rate of return on capital, will reduce the real wages (the purchasing power of the money wages) of the working people, and this reduction may encourage unions to bargain for higher wages, assuming that unions do not suffer from money illusion defined as the failure to perceive that a money unit, such as the dollar, shrinks and expands in value. Suppose unions were able to raise wages in the two sectors (industries) to ($40) and ($30), respectively, the new prices would be

$$P = \begin{bmatrix} 1.573423 & 0.885449 \\ \\ 0.687974 & 2.006593 \end{bmatrix} \begin{bmatrix} 40 \\ \\ 30 \end{bmatrix} = \begin{bmatrix} 89.2 \\ \\ 87.2 \end{bmatrix}.$$

The foregoing arguments may suggest that inflation is a power phenomenon in that price increases are generated by profit inflation, which will trigger wage increases that reinforce the original increases in prices. This price-wage spiral may continue until a recession appears, a situation describing the American economy during the 1970s.

Problems

1.   For this two-sector economy whose transaction matrix is

	S_1	S_2	H	Y
S_1	30	20	10	70
S_2	0	28	7	45
H	5	8	3	25

find $\mathbf{A}$, $(\mathbf{I} - \mathbf{A})$, $(\mathbf{I} - \mathbf{A})^{-1}$, $(\mathbf{I} - \mathbf{A}^*)$, and $(\mathbf{I} - \mathbf{A}^*)^{-1}$.

2.   For the two sector-economy of problem 1, find Type (I) and Type (II) income multipliers and interpret the results.

3.   For the two sector-economy of problem 1, find Type (I) and Type (II) employment multipliers if $\mathbf{L}^* = [0.008 \quad 0.07 \quad 0.006]$. Interpret the meaning of each multiplier.

4.   For a two-sector economy whose technological matrix in physical units and the capital requirement matrix are

$$A = \begin{bmatrix} 0.15 & 0.30 \\ 0.20 & 0.25 \end{bmatrix} \quad \text{and} \quad B = \begin{bmatrix} 0.08 & 0.10 \\ 0.15 & 0.20 \end{bmatrix}$$

and whose wage vector is $\mathbf{W}^t = [30 \quad 25]$ and whose rate of return (r) is 20 percent, find the price vector $\mathbf{P}^t = [P_1 \quad P_2]$. If (r) becomes 30 percent, find the price vector.

5.   For a two-sector economy, the following information is given:

$$T = \begin{bmatrix} 50 & 150 \\ 120 & 80 \end{bmatrix}, \quad Y = \begin{bmatrix} 300 \\ 1000 \end{bmatrix}, \quad \text{and } X = \begin{bmatrix} 800 \\ 1200 \end{bmatrix}.$$

Find the direct backward and forward linkages for the two sectors. Find the total backward and forward linkages for the two sectors.

CHAPTER FOUR

Optimization Theory: The Calculus Approach

Optimization of mathematical functions is a process in which minimization and maximization of functions can be determined. In this chapter, the *calculus approach* to optimization theory is used in detail. Chapter 7 and 8, however, will use a noncalculus approach to optimization theory of linear functions, an approach called *linear programming*.

Using the calculus approach, several mathematical rules are available to optimize functions of one variable, of several variables, and of functions of several variables subject to constraints. In other words, the first type of optimization is called *unconstrained optimization* (the first two sections), whereas the second type is called *constrained optimization* (the third section).

Optimization of Functions of One Variable

Take a mathematical function such as $y = f(x)$, for which we want to find its optimum value. To find such a value, we differentiate the function and set its first derivative equal to zero (Dowling 1980; McGuigan and Moyer 1986). That is,

$$f'(x) = dy/dx = 0.$$

The second step is to use the first derivative to solve for the critical point (x_c) (or points) of the function. These critical points are also called the "stationary points," points at which the function will have either maximum or minimum values or neither. The third step is to find the second derivative of the function, that is, $d^2y/dx^2 = f''(x)$. After finding the second derivative, substitute the critical point(s) we found in step 2 in the second derivative to find whether the second derivative is positive or negative. If it is positive, the function has a minimum value at the critical point(s). In contrast, if the second derivative is negative, the function has a maximum value at the critical point(s). Otherwise, the test fails and the function may have an inflection point.

Example 1: Optimize the function $y = 3x^2 - 12x$.
Solution: Find the first derivative and set it equal to zero. That is,

$$f'(x) = dy/dx = 6x - 12 = 0$$

and solving for the critical point x_c yields

$$6x = 12$$

and $x_c = 2$. Now, find the second derivative for the function

$$d^2y/dx^2 = f''(x) = 6.$$

Because the second derivative is positive, the function has a minimum value at the critical point $x_c = 2$. Also, if we substitute various values of x in our function, the y's values (or the values of the function) will be

x	-2	-1	0	1	2	3
y	36	15	0	-9	-12	-9

As can be seen, the function has a minimum value of (-12) at the critical point $x_c = 2$. One should note from this example that we can find the minimum value of the function by using the first derivative only. As we know the critical value, which is $x_c = 2$, we can take other values for x, such as x = 1 (which is less than the critical value) and x = 3 (which is higher than the critical value), and after substituting these values in the first derivative we can obtain $f'(x) = -6$ and $f'(x) = 6$. Because the first derivative changes signs from negative to positive, the function must have a minimum value at the critical point.

Example 2: Optimize the function $y = f(x) = -2x^2 + 20x - 2$.
Solution: The first derivative is

$$dy/dx = -4x + 20 = 0 \text{ , and hence } x_c = 5.$$

The second derivative is

$$d^2y/dx^2 = -4.$$

As the second derivative is negative, the function has a maximum value at the critical point $x_c = 5$. One should note that by substituting various values of x in the given function, we can find the maximum value of the function. This is shown below:

x	-1	0	1	2	3	4	5
y	-24	-2	16	30	40	46	48

Similarly, by using the first derivative alone, one can determine the maximum value of the function. Take two points such as x = 4, which is less than the critical point, and x = 6, which is higher than the critical point, and use these two points to evaluate the first derivative. Having done so, we obtain $f'(x) = 4$ and $f'(x) = -4$. Because the first derivative changes signs from positive to negative, the function must have a maximum value at the critical point.

Example 3: Optimize the function $y = f(x) = x^3 - 12x$.
Solution: The first derivative is

$$dy/dx = 3x^2 - 12 = 0$$

or

$$= x^2 - 4 = 0.$$

Solving for the critical points, we find

$$(x - 2)(x + 2) = 0.$$

Using this equation, the first critical point is found by setting x - 2 = 0, and hence $x_c = 2$; the second critical point is found by setting x + 2 = 0, and hence $x_c = -2$. The second derivative of the function would be

$$d^2y/dx^2 = 2x.$$

After substituting the critical point ($x_c = 2$) into the second derivative, we find that $d^2y/dx^2 = 4$, and if we substitute the second critical point ($x_c = -2$) into the second derivative we obtain $d^2y/dx^2 = -4$. Thus, we conclude that the function does have a minimum value at the first critical point ($x_c = 2$), because the second derivative evaluated at this point is equal to (4), a positive value. Conversely, the function does have a maximum value at ($x_c = -2$), because the second derivative evaluated at this point is (- 4), a negative value.

Example 4: Optimize the function $y = f(x) = 6x + 12$.
Solution: The first derivative is

$$dy/dx = 6$$

and no critical point can be found. The second derivative is equal to zero, and hence the function does not have a maximum nor does it have a minimum—an inflection point.

Example 5: Optimize the function $y = f(x) = (x - 3)^2$.
Solution: The first derivative is

$$dy/dx = 2(x - 3) = 0$$

and the critical point is $x_c = 3$. The second derivative is

$$d^2y/dx^2 = 2.$$

As the second derivative is positive, the function has a minimum value at the critical point $x_c = 3$. If we are interested in using the first derivative, we can assume values of x such as $x = 2$ and $x = 4$. Evaluating the first derivative at these points, we can find $f'(x) = -2$ and $f'(x) = 2$. That is, $f'(x_c)$ changes its signs from negative to positive, and hence the function must have a minimum value at $x_c = 3$.

 Example 6: If a producer faces a demand curve of the form of $P = 81 - Q$, and the average cost curve is $Q^2 - Q + 6$, find the output level that maximizes the profit.
Solution: Total revenue (TR) is defined by

$$TR = PQ$$

where P and Q are the price and output, respectively. Thus,

$$TR = (81 - Q)Q = 81Q - Q^2.$$

In contrast, the total cost, TC, is defined by

$$TC = (AC)Q,$$

where AC is the average cost. Thus,

$$TC = (Q^2 - Q + 6)Q = Q^3 - Q^2 + 6Q.$$

As the total profit (TP) is the difference between total revenue and total cost, that is, $TP = TR - TC$, therefore

$$TP = 81Q - Q^2 - Q^3 + Q^2 - 6Q = 75Q - Q^3.$$

To maximize total profit, we differentiate TP with respect to output (Q), which yields

$$d(TP)/dQ = 75 - 3Q^2 = 0$$

and the critical points are

$$Q_c = -5 \text{ and } Q_c = 5.$$

The second derivative would be

$$d^2(TP)/dQ^2 = -6Q.$$

Thus, at $Q_c = -5$, the second derivative is positive, indicating that this level of output does minimize the profit, a level that is not reasonable in economics. On the contrary, at $Q_c = 5$, the second derivative is negative, suggesting that the producer must produce 5 units of output in order to maximize his or her profit, a behavior deemed is rational according to economic theory.

Example 7: Baumol's Theory of Demand for Money. Let Y_j be the real income per period, say a year, which is held in the form of bonds. The individual is assumed to withdraw money by converting some bonds into money in lot-size units of C_j dollars evenly spaced (Baumol 1952). In other words, C_j is the demand for cash for transaction purposes. Number of withdrawals made by the individual during the period would be Y_j/C_j. For each withdrawal the individual pays a transaction cost of b_j dollars in order to convert some bonds into money. Thus, b_jY_j/C_j is the inventory replenishment cost, which includes brokerage fees, transfer taxes, the cost of inconvenience of doing so, and so on.

Let $C_j/2$ be the individual's average cash balance held halfway through the interval from one withdrawal to another. If this is so, then $i(C_j/2)$ is the cost of holding cash: It is the interest that could have been received had the individual held the money in cash. Therefore, the total cost of holding the inventory of cash is T_j, which is equal to

$$T_j = b_j(Y_j/C_j) + i(C_j/2).$$

To find the demand for money C_j which minimizes the total cost, we differentiate the above function with respect to C_j. That is,

$$dT_j/dC_j = - b_j Y_j/C_j^2 + i/2 = 0;$$

solving for C_j yields

$$C_j = (2b_j Y_j/i)^{1/2},$$

which says that the demand for money is related positively to the square root of b_j and Y_j and negatively to i. The second-order derivative is

$$d^2T_j/dC_j^2 = 2b_j Y_j/C_j^3 > 0,$$

which indicates that the function has a minimum value at the critical point C_j. For example, if $b = 0.10$, $i = 0.08$, and Y is $500, the demand for cash would be $[2(0.10)(500/0.08)]^{1/2} = \$35.35$.

Optimization of Functions of Several Variables

To optimize a function of the form $Z = f(x, y)$, we follow similar steps to the ones used for optimizing functions of one variable (Chiang 1984; Lambert 1985). The first step is to differentiate the function partially with respect to x and y and set these partial derivatives equal to zero. This process is called the *first-order conditions*. Mathematically,

$$f_x = 0 \tag{1}$$

$$f_y = 0. \tag{2}$$

The second step is to solve for the critical values x_c and y_c, a solution obtained by solving equations (1) and (2) simultaneously. The third step is to take the direct and cross-partial derivatives for equations (1) and (2) with respect to x and y (the second-order conditions) so as to form the Hessian determinant. In other words, we formulate

$$IHI = \begin{vmatrix} f_{xx} & f_{xy} \\ f_{yx} & f_{yy} \end{vmatrix}.$$

The next step is to find the value of $IHI = f_{xx}f_{yy} - f_{xy}f_{yx}$. If $f_{xx} > 0$ and $IHI > 0$, the function has a minimum value at the critical points. In contrast, if fxx < 0 and IHI > 0, the function has a maximum value at the critical points; otherwise the test fails, and the function may have an inflection or saddle point.

For a function of three variables such as $Z = f(x, y, w)$, we follow the same procedure. That is, we obtain the first-order conditions for the function as follows:

$$f_x = 0$$

$$f_y = 0$$

$$f_w = 0$$

and solve for the critical points x_c, y_c, and w_c. Having done so, we obtain the second-order conditions by finding the direct and cross-partial derivatives as shown: f_{xx}, f_{xy}, f_{xw}, f_{yx}, f_{yy}, f_{yw}, f_{wx}, f_{wy}, and f_{yy}, and the Hessian determinant is

$$IHI = \begin{vmatrix} f_{xx} & f_{xy} & f_{xw} \\ f_{yx} & f_{yy} & f_{yw} \\ f_{wx} & f_{wy} & f_{ww} \end{vmatrix}$$

If $f_{xx} < 0$, $\begin{vmatrix} f_{xx} & f_{xy} \\ f_{yx} & f_{yy} \end{vmatrix} > 0$, and IHI <0 the function has a maximum value at the critical points. In other words, if these determinants, whatever the number of variables may be, alternate the signs from negative, positive, negative, positive and so on, the function has a maximum value at the critical points. In

contrast, if $f_{xx} > 0$, $\begin{vmatrix} f_{xx} & f_{xy} \\ f_{yx} & f_{yy} \end{vmatrix} > 0$, and IHI> 0 the function has a minimum value

at the critical points. In other words, if these determinants, whatever the number of variables may be, are positive, the function has a minimum value at the critical points.

Example 1: Optimize the function $Z = 4x^2 - 7x - 2xy - 5y + 4y^2$.
Solution: The first-order conditions are

$$Z_x = 8x - 7 - 2y = 0$$

$$Z_y = -2x - 5 + 8y = 0$$

where Z_x and Z_y are the partial derivatives of the function with respect to x, f_x, and y, f_y, respectively. By using the methods of chapter 1, it is possible to solve for x and y from the first-order conditions to obtain the critical points x_c and y_c. Arranging the first-order conditions in two equations

$$8x - 2y = 7$$

$$-2x + 8y = 5$$

and using Cramer's rule, we obtain

$$IAI = \begin{vmatrix} 8 & -2 \\ -2 & 8 \end{vmatrix} = 60, \quad IA_1I = \begin{vmatrix} 7 & -2 \\ 5 & 6 \end{vmatrix} = 66, \text{ and } IA_2I = \begin{vmatrix} 8 & 7 \\ -2 & 5 \end{vmatrix}.$$

Hence, x = 64/60 and y = 54/60.

The second-order conditions are

$$Z_{xx} = 8, Z_{xy} = -2, Z_{yx} = -2, \text{ and } Z_{yy} = 8,$$

and the Hessian determinant is

$$IHI = \begin{vmatrix} 8 & -2 \\ -2 & 8 \end{vmatrix} = 64 - 4 = 60$$

As Z_{xx} is positive and so is IHI, the function has a minimum value at the critical points.

Example 2: Optimize the function $Z = 16x + 17y - 3x^2 - 4xy - 2y^2$.
Solution: The first-order conditions are

$$Z_x = 16 - 6x - 4y = 0$$

$$Z_y = 17 - 4x - 4y = 0.$$

Solving for the critical points from the first-order conditions by the Gauss-Jordan method, that is,

$$-6x - 4y = -16$$

$$-4x - 4y = -17$$

then,

$$\begin{vmatrix} -6 & -4 & \vdots & -16 \\ -4 & -4 & \vdots & -17 \end{vmatrix}$$

$$\begin{vmatrix} 1 & 4/6 & \vdots & 16/6 \\ 0 & -8/6 & \vdots & -38/5 \end{vmatrix}$$

$$\begin{vmatrix} 1 & 0 & \vdots & -1/2 \\ 0 & 1 & \vdots & 38/8 \end{vmatrix} .$$

Hence, x = -1/2 and y = 38/8. The second-order conditions are

$$Z_{xx} = -6, Z_{xy} = -4, Z_{yx} = -4, \text{ and } Z_{yy} = -4,$$

and the Hessian determinant is,

$$|H| = \begin{vmatrix} -6 & -4 \\ -4 & -4 \end{vmatrix} .$$

As Z_{xx} is negative and $|H|$ is positive, the function has a maximum value at the critical points.

Example 3: Suppose a producer faces two demand curves for two commodities (a) and (b) she produces of the form

$$P_a = 120 - 3Q_a - 2Q_b$$

$$P_b = 150 - Q_a - 4 Q_b$$

The total cost of producing the two commodities (a) and (b) is

$$TC = Q_a^2 + 3Q_aQ_b + 3Q_b^2 + 60.$$

Find the levels of Q_a and Q_b that maximize the total profits ($Z = TP$).
Solution: As $TP = TR - TC$ and $TR = P_aQ_a + P_bQ_b$, therefore

$$Z = TP = P_aQ_a + P_bQ_b - TC.$$

Using the demand equations and the total cost equation yields

$$Z = TP = (120 - 3Q_a - 2Q_b)Q_a + (150 - Q_a - 4Q_b)Q_b - Q_a^2 - 3Q_aQ_b - 3Q_b^2 - 60;$$

thus,

$$Z = TP = 120Q_a - 4Q_a^2 - 6Q_aQ_b + 150Q_b - 7Q_b^2 - 60.$$

The first-order conditions are

$$Z_{qa} = 120 - 8Q_a - 6Q_b = 0$$

$$Z_{qb} = 150 - 6Q_a - 14Q_b = 0.$$

Solving these two equations yields $Q_a = 390/38$ and $Q_b = 240/38$, output levels that maximize profits should the second-order conditions hold.
   The second-order conditions are

$$Z_{qaqa} = -8, \quad Z_{qaqb} = -6$$

$$Z_{qbqa} = -6, \text{ and } Z_{qbqb} = -14,$$

and the Hessian determinant is

$$|H| = \begin{vmatrix} -8 & -6 \\ -6 & -14 \end{vmatrix} = 112 - 36 = 76.$$

Because Z_{qaqa} is negative and $|H|$ is positive, the function has a maximum value at the critical points. And students should be able to find TR, TC, and Z.

Example 4: Optimize the function

$$Z = f(x, y, w) = -4x^2 + 8x + 2xw - 3y^2 + 5y + yw - 5w^2 + 64.$$

Solution: The first-order conditions are

$$Z_x = -8x + 8 + 2w = 0$$

$$Z_y = -6y + 5 + w = 0$$

$$Z_w = 2x + y - 10w = 0.$$

Solving for the critical points xc, yc, and wc by the inverse method,

$$
\begin{bmatrix} X \\ Y \\ Z \end{bmatrix} = \begin{bmatrix} -8 & 0 & 2 \\ 0 & -6 & 1 \\ 2 & 1 & -10 \end{bmatrix} \begin{bmatrix} -8 \\ -5 \\ 0 \end{bmatrix} = \begin{bmatrix} 013169 & -0.00446 & -0.02678 \\ -0.00446 & -0.13964 & -0.01785 \\ -0.02678 & -0.01785 & -0.10714 \end{bmatrix} \begin{bmatrix} -8 \\ -5 \\ 0 \end{bmatrix} = \begin{bmatrix} 1.08 \\ 0.88 \\ 0.30 \end{bmatrix}.
$$

The second-order conditions are

$$Z_{xx} = -8, Z_{xy} = 0, Z_{xw} = 2$$

$$Z_{yx} = 0, Z_{yy} = -6, Z_{yw} = 1$$

$$Z_{wx} = 2, Z_{wy} = 1, \text{ and } Z_{ww} = -10,$$

and the Hessian determinant is

$$
|H| = \begin{vmatrix} -8 & 0 & 2 \\ 0 & -6 & 1 \\ 2 & 1 & -10 \end{vmatrix}.
$$

Because Z_{xx} is negative, $\begin{vmatrix} Z_{xx} & Z_{xy} \\ Z_{yx} & Z_{yy} \end{vmatrix}$ is positive, and $|H|$ is negative

(determinants alternate signs), the function has a maximum value at the critical points.

Example 5: Optimize the function

$$Z = f(x, y, w) = 4x^2 + 8x + 2xw + 3y^2 + 5y + yw + 5w^2 + xy.$$

Solution: The first-order conditions are

$$Z_x = 8x + y + 8 + 2w = 0$$

$$Z_y = 6y + x + 5 + w = 0$$

$$Z_w = 2x + y + 10w = 0.$$

Solving for the critical points by using the inverse method,

$$
\begin{bmatrix} X \\ Y \\ Z \end{bmatrix} = \begin{bmatrix} 8 & 1 & 2 \\ 1 & 6 & 1 \\ 2 & 1 & 10 \end{bmatrix}^{-1} \begin{bmatrix} -8 \\ -5 \\ 0 \end{bmatrix} = \begin{bmatrix} 0.133484 & -0.01809 & -0.02488 \\ -0.01809 & 0.171945 & -0.01357 \\ -0.02488 & -0.01357 & 0.106334 \end{bmatrix} \begin{bmatrix} -8 \\ -5 \\ 0 \end{bmatrix} = \begin{bmatrix} -0.98 \\ -0.71 \\ 0.27 \end{bmatrix}.
$$

The second-order conditions are

$$Z_{xx} = 8, Z_{xy} = 1, Z_{xw} = 2$$

$$Z_{yx} = 1, Z_{yy} = 6, Z_{yw} = 1$$

$$Z_{wx} = 2, Z_{wy} = 1, \text{ and } Z_{ww} = 10,$$

and the Hessian determinant is

$$
|H| = \begin{vmatrix} 8 & 1 & 2 \\ 1 & 6 & 1 \\ 2 & 1 & 10 \end{vmatrix} = 432.
$$

Because Z_{xx} is positive and so are $\begin{vmatrix} Z_{xx} & Z_{xy} \\ Z_{yx} & Z_{yy} \end{vmatrix}$ and $|H|$, the function has a minimum value at the critical points.

Example 6: Optimize the function $Z = 4x^2 - 28x + 3xy - 2y^2 + 6y - 21$.
Solution: The first-order conditions are

$$Z_x = 8x - 28 + 3y = 0$$

$$Z_y = 3x - 4y + 6 = 0.$$

Solving for the critical points yields $x = 2.29$ and $y = 3.22$.
The second-order conditions are

$$Z_{xx} = 8, Z_{xy} = 3, Z_{yx} = 3, \text{ and } Z_{yy} = -4,$$

and the Hessian determinant is

$$\mathrm{IHI} = \begin{vmatrix} 8 & 3 \\ 3 & -4 \end{vmatrix} = -32 - 9 = -41$$

As Z_{xx} is positive and IHI is negative, the function cannot be optimized at the critical points. In this case, Dowling (1980, 92) argues that the function has a saddle point at the critical points. This is so because Z_{xx} and Z_{yy} have opposite signs and $(Z_{xx}Z_{yy})$ is less than $(Z_{xy}Z_{yx})$. As long as this situation occurs, the function has a saddle point.

Example 7: Optimize the function $Z = 7x - 2x^2 + 11xy - 11y^2 + 5y + 33$.
Solution: The first-order conditions are

$$Z_x = 7 - 4x + 11y = 0$$

$$Z_y = 11x - 22y + 5 = 0.$$

Solving for the critical points, we obtain $x = -6.33$ and $y = -2.94$.
The second-order conditions are

$$Z_{xx} = -4, Z_{xy} = 11$$

$$Z_{yx} = 11, \text{ and } Z_{yy} = -22,$$

and the Hessian determinant is

$$|H| = \begin{vmatrix} -4 & 11 \\ 11 & -22 \end{vmatrix} = 88 - 121 = -33.$$

Because Z_{xx} is negative and so is $|H|$, the function cannot be optimized at the critical points. Dowling (1980, 92) argues that since Z_{xx} and Z_{yy} have the same signs but $Z_{xx}Z_{yy}$ is less than $Z_{xy}Z_{yx}$, the function has an inflection point at the critical points.

Example 8: Demand for factors of production. If a producer faces a production function of the form

$$Q = 10\, L^{0.6}L^{0.4}$$

and a linear total cost of the form

$$TC = 3L + 5K = 80,$$

find the quantity demanded for labor and capital (Henderson and Quandt 1980; Varian 1996) that maximizes profit if the price of the product is $4.00.

Solution: Total profit (Z) is the difference between total revenue and cost. Mathematically,

$$Z = PQ - TC,$$

or

$$Z = 4[10K^{0.6}L^{0.4}] - 3L - 5K.$$

The first-order conditions are

$$Z_k = 24K^{-0.4}L^{0.4} - 5 = 0 \tag{3}$$

$$Z_l = 16K^{0.6}L^{-0.6} - 3 = 0 \tag{4}$$

Dividing equations (3) and (4) yields

$$L = (10/9)K. \tag{5}$$

Inserting equation (5) in the cost equation yields,

$$K = 9.6. \tag{6}$$

Using equation (6) in equation (5) we obtain

$$L = 10.67. \tag{7}$$

Equations (6) and (7) represent the quantity demanded for capital and labor, respectively. These quantities maximize profit if the second-order conditions are satisfied, and students should verify this by finding Z_{kk}, Z_{kl}, Z_{lk}, and Z_{ll} from the first-order conditions and the Hessian determinant. At any rate, using equations (6) and (7) in the production function, the output level Q turns out to be Q = 100.1 units. Therefore, the total revenue is (4)(100.1) = \$400.1, and as the total cost is \$80.00, the profit must be \$320.1.

Constrained Optimization of Functions of Several Variables

Given a function of the form $Z = f(X,Y)$, which is subject to a functional constraint of the form $g(X,Y)$, the optimization of this function can be achieved through the following procedure: Introduce a new variable called the *Lagrangian multiplier* λ and write the Lagrangian function (Z) in this form

$$Z = f(X,Y) + \lambda g(X,Y).$$

Differentiate the function Z with respect to x, y, and λ to obtain the first-order conditions. Mathematically,

$$f_x = 0$$

$$f_y = 0$$

$$f_\lambda = 0.$$

After solving for the critical points by using the first-order conditions, find the second-order conditions by differentiating the first-order conditions with respect to x, y, and λ. In other words, we must find

$$f_{xx}, f_{xy}, g_x$$

$$f_{yx}, f_{yy}, g_y$$

$$f_{\lambda x}, \text{ and } f_{\lambda y}$$

where g_x and g_y are the partial derivatives of the constraint function g with respect to x and y, respectively. Having done so, we formulate the Hessian determinant as follows:

$$IHI = \begin{vmatrix} f_{xx} & f_{xy} & g_x \\ f_{yx} & f_{yy} & g_y \\ g_x & g_y & 0 \end{vmatrix}.$$

If IHI is negative, the function has a minimum value at the critical points, and if IHI is positive, the function has a maximum value at the critical points. One should note that the above Hessian determinant is also called the *bordered Hessian*, because the border is the first partial derivative of g with respect to x, y, and λ.

For a function of three variables such as Z = f(x, y, w), which is subject to the restriction g(x, y, w), the procedure for optimizing this function is the same but with a Hessian determinant of a higher order: 4 x 4. Write the Lagrangian function (Z) as

$$Z = f(x, y, w) + \lambda g(x, y, w),$$

and the first-order conditions are

$$f_x = 0$$

$$f_y = 0$$

$$f_w = 0$$

$$f_\lambda = 0.$$

After solving for the critical values, we must obtain the second-order conditions whose Hessian determinant is

$$IHI = \begin{vmatrix} f_{xx} & f_{xy} & f_{xw} & g_x \\ f_{yx} & f_{yy} & f_{yw} & g_y \\ f_{wx} & f_{wy} & f_{ww} & g_w \\ g_x & g_y & g_w & 0 \end{vmatrix}.$$

$$\text{If } |\mathbf{H}_2| = \begin{vmatrix} f_{xx} & f_{xy} & f_{xw} \\ f_{yx} & f_{yy} & f_{yw} \\ f_{wx} & f_{wy} & f_{ww} \end{vmatrix} \text{ is negative and so is } |\mathbf{H}|, \text{ the function}$$

has a minimum value at the critical points. In contrast, if $|\mathbf{H}_2|$ is positive and $|\mathbf{H}|$ is negative, the function has a maximum value at the critical points.

Example 1: Optimize the function $Z = 5x^2 + 5xy + 4y^2$, which is subject to $x + 2y = 46$.
Solution: the Lagrangian function (Z) is

$$Z = 5x^2 + 5xy + 4y^2 + \lambda(x + 2y - 46).$$

The first-order conditions are

$$Z_x = 10x + 5y + \lambda = 0$$

$$Z_y = 5x + 8y + 2\lambda = 0$$

$$Z_\lambda = x + 2y - 46 = 0.$$

As you can see, the first-order conditions represent a system of three equations. That is,

$$10x + 5y + \lambda = 0$$

$$5x + 8y + 2\lambda = 0$$

$$x + 2y = 46$$

The solution of this system is obtained by using the inverse method as follows:

$$\begin{bmatrix} X \\ Y \\ \lambda \end{bmatrix} = \begin{bmatrix} 10 & 5 & 1 \\ 5 & 8 & 2 \\ 1 & 2 & 0 \end{bmatrix}^{-1} \begin{bmatrix} 0 \\ 0 \\ 46 \end{bmatrix} = \begin{bmatrix} 0.142857 & -0.07142 & -0.07142 \\ -0.07142 & -0.035714 & 0.535714 \\ -0.07142 & 0.535714 & -1.96428 \end{bmatrix} \begin{bmatrix} 0 \\ 0 \\ 46 \end{bmatrix} = \begin{bmatrix} -3.285 \\ 24.64 \\ -90.35 \end{bmatrix}.$$

The second-order conditions are

$$Z_{xx} = 10, \ Z_{xy} = 5, Z_{x\lambda} = 1$$

$$Z_{yx} = 5, Z_{yy} = 8, Z_{y\lambda} = 2$$

$$Z_{\lambda x} = 1, Z_{\lambda y} = 2, \text{ and } Z_{\lambda\lambda} = 0,$$

and the Hessian determinant is

$$|H| = \begin{vmatrix} 10 & 5 & 1 \\ 5 & 8 & 2 \\ 1 & 2 & 0 \end{vmatrix}.$$

Because $|H|$ is negative, the function has a minimum value at the critical points.

Example 2: Optimize the function $Z = 4xy$ subject to $2x + 3y = 62$.
Solution: The Lagrangian function (Z) is

$$Z = 4xy + \lambda(2x + 3y - 62).$$

The first-order conditions are

$$Z_x = 4y + 2\lambda = 0$$

$$Z_y = 4x + 3\lambda = 0$$

$$Z_\lambda = 2x + 3y - 62 = 0,$$

and this is a system of three equations whose solution can be obtained by

$$\begin{bmatrix} X \\ Y \\ Z \end{bmatrix} = \begin{bmatrix} 0 & 4 & 2 \\ 4 & 0 & 3 \\ 2 & 3 & 0 \end{bmatrix}^{-1} \begin{bmatrix} 0 \\ 0 \\ 62 \end{bmatrix} = \begin{bmatrix} -0.1875 & 0.125 & 0.25 \\ 0.125 & -0.08333 & 0.166666 \\ 0.25 & 0.166666 & -0.33333 \end{bmatrix} \begin{bmatrix} 0 \\ 0 \\ 62 \end{bmatrix} = \begin{bmatrix} 15.5 \\ 10.33 \\ -20.87 \end{bmatrix}.$$

The second-order conditions are

$$Z_{xx} = 0, Z_{xy} = 4, Z_{x\lambda} = 2$$

$$Z_{yx} = 4, Z_{yy} = 0, Z_{y\lambda} = 3$$

$$Z_{\lambda x} = 2, Z_{\lambda} = 3, \text{ and } Z_{\lambda\lambda} = 0,$$

and the Hessian determinant would be

$$|H| = \begin{vmatrix} 0 & 4 & 2 \\ 4 & 0 & 3 \\ 2 & 3 & 0 \end{vmatrix} = 48.$$

As |H| is positive, the function has a maximum value at the critical points.

Example 3: Deriving the output demand curves.   Suppose a consumer has a utility function of the form $U = Q_1Q_2$ and the budget restriction has the form $P_1Q_1 + P_2Q_2 = Y$, where P_1 and P_2 are the prices of the two commodities, Q_1 and Q_2 are the quantities of these two commodities, and Y is the consumer's income. We are interested in deriving the demand curves for the two commodities (Binger and Hoffman 1988; Silberberg 1990; Henderson and Quandt 1980).

Solution: To find the demand curves we maximize the utility function subject to the budget restriction. That is, the Lagrangian function (Z) takes the form

$$Z = Q_1Q_2 + \lambda(P_1Q_1 + P_2Q_2 - Y).$$

The first-order conditions are

$$Z_{q1} = Q_2 + \lambda P_1 = 0$$

$$Z_{q2} = Q_1 + \lambda P_2 = 0$$

$$Z_{\lambda} = P_1Q_1 + P_2Q_2 - Y = 0.$$

This is a system of three equations, which can be solved for Q_1, Q_2, and λ. Arranging the system,

$$0Q_1 + Q_2 + \lambda P_1 = 0$$

$$Q_1 + 0Q_2 + \lambda P_2 = 0$$

$$P_1Q_1 + P_2Q_2 = Y$$

solve for the unknowns by using Cramer's rule

$$IAI = \begin{vmatrix} 0 & 10 & P_1 \\ 10 & 0 & P_2 \\ P_1 & P_2 & 0 \end{vmatrix} = 20P_1P_2$$

$$IA_1I = \begin{vmatrix} 0 & 10 & P_1 \\ 0 & 0 & P_2 \\ Y & P_2 & 0 \end{vmatrix} = 10YP_2$$

$$IA_2I = \begin{vmatrix} 0 & 0 & P_1 \\ 10 & 0 & P_2 \\ P_1 & Y & 0 \end{vmatrix} = 10P_1Y$$

$$IA_3I = \begin{vmatrix} 0 & 10 & 0 \\ 10 & 0 & 0 \\ P_1 & P_2 & Y \end{vmatrix} = -102Y.$$

Therefore, the demand curve for commodity Q_1 is $Q_1 = Y/2P_1$, the demand curve for commodity Q_2 is $Q_2 = Y/2P_2$, and $\lambda = -Y/2P_1P_2$.

The second-order conditions are

$$Z_{q1q1} = 0, Z_{q1q2} = 1, Z_{q1\lambda} = P_1$$

$$Z_{q2q1} = 1, Z_{q1q1} = 0, Z_{q2\lambda} = P_2$$

$$Z_{\lambda q1} = P_1, Z_{\lambda 2} = P_2, \text{ and } Z_{\lambda\lambda} = 0,$$

and the Hessian determinant is

$$\text{IHI} = \begin{vmatrix} 0 & 10 & P_1 \\ 10 & C & P_2 \\ P_1 & P_2 & 0 \end{vmatrix} = 20P_1P_2 > 0.$$

Hence, the function has a maximum value at the critical points: the quantity demanded for Q_1 and Q_2.

Example 4: A rational consumer is interested in maximizing the utility function subject to income constraint. The utility function is

$$U = 2Q_1Q_2,$$

where Q_1 and Q_2 are two different commodities, and the budget restriction is

$$2Q_1 + 4Q_2 = 70,$$

where $P_1 = \$2.00$ and $P_2 = \$4.00$, which are the prices of commodities Q_1 and Q_2, and the $\$70$ represents the consumer's total income. The problem is to maximize the utility function subject to the budget constraint. That is, we would like to find the quantity demanded of Q_1 and Q_2 the consumer should buy in order to maximize his or her utility.

Solution: Formulate the Lagrangian function (Z),

$$Z = 2Q_1Q_2 + \lambda(2Q_1 + 4Q_2 - 70),$$

and the first-order conditions are

$$Z_{q1} = 2Q_2 + 2\lambda = 0$$

$$Z_{q2} = 2Q_1 + 4\lambda = 0$$

$$Z_u = 2Q_1 + 4Q_2 - 70 = 0.$$

Solving for the critical points yields $Q_1 = 17.5$, $Q_2 = 8.75$, and $u = -8.75$. The second-order conditions are

$$Z_{q1q1} = 0, Z_{q1q2} = 2, Z_{q1\lambda} = 2$$

$$Z_{q2q1} = 2, Z_{q2q2} = 0, Z_{q2\lambda} = 4$$

$$Z_{\lambda q1} = 2, Z_{\lambda q2} = 4, \text{ and } Z_{\lambda\lambda} = 0,$$

and the Hessian determinant is

$$|H| = \begin{vmatrix} 0 & 2 & 2 \\ 2 & 0 & 4 \\ 2 & 4 & 0 \end{vmatrix} = 32.$$

As |H| is positive, the function has a maximum value at the critical points.
Example 5: Maximization of production. Given the production function of the form

$$Z = 10K^{0.6}L^{0.4}$$

and the total cost of the form

$$TC = 3L + 5K = 80,$$

maximize the total output Z.
Solution: Form the Lagrangian function

$$Z = 10K^{0.6}L^{0.4} + \lambda(3L + 5K - 80).$$

The first-order conditions are

$$Z_k = 6K^{-0.4}L^{0.4} + 5\lambda = 0 \qquad\qquad (8)$$

$$Z_l = 4K^{0.6}L^{-0.6} + 3\lambda = 0 \qquad\qquad (9)$$

$$Z_\lambda = 3L + 5K - 80 = 0 \qquad\qquad (10)$$

To solve for L and K, we divide equation (8) by equation (9), which yields

$$L = (10/9)K \text{ and } K = (9/10)L.$$

Using L value in equation (10) yields K = 9.6, and hence L = 10.67. Inserting these values in the production function, we find the total production Z = 100.1. To make sure that the level of output is at maximum, we have to find the second-order conditions and a positive Hessian determinant; this task is left to students for verification.

Example 6: Deriving the input demand curves. Let us take the production function and the cost equation of example 5 to derive the demand for factors of production (inputs). To do so, we minimize the cost equation subject to the production function assuming a given output level of Y.
Mathematically, the Lagrangian function (Z) is

$$Z = rL + sK + \lambda(10K^{0.6}L^{0.4} - Y),$$

where r and s are the prices of labor and capital, respectively.
The first-order conditions are

$$Z_l = r + 4 \lambda K^{0.6}L^{-0.6} = 0 \tag{11}$$

$$Z_k = s + 6 \lambda K^{-0.4}L^{0.4} = 0 \tag{12}$$

$$Z_\lambda = 10K^{0.6}L^{0.4} - Y = 0.$$

Dividing equation (11) by equation (12) yields

$$L = (2s/3r)K \tag{13}$$

and

$$K = (3r/2s)L. \tag{14}$$

Equation (13) or (14) is called the "expansion path." Using equations (13) and (14) in the production function repeatedly, we obtain the demand curves for L and K. That is,

$$L = (0.08Y) / (r/s)^{0.6} \tag{15}$$

and

$$K = (0.12Y) / (s/r)^{0.4}. \tag{16}$$

Students should verify that the Hessian determinant will hold, that is, it will be negative in order for the function to have a minimum value at the critical points. In any event, if s = 5, r = 3, and Y = 100, using equations (15) and (16) we find that L = 10.7 and K = 9.7, a solution similar to the one we obtained previously. One should note that if the price of capital increases from 5 to 7, assuming everything else is constant and using equation (16), the demand for capital will be 8.57. That is, as the price of capital increases the demand for capital will decline: The law of demand, and a similar argument, can be made with respect to labor.

Example 7: Deriving the compensated demand functions. Given the utility function and the budget restriction of example 3, we are interested in finding the compensated-demand functions.
Solution: To do so, we minimize the total expenditure subject to the utility function. Mathematically, the Lagrangian function (Z) becomes:

$$Z = P_1Q_1 + P_2Q_2 + v(Q_1Q_2 - Uo),$$

where v is the Lagrangian multiplier and Uo is a given amount of utility.
The first-order conditions are

$$Z_{q1} = P_1 + vQ_2 = 0$$

$$Z_{q2} = P_2 + vQ_1 = 0$$

$$Z_v = Q_1Q_2 - Uo = 0.$$

Solving for the critical points, we obtain

$$Q_1 = [P_2Uo/P_1]^{1/2}$$

$$Q_2 = [P_1Uo/P_2]^{1/2}.$$

Q_1 and Q_2 are the compensated demand functions for the two commodities should the Hessian determinant be negative.

Example 8: Find the compensated demand for the utility function and the budget restriction used in example 4.
Solution: We minimize the total expenditure subject to the utility function. That is,

$$Z = 2Q_1 + 4Q_2 + v(2Q_1Q_2 - Uo).$$

The first-order conditions are

$$Z_{q1} = 2 + 2vQ_2 = 0 \tag{17}$$

$$Z_{q2} = 4 + 2vQ_1 = 0 \tag{18}$$

$$Z_v = 2Q_1Q_2 - Uo = 0. \tag{19}$$

Dividing equation (17) by (18) yields

$$1/2 = Q_2/Q_1,$$

or

$$Q_1 = 2Q_2 \text{ and } Q_2 = (1/2)Q_1. \tag{20}$$

Using equation (20) repeatedly in equation (19), we obtain

$$Q_1 = [Uo]^{1/2}$$

$$Q_2 = [(1/4)Uo]^{1/2}.$$

Accordingly, if Uo is specified at 100 utils, then Q_1 and Q_2 are 10 and 5 units, respectively.

The second-order conditions are

$$Z_{q1q1} = 0, Z_{q1q2} = 2V, Z_{q1v} = 2Q_2,$$

$$Z_{q2q1} = 2V, Z_{q2q2} = 0, Z_{q2v} = 2Q_1,$$

$$Z_{vq1} = 2Q_2, Z_{vq2} = 2Q_1, \text{ and } Z_{vv} = 0,$$

and the Hessian determinant is

$$|H| = \begin{vmatrix} 0 & 2V & 2Q_2 \\ 2V & 0 & 2Q_1 \\ 2Q_2 & 2Q_1 & 0 \end{vmatrix}.$$

As we know Q_1 and Q_2, after substituting the value of Q_2 in equation (21), we obtain $V = -1/5$; hence, $|H|$ would be

$$|H| = \begin{vmatrix} 0 & -2/5 & 10 \\ -2/5 & 0 & 20 \\ 10 & 20 & 0 \end{vmatrix} = -160$$

and the function has a minimum value at the critical points, because the Hessian determinant is negative.

Problems

1.   Optimize the following functions:

   (a) $y = 2x^2 + 16x$ (b) $y = -2x^2 + 16x$ (c) $y = 3x^2 + 14$

   (d) $y = 5x^2 + 5x - 6$ (e) $y = x^3 + 3x^2$ (f) $y = 2x^3 + 3x^2 - 18x$

2.   A firm produces two commodities Q_1 and Q_2. The revenue functions are $R_1 = 60Q_1 - 3Q_1^2$ and $R_2 = 40Q_2 - 2Q_2^2$ and the cost function is $C = 2Q_1 Q_2$. Find the best level of Q_1 and Q_2 that maximizes profit.

3.   A firm produces two commodities Q_1 and Q_2. The revenue functions are $R_1 = 40Q_1 - 2Q_1^2$ and $R_2 = 30Q_2 - Q_2^2$. If the cost function is $20(Q_1 + Q_2)$ find the output maximizing profits.

4.   A firm produces one commodity Q. The revenue and cost functions are $R = 20Q - 2Q^2$ and $C = Q^3 - 15Q^2 + 20Q$. At what level of output Q is profit maximized? Also, maximize the revenue function and minimize the cost function. Compare your answers.

5.   Optimize the following functions:

   (a) $Z = 8x^2 - 6x - 4xy - 3y + 5y^2$ (b) $Z = 8x^2 - 4xy + y^2$

   (c) $Z = -5x^2 + 2xy - y^2$.   (d) $Z = -3x^2 + 7x + xw - 2y^2 + 4y + 2yw - 4w^2$

6.   Optimize the functions

   (a) $U = xy$ subject to $2x + 4y = 32$

   (b) $U = 3x^2 + 4y^2$ subject to $x + y = 12$

   (c) $U = x^{1/2}y^{1/2}$ subject to $5x + 3y = 25$

7.   Find the ordinary quantity demanded if the utility function is $U = 2xy$ and the budget constraint is $3x + 6y = 120$.

8.   Use the information in problem 7 to find the compensated quantity
         demanded for x and y, assuming utility U equal to 80 utils.

9.   If a firm has a production function of the form $Q = L^{1/2}K^{2/3}$ and the cost
         equation is $2L + 7K = 260$, find the quantity demanded for labor L and
         capital K that minimizes the production cost.

CHAPTER FIVE

The Inventory Model

What is important in this chapter is the significance of the inventory model to modern firms and its fundamental objectives. Basically, the goal of the inventory model is to minimize the total inventory cost, a minimum that provides the optimal units (or quantity) of goods a firm should store (or carry). Why is this model important? Various reasons force firms to store units of products. In reality, demand and supply may not be at equilibrium initially. If demand for a product is greater than the available supply, customers might purchase the product from another firm, a switch that leads to a loss of revenue for the first firm that it could have received had it stored units of that product. Similarly, if the demand for the product is less than supply, the firm can store an optimum quantity with minimum cost of inventory, a quantity that can be used in due time to satisfy customers' demand. Accordingly, one can state that inventory is not only a means to meet demand's fluctuation but it is also a way to maintain good business relations with customers.

A firm can use the inventory model to make more profit by taking advantage of changes in prices. For example, if today the firm expects that the price of a barrel of oil will increase from its current price of $13.00 to, say, $18.00 within the next two weeks, then it is advantageous to the firm to store oil now and sells it in the future to make $5.00 per barrel, assuming the price does increase to $18.00. Similarly, if the firm expects the price to decline, it will have two options: either sell oil now, or store it until the price increases in the future.

This chapter analyzes various inventory models that help business firms understand how to find the optimum quantity that must be stored in order to minimize the total inventory cost. The first section explains the economic order quantity (EOQ) model, and the second section analyzes the optimal quantity model or economic lot size model. The third section examines the inventory model with planned shortage.

The Economic Order Quantity (EOQ) Model

To analyze this model it is assumed that demand for inventory is known with certainty; the ordering firm receives its order (a product) when an order for that product is placed—that is, inventory renewal is instantaneous; carrying and ordering costs per unit are fixed; and inventory is renewed only when inventory level reaches zero.

These assumptions suggest that when the demand for inventory is known with certainty and inventory level reaches its optimum point at time t_o, then declines to zero at time t_1 (inventory cycle), the firm has to reorder at time t_1 and the inventory level is replenished to its optimum level again. Figure 5.1 describes this argument.

Figure 5.1. **Inventory Cycle**

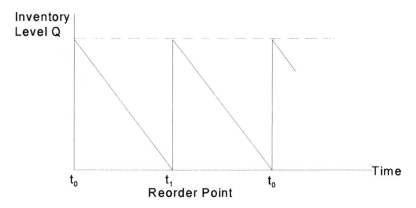

Mathematically, let CC be the annual inventory carrying cost per unit of output, a cost that is associated with storing an item. This cost is a certain ratio of the value of the inventory item V. Let Cc be the per unit cost of carrying or storing (holding) an item for a year, a cost that consists of deterioration cost, damage cost, interest that could have been obtained had the item not been stored (opportunity cost), taxes, insurance cost, security cost, rent of the warehouse, electricity of the warehouse, and so forth. Cc can be written as

$$Cc = CC \times V.$$

For example, if the value of the inventory item is \$100 and CC is 5 percent of this value, then Cc, the annual cost of carrying this item, is equal to (\$100.00)(0.05) = \$5.00.

As we know Cc, it becomes easier to find the total annual carrying cost (TC) if the annual inventory level, say Q, is known. In reality, we know two things: the maximum inventory level, Q, and the minimum inventory level, which is 0Q, no inventory. On average, the firm has an inventory level of

$$(1Q + 0Q) / 2 = 1/2(Q).$$

Accordingly, the total annual carrying cost TC is the multiplication of the average inventory (or the order quantity: the amount ordered by the firm each time) and the annual cost of carrying an item, that is,

$$TC = (1/2)Q \ Cc. \tag{1}$$

This cost is shown in Figure 5.2. TC increases and decreases in relation to Q.

Figure 5.2. **Total Annual Carrying Cost (TC)**

The total annual carrying cost is one part of the total inventory cost TV, which consists of two components: the total annual carrying cost of inventory items TC and the total annual cost of ordering inventory items, say TO (Bierman et al. 1977; Brown 1967). The TO consists of costs of overhead, clerical help, searching sources of supply, and so forth. The issue is how TO can be modeled. This cost must reflect the cost of making (placing) an order and the number of orders the firm makes annually. Assume the cost of making an order is CO. This cost contains the cost of individuals making the order: wages and salaries, the cost of making the order such as telephone calls, paperwork, and transportation associated with an order, and the cost of receiving the order. What we need now is the number of orders, N. If the annual demand for the product is D and the inventory level or the order quantity (the replenishment size) is Q, then the total annual ordering cost, TO, is

$$TO = (D/Q)CO = N \ CO \tag{2}$$

where $N = D/Q$. This cost is shown in Figure 5.3.

Figure 5.3. **Total Ordering Cost (TO)**

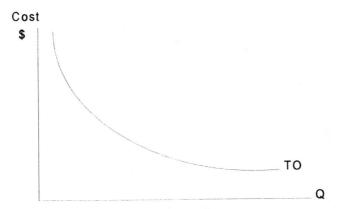

TO decreases as Q increases, because the larger the Q, the smaller the number of orders will be. Therefore, the annual total inventory cost, TV, is the sum of equations (1) and (2), that is,

$$TV = TC + TO = (1/2)Q\ Cc + (D/Q)CO \qquad (3)$$

and Figure 5.4 shows this cost.

Figure 5.4. **Total Inventory Cost (TV)**

As can be seen, TV starts decreasing as Q increases untill TV reaches its minimum at Q* then starts increasing again. This minimum provides the optimum quantity that should be stored. Usually, business firms are interested in finding the order quantity, Q (the inventory level), that minimizes the total inventory cost TV (Hadley and Whitin 1963). How do we do that? Calculus can provide us with the required solution. We can minimize equation (3) by differentiating it with respect to Q and set the outcome equal to zero. This enables us to find the critical point Q*. Then we find the second derivative, which must be positive if the equation has a minimum. Thus,

$$d(TV) / dQ = (1/2)Cc - (D/Q^2)CO = 0$$

$$(1/2)\,Cc = (D/Q^2)CO$$

$$Q^2 = [(2D/Cc)]CO$$

$$Q^* = ([2DCO/Cc]^{1/2}, \tag{4}$$

which is the economic order quantity (or the critical point). The second derivative is

$$d^2(TV)/dQ^2 = -(2Q)(-D)/Q^4 = 2D/Q^3 > 0.$$

Figure 5.5 shows this minimum cost and all the other cost curves.

Figure 5.5. **Inventory Cost Curves and Best Level of Q**

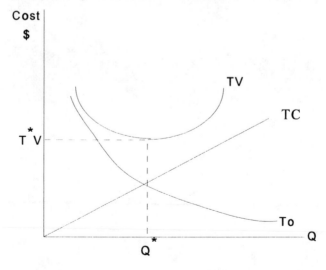

It should be noted that Q* can also be obtained if TC is set equal to TO, and this exercise is left to students to do.

Example 1: The Washington Bookstore faces an annual demand for Paul Kennedy's book of 1000 units. Each book costs $10. It was estimated that each order costs $74.89, and the inventory carrying cost per book is 15 percent. Find Q^*, TV, TO, TC, maximum inventory, average inventory, and number of orders per year.
Solution: Cc = (CC)(V) = ($10.00)(0.15)= $1.5. As D = 1000 and CO = $74.89,

$$Q^* = [2(1000)(\$74.89)/\$1.5]^{1/2} = 316 \text{ books}$$

$$TC = (1/2)Q^* Cc = (1/2)(316)(\$1.5) = \$237$$

$$TO = (D/Q^*)CO = (1000/316)(74.89) = \$237$$

$$TV = TC + TO = 237 + 237 = \$474$$

Maximum inventory level = Q^* = 316
Average inventory level = $(1/2)Q^*$ = (1/2)(316) = 158 books
Number of orders per year, N = D/Q^* = 1000/316 = 3.16 = 3 orders

Example 2: Vary Q* from 0 to 400 and find the effects of these changes on the cost curves. (Also graph your results.)
Solution: By varying the economic order quantity from zero to 400 we are actually performing what is called "sensitivity analysis," that is, how sensitive these costs are to the varied amount of Q*. These results are shown in Table 5.1, and Figure 5.6 shows the cost curves.

Table 5.1. **Sensitivity Analysis to Order Quantity**

Q*	TC	TO	TV
50	37.50	1497.80	1535.30
100	75.00	998.53	1073.53
150	112.50	499.27	611.77
200	150.00	374.45	524.45
250	187.50	299.56	487.06
300	225.00	249.63	474.63
315	236.25	237.75	474.00
316	237.00	237.00	474.00
317	237.75	236.25	474.00
350	262.50	213.97	476.47
400	300.00	187.23	487.23

Figure 5.6. **The Cost Curves**

In the above discussion we have learned how to find the quantity the firm must order so as to minimize its total inventory cost. We want to know how often the firm has to order—for example, should it order every 10 days or every 15 days after placing the first order? In other words, one has to know what is termed the *inventory cycle*, CT, the period of time between two consecutive orders. Moreover, we must know at which level of inventory the firm must order or reorder—the reorder point, RO.

The inventory cycle can be found by calculating the ratio of the number of working days in a year and the number of orders, N. We know that the number of orders N is equal to

$$N = D/Q^*$$

and if we assume that each year consists of 250 working (business) days, then the inventory cycle, CT, is

$$CT = 250/N = [250] / [D/Q^*].$$

For the Washington Bookstore of example 1, the inventory cycle is

$$CT = 250/1000/316 = 83 \text{ days,}$$

which suggests that the bookstore must order every 83 working days.

With respect to the reorder point, we need to know the following. If the publisher of the book has guaranteed Washington that a four-day delivery period is needed to deliver a shipment of books (or to meet any order placed by the bookstore), then this information provides us with what is called the *lead time*, LT. If the demand per business day for Mr. Kennedy's book is estimated by the bookstore to be dd (demand divided by number of business days), then the reorder point, RO, is equal to

$$RO = (dd)(LT) = (D/250)(LT).$$

For example 1, the level of inventory Q at which the bookstore must place an order, the reorder point, if dd is equal to (1000/250), which is 4 books, is

$$RO = (4)(4) = 16 \text{ books.}$$

In other words, the bookstore has to reorder books if the inventory level reaches 16 books. Figure 5.7 shows the inventory cycle for the Washington Bookstore.

Figure 5.7. **Inventory Cycle and Reorder Point for Washington Bookstore**

Example 3: Super Buy specializes in selling various brands of TVs, grills, dryers, refrigerators, and other appliances. Suppose that Super Buy is the dealer of a certain brand of refrigerators. If the annual demand is 720 units, the carrying cost is $90.00 per unit, and the ordering cost is $25.00 per order. Find the optimum number of refrigerators that should be stored (ordered) in order to minimize total inventory cost. Also, find TC, TO, TV, N, CT, and RO, assuming 3 days of lead

time and 250 working days.

Solution:

$$Q* = [(2)(25)(720)/90]^{1/2} = 20 \text{ units}$$

$$TC = (1/2)(20)(90) = \$900.00$$

$$TO = (720/20)(25) = \$900.00$$

$$TV = TC + TO = \$1800.00$$

$$N = D/Q* = 720/20 = 36 \text{ orders}$$

$$CT = 250/36 = 7 \text{ days between consecutive orders}$$

$$RO = (720/250)(3) = 8.6 \text{ days}$$

The EOQ model can be applied to the production process if the ordering cost per order, CO, is replaced by the setup cost, SC, per production run (Hillier and Lieberman 1980; Draper and Klingman 1972). This cost is associated with the preparation of the production process to a new product line. For example, a production process can be changed from the production of a book to a newspaper. This production shift requires expenditures for materials and other items in order to set up the new production run. The next example illustrates the point.

Example 4: The Lincoln Company must provide one of its retailers with 4000 air conditioning units annually. The yearly carrying cost per unit is $50.00, and the setup cost for this new production run is $160.00. Find the number of units that should be produced in each production run in order to minimize the inventory cost. Also, find total annual setup cost, TSC, number of production runs NP, TC, and TV.

Solution: D = 4000, Cc = $50.00 per unit, and set up cost SC = $160.00. Thus,

$$Q* = [(2)(4000)(160)/(50)]^{1/2} = 160 \text{ units}$$

$$TSC = SC(D/Q*) = 160(4000/160) = \$4000.00.$$

Number of inventory cycles (or number of production runs) NP = D/Q* = 4000/160 = 25 cycles (or production runs) per year

$$TC = (1/2)Q*Cc = (1/2)(160)(50) = \$4000.00$$

$$TV = TC + TSC = 4000.00 + 4000.00 = \$8000.00$$

This inventory model can be used in a situation when there is a discount (Winston 1987). In the business world, manufacturers provide discounts to retailers if they purchase large quantities of products. A retailer who needs to decide whether to take a discount has to compare the two costs of inventory with and without discounts and select the minimum cost. In this situation, the total inventory cost TV^* is modified to include the purchasing cost PC, that is,

$$TV^* = (V_i.CC)Q/2 + CO(D/Q) + V_i.D$$

$$= TC + TO + PC$$

where V_i, $i = 1$ and 2 is the price of the item with and without discount; and $V_i.D$ is the purchasing cost with and without the discount. The remaining variables have the same definitions as before.

As an example, consider the following information and select whether the best action is to take a discount: $D = 250$ TV, $CC = 0.30$, $CO = 15$; $V_1 = \$80$, price without a discount; $V_2 = \$70$, price with a discount. The solution, which can be obtained by using TV^*, is as follows:

	Discount	Without Discount
Q*	19.0	18.0
TC	199.5	216.0
TO	197.4	208.3
PC	17,500.0	20,000.0
TV*	$17,915.9	$20,442.3

The decision is to take the discount, because the discount minimizes the inventory cost, TV^*.

The Optimal Order Quantity Model

The economic order quantity (EOQ) model can be extended by assuming that the ratio D/P is not equal to zero. In other words, it is assumed that the product is received daily at a constant rate (or the uniform replenishment rate) of P; D is the demand (use) rate for the item. Hence, D/P is the percentage of demand satisfied by P. In this model it is assumed that P is greater than D $(P > D)$ for the inventory level Q to be materialized. (It should be noted that D/P was not used in the previous model, because the inventory was replenished immediately.) If t is number of days, then the maximum level of inventory, Qmax, is actually the multiplication of excess replenishment rate (P - D) and t. That is,

$$Qmax = (P - D)t.$$

We know

$$Q = Pt$$

so the period (here in days) required to receive an order is

$$t = Q/P.$$

Therefore

$$Qmax = (P - D)t = (P - D)Q/P = PQ/P - DQ/P = (1 - D/P)Q = Q - QD/P.$$

But the minimum inventory level is zero, that is

$$Qmin = 0.$$

It follows that the average inventory level is

$$(1/2) (1 - D/P)Q = 1/2[Q - QD/P].$$

As we know that the annual carrying cost per unit is Cc, the total annual carrying cost, TC, which is the first part of the total inventory cost, must be equal to

$$TC = [(1/2)(1 - D/P)Q] Cc. \qquad (5)$$

The second component of the total annual inventory cost is the total ordering cost, TO. As the number of order is D/Q, and the cost per order is CO, then

$$TO = (D/Q) CO, \qquad (6)$$

which is the same cost as it was with the EOQ model. Accordingly, the total annual inventory cost, TV, is equal to the sum of TC (equation 5) and TO (equation 6), that is,

$$TV = TC + TO = [(1/2)(1 - D/P)Q] Cc + (D/Q)CO.$$

To find the optimal order quantity Q*, TV has to be minimized; that is,

$$d(TV)/dQ = (1/2)(1 - D/P)Cc - (D/Q^2) CO = 0.$$

Solving for the critical point Q* yields

$$Q^* = ([2DCO] / [(1 - D/P)Cc])^{1/2}. \tag{7}$$

As can be seen, if D/P is set equal to zero, equation (7) will be reduced to equation (4). This suggests that the difference between the EOQ and the OEM is D/P, the ratio of demand rate to replenishment rate.

Example 5: The Washington bookstore faces an annual demand for Paul Kennedy's book of 1000 books, and the replenishment rate is 2000 volumes. Each book costs $10. It was estimated that the cost per order is $74.89, and the inventory carrying (holding) cost per book is 15 percent. Find Q*, N, t, TC, TO, TV, and CT if the working days per year is 250, and RO if the lead time is 4 days. Also, graph the inventory cycle.
Solution:

$$Q^* = ([(2)(1000)(\$74.89)]/[(1 - 1000/2000)(\$1.5)])^{1/2} = /149780/0.75 = 447$$

$$N = D/Q^* = 1000/447 = 2.24$$

$$CT = 250/N = 250/2.24 = 112 \text{ days}$$

$$RO = (4)(4) = 16$$

$$Qmax = 447 - (447/2000)(1000) = 223.5 \text{ books}$$

$t = Q^*/P = 447/2000 = 0.2235$ of year [or $(250)(0.2235) = 56$ days] to receive an order, which can be called the *order receipt period*, a time at which Q returns to its maximum level.

$$TC = [1/2(1 - 1000/2000)447] 1.5 = \$167$$

$$TO = (1000/447)(74.89) = \$167$$

$$TV = 167 + 167 = \$334$$

The order receipt period, which is the number of units demanded during period t, is $DQ^*/P = (1000/2000)(447) = 223.5$ books.

Percentage of P satisfying demand is $D/P = 1000/2000 = 50$ percent
Period of order depletion = maximum inventory/demand rate = 223.5/4
Period of order receipt = maximum inventory/replenishment rate = 223.5/8
The graph of the inventory cycle is shown in Figure 5.8.

Figure 5.8. **Inventory Cycle**

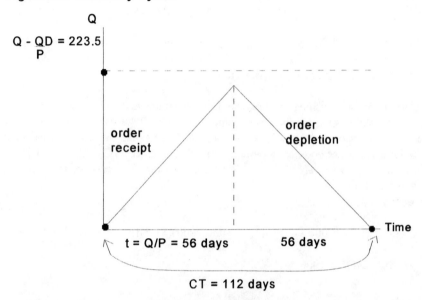

Example 6: Consider the following information:
Carrying cost per unit = $26.00, ordering cost per unit = $10.00, annual demand = 210, working days = 210, demand rate per day = 210/210 = 1 unit, daily receipt rate $P = 2$ units, and annual receipts are $(2)(210) = 420$.
Solution:

$$Q^* = [(2)(10)(210)/26(1 - 1/2)]^{1/2} = 18 \text{ units}$$

$$TC = [1/2(1 - 210/420)\,18]\,(26) = \$117$$

$$TO = (210/18)(10) = \$117$$

$$TV = TC + TO = \$234$$

$$N = D/Q^* = 210/18 = 11.67$$

$$CT = 210/N = 18$$

Period of order receipt is $t = Q^*/P = 18/2 = 9$

Period of order depletion is $Q^*/P = 18/2 = 9$

As was indicated in the last section, this model can also be applied to the production process if the cost per order is replaced by the setup cost per production run, SC. In addition, P is called in this context the *annual productive capacity* (or production rate). The next two examples illustrate this point.

Example 7: The Washington Bookstore faces an annual demand of 1000 books for Paul Kennedy's book, and the production line has an annual capacity of 2000 books. Each book costs $10. It was estimated that the setup cost per production run is $74.89, and the inventory carrying cost per book is 15 percent. Find Q^*, N, and CT if the working number of days per year is 250, and RO if the lead time is 4 days.
Solution.
$Q^* = ([(2)(1000)(\$74.89)]/[(1 - 1000/2000)(\$1.5)])^{1/2} = 149780/0.75 = 447$

$Qmax = (P - D)Q^*/P = (2000 - 1000) (447/2000) = 223.5$

Average inventory $= 1/2 (1 - D/P)Q^* = 223.5$

Length of production phase $= Q^*/P = 447/2000 = 0.2235$ year (or 56 days)

Length of inventory depletion $= (P - D)Q^*/PD =$
    $[(2000 - 1000)/(2000)(1000)](447) = 0.2235$ year

Number of inventory cycles $= D/Q^* = 1000/447 = 2.24$

$CT = 56 + 56 = 112$ days

$TSC = SC [D/Q^*] = 74.89 [1000/447] = \$167.5$

Example 8: Clinton Company must provide 500 tractors a month to one of its retailers. The monthly carrying cost per tractor is $10, and the setup cost for a production run is $200. Production is at a constant rate of 1000 tractors per month. Find the number of tractors that must be produced in order to minimize inventory cost.
Solution:

$D = 500$, $Cc = \$10$, SC (setup cost per run) $= 200$, and $P = 1000$; hence,

$Q* = ([(2)(500)(200)]/[(1 - 500/1000)10])^{1/2} = 200$ units.

$Qmax = (P - D)Q*/P = (1000 - 500)/1000)(200) = 100$

Average inventory $= 1/2 (1 - D/P)Q* = 1/2(1 - 500/1000)(200) = 50$

Length of production phase $= Q*/P = 200/1000 = 0.2$ year

Length of inventory depletion $= (P - D)Q*/PD = [(1000 - 500)/(1000)(500)] = 0.2$ year

Number of inventory cycles $= D/Q* = 500/200 = 2.5$ cycles per year

Example 9: Hayder's Company needs 2500 fans per quarter. It costs $3.00 a month to store a fan. The cost of ordering a supply of fans is $0.50 per quarter. Hayder's Company has two options: (1) to purchase the fan periodically in lots or (2) to purchase the fan periodically from a supplier who sends them at a rate of 1500 per month until an order is filled. Find the quarterly cost of the optimal option.
Solution: $D = 2500$, $CO = \$0.50$, $Cc = (3)(3) = \$9.00$ per quarter, and $P = (1500)(3) = 4500$ per quarter; hence, the optimal order quantity for option 1 is

$$Q* = [(2)(0.50)(2500)/9]^{1/2} = 50/3$$

and

$$TV_1 = 9(50/3)/2 + (1/2)(2500)/(50/3) = \$150.$$

The optimal order quantity for option 2 is given by

$$Q* = ([(2)(0.50)(2500)]/ [9(1 - 2500/4500)])^{1/2} = 25$$

and

$$TV_2 = (1/2)(9)(25)(1 - 5/9) + (1/2)(2500)/25 = \$100.$$

Therefore, option 2 whose TV is less than option 1 is the best choice.

Inventory With Planned Shortage

Managers cannot always keep materials in inventories because of high cost of inventory and space limitation. It follows that demand by customers is not satisfied immediately, and orders have to be made to meet the demand, a situation indicating a waiting period for the customers. The aim is to formulate the inventory model with this planned shortage. In this model the total inventory cost, TV, consists of three different cost components: total ordering cost, total carrying cost, and total shortage (or stockout) cost (or cost of back orders). The total carrying cost is discussed as follows. If the quantity of shortage back-ordered per an order is S, a quantity that is equivalent to the number of back orders the firm has to make to satisfy demand, then the maximum inventory level is

$$Q - S,$$

where Q is the order quantity. The minimum inventory is zero, and the average inventory level is $(1/2)(Q - S)$.

Because customers' demand is satisfied by the available inventory and back order, the total cycle time (or inventory cycle), CT, has to be divided into two periods: CT_1 and CT_2. CT_1 represents time over which the inventory satisfies all demand—no back order of stock is on hand; CT_2 represents time over which the firm has to make back orders in order to meet demand—a stockout condition, no inventory. If this is the case, the average inventory level over CT_1 becomes

$$[Q - S](CT_1)/2.$$

With respect to the CT_2 period, one can argue that the inventory level is zero because the demand is met by making back orders. In sum, the average inventory level over the entire period, CT, has to be

$$(Q - S)(CT_1)/ 2CT. \tag{8}$$

Also, note that the inventory cycle is

$$CT = Q/D \tag{9}$$

and

$$CT_1 = (Q - S) / D, \tag{10}$$

that is, $CT_2 = S/D$, because $CT = CT_1 + CT_2$. And $CT_2 = Q/D - (Q - S)/D$. Using equations (9) and (10) in equation (8), the average inventory level becomes

$$(Q - S)[Q - S)/D] / [2Q/D] = (Q - S)^2/2Q \tag{11}$$

and the total annual cost of holding inventory items is the multiplication of Cc and equation (11). That is,

$$TC = [(Q - S)^2/2Q]Cc. \tag{12}$$

The second component of the total inventory cost is the ordering cost. This cost is the same as the one shown in equation (2), that is,

$$TO = (D/Q) \, CO.$$

The third component of the total inventory cost that must be considered in this model is the cost of shortage (or the cost of back order). To formulate this cost, one has to find the average level of shortage (back orders) over the period CT_2 only, because the shortage level over the period CT_1 is zero. The minimum shortage level of S is zero, and the maximum level is S; hence, the average is S/2. In addition, over the period CT_2, S/2 becomes $(S/2)(CT_2)$, and the average shortage level over the entire cycle CT is

$$S/2(CT_2)/CT. \tag{13}$$

And the period of shortage CT_2 is

$$CT_2 = S/D. \tag{14}$$

Using equations (12) and (7) in equation (11), the average shortage level becomes

$$[(S/2)(S/D)]/[Q/D] = S^2/2Q. \tag{15}$$

If the per unit cost of shortage (or cost of a back order) is C_d, then the annual cost of shortage T_d is the multiplication of C_d and equation (13). That is,

$$T_d = (S^2/2Q)C_d. \tag{16}$$

Accordingly, the total annual inventory cost, TV, is the sum of equations (2), (12), and 16); that is,

$$TV = TC + TO + T_d$$

or

$$TV = [(Q - S)^2/2Q]Cc + (D/Q)CO + (S^2/2Q)C_d. \tag{17}$$

In this equation, there are two unknowns, Q (order quantity) and S (planned shortage level). To minimize equation (17), the equation has to be differentiated partially with respect to Q and S. In other words, the technique of *minimization of functions of several variables* has to be used. It follows that

$$\partial TV/\partial S = [2(Q - S)/2Q](-1)Cc + (2S/2Q)C_d = 0$$

$$\partial TV/\partial S = -Cc + SCc/Q + (S/Q)C_d = 0$$

or

$$S = Q[Cc/(Cc + C_d)] \tag{18}$$

and

$$\partial TV/\partial Q = Cc/2 - DCO/Q^2 - (Cc + C_d)S^2/2Q^2 = 0$$

or

$$Q^2 = (2/Cc)[DCO + (1/2)(Cc + C_d)S^2]. \tag{19}$$

Using equation (18) in equation (19) and solving for Q yields

$$Q^* = [(2DCO)(Cc + C_d)/CcC_d)]^{1/2}. \tag{20}$$

Now using equation (20) in equation (18) yields

$$S^* = \{2DCO[(Cc + C_d)/(CcC_d)]\}^{1/2}[(Cc)/(Cc + C_d)]$$

$$= Q^*[(Cc)/(Cc + C_d)].$$

Example 10: Super Buy is trying to use a new inventory policy that allows for planned shortages in order to minimize total inventory cost. Given the following information related to one of the products—annual demand D = 4000, carrying cost per unit Cc = \$20, ordering cost per order CO = \$50, and shortage cost per unit C_d = \$60—find the optimum order quantity, optimum shortage level, CT, and TV. Solution:

$$Q^* = ([2(4000)(50)/20] [(20 + 60)/(60)])^{1/2} = \text{optimal level of order quantity} = 141$$

$$S^* = Q^*[(20/(20 + 60)] = 141 [20/80] = \text{Optimal level of shortage} = 35$$

This model can also be used in production if some assumptions are made. If the ordering cost per order is replaced by the setup cost, if it is assumed that production orders are filled without delay, and if the demand is constant, then this model can be applied to the production process. The following example illustrates this point.

Example 11: The Lincoln Company must provide Famous.Tarr with 1350 chairs annually. The annual storage cost is $40 per chair, the shortage cost is $50 per chair short per year, and it costs $150 to start a production run (setup cost). If production orders are filled without delay and demand is at a constant rate, determine Q* and S*.
Solution: Cd = $50 per unit short a year, D = 1350, SC (setup cost) = CO = $150, and Cc = $40 per unit; hence,

$$Q* = ([2(1350)150/40][(40 + 50)/(50)])^{1/2} = [10125\ (1.8)]^{1/2} = 135.$$

$$S* = 135[(40/90)] = 60$$

and

$$D/Q* = 1350/135 = 10.$$

Problems

1. A bookstore faces an annual demand for a book of 800 units. Each book costs $20.00, and each order costs $80.00. The carrying cost per book is 5 percent. Find Q* , TV, TO, TC, and number of orders per year. Also, find the inventory cycle if each year is assumed to consist of 250 business days.

2. A department store faces a demand for topsoil of 10,000 bags a year. Each bag costs $1.10 and each order costs $100.00. The inventory carrying cost per bag is 5 percent. Find Q*, TV, TO, and number of orders annually. Also, find the inventory cycle if the year is assumed to have 250 business days and the reorder   point if the leading time is 5 days.

3. A department store is selling a certain brand of dryers. If the annual demand is 2000 units, the carrying cost is $80.00 per unit, and the ordering cost is $20.00, find the optimal number of dryers that should be ordered (or stored). Also, find TC, TO, TV, N, CT, and RO, assuming there are 3 days lead time and 250 business day in the year.

4. For problem 1, if the replenishment rate is 1600 books, use all the previous information to find Q*, N, CT, RO if the lead time is 2 days, and also Qmax. Moreover, find TC, TO, and TV.

5.   A store is selling IBN computers. The annual demand is 10,000 units, and the annual working days are 200. The carrying cost is $30, and the ordering cost is $15.00 per unit. Assuming the daily replenishment (receipt) rate is 100 units, find Q*, TC, TO, TV, N, CT, period of order receipt, and period of order depletion.

6.   A store is trying to use a new inventory policy allowing for planned shortages of dryers in order to minimize the total inventory cost. Assume the following information: The annual demand for dryers is 3500, carrying cost per dryer is $25.00, cost per order is $60.00, and cost of a back order is $70.00; find Q*   and S*.

7.   A firm must provide one of its retailers with 3000 units of a certain brand of radio. The annual carrying cost is $5.00, and the setup cost for this new production run is $100.00. How many units should be produced in order to minimize the inventory cost? Also, find TSC, NP, TC, and TV.

8.   A supplier provides a department store with 2000 tires annually. The carrying cost is $30.00 per tire, the shortage cost is $40.00 per year, and setup cost is $120.00. Find Q* and S* assuming demand is at constant rate and the production orders are filled without delay.

CHAPTER SIX

Dynamic Techniques

In this chapter various dynamic techniques along with some of their applications in business and economics will be explored. These dynamic techniques are definite and indefinite integration, first- and second-order linear difference equations, and first- and second-order linear differential equations. These techniques have various applications in both business and economics. For example, the integral calculus can be used to find functions reflecting time paths for variables such as consumption and investment. Also, first-order linear difference equations can be used to find the dynamic equilibrium of price and investment. Similarly, first- and second-order differential equations have various applications in dynamic economics.

Definite and Indefinite Integration

Integration is in general a procedure termed *antidifferentiation* (Chiang 1984; Bressler 1975). A function such as $y = 3x$ has a derivative of $dy/dx = 3$. The integration of the derivative 3 is a process that generates the original function $y = 3x$. That is, $\int 3dx = 3x + c$, where c is the undetermined constant. Because the value of c is unknown, the integration is called *indefinite* because the outcome $3x + c$ has no definite value even if the value of x is known. In any event, for $\int 3dx$, the sign $\int$ is called the *integral sign*; dx means the integration is performed with respect to x; and the 3 [or any function of x, f(x)] is called the *integrand*.

Similar to differentiation, there are useful rules that can be used to perform the integration process. Here are the most important rules used in integral calculus:

1. $\int X^n \, dx = 1/(n + 1) X^{n+1} + c$, where $n \neq -1$

For example, $\int x^3 \, dx = 1/4x^4 + c$ and $\int x^6 \, dx = 1/7x^7 + c$.

2. $\int 1 \, dx = x + c$.

For example, $\int 3dx = 3x + c$ and $\int 5dx = 5 \int dx = 5x + c$.

3. $\int kf(x)dx = k\int f(x)dx$, where k is a constant.

For example, $\int 4x^2dx = 4\int x^2dx = 4/3\ x^3 + c$ and $\int 10x^4dx = 10/5\ x^5 + c = 2x^5 + c$. Also, $\int -3x^2dx = -x^3 + c$.

4. $\int [f(x) + g(x)]dx = \int f(x)dx + \int g(x)dx$

For example, $\int [x + x^2]dx = \int xdx + \int x^2dx = (1/2)x^2 + c_1 + (1/3)x^3 + c_2$ which is equal to $(1/2)x^2 + (1/3)x^3 + c$, where $c = c_1 + c_2$. And $\int [2x - 3x^2]dx = \int 2xdx - \int 3x^2dx = x^2 - x^3 + c$.

5. $\int [f'(x)/f(x)]dx = \ln f(x) + c$, if $f(x) > 0$, where $f'(x)$ is the derivative of $f(x)$, or $\int [f'(x)/f(x)]dx = \ln If(x)I + c$, if $f(x) < 0$.

For example, $\int [4x/2x^2]dx = \ln (2x^2) + c$, for $4x = 8$. Or $\int [4x/2x^2]dx = \ln I2x^2I + c$, for $4x = -8$.

It should be noted that at times the integrand can be manipulated such that the rule can be used. For example, to find $\int [x/x^2]dx$, we can multiply the integrand by 2/2. The function becomes $\int [2x/2x^2]dx$, which is $(1/2)\int [2x/2x^2]dx = (1/2)[\ln x^2] + c]$.

6. $\int x^{-1}dx = \int (1/x)dx = \ln x + c$, if $x > 0$. Or $\int (1/x)dx = \ln IxI + c$, if $x < 0$.

For example, $\int x^{-4}dx = \int (1/x^4)dx = (1/-5)x^{-5} + c$.

7. $\int e^{kx}dx = (e^{kx}/k) + c$. For example, $\int e^{3x}dx = (e^{3x}/3) + c$. For $3\ e^{4x}dx = 3e^{4x}/4 + c = (3/4)e^{4x} + c$. And the integral of the function e^xdx is $e^x + c$.

8. $\int (a)^{kx}dx = [(a)^{kx}/k\ \ln(a)] + c$, where a and k are constants.

For example, $\int (3)^{2x}dx = [(3)^{2x}/2\ \ln(3)] + c$. Also, $\int (2)^{5x}dx = [(2)^{5x}/5\ \ln(2)] + c$.

9. $\int f'(x)e^{f(x)}dx = e^{f(x)} + c$, where $f'(x)$ is the derivative of $f(x)$.

For example, $\int 4xe^{2x^2}dx = e^{2x^2} + c$. And $\int 2e^{2x}dx = e^{2x} + c$, because 2 is the derivative of 2x. Similarly, the integrand can be manipulated to perform this integration. For example, $\int e^{2x}dx$ can be rewritten as

$$(2/2)e^{2x}dx = (1/2)\int 2e^{2x}dx = (1/2)e^{2x} + c.$$

If one knows the initial and boundary conditions, the constant (c) can be determined. For example, given $y = \int 3dx$ and the boundary condition is $y = 5$ when $x = 1$, then $y = 3x + c$. Using the boundary condition, $5 = 3(1) + c$. Hence, c $= 2$. Consequently, $y = 3x + 2$. Similarly, the initial condition can be used to find c. For the initial condition $y = 5$, when $x = 0$; $y = 3x + c$ becomes $5 = 3(0) + c$, and c = 5. Therefore, y = 3x + 5.

10. $y = \int u^n du = [(u^{n+1})/(n + 1)] + c$, where u is a function of x.

For example, $y = \int (x + 3)^3 dx = [(x + 3)^4/4] + c$.

11. $y = \int u e^u du = e^u(u - 1)$, where u is a function of x.

For example, $y = \int 3xe^{3x} dx = e^{3x}(3x - 1)$.

Integration by Substitution

Under this rule of integration the integrand f(x) can be expressed by another function u and its derivative du/dx. That is, f(x) becomes udu/dx. In general, the given function can be written as

$$\int f(x)dx = \int (u\, du/dx)dx = \int udu.$$

For example, $y = \int 3x^2(x^3 + 4)dx$ can be integrated as follows. Let

$$u = x^3 + 4 ,$$

then $du/dx = 3x^2$; hence,

$$dx = du/3x^2.$$

After using (u) and (dx) in the given function y, we obtain

$$y = \int 3x^2 . u . du/3x^2.$$

Or
$$y = \int udu = (1/2)u^2 + c = (1/2)(x^3 + 4)^2 + c, \text{ where } x^3 + 4 = u.$$

Similarly, to find $y = \int x^6(2x^7 + 15)dx$, let $u = 2x^7 + 15$, then $du/dx = 14x^6$ and dx = $du/14x^6$. Using (u) and (dx) in the given function, we obtain

$$y = \int x^6 . u . du/14x^6 = \int (1/14)udu = (1/28)u^2 + c = (1/28)(2x^7 + 15)^2 + c.$$

To find $y = \int 8e^{4x+6}dx$, we can follow the same procedure. Let $u = 4x + 6$, then du/dx = 4, and dx = du/4. Using (u) and (dx) in the given function, we obtain

$$y = \int 8e^u du/4 = \int 2e^u du = 2e^u + c = 2e^{4x + 6} + c, \text{ where } 4x + 6 = u.$$

Integration by Parts

To perform this integration the given function has to be expressed as $\int f(x)g'(x)dx$. That is, $f(x)$ and $g'(x)$ must be specified from the given function. And this expression is equal to $f(x)g(x) - \int g(x)f'(x)dx$. To find $y = \int 4xe^x dx$, we have to put the given function in the expression $\int f(x)g'(x)dx$. Thus, $f(x) = 4x$ and $g'(x) = e^x$. It follows that $f'(x) = 4$ and $g(x) = \int g'(x)dx$ which is equal to $e^x dx = e^x$. Using

$$\int f(x)g'(x)dx = f(x)g(x) - \int g(x)f'(x)dx,$$

we obtain

$$\int 4x.e^x dx = 4x.e^x - \int e^x.4dx = 4x.e^x - 4e^x + c.$$

To check the answer, differentiate the outcome of the integration with respect to x, that is, find dy/dx, which is equal to $4e^x + e^x 4x - 4e^x = 4xe^x$; and this is the given function.

Another example may illustrate the technique further. Assume we are given the function $y = \int 4 \ln x \, dx$. To integrate the function by parts we need to use

$$\int f(x)g'(x)dx = f(x)g(x) - \int g(x)f'(x)dx.$$

So, let $f(x) = 4 \ln x$, then $f'(x) = 4/x$. Also, let $g'(x) = 1$, then $g(x)$ is $\int g'(x)dx = \int 1 \, dx = x$. Use these results in the above formula to get

$$\int 4 \ln x.1.dx = 4 \ln x.x - \int x.(4/x)dx$$

$$= 4 \ln x.x - \int 4dx$$

$$= 4x \ln x - 4x + c$$

and $dy/dx = 4 \ln x + (1/x)4x - 4 = 4 \ln x$, which is the given function.

The integration technique has various applications. It can be applied to find the time path function of capital stock, $K(t)$, if the function of the investment rate $I(t)$ is given. If $I(t) = 30t^{0.5}$, then $K(t) = \int 30t^{0.5}dt = (30/1.5)t^{1.5} + c$. As indicated previously, if the initial condition is given, one can determine c. If $K(t)$ at time zero is 80—that is, $K(0) = 80$—then $80 = (30/1.5)(0)^{1.5} + c$; hence c, the initial value of capital, is equal to 80; and $K(t) = (30/1.5)t^{1.5} + 80$.

If we know the marginal propensity to consume, the time path function of consumption $C(t)$ can be determined. For example, if MPC = 0.9, then $C(t) = \int 0.9dt = 0.9t + c$. If at time zero $C(t) = 100$, then c = 100 and the time path function of the consumption becomes $C(t) = 0.9t + 100$. It should be noted that if the integration is performed with respect to income y, the consumption function becomes $C = 0.9y + 100$.

The foregoing discussion centers upon the indefinite integration where the value of the function was not obtained. If we are interested in finding such values we need to use the definite integration. This technique intends to measure areas under curves. The previous rules will be utilized, and the constant of integration is eliminated. The definite integration of $f(x)$ between x greater than (a) but no less than (b), where (a) and (b) are constants, can be performed in this way:

$$_a\int^b f(x)dx = F(x) \,_a|^b = F(b) - F(a)$$

For example, $_2\int^5 2xdx = x^2 \,_2|^5 = (5)^2 - (2)^2 = 21$. Graphically, the function $y = 2x$ is shown in Figure 6.1.

Figure 6.1. **Area of 21 Under the Curve**

Important applications of the definite integration are the *consumer surplus* and the *producer surplus* (Henderson and Quandt 1980). The consumer surplus (C.S) is written as

$$C.S. = {_0}\int^{Qo} f(Q)dQ - PoQo$$

where $f(Q)$ is the inverse demand curve; and Po and Qo are the equilibrium price and quantity, respectively. The consumer surplus can be shown graphically in Figure 6.2.

Figure 6.2. **Consumer Surplus Under f(Q)**

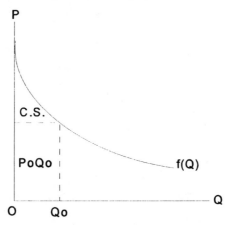

Example: If the inverse demand curve is P = 50 - 5Q and Po is $5, find C.S.
Solution: To find C.S., we need to get Qo from the inverse demand curve. That is,
5 = 50 -5Q, which is 45/5 = Qo = 9. Hence, PoQo = 5(9) = 45. Accordingly,

$$C.S. = {}_0\!\int^{Qo} (50 - 5Q)dQ - 45$$

$$= (50Q - 2.5Q^2) - 45$$

$$= 50(9) - 2.5(81) - 45$$

$$= 450 - 202.5 - 45 = 202.5$$

Similarly, the producer surplus, P.S., can be obtained from the inverse supply
curve. That is,

$$P.S. = PoQo - {}_0\!\int^{Qo} f(Q)dQ.$$

The P.S. is shown in Figure 6.3.

Figure 6.3. **The Producer Surplus Above f(Q)**

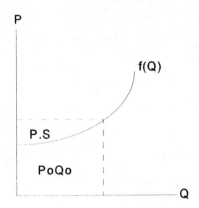

Example: If the inverse supply function is $P = 2Q + 1$ and $P_o = 49$, find the producer surplus.

Solution: To find P.S. we need to find Q_o, which is equal to $49 = 2Q + 1$; hence, $Q_o = 24$. Consequently,

$$P.S. = 24(49) - {}_o\int^{24} (Q + 1)dQ$$

$$= 24(49) - [(0.5Q^2 + Q)]$$

$$= 24(49) - [0.5(24)^2 + 24]$$

$$= 1176 - [288 + 24] = 864.$$

Another application of the definite integration is finding the present value of (n) year revenue stream, given the annual discount rate. In this case, the revenue is discounted according to the following formula:

$$\text{Present Value} = \text{future Value} * e^{-rt}$$

or

$$PV = FVe^{-rt}.$$

Therefore, for (n) year stream of annual revenue of R, the present value becomes

$$PV = {}_o\int^n R(t)e^{-rt}.$$

Thus, if the annual revenue is $1000, the discount rate is 0.02, and for 5 years, the present value would be

$$PV = {_0}\int^5 1000^{e-0.02t}$$

$$= (-1000/0.02)e^{-0.02t}$$

$$= -1000/0.02[e^{-0.02(5)} - e^{-0.02(0)}]$$

$$= 4759.$$

The definite integration can also be used in probability theory. For instance, if f(x) is a probability function, one can find the probability that the random variable (x) is between 1 and 3. That is,

$$P(1 < x < 3) = \int f(x)dx.$$

So, if f(x) = 0.2, then

$$P(1 < x < 3) = {_1}\int^3 0.2dx = 0.2x] = 0.2(3) - 0.2(1) = 0.4.$$

First-Order Linear Difference Equations

A difference equation is used to find the time path of a variable in discrete time, that is, over one day, one month, one year, and so forth. This dynamic analysis is also called *period analysis*. If a variable y is taken into consideration, the first difference between two periods is written as

$$\Delta y = y_t - y_{t-1},$$

where y_t means the value of the variable y in time t, and y_{t-1} means the value of the variable y in time t-1; if t is Monday, then t-1 is Sunday. If Δy is equal to 4, then the pattern of change can be described as

$$\Delta y = y_t - y_{t-1} = 4,$$

which is a first-order nonhomogeneous linear difference equation. If Δy is written as

$$\Delta y = y_t - y_{t-1} = 0,$$

the equation is called a *linear first-order homogeneous difference equation*. At any rate, the general form of a nonhomogeneous linear difference equation is

$$y_t = a_1y_{t-1} + a_2y_{t-2} + a_3y_{t-3} + ... + a_ny_{t-n} + c.$$

In this section we are interested in finding a solution for a linear first order difference equation (Chiang 1984; Goldberg 1971; Gondolfo 1971). The starting point is the first-order linear homogeneous difference equation taking the form

$$y_t - ay_{t-1} = 0,$$

where (a) is a constant coefficient. This equation is linear, because the variables y_t and y_{t-1} are raised to the first power. The equation is of first order, because the difference between the variables y_t and y_{t-1} is one period. The solution to the equation must satisfy two conditions: (1) It must satisfy the difference equation for all values of t, and (2) it must satisfy the initial condition, the value of y at time zero: $Y(t = 0) = Y_o = K_o$. To find the solution, rewrite the above equation as

$$y_t = ay_{t-1}. \tag{1}$$

At $t = 1$, equation (1) becomes

$$y_1 = ay_o, \tag{2}$$

but if $y_o = K_o$, the initial condition, then equation (2) becomes

$$y_1 = ay_o = a\,K_o. \tag{3}$$

At $t = 2$, equation (1) becomes, after using equation (3),

$$y_2 = ay_1 = a\,(a\,K_o) = a^2K_o.$$

If we continue doing that, we arrive at the general solution for the first-order homogeneous difference equation as

$$Y_t = (a)^tK_o = (a)^ty_o \tag{4}$$

where K_o (or y_o) is the initial condition.

To demonstrate that equation (4) is indeed the general solution, check the two conditions described previously. First, by lagging the solution by one period, we obtain

$$Y_{t-1} = (a)^{t-1}y_o. \tag{5}$$

If we use equations (4) and (5) in equation (1), the solution does satisfy the difference equation (1): $y_t = y_t$. Second, using $t = 0$ in the general solution equation (4), we find that the initial condition is satisfied: $Y_o = K_o$.

Example 1: Find the general solution for $y_t - 0.9y_{t-1} = 0$.
Solution: Write the difference equation as $y_t = 0.9y_{t-1}$; hence, the general solution is $y_t = y_o(0.9)^t$. If $y_o = 150$, the definite solution is $y_t = 150(0.9)^t$, a solution that describes the time path function of the variable y. For various values of t, the definite solution is shown in Figure 6.4.

Figure 6.4. **The Definite Solution for Various Values of t**

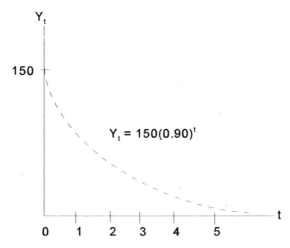

$$Y_t = 150(0.90)^t$$

Example 2: Given the following model

$$y_t = C_t + I_o,$$

where $I_o = 0$ and $C_t = 0.9y_t$, find the time path function of y if y_o, the initial condition, is 1000.
Solution: Using Io and C_t in y_t, we obtain the first order homogeneous equation $y_t = 0.9y_t$ whose solution is $y_t = y_o(0.9)^t = 1000(0.9)^t$. This solution shows the time path function of the variable y_t.

Example 3: The Harrod Model of Economic Growth. To explain the economic growth of a capitalistic economy, Harrod used the Keynesian saving and investment functions. Saving is specified as a proportional function of income y_t. That is,

$$S_t = by_t.$$

Similarly, investment is specified as proportional to the first difference of income. That is,

$$I_t = c(y_t - y_{t-1}).$$

The equilibrium condition of income is achieved when investment is equal to saving. That is,

$$by_t = c(y_t - y_{t-1}).$$

After simplification, we get a first-order linear homogeneous difference equation

$$y_t = [c/(c - b)]y_{t-1}$$

whose solution (or the time path function of income) is

$$y_t = y_0[c/(c - b)]^t,$$

where $[c/(c - b)] - 1$ is the warranted rate of economic growth, which creates a state of mind conducive to economic growth. For example, if $c = 2$ and $b = 0.15$, then the warranted rate of economic growth is $[2/(2 - 0.15)] - 1 = 8.1$ percent.

If the first-order linear difference equation is nonhomogeneous, it takes the form

$$y_t - ay_{t-1} = c,$$

where c is a constant. To find a solution for such an equation, we need to find and combine two solutions. The first solution is obtained for the homogeneous part of the difference equation, a solution called the *general solution*, and the second solution is called the *particular solution*, obtained by trying the solution $k = y_{t-1} = y_t$, where k is a constant, in the given nonhomogeneous difference equation.

Example 4: Solve the equation $y_t - ay_{t-1} = c$.
Solution: The general solution for $y_t - ay_{t-1} = 0$ is $y_t = A (a)^t$, where A is an undetermined constant to be obtained from the initial condition. For a particular solution, we try the solution $k = y_{t-1} = y_t$ in the given difference equation to obtain $k - ak = c$. Hence, the particular solution is $k = c/(1 - a)$. Combine the particular solution and the general solution to obtain the complete solution:

$$y_t = A (a)^t + c/(1 - a).$$

To make the complete solution definitive, we need to find a value for A by using the initial condition in the complete solution. At $t = 0$, the complete solution becomes

$$y_o = A + c/(1 - a)$$

hence,

$$A = y_o - c/(1 - a).$$

After using (A) into the complete solution, we obtain the definitive complete solution,

$$y_t = [y_o - c/(1 - a)] (a)^t + c/(1 - a) .$$

Example 5: Given the following Keynesian macroeconomic model

$$y_t = C_t + I_t,$$

where $C_t = 0.8y_{t-1}$ and $I_t = 50$, find the time path function of income if the initial condition is $y_o = 750$.
Solution: Using C_t and I_t in the equilibrium equation, we obtain

$$y_t = 0.8y_{t-1} + 50.$$

This is a first-order nonhomogeneous linear difference equation. The solution of the homogeneous part of this equation is

$$y_t = A (0.8)^t.$$

To find the particular solution, we try $k = y_{t-1} = y_t$ in the difference equation to obtain

$$k = 0.8k + 50.$$

Hence, $k = 250$, which is the particular solution. We combine the two solutions to obtain the complete solution

$$y_t = A (0.8)^t + 250.$$

To make the solution definitive, we use the initial condition. Using $t = 0$ in the complete solution we get,

$$750 = A + 250.$$

Hence, A is 500. Thus, the definitive complete solution is

$$y_t = 500(0.8)^t + 250.$$

Example 6: Solve $y_t = y_{t-1} + 10$, and $y_o = 30$.
Solution: The solution of the homogeneous part of the equation is $y_t = A(1)^t$. By trying the solution $k = y_t = y_{t-1}$ in the difference equation, we obtain no value for k, the particular solution. Consequently, we try another solution such as $y_t = k*t$. If this solution is correct, then $y_{t-1} = k*(t-1)$. After using y_t and y_{t-1} in the difference equation, we obtain

$$k*t = k*(t-1) + 10$$

$$k*t = k*t - k + 10.$$

Hence, k, the particular solution, is equal to 10. Combining the two solutions, the complete solution is

$$y_t = A(1)^t + 10.$$

Using the initial condition $t = 0$ in the above solution, we obtain $A = 20$; hence, the definitive complete solution is

$$y_t = 20(1)^t + 10.$$

Example 7: Given the following market model $D_t = -3P_t + 120$ and $S_t = 2P_{t-1} - 30$, and the initial condition (at $t = 0$) is $Po = 25$, find the time path function for P.
Solution: Equating S_t and D_t, we obtain

$$-3P_t + 120 = 2P_{t-1} - 30$$

$$-3P_t = 2P_{t-1} - 150.$$

After multiplying by -1 and dividing by 3, the equation becomes

$$P_t = (-2/3)P_{t-1} + 50,$$

which is a first-order nonhomogeneous linear difference equation. The first solution is

$$P_t = A(-2/3)^t.$$

To obtain the particular solution, try $k = P_t = P_{t-1}$ in the difference equation to get $k = (-2/3)k\ 50$. Hence, $k = 30$. The complete solution becomes

$$P_t = A(-2/3)^t + 30.$$

At $t = 0$, $Po = 25$. That is, $25 = A + 30$ and $A = -5$. The definitive complete solution becomes

$$P_t = (-5)(-2/3)^t + 30.$$

Taking the limit of P_t as t approaches infinity, we find $P = 30$, which is the dynamic equilibrium price, a price that can also be obtained by equating the demand and supply curves given previously.

Finally, it should be noted that the time path of P is convergent to an equilibrium point if the absolute value of (a) is less than one. If the absolute value of (a) is greater than one, the time path of P is divergent. In the above example, the absolute value of (a) is 2/3, which is less than one; hence, the time path of P is convergent to the dynamic equilibrium price 30. Students can graph the solution to see the time path of P.

Second-Order Linear Difference Equations

The second-order linear nonhomogeneous difference equation reflects the second difference $\Delta^2 y_t$ taking the form

$$\Delta^2 y_t = \Delta(\Delta y) = \Delta(y_t - y_{t-1}) = \Delta y_t - \Delta y_{t-1}$$

but

$$\Delta y_t = y_t - y_{t-1} \text{ and } \Delta y_{t-1} = y_{t-1} - y_{t-2}.$$

Hence,

$$\Delta^2 y_t = \Delta(\Delta y) = y_t - 2y_{t-1} + y_{t-2}.$$

This means that the second difference contains the value of y, say on Monday y_t, and the value on Sunday y_{t-1}, and the value on Saturday y_{t-2}. In any event, one can state the second-order linear nonhomogeneous difference equation as

$$y_t + a_1 y_{t-1} + a_2 y_{t-2} = c,$$

where a_1, a_2, and c are constant coefficients. We can solve this equation by finding a solution to the homogeneous part of the equation (i.e., when c = 0). If this is so, then we try the solution $A(b)^t$, which is not equal to zero. This solution suggests the following: $y_{t-1} = A(b)^{t-1}$ and $y_{t-2} = A(b)^{t-2}$. After inserting these solutions in the second-order linear homogeneous difference equation, we obtain

$$A(b)^t + a_1 A(b)^{t-1} + a_2 A(b)^{t-2} = 0.$$

After dividing the above equation by $(b)^{t-2}$ and factoring A, we obtain

$$A[b^2 + a_1 b + a_2] = 0$$

(we should note that to solve the second-order difference equation we need to state the equation in terms of this quadratic equation by making b^2 a coefficient of y_t, b the coefficient of y_{t-1}, and the constant a_2 the coefficient of y_{t-2}). At any rate, the quadratic equation has two roots, b_1 and b^2, whose values are obtained from

$$b_1, b_2 = -a_1 \pm (a_1^2 - 4a_2)^{1/2} / 2.$$

This suggests that there are two linearly independent solutions. From the quadratic formula, there are three possibilities:

1. If $a^2_1 > 4a_2$, there are distinct roots, and the solution to the second-order linear homogeneous difference equation is

$$y_t = A_1(b_1)^t + A_2(b_2)^t,$$

where A_1 and A_2 are obtained by using the two initial conditions (yo and y_1 obtained by setting t = 0 and t = 1) in the solution.

2. If $a^2_1 = 4a_2$, there are repeated (equal) roots, and the solution becomes

$$y_t = A_1(b)^t + A_2 t(b)^t.$$

3. If $a^2_1 < 4a_2$, the root is complex, and the solution is

$$y_t = (K)^t(B_1 \cos t\theta + B_2 \sin t\theta)$$

(see example 4 below).

Example 1: Solve $y_t - 4y_{t-1} + 3y_{t-2} = 0$, given the initial conditions $y_0 = 150$ and $y_1 = 180$.
Solution: The quadratic equation for this difference equation can be written as $b^2 - 4b + 3 = 0$, which is (b - 3)(b - 1) = 0. That is, $b_1 = 3$ and $b_2 = 1$, a solution having

distinct roots: $a^2_1 = 16 > 4a_2 = 12$. Hence, the solution is $y_t = A_1(3)^t + A_2(1)^t$. To find A_1 and A_2, we use the initial conditions in the solution. For $t = 0$ and $t = 1$, the solution gives

$$y_0 = A_1 + A_2 = 150$$

$$y_1 = 3A_1 + A_2 = 180.$$

Solving by Cramer's rule, A_1 is 15 and A_2 is 135. After inserting these values in the solution, we obtain $y_t = 150(3)^t + 135(1)^t$, which describes the time path function of y_t.

Example 2: Solve $y_t - 4y_{t-1} + 4y_{t-2} = 0$, given the initial conditions $y_0 = 10$ and $y_1 = 30$.

Solution: The quadratic equation for this difference equation is $b^2 - 4b + 4 = 0$ whose roots are equal. That is, $b_1 = 2$ and $b_2 = 2$. The solution becomes

$$y_t = A_1(2)^t + A_2t(2)^t.$$

To find A_1 and A_2, we use the values of the solution at $t = 0$ and $t = 1$; this would give

$$10 = A_1$$

$$30 = 2A_1 + 2A_2.$$

Therefore, $A_1 = 10$ and $A_2 = 5$. The solution becomes $y_t = 10(2)^t + 5t(2)^t$, which describes the time function of y_t.

Example 3: Solve $y_t + 2y_{t-1} - 8y_{t-2} = 15$ with the initial conditions $y_0 = 10$ and $y_1 = 15$.

Solution: This is a second-order linear nonhomogeneous difference equation. To solve this equation, a solution must be found for the homogeneous part and a particular solution must also be found. To obtain the first solution, the quadratic equation can be stated as $b^2 + 2b - 8 = 0$ whose distinct roots are $b_1 = -4$ and $b_2 = 2$. The solution becomes $y_t = A_1(-4)^t + A_2(2)^t$. To find the particular solution, try $(y_t = k = y_{t-1} = y_{t-2})$ in the given difference equation to obtain $k - 2k - 8k = 15$. (If $y_t = k$ does not work, try $y_t = k*t$.) That is, $-5k = 15$; hence, $k = -3$. The complete solution is the combination of the two solutions. Thus, $y_t = A_1(-4)^t + A_2(2)^t - 3$. To make the solution definitive, we use the initial conditions y_0 ($t = 0$) and y_1 ($t = 1$) in the complete solution. That is,

$$10 = A_1 + A_2 - 3$$

$$15 = -4A_1 + 2A_2 - 3.$$

And A_1 is 8/6 and A_2 is 70/6. Using these values in the complete solution, we obtain the definitive complete solution

$$y_t = (8/6)(-4)^t + (70/6)(2)^t - 3.$$

Example 4: Solve $y_t + 2y_{t-2} = 10$, given the initial conditions $y_o = 7$ and $y_1 = 10$. Solution: The quadratic equation for this difference equation is

$$b^2 + a_1 b + a_2 = 0$$

giving complex roots because $a^2_1 < 4a_2$ [0 < 4 (2)]. The roots are

$$b_1, b_2 = -a_1 + i\ (4a_2 - a^2_1)^{1/2} / 2$$

$$b_1, b_2 = h \pm f\ i$$

where $h = -(1/2)a_1$ and $f = (1/2)\ (4a2 - a^2_1)^{1/2}$; h and f are the two sides of the triangle shown in Figure 6.5.

Figure 6.5. Sides of the Triangle in a Circle

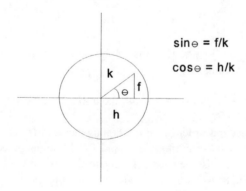

$$\sin\ominus = f/k$$
$$\cos\ominus = h/k$$

Also, $K^2 = h^2 + f^2$, and $K = (h^2 + f^2)^{1/2}$. Using h and f, one can find $K = (a_2)^{1/2}$. Accordingly, one can write the complete solution as

$$y_t = (k)^t\ (B_1 \cos t\theta + B_2 \sin t\theta).$$

For the given difference equation, the following information may be obtained: h $= - (1/2)a_1 = (1/2)(0) = 0$ and $f = (1/2)\ (4a_2 - a^2_1\ )^{1/2} = (1/2)\ [4(2)]^{1/2} = 1.41$, and K

$= (a_2)^{1/2} = (2)^{1/2} = 1.41$. Thus, $\sin \theta = f/K = 1.41/1.41 = 1$ and $\cos \theta = h/K = 0$. For $\sin \theta = 1$ and $\cos \theta = 0$, we can find angle of $\theta = \pi/2$. The complete solution would be

$$y = (1.41)^t [B_1 \cos (\pi/2)t + B_2 \sin (\pi/2)t].$$

For the particular solution, try $y_t = k$ in the given difference equation; we find $k + 2k = 10$. Therefore, $k = 3.3$. Combining this solution with the first solution, we obtain the complete general solution

$$y_t = (1.41)^t [B_1 \cos (\pi/2)t + B_2 \sin(\pi/2)t] + 3.3.$$

Use $t = 0$ and $t = 1$ in this solution to obtain B_1 and B_2. That is, at $t = 0$, $y_0 = 6 = B_1 + 3.3$; hence, $B_1 = 3.7$. At $t = 1$, $y_1 = 10 = (1.41)[B_1 \cos (\pi/2)(1) + B_2 \sin (\pi/2)(1)] + 3.3$. Hence, $B_2 = 6.7$ because $\cos \pi/2 = 0$ and $\sin \pi/2 = 1$ ($\pi = 180$). The definitive complete solution becomes

$$y_t = (1.41)^t [3.7\cos (\pi/2)t + 6.7\sin(\pi/2)t] + 3.3.$$

Example 5: Samuelson's Model of the Interaction Between the Accelerator and the Multiplier

Samuelson's (1939) model consists of the following equations:

$Y_t = C_t + I_t + 100$, where 100 represents government expenditures

$C_t = 20 + 0.9Y_{t-1}$

$I_t = 10 + 0.1(C_t - C_{t-1})$.

We try to find the time path function of the variable Y_t.
Solution: Lag C_t by one period to obtain

$$C_{t-1} = 0.9Y_{t-2}.$$

Use C_t and C_{t-1} in the investment function to get

$$I_t = 10 + 0.1[20 + 0.9Y_{t-1} - 0.9Y_{t-2}] = 10 + 2 + 0.09Y_{t-1} - 0.09Y_{t-2}$$

$$I_t = 12 + 0.09Y_{t-1} - 0.09Y_{t-2}.$$

Using I_t and C_t in the income equation, we obtain

$$Y_t = 20 + 0.9Y_{t-1} + 100 + 12 + 0.09Y_{t-1} - 0.09Y_{t-2}$$

$$Y_t = 132 + 0.99Y_{t-1} - 0.09Y_{t-2}.$$

This equation is a second-order linear nonhomogeneous difference equation because it takes the form

$$Y_t - 0.99Y_{t-1} + 0.09Y_{t-2} = 132,$$

whose quadratic equation is $b^2 - 0.99b + 0.09 = 0$. Students are encouraged to find the time path function of Y_t, that is, the solution of the above equation. (For the particular solution, try $Y_t = k$).

First-Order Linear Differential Equations

The first order linear differential equation takes the form

$$dy/dt + u(t)y = w(t),$$

where $u(t)$ and $w(t)$ are both functions of t. If $w(t)$ is equal to zero, the equation is said to be *homogeneous*; otherwise, it is *nonhomogeneous*. Also, these two functions may be constant. If they are constant, the differential equation is said to be of *constant coefficient* and *constant term*, and this equation shall be used in this section. The differential equation is said to be of *first order*, because there is the first derivative dy/dt only. It is said to be of *first degree*, because the derivative dy/dt is raised to the first power; if the derivative is raised to the second power, $(dy/dt)^2$, the equation is termed *second degree*. If there was a second derivative d^2y/dt^2 in lieu of the first derivative, the equation would be called of *second order*.

In this section we are interested in finding a solution to this differential equation. Similar to the first-order difference equation, we try a solution to the homogeneous part of the equation and try a particular solution to the nonhomogeneous part. Then the two solutions are combined to give the complete solution.

Example 1: Solve $dy/dt + ay_t = 0$ (or $dy/dt = -ay_t$), given the initial condition

$$y_0 = 5.$$

Solution: Try the solution $y_t = Ae^{-at}$, where A can be obtained from the initial condition. Then $dy/dt = -aAe^{-at}$. Using y_t and dy/dt in the given differential equation, we obtain $-aAe^{-at} + aAe^{-at} = 0$; thus, the solution does satisfy the differential equation. For $t = 0$, $y_0 = A = 5$. The complete definitive solution becomes $y_t = y_0e^{-at} = 5e^{-at}$.

Example 2: Solve $2dy/dt = -6y_t$, given $y_o = 10$.
Solution: Dividing the differential equation by 2, we obtain $dy/dt = -3y_t$. Accordingly, the solution is $y_t = Ae^{-3t}$. At $t = 0$, $y_o = A = 10$. The definitive solution is $y_t = 10e^{-3t}$, which is the time path function of y_t. One should note that if the given differential equation is rewritten in this way

$$dy/y = -3dt,$$

and both its sides are integrated, one obtains $\ln |y| + c_1 = -3t + c_2$, or $\ln |y| = -3t + c$, where $c = c_2 - c_1$. Taking the antilog of both sides, assuming y is positive, we obtain $y_t = Ae^{-3t}$, where $A = e^c$.
Example 3: Solve $dy/dt + 0.6y_t = 0$, given $y_o = 3$.
Solution: $y_t = Ae^{-0.6t}$. At $t = 0$, $y_o = A = 3$. Hence, $y_t = 3e^{-0.6t}$. The time path function of y is convergent to an equilibrium point, because the absolute vale of -0.6 is less than one. If it was greater than one, the time path function would be divergent from an equilibrium point; the time path function is graphically presented in Figure 6.6.

Figure 6.6. **Time Path Function for y_t**

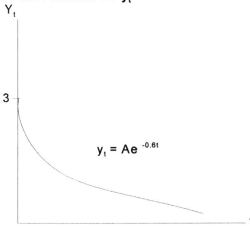

Example 4: Solve $dy/dt + 0.5Y = 5$, given $y_o = 5$.
Solution: This is a first-order nonhomogeneous differential equation. The solution of the homogeneous part is $y_t = Ae^{-0.5t}$. To obtain the particular solution, try $y = k$, where k is a constant; then $dy/dt = 0$. Using $y = k$ and dy/dt in the given differential equation, we obtain $0 + 0.5k = 5$; hence, $k = 10$. After combining the two solutions, we can obtain the complete definitive solution (or the time path function of y):

$$Y_t = Ae^{-0.5t} + 10.$$

At $t = 0$, yo $= 5 = A + 10$ and $A = -5$. Hence, the complete solution is

$$y_t = -5e^{-0.5t} + 10.$$

Example 5: If the demand curve is $D = 2 - 0.5P$, and the supply curve is $S = -3 + 0.5P$, find the time path function for P, assuming $dp/dt = 0.5(D - S)$, where 0.5 is the adjustment coefficient. The initial condition is $P_o = 7$.
Solution: At equilibrium, $D = S$, the equilibrium price is 5. Now, $dp/dt = 0.5 (2 - 0.5P + 3 - 0.5P) = 2.5 - 0.5P$, which is a nonhomogeneous linear differential equation. The first solution is

$$P_t = Ae^{-0.5t}.$$

For the second solution, try $P = k$ and $dk/dt = 0$. Insert both in the given differential equation to obtain

$$0 = 2.5 - 0.5k.$$

Hence, $k = 5$. Combining the two solutions, we obtain the complete solution,

$$P_t = Ae^{-0.5t} + 5.$$

To make the solution definite, use the initial condition (P at time $t = 0$, i.e. $P_o = 7$) in the complete solution to get $7 = A(1) + 5$; hence, $A = 2$. Thus, the definitive complete solution is

$$P_t = 2e^{-0.5t} + 5.$$

Also, the limit of P_t as t approaches zero is 5, which is the dynamic equilibrium price. The time path function of P is shown in Figure 6.7.

Figure 6.7. **Time Path Function for P_t**

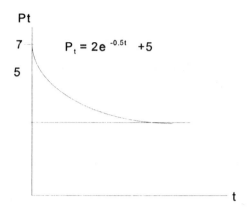

It should be noted that for the differential equation $dy/dt + u(t)y = w(t)$, the definitive complete solution can be stated as

$$y_t = e^{-\int u dt} [A + \int w e^{\int u dt}\, dt].$$

For example, if $dy/dt + 2y = 10$, then $u = 2$ and $w = 10$. $\int 2dt = 2t$ and $\int 10e^{2t}dt = 5e^{2t}$. Thus, the above solution becomes

$$y_t = e^{-\int 2dt} [A + \int 10 e^{\int 2dt}\, dt],$$

which is equal to

$$y_t = e^{-2t} [A + 5e^{2t}] = Ae^{-2t} + 5.$$

If the initial condition is $y_0 = 7$, then $7 = A + 5$, and $A = 2$. The complete solution is

$$y_t = 2e^{-2t} + 5.$$

In fact, the above general solution, which is obtained by using an integrating factor $\int u dt$ in the given differential equation, can be used whether $u(t)$ and $w(t)$ are constant or functions of t.

Example 6: The Domar Model of Economic Growth
Domar (1946) used the Keynesian tools to find out the time path function of investment, which has two effects on aggregate demand (income y) and capacity (potential) output (C). In Keynesian analysis the marginal propensity to save (s) can be used to find the multiplier (k), where ($k = 1/s$). The change in investment over

time (dI/dt) generates a change in income (dy/dt) through the multiplier (k) as follows:

$$dy/dt = kdI/dt.$$

Also, the investment rate (I) influences the change in capacity (potential) output (C) by an amount of (a). That is,

$$dC/dt = aI$$

Also, $a = C/K$, where C is capacity output and K is capital stock. In equilibrium, capacity output (C) should equal to aggregate demand (or income y). That is,

$$C = y.$$

It follows that

$$dC/dt = dy/dt.$$

Combining the equations, we obtain

$$kdI/dt = aI$$

or

$$dI/dt = (a/k)I.$$

This is a homogeneous first-order linear differential equation whose solution is

$$I_t = Ae^{(a/k)t}.$$

If the initial condition (A) is equal to (Io), the time path function of investment becomes

$$I_t = Ioe^{(a/k)t} = Ioe^{(sa)t}.$$

Second-Order Linear Differential Equations

This equation is similar to the second-order difference equation. Here the second difference is replaced by the second-order time derivative of y with respect to t, and the first difference is replaced by the first derivative (Kamien and Schwartz 1981). The form of this equation is

$$d^2y_t/dt^2 + a_1 dy/dt + a_2 y_t = c$$

or

$$y''_{(t)} a_1 y'_{(t)} + a_2 y_{(t)} = c.$$

The solution of this equation provides the time path function of the variable y. To solve this equation, we try the solution $y_{(t)} = Ae^{bt}$, then $y'_{(t)} = Abe^{bt}$, and $y''_{(t)} = Ab^2e^{bt}$. Using these derivatives in the homogeneous part of the differential equation, we obtain

$$Ab^2e^{bt} + a_1 Abe^{bt} + a_2 Ae^{bt} = 0.$$

After simplification, we obtain

$$Ae^{bt}[b^2 + a_1 b + a_2] = 0.$$

The two roots of the quadratic equation are

$$b_1, b_2 = -a_1 \pm (a^2_1 - 4a_2)^{1/2} / 2.$$

And there are three possibilities:

1. If $a^2_1 > 4a_2$, the roots are distinct, and the solution of the homogeneous part of the differential equation is

$$y_{(t)} = A_1 e^{b1t} + A_2 e^{b2t}.$$

The second solution is obtained by trying a solution such as $y_{(t)} = k$ in the given differential equation. (Remember, if $y_{(t)} = k$, then $y'_{(t)} = 0$ and $y''_{(t)} = 0$.) We get the second solution, then a combination of the two solutions provides the complete solution. By using the initial conditions in the complete solution to obtain A_1 and A_2, these values can be used in the complete solution to give the definitive complete solution.

2. If $a^2_1 = 4a_2$, the roots are repeated, and the solution of the homogeneous part is

$$y_{(t)} = A_1 e^{b1t} + A_2 t e^{b2t}.$$

3. If $a^2_1 < 4a_2$, the roots are complex, and the solution to the homogeneous part is

$$y_{(t)} = e^{ht}(B_1 \cos f t + B_2 \sin f t).$$

where $h = (-1/2)a_1$ and $f = (1/2) (4a_2 - a^2_1)^{1/2}$.

Example 1: Solve $y''_{(t)} - 5y'_{(t)} + 6y_{(t)} = 5$ where the initial conditions are $y_o = 7$ and $y'_{(0)} = 8$.

Solution: The quadratic equation for the homogeneous part is $b^2 - 5b + 6 = 0$, given the two distinct roots $b_1 = 2$ and $b_2 = 3$. Thus, the first solution is $y_{(t)} = A1e^{2t} + A2e^{3t}$. For the particular solution, try $y = k$, then $dy/dt = 0$ and $d^2y/dt^2 = 0$. Using these derivatives in the differential equation, we get $6k = 5$ and $k = 5/6$. Combining the two solutions we get $y_{(t)} = A_1e^{2t} + A_2e^{3t} + 3$. To solve for A_1 and A_2, we use the initial conditions in the complete solution—that is, at $t = 0$,

$$7 = A_1 + A_2 + 5/6$$

and $dy/dt = 2A_1e^{2t} + 3A_2e^{3t}$; then at $t = 0$,

$$y'_{(0)} = 8 = 2A_1 + 3A_2.$$

Solving these two equations for A_1 and A_2, we find $A_1 = 56$ and $A_2 = -3.6$. Hence, the definitive complete solution is $y_{(t)} = 56e^{2t} -3.6e^{3t} + 3$.

Example 2: Solve $y''_{(t)} - 6y'_{(t)} + 9y_{(t)} = 18$ with the initial conditions $y_o = 10$ and $y'(o) = 30$.

Solution: The quadratic equation is $b^2 - 6b + 9 = 0$ with two repeated roots $b_1 = 3$ and $b_2 = 3$. The solution is $y_{(t)} = A_1e^{3t} + A_2te^{3t}$. For the particular solution try $y = k$ in the differential equation to obtain $k = 2$, The complete solution is $y_{(t)} = A_1e^{3t} + A_2te^{3t} + 2$. Using the initial conditions $[y_{(0)} = 10$ and $y'(o) = 30]$ in the complete solution, we obtain $A_1 = 8$ and $A_2 = 6$. Therefore, the complete definitive solution becomes $y_{(t)} = 8e^{3t} + 6te^{3t} + 3$.

Example 3: Solve $y''_{(t)} + y'_{(t)} + 5y_{(t)} = 10$.

Solution: The quadratic equation is $b^2 + b + 5 = 0$ giving complex roots because $a^2 1 < (4)(a_2 = 5)$. Here, $h = (-1/2)a_1 = (-1/2)(1) = -1/2$ and $f = (1/2) (4a_2 - a^2_1)^{1/2} = (1/2)(19)^{1/2} = 2.18$. As the solution is

$$y_{(t)} = e^{ht} (B_1\cos f\,t + B_2 \sin f\,t),$$

therefore,

$$y_{(t)} = e^{-0.5t} (B_1\cos 2.8t + B_2 \sin 2.8t).$$

Try $y = k$ in the differential equation to obtain $k = 2$. The complete solution is

$$y_{(t)} = e^{-0.5t} (B_1\cos 2.8t + B_2 \sin 2.8t) + 2.$$

Problems

1. Integrate the following:

   (a) $y = 3x$ (b) $y = 2 + 2x$ (c) $y = x^2 + 2x$ (d) $y = 2x/x^2$

   (e) $y = e^{12x}$ (f) $y = (2)^{5x}$ (g) $y = x^4 (2x^2 + 2)$

   (h) $y = x^3(5x^2 + 5)$ (i) $y = 2x^{ex}$ (j) $y = 8 \ln (2x)$ (k) $y = 3x + 10x^3$

2. Evaluate

   (a) $_2\int^3 (2x + 2)dx$ (b) $_2\int^5 x^2 dx$ (c) $_1\int^4 x^3 dx$ (d) $_2\int^3 (1/x) \, dx$

   (e) $_1\int^6 4dx$ (f) $_1\int^3 (5x + 3x^2)dx$ (g) $_1\int^6 (4 + x)dx$

3. If the marginal propensity to consume is MPC = 0.95, find the consumption function.

4. If the marginal cost function is $MC = Q^2 + 2Q + 6$, find the cost function.

5. If the marginal revenue function is $MR = 2Q$, find the revenue function.

6. If $P = 40 - 2Q$, find consumer surplus if $P = 2$.

7. Solve the following difference equations:

   (a) $y_t - 0.5y_{t-1} = 0$ (b) $2y_t - 3y_{t-1} = 0$

   (c) $y_t - 2y_{t-1} = 5$ (d) $y_t - 10y_{t-1} = 20$

8. Find the time path function for income yt from this model given $y_0 = 500$:

$$y = C + I$$

$$C_t = 0.7y_{t-1}$$

$$I = 50$$

9. Find the time path function for price P_t from this market model given $P_0 = 10$:

$$D_t = -2Pt + 100$$

$$S_t = P_{t-1} - 20$$

$$D_t = S_t$$

10.   Solve the following difference equations:

(a) $y_t - 3y_{t-1} - 4y_{t-2} = 10$ (b) $y_t + 4y_{t-2} = 12$ (c) $y_t - 7y_{t-1} + 12y_{t-2} = 0$

(d) $y_t + 16y_{t-2} = 0$

11.   Solve the following differential equations:

(a) $dy/dt = 5y_t$ $(y = 5)$ (b) $dy/dt + 0.3y_t = 0$ $(y_o = 5)$

(c) $dy/dt + 0.5yt = 5$ $(y_o = 8)$ (d) $dy/dt + 5y_t = 15$

12.   Find the time path function for this market model:

$D_t = 3 - P_t$ and $S_t = -3 + P_t$ and $dP/dt = 0.3 (D_t - S_t)$.

13.   Solve the following differential equations:

(a) $y_t + 3y_t - 10y_t = 0$ (b) $y_t - 7y_t + 12 y_t = 15$ (c) $y_t - 8y_t + 16y_t = 5$

(d) $y_t + 2y_t + 10 y_t = 0$ (e) $y_t + 3y_t + 15y_t = 5$

CHAPTER SEVEN

Linear Programming I: The Simplex Method

Economics was defined by Lionel Robbins (1932) as the science of studying the allocation of scarce economic resources among competing ends, that is, economics is concerened with making choices and decisions. Similarly, *linear programming* is a mathematical theory by which the available economic resources can be allocated efficiently for achieving a certain goal .

Linear programming was developed independently by Leonid Kantorovich and T.C. Koopmans; both shared the Nobel prize in economics in 1975 for developing this mathematical model (Kantorovich 1960, 1965; Koopmans 1951). Kantorovich was able to find a mathematical model by which the available economic resources in the Soviet Union could be allocated efficiently. Kantorovich, however, was not able to develop an algorithm by which a linear mathematical program can be solved. This task was left to George Dantzig to develop in 1947 (Dantzig 1963). Since then economists such as Dorfman (1953), Dorfman et al. (1958), and Baumol (1977) have applied the model of linear programming to a variety of real world problems in transportation, accountancy, finance, diet, the military, agriculture, and human resources, to mention a few.

A Problem's Formulation and Assumptions

The most difficult part of linear programming is the formulation of a particular segment of the real world in a linear mathematical programming context (Taha 1987; Thompson 1976; Lapin 1991). In fact, the formulation of a linear programming problem is an art that must be learned from experience rather than a textbook. Mathematically, a mathematical linear program is written as

$$\text{Maximize } Z = c_1X_1 + c_2X_2 + c_3X_3 + \dots + c_nX_n$$

Subject to

$$a_{11}X_1 + a_{12}X_2 + \dots + a_{1n}X_n \le b_1$$

$$a_{21}X_1 + a_{22}X_2 + ... + a_{2n}X_n \le b_2$$

$$a_{31}X_1 + a_{32}X_2 + ... + a_{3n}X_n \le b_3$$

....

$$a_{m1}X_1 + a_{m2}X_2 + ... + a_{mn}X_n \le b_m$$

$$X_1 \ge 0, \ X_2 \ge 0, \ ..., X_n \ge 0$$

This mathematical model suggests that there are (n) different activities $(X_1, X_2, ..., X_n)$. These activities (doing something) may take the form of the production of output such as TV sets (X_1), automobile (X_2), corn (X_3), and so forth. Conversely, the model contains the quantities of several economic resources designated by $(b_1, b_2, ..., b_m)$. For example, (b_1) may be the number of hours available, (b_2) may be the amount of loan that can be obtained to produce a unit of output, and (bm) may be the amount of fertilizer available. The linear programming model is primarily designed for allocating these economic resources to each economic activity in order to achieve a specified goal such as profit maximization, given the knowledge of the coefficients (c_j), $j = 1,2,..., n$; the technological coefficients (a_{ij}); and b_i, $i = 1, 2, ...m$.

The coefficients of (c_j) indicate the contribution of each activity to the objective function. For example, if the objective function is to maximize profit, then (c_1) may be the contribution of one unit of (X_1) to total profit; (c_2) may be the contribution of one unit of (X_2) to total profit; and (c_n) may be the contribution of one unit of (X_n) to the profit. In other words, each unit of output (X_1), (X_2), and (X_n) generates a profit of (c_1), (c_2), and (c_n).

As can be seen from the model, the objective function is restricted by several linear constraints, each of which describes the resource requirements per unit of output. For example, the first restriction indicates that the production of one unit of (X_1) requires (a_{11}) from the first resource (b_1); the production of one unit of (X_2) requires (a_{12}) from the first resource; and the production of one unit of (X_n) requires (a_{1n}) from the first resource. The other resources are utilized similarly in the production of (X_1), (X_2), and (X_n). In other words, the $(a_{ij}$'s) are the resource requirement coefficients per unit of output.

The last part of the linear restrictions is the nonnegativity constraint, suggesting that the production level of each economic activity must be zero or greater than zero. That is, a negative amount of production is not allowed in this model.

Like other mathematical models, linear programming is based on several assumptions (Thompson 1976). First, the model assumes that the proportionality or linearity condition, whether in the objective function or the constraints, is held (or satisfied). That is, there is a linear (proportional) relationship between, for example, profit (our goal) and the level of output, assuming that the profit per unit of output (c_j) is constant. Similarly, there is a proportional (linear) relationship between the amount of a certain economic resource and the level of production (activity), assuming that the rate of resource utilization (a_{ij}) is fixed. Should nonlinearity exist in the objective function and constraints, nonlinear programming is used.

Second, the model assumes the additivity condition to be met. This assumption means that total profit and total utilization of a certain economic resource are obtained by adding up the total profit and total resource utilization from each activity. Third, the model assumes that divisibility is held. This assumption means that the solution can take any value on the real line, integer and noninteger. If an integer solution is required, integer programming must be used. Fourth, the model assumes that the coefficients (c_j) and (a_{ij}) and the quantity of resources (b_i) are known. That is, they are not determined by a chance (probabilistic) process. If they are determined by a probabilistic process, *stochastic linear programming* is employed.

Example 1: Resource Allocation in Agriculture. A farmer has a cropland of 120 acres. The farmer claims that the most critical limitations on production are land acreage, amount of fertilizer, and labor. The amounts of labor hours and fertilizer available to the farmer are 700 hours and 200 pounds (lb), respectively. Available data indicate that 100 bushels of corn require 7 hours of labor, 2 acres of land, and 10 lb of fertilizer. In addition, the data reveal that 100 bushels of soybeans require 30 hours of labor, 4 lb of fertilizer, and 1 acre of land. Moreover, the prices of corn and soybeans are determined by market forces at $3.00 for corn and $5.00 for soybeans. But each bushel of corn and soybeans costs the farmer $2.80 and $4.55, respectively. How can our farmer allocate economic resources efficiently in order to maximize profit?

Solution: Let X_1 and X_2 be the quantities (in hundreds) of corn and soybeans. The profits from 100 bushels of corn and soybeans are $20.00 $[(100)(3) - (2.8)(100)]$ and $45.00 $[(100)(5) - (4.55)(100)]$, respectively. Therefore, the mathematical program becomes

Maximize $20X_1 + 45X_2$

Subject to

$$2X_1 + 1X_2 \leq 120$$

$$7X_1 + 30X_2 \leq 700$$

$$10X_1 + 4X_2 \leq 200$$

$$X_1 \geq 0, X_2 \geq 0, \text{ and } X_3 \geq 0$$

and the optimal feasible solution is $X_1 = 11.77$, $X_2 = 20.58$, and $Z = 1161.77$.

Example 2: Resource Allocation in Industry. A firm that produces two products has limitations on its machine and labor time (Boulding and Spivey 1960). There are 240 hours of machine time and 300 hours of labor time available during the production period. A unit of the first product requires 4 hours of machine time and 3 hours of labor time. The second product takes 6 and 8 hours of machine and labor time, respectively. A unit of product 1 and product 2 generates profits of $10.00 and $12.00, respectively. The economic problem is to find the levels of products 1 and 2 that maximize profit and allocate economic resources efficiently.
Solution: Let X_1 and X_2 be the quantities of products 1 and 2. Therefore, the program can be formulated as follows:

Maximize $10X_1 + 12X_2$

Subject to

$$4X_1 + 6X_2 \leq 240$$

$$3X_1 + 8X_2 \leq 300$$

$$X_1 \geq 0 \text{ and } X_2 \geq 0$$

and the optimal feasible solution is $Z = 600$, $X_1 = 60$, and $X_2 = 0$. That is, the producer should allocate 180 hours for the production of products 1 and 2, respectively and 240 hours of machine time for the production of products 1 and 2, respectively.

Example 3: Portfolio Selection. A university president has saved $150,000.00 during his tenure at XXU. He has decided to invest his saving in four investment alternatives: real estate, Sam Pizza, government bonds, and IBN (Anderson et al. 1978 and 1985). His choice was based on a recommendation made by a private financial analyst, who calculated the past rates of return as follows:

Real estate, 8%
Sam Pizza,7.5%
Government bonds,7%
IBN, 9%

The financial analyst has suggested the following investment guideline:

1. Investment in real estate and pizza should not exceed 50 percent of the total investment.

2. Investment in government bonds should not exceed 30 percent of the investment in real estate and Sam Pizza.

3. Investment in IBN, considered a risky alternative, should be at most $60,000.

Our task is to determine the best portfolio that the retired university president should make in order to maximize his return.

Solution: Let X_1, X_2, X_3, and X_4 be the dollars invested in the four investment opportunities. Consequently, the program becomes

$$\text{Maximize } 0.08X_1 + 0.075X_2 + 0.07X_3 + 0.09X_4$$

Subject to

$$X_1 + X_2 + X_3 + X_4 = 150,000$$

$$X_1 + X_2 \leq 75,000$$

$$-0.30X_1 - 0.30X_2 + X_3 \leq 0$$

$$X_4 \leq 60000$$

$$X_1 \geq 0, X_2 \geq 0, X_3 \geq 0, \text{ and } X_4 \geq 0$$

and the optimal feasible solution is $X_1 = \$75,000.00$, $X_2 = \$0.00$, $X_3 = \$15,000.00$, $X_4 = \$60,000.00$, and $Z = \$12,450.00$.

Example 4: The Transportation Problem. A company has two factories supplying two of its warehouses with units of one of its products. The table below shows the transportation cost per unit of output between the two factories and the warehouses. In addition, the table shows the production level of each factory as well as the demand for the product in each warehouse (destination).

| | Warehouse | | |
Factory	1	2	Production
1	$10	14	60
2	14	10	50
Demand	80	30	

The company is interested in finding the route(s) that minimizes the transportation cost between the factories and the warehouses. In other words, how many units of the product must be shipped to each destination in order to minimize the transportation cost (Z)?

Solution: Let X_{ij} be the number of units shipped from the *ith* factory to the *jth* warehouse. Therefore, the program becomes

$$\text{Minimize } Z = 10X_{11} + 14X_{12} + 14X_{21} + 10X_{22}$$

Subject to

$$X_{11} + X_{12} = 60$$

$$X_{21} + X_{22} = 50$$

$$X_{11} + X_{21} = 80$$

$$X_{12} + X_{22} = 30$$

$$X_{ij} \geq 0$$

and the optimal feasible solution is $X_{11} = 60$ units, $X_{12} = 0$ units, $X_{21} = 20$ units, $X_{22} = 30$ units, and the transportation cost $Z = \$1180$. The solution suggests that the company should not ship any unit of the product from the second factory to the second destination.

Example 5: An Advertising Problem. Young Nasr wishes to spend $50,000 for advertising on a Nasr XLT in the Springfield area. Nasr suggests that at least $10,000 be spent on TV advertising. In addition, no more than 30 percent of the budget should be allocated for newspaper ads and that newspaper allocation should not exceed 40 percent of the TV expenditures. From past experience, Nasr knows that a radio spot that costs $150 generates 50 audience points, a TV spot that costs $800 generates 180 points, and a newspaper insertion that costs $300 generates 250 points. Determine the dollars that should be allocated to each advertising alternative so that the total number of audience points is maximized.

Solution: Let X_1, X_2, and X_3 be the dollars spent on a radio spot, a TV spot, and a newspaper insertion. Point per dollar ratios that measure the effectiveness of advertisement are 50/150, 180/800, and 250/300 for the three alternatives. Accordingly, the program becomes

$$\text{Maximize } (50/150)X_1 + (180/800)X_2 + (250/300)X_3$$

Subject to

$$X_1 + X_2 + X_3 = 50,000$$

$$X_2 \geq 10,000$$

$$X_1 \leq 0.30(50,000) = 15,000$$

$$X_1 - 0.40X_2 \leq 0$$

$$X_1 \geq 0, X_2 \geq 0, \text{ and } X_3 \geq 0$$

and the optimal feasible solution is $X_1 = \$0$, $X_2 = \$10,000.00$, $X_3 = \$40,000.00$, and $Z = \$35,500$. That is, Nasr must not use the radio option for advertisement.

Graphical Solution of Linear Programming Problems

A mathematical linear program can be solved graphically. Suppose that the following program is available:

Maximize $6X_1 + 8X_2$

Subject to

$$2X_1 + 2X_2 \leq 20$$

$$2X_1 + 4X_2 \leq 24$$

$$X_1 \geq 0 \text{ and } X_2 \geq 0.$$

Figure 7.1 shows the complete solution of the program.

Figure 7.1. **Graphical Solution of the Linear Program**

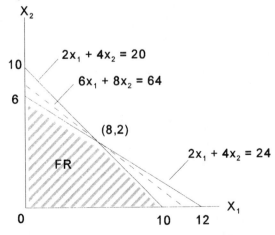

But how is the figure obtained? It is obtained as follows: Each constraint is plotted by replacing the inequality by an equality sign. The first restriction is written as

$$2X_1 + 2X_2 = 20.$$

After setting X_1 equal to zero and solving for X_2, we obtain

$$2X_2 = 20 \text{ and } X_2 = 10.$$

Determine the point (X_1, X_2) or $(0, 10)$ on the vertical axis. Next, setting X_2 equal to zero and solving for X_1, we have

$$2X_1 = 20 \text{ and } X_1 = 10.$$

Determine the point $(X_1 = 10 \text{ and } X_2 = 0)$ on the horizontal axis of Figure 7.1. Connecting the two points we obtain a line representing the first constraint. Similarly, and using the same procedure, the second restriction can be plotted. That is, setting X_1 equal to zero and solving for X_2 yields

$$4X_2 = 24 \text{ and } X_2 = 6.$$

Thus, we have the point $(X_1 = 0 \text{ and } X_2 = 6)$, which can plotted on the vertical axis. Next, setting X_2 equal to zero and solving for X_1 yields

$$2X_1 = 24 \text{ and } X_1 = 12.$$

Accordingly, we have the point $(X_1 = 12 \text{ and } X_2 = 0)$, which can be plotted on the horizontal axis. Finally, after connecting these points we obtain a line representing the second constraint.

The shaded area of Figure 7.1 indicates the feasibility region of the program. As shown in the figure, there are four corner points, one of which must be the optimal feasible solution: The solution is optimal because it is the best; it is feasible because it does satisfy the constraints. The values associated with the objective function, evaluated at the corner points, are listed below.

Corner Points	Value of Objective Function	Maximum Solution
$(X_1,X_2) = (0,0)$	$6(0) + 8(0) = 0$	
$(X_1,X_2) = (0,6)$	$6(0) + 8(6) = 48$	
$(X_1,X_2) = (8,2)$	$6(8) + 8(2) = 64$	64
$(X_1,X_2) = (10,0)$	$6(10) + 2(0) = 60$	

One should note that the third corner point is obtained by solving the two constraints simultaneously. As shown, the best solution is $X_1 = 8$, $X_2 = 2$, and $Z = 64$.

Example 1: Suppose we have a mathematical program whose minimum value is sought, such as

$$\text{Minimize} \quad 160X_1 + 240X_2$$

Subject to

$$4X_1 + 4X_2 \geq 48$$

$$2X_1 + 4X_2 \geq 32$$

$$X_1 \geq 0 \text{ and } X_2 \geq 0.$$

Figure 7.2 shows the lines representing the two restrictions and the objective function.

Figure 7.2. **Graphical Solution of the Minimization Program**

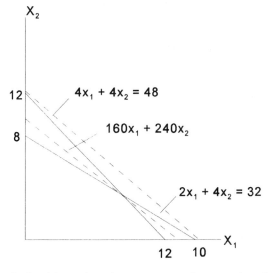

Figure 7.2 is obtained by using the same procedure employed in plotting the constraints of the maximization problem. The values of the objective function evaluated at each corner point are as follows:

Corner Points	Value of the Objective Function	Minimum Solution
$(X_1, X_2) = (0, 12)$	$160(0) + 240(0) = 2880$	
$(X_1, X_2) = (8,4)$	$160(8) + 240(4) = 2240$	2240
$(X_1, X_2) = (16,0)$	$160(16) + 240(0) = 2560$	

Hence, the best solution is $Z = 2240$, $X_1 = 8$, and $X_2 = 4$.

The Simplex Method: Maximization Problems

Suppose that we are interested in the program

Maximize $6X_1 + 8X_2$

Subject to

$$2X_1 + 2X_2 \le 20$$

$$2X_1 + 4X_2 \le 24$$

$$X_1 \ge 0 \text{ and } X_2 \ge 0.$$

Before applying the simplex method, we must put the program in a standard form. To do so, we convert the sign of equal or less than ($\le$) into the equality sign ($=$). This can be done by introducing a variable called a *slack variable*, a fictitious activity utilizing any unused capacity of the available economic resource, to each constraint having the sign of equal or less than (Gass 1985; Hadley 1962). As we have two restrictions, we must add two slack variables, (X_3) and (X_4). Accordingly, the two restrictions become

$$2X_1 + 2X_2 + X_3 = 20$$

$$2X_1 + 4X_2 + X_4 = 24.$$

The slack variables must have zero coefficients in the objective function. That is, after introducing the slack variables (X_3) and (X_4), the objective function can be rewritten as

$$Z = 6X_1 + 8X_2 + 0X_3 + 0X_4.$$

Combining the objective function and the two restrictions, the entire mathematical program becomes

Maximize $Z = 6X_1 + 8X_2 + 0X_3 + 0X_4$

Subject to

$$2X_2 + 2X_2 + X_3 = 20$$

$$2X_1 + 4X_2 + X_4 = 24$$

$$X_1 \geq 0 \text{ and } X_2 \geq 0.$$

After transferring the right-hand side variables of the objective function to the left-hand side, the standard form of the program can be written as

$$Z - 6X_1 - 8X_2 - 0X_3 - 0X_4 = 0$$

$$2X_1 + 2X_2 + 1X_3 + 0X_4 = 20$$

$$2X_1 + 4X_2 + 0X_3 + 1X_4 = 24.$$

Having done so, we are ready to put the coefficients of the standard form in the simplex tableau (Tableau I) as follows

Tableau I

	Z	X_1	X_2	X_3	X_4	RHS	
Z	1	-6	-8	0	0	0	
X_3	0	2	2	1	0	20	20/2 = 10
X_4	0	2	4	0	1	24	24/4 = 6

One should note that the first column of the variables on the left-hand side of Tableau I is called the *basis*, because it contains the basic variables. In addition, the columns headed by (X_3) and (X_4) also contain the basic variables. As can be seen from Tableau I, the basis consists of the slack variables (X_3) and (X_4) as well as the variable (Z), which indicates the current value (solution) of the objective function. It is a general rule to put the slack variables in the basis. Tableau I indicates the initial solution to the program: $Z = 0$, $X_3 = 20$, and $X_4 = 24$.

But the question is whether the initial solution is indeed the optimal solution. The answer is no, because it is a rule that as long as the top row of Tableau I has negative elements, (-6) and (-8), there is no optimal solution; and as long as these negative elements exist in the top row of Tableau I we can improve the initial solution until we reach the optimal feasible solution. And the initial solution can be improved by entering a new incoming variable at the same time we allow another variable (the outgoing variable) to leave the basis. How do we do this?

The incoming variable can be selected by determining the most negative element in the top row of Tableau I, and the most negative element is (-8), which is located in the third column of Tableau I. Hence, (X_2) is the incoming variable, that is, X_2 must enter the basis. Having determined the incoming variable, we need to determine the outgoing variable by the minimum ratio rule. This rule works as follows: Divide the elements of the right-hand side of Tableau I, ignoring the elements of the top row and first column, by the elements of column 3 of Tableau I. That is, $(20/2) = 10$ and $(24/4) = 6$. The minimum is (6) as shown in Tableau I; hence, (X_4) is the outgoing variable, which is to be replaced by (X_2), and the third row of Tableau I is the pivotal row whose element must become (1). To convert the element to (1), we must multiply the third row of Tableau I by (1/4) and write the resulting outcome in the third row of Tableau II.

Tableau II

	Z	X_1	X_2	X_3	X_4	RHS	
Z	1	-2	0	0	2	48	
X_3	0	1	0	1	-1/2	8	8/1 = 8
X_2	0	1/2	1	0	1/4	6	6/1/2 = 12

Consequently, our pivotal row is actually the third row of Tableau II and our pivotal element is (1)—the previous element of Tableau I.

Having done so, we need to make all elements above and below the element of Tableau I zeros, and this can be done by using the pivotal row of Tableau II. To make the element (2) in the second row of Tableau I zero, we multiply the pivotal row of Tableau II by (-2) and add the outcome to the second row of Tableau I and report the results in the second row of Tableau II. Next, to convert the element (-8) in the first row of Tableau I to zero, we multiply the pivotal row by (8) and add the outcome to the first row of Tableau I and report the results in the first row of Tableau II.

By completing Tableau II, the first iteration is said to be finished, and we have to ask whether we have reached an optimal solution or not. If the optimal solution has not been obtained, we will repeat the same procedure we have used to complete the first iteration. Once the readers understand the mechanism of the first iteration, the other iterations will be completed similarly. If the optimal solution has been reached, we will terminate (stop) the simplex algorithm.

Now, the first question we ask after looking at Tableau II is whether we have an optimal solution. The answer is no, because we still have a negative element in the top row, (-2). The second question is to determine the incoming variable, and it is the variable with the largest negative element in the top row: (X_1). The third question is to determine the outgoing variable. To answer this question we use the minimum ratio rule as shown in Tableau II. That is, $(8/1 = 8)$ and $(6/1/2 = 12)$, and the minimum ratio is 8; hence, (X_3) is the outgoing variable, which is to be replaced by (X_1), the incoming variable. It follows that the second row of Tableau II will become the pivotal row, and the pivotal element need not be converted to (1) because it is already so. Thus, the second row of Tableau II will be reported as the second row of Tableau III.

Tableau III

	Z	X_1	X_2	X_3	X_4	RHS
Z	1	0	0	2	1	64
X_1	0	1	0	1	-1/2	8
X_2	0	0	1	-1/2	1/2	2

By the same token, the elements above and below the pivotal element must be converted to zeros. To convert the element (-2) to zero, we multiply the pivotal row by (2) and add the outcome to the first row of Tableau II, reporting the results in the first row of Tableau III. Next, the element (1/2) in the third row of Tableau II must be converted to zero by multiplying the pivotal row of Tableau III by (-1/2) and add the outcome to the third row of Tableau II, and the results must be reported in the third row of Tableau III.

Having completed the second iteration, we have to ask whether we have reached the optimal solution or not. Because there is no negative element in the top row of Tableau III, the optimal solution has been found. In other words, the objective function (Z) is equal to (64), (X_1) is equal to (8), and (X_2) is equal to (2).

Example 2: Solve the following mathematical program:

Maximize $300X_1 + 160X_2$

Subject to

$$2X_1 + 2X_2 \le 1200$$

$$8X_1 + 4X_2 \le 4000$$

$$X_1 \ge 0 \text{ and } X_2 \ge 0.$$

Solution: To each restriction we must add a slack variable to convert the sign ($\le$) to the equality sign, (=). Thus, two slack variables, (X_3) and (X_4), are added to the first and second restriction, respectively. After transferring the right-hand side of the objective function to the left-hand side, the mathematical linear program becomes

$$Z - 300X_1 - 160X_2 + 0X_3 + 0X_4 = 0$$

$$2X_1 + 2X_2 + X_3 + 0X_4 = 1200$$

$$8X_1 + 4X_2 + 0X_3 + X_4 = 4000$$

and the first simplex tableau becomes

Tableau Ia

	Z	X_1	X_2	X_3	X_4	RHS	
Z 1		-300	-160	0	0	0	
X_3 0		2	2	1	0	1200	1200/2 = 600
X_4 0		8	4	0	1	4000	4000/8 = 500

As can be seen, there is no optimal solution because there are negative elements in the top row of Tableau Ia. The incoming variable is (X_1), which must enter the basis, because it has the largest negative element, (-300). The outgoing variable is (X_4), which must leave the basis, because it has a minimum ratio of (500). Parenthetically, one should note that in obtaining the minimum ratio, readers, should never divide the right-hand side by a negative number or zero. In any event, the pivotal element is (8), which is located in the third row of Tableau Ia. To make this element (1), we multiply the third row of Tableau Ia by (1/8) and report the results in the third row of Tableau IIa.

Tableau IIa

	Z	X_1	X_2	X_3	X_4	RHS	
Z 1		0	-10	0	75/2	150000	
X_3 0		0	1	1	-1/4	200	200/1 = 200
X_1 0		1	1/2	0	1/8	500	500/1/2 = 1000

Next, we multiply the pivotal element of Tableau IIa by (-2) and add the outcomes to the second row of Tableau Ia, and we report the results in the second row of Tableau IIa. Finally, to convert the (-300) to zero we multiply the pivotal row of Tableau IIa by (300) and add the results to the first row of Tableau Ia; the results must be reported in the first row of Tableau IIa.

As Tableau IIa indicates, we have not reached the optimal solution to the program, and the solution can be improved as there is a negative element in the top row, (-10). Consequently, the incoming variable is (X_2). After applying the minimum ratio rule, one can select (X_3) to be the outgoing variable as it has a minimum ratio of (200). It follows that the pivotal element is (1) and the pivotal row is the second row of Tableau IIa, which is reported in Tableau IIIa.

	Z	X_1	X_2	X_3	X_4	RHS
Z	1	0	0	10	35	152000
X_2	0	0	1	1	-1/4	200
X_1	0	1	0	-1/2	1	400

Tableau IIIa

To convert the (-10), located in the top row of Tableau IIa, to zero, we multiply our pivotal row by (10) and add the outcome to the first row of Tableau IIa, and the results must be reported in the first row of Tableau IIIa. Next, we convert the (1/2), located in the third row of Tableau IIa, to zero by multiplying our pivotal row by (-1/2) and add the outcome to the third row of Tableau IIa, and report the results in the third row of Tableau IIIa. As there are no negative elements in the top row of Tableau IIIa, the optimal feasible solution ($Z = 152000$, $X_1 = 400$, and $X_2 = 200$) has been obtained.

Example 3: Maximize the program

$$Z = 2X_1 + 4X_2$$

Subject to

$$2X_1 + 2X_2 \leq 8$$

$$2X_1 \geq 2$$

$$X_1 \geq 0 \text{ and } X_2 \geq 0.$$

Solution: This program is different from the previous ones in one aspect: The second restriction contains the sign of equal to and greater than, ($\geq$), which requires a new treatment. As a rule, if the sign ($\geq$) exists in one constraint, readers should add a negative surplus variable ("a negative slack variable to absorb any excess resulting from the overfulfillment of the minimum resource requirement" (Thompson 1976, p. 219), say (-X_4), and an artificial variable ["a simple device permits us to get started with an initial basic feasible solution"(Thompson 1976, p. 213)], say (X_5), to that restriction. In addition, the surplus variable must have a coefficient of zero in the objective function, and the artificial variable must have a large negative coefficient in the objective function in order to make this variable unattractive as a basic variable. The large negative coefficient may be (100), (1000), (1,000,000). In other words, it must be three to four times larger than the coefficients of the program.

Accordingly, the standard form of our program becomes

$$\text{Maximize} \quad Z = 2X_1 + 4X_2 - 100X_5$$

Subject to

$$2X_1 + X_2 + X_3 = 8$$

$$2X_1 - X_4 + X_5 = 2$$

$$X_1 \geq 0 \text{ and } X_2 \geq 0.$$

where (X_3) is a slack variable added to the first constraint. After transferring the right-hand side of the objective function to the left-hand side, the standard form becomes

$$Z - 2X_1 - 4X_2 + 100X_5 = 0$$

$$2X_1 + 2X_2 + X_3 = 8$$

$$2X_1 - X_4 + X_5 = 2$$

and the coefficients of the standard form are reported in Table 7.1b, the pre-simplex table, we obtain

The Pre-Simplex Table 7.1b

	Z	X_1	X_2	X_3	X_4	X_5	RHS
Z	1	-2	-4	0	0	-100	0
X_3	0	2	2	1	0	0	8
X_5	0	2	0	0	-1	1	2

Before proceeding further, two comments must be mentioned. First, the basis of Table 7.1b indicates that (X_3) and (X_5) are introduced but not (X_4), the surplus variable. As a rule, we should never bring the surplus variable into the basis. Second, before starting the simplex method, the (-100) in the first row of Table 7.1b must be removed, that is, it must be converted to zero. To do so, we multiply the third row of table 7.1b by (100) and add the outcome to the first row. The results must be reported in Tableau Ib, the simplex tableau, as shown below.

Tableau Ib

	Z	X_1	X_2	X_3	X_4	X_5	RHS	
Z	1	-202	-4	0	100	0	-200	
X_3	0	2	2	1	0	0	8	$8/2 = 4$
X_5	0	2	0	0	-1	1	2	$2/2 = 1$

As can be seen, there is no optimal solution because there are negative elements in the top row of Tableau Ib. The incoming variable is (X_1), as it is associated with the largest negative element, and (X_5) is the outgoing variable as it is associated with a minimum ratio of (1). Hence, the pivotal element is (2), and the pivotal row is the third row of Tableau Ib. To convert the pivotal element to (1), we multiply the pivotal row by (1/2) and report the outcome in Tableau IIb. This pivotal row is also used to convert (2) and (-202) in the second and first row of Tableau Ib to zeros. These results are reported in Tableau IIb.

Tableau IIb

	Z	X_1	X_2	X_3	X_4	X_5	RHS	
Z	1	0	-4	0	-1	101	2	
X_3	0	0	2	1	1	-1	6	$6/2 = 3$
X_1	0	1	0	0	-1/2	1/2	1	

Tableau IIb indicates that there is no optimal solution because there is still a negative element, (-4), in the top row. Thus (X_2) is the incoming variable, and (X_3) is the outgoing variable as it is associated with a minimum ratio of (3). Next, the element (-4) must be converted to zero. To do so, we multiply the pivotal row of Tableau IIIb by (4) and add the outcome to the first row of Tableau IIb, and report the results in the first row of Tableau IIIb. Because the element that is located below the pivotal element of Tableau IIb is already zero, the third row of Tableau IIb is reported as the third row of Tableau IIIb.

Tableau IIIb

	Z	X_1	X_2	X_3	X_4	X_5	RHS
Z	1	0	0	2	1	99	14
X_2	0	0	1	1/2	1/2	-1/2	3
X_1	0	1	0	0	-1/2	1/2	1

As there is no negative element in the top row of Tableau IIIb, the optimal feasible solution is

$$Z = 14, X_2 = 3, \text{ and } X_1 = 1.$$

Example 4: Maximize the program

$$Z = 18X_1 + 12X_2$$

Subject to

$$5X_1 + 6X_2 \le 36$$

$$X_1 + 3X_2 = 9$$

$$X_1 \ge 0 \text{ and } X_2 \ge 0.$$

Solution: The difference between this program and the previous ones is that the current program has the equality sign in the second constraint. In this case, we only add an artificial variable (X_4) to the second constraint, treating the first restriction as before, that is, we add a slack variable (X_3). In addition, we attach a large negative coefficient, say (-100), to the artificial variable in the objective function. Accordingly, the standard form of the program becomes:

$$Z - 18X_1 - 12X_2 + 100X_4 = 0$$

$$5X_1 + 6X_2 + X_3 = 36$$

$$X_1 + 3X_2 + X_4 = 9$$

and the program's coefficients are reported in the pre-simplex Table 7.1c.

Pre-Simplex Table 7.1c

	Z	X_1	X_2	X_3	X_4	RHS
Z	1	-18	-12	0	100	0
X_3	0	5	6	1	0	36
X_4	0	1	3	0	1	9

As before, we have to convert the (100) in the top row of of the pre-simplex Table 7.1c to zero by multiplying the third row of the table by (-100) and adding the outcome to the top row of the table, and report the results in simplex Tableau Ic.

Tableau Ic

	Z	X_1	X_2	X_3	X_4	RHS	
Z	1	-118	-312	0	0	-900	
X_3	0	5	6	1	0	36	36/6 = 6
X_4	0	1	3	0	1	9	9/3 = 3

Tableau Ic indicates that there is no optimal solution. Following the same procedure, Tableaus IIc and IIIc are obtained, and the optimal solution is shown in Tableau IIIc.

Tableau IIc

	Z	X_1	X_2	X_3	X_4	RHS	
Z	1	-14	0	0	312/3	36	
X_3	0	3	0	1	-2	18	18/3 = 6
X_2	0	1/3	1	0	1/3	3	3/1/3 = 9`

Tableau IIIc

	Z	X_1	X_2	X_3	X_4	RHS
Z	1	0	0	14/3	284/3	120
X_1	0	1	0	1/3	-2/3	6
X_2	0	0	1	-1/9	5/9	1

Example 5: Maximize the program

$$Z = 2X_1 + 3X_2$$

Subject to

$$X_1 + 2X_2 = 6$$

$$4X_1 + X_2 \geq 8$$

$$3X_1 + 3X_2 \leq 12$$

$$X_1 \geq 0 \text{ and } X_2 \geq 0.$$

Solution: This program consists of all types of equality and inequalities that researchers and students might assign to various restrictions. As mentioned, an artificial variable (X_3) must be added to the first restriction; a surplus variable (X_4) must be subtracted —or added with a minus sign—from the second restriction, and an artificial variable (X_5) must be added; a slack variable (X_6) must be added to the third constraint. Accordingly, the program can be written as

$$Z - 2X_1 - 3X_2 + 100X_3 + 100X_5 = 0$$

$$X_1 + 2X_2 + X_3 = 6$$

$$4X_1 + X_2 - X_4 + X_5 = 8$$

$$3X_1 + 3X_2 + X_6 = 12$$

and the pre-simplex Table 7.1d shows the coefficients of the problem

The Pre-Simplex Table 7.1d

	Z	X_1	X_2	X_3	X_4	X_5	X_6	RHS
Z	1	-2	-3	100	0	100	0	0
X_3	0	1	2	1	0	0	0	6
X_5	0	4	1	0	-1	1	0	8
X_6	0	3	3	0	0	0	1	12

The pre-simplex Table 7.1d will be ready for the simplex method if we eliminate the (100s) in the top row. First, multiply the second row by (-100) and add the results to the first row of the table, we obtain the pre-simplex Table 7.2d.

The Pre-Simplex Table 7.2d

	Z	X_1	X_2	X_3	X_4	X_5	X_6	RHS
Z	1	-102	-203	0	0	100	0	-600
X_3	0	1	2	1	0	0	0	6
X_5	0	4	1	0	-1	1	0	8
X_6	0	3	3	0	0	0	1	12

Second, by multiplying the third row of the pre-simplex Table 1d or 2d by (-100) and adding the results to the first row of the pre-simplex Table 7.1d or 7.2d, we obtain the simplex Tableau Id:

Tableau Id

	Z	X_1	X_2	X_3	X_4	X_5	X_6	RHS	
Z	1	-502	-303	0	100	0	0	-1400	
X_3	0	1	2	1	0	0	0	6	6/1 = 6
X_5	0	4	1	0	-1	1	0	8	8/4 = 2
X_6	0	3	3	0	0	0	1	12	12/3 = 4

Now, we are ready to use the simplex method on Tableau Id. As can be seen from the table, the incoming variable is (X_1) and the outgoing variable is (X_5); hence, the pivotal element is (4), and the pivotal row is the third row of Tableau Id. Following the same mathematical procedure, the complete iterations are shown below, and the optimal solution is $Z = 10$, $X_1 = 2$, and $X_2 = 2$.

Tableau IId

	Z	X_1	X_2	X_3	X_4	X_5	X_6	RHS
Z	1	0	-355/2	0	-51/2	502/4	0	-396
X_3	0	0	7/4	1	1/4	-1/4	0	4
X_1	0	1	1/4	0	-1/4	1/4	0	2
X_6	0	0	9/4	0	3/4	-3/4	1	6

Tableau IIId

	Z	X_1	X_2	X_3	X_4	X_5	X_6	RHS
Z	1	0	0	710/7	-1/7	5608/56	0	68/7
X_2	0	0	1	4/7	1/7	-1/7	0	16/7
X_1	0	1	0	-1/7	-2/7	2/7	0	10/7
X_6	0	0	0	-9/7	3/7	-3/7	1	6/7

Tableau IVd

	Z	X_1	X_2	X_3	X_4	X_5	X_6	RHS
Z	1	0	0	101	0	100	1/3	10
X_2	0	0	1	1	0	0	-1/3	2
X_1	0	1	0	-1	0	0	2/3	2
X_4	0	0	0	-3	1	-1	7/3	2

To sum up, in a maximization problem we add a slack variable to each constraint having the inequality ($\leq$). The slack variable will have a coefficient of zero in the objective function. For each constraint having the sign ($\geq$), we subtract a surplus variable and add an artificial variable to that constraint. The artificial variable will have a large negative coefficient, say (-100), in the objective function. Moreover, for each constraint having the equals sign (=), we add an artificial variable to that constraint; the artificial variable must have a large negative coefficient in the objective function.

The Simplex Method: Minimization Problems

Assume that we are interested in minimizing the following program:

$$Z = 2X_1 + 3X_2$$

Subject to

$$4X_1 - 2X_2 \geq 3$$

$$20X_1 + X_2 \geq 10$$

$$X_1 \geq 0 \text{ and } X_2 \geq 0.$$

To solve the program by the simplex method, we follow the same procedure we have used in maximization problems. That is, to each constraint having the sign ($\leq$) we add a slack variable; for each constraint having the sign ($\geq$), we subtract a surplus variable and add an artificial variable; and to each constraint having the equality sign (=), we add an artificial variable. In minimization, however, the artificial variables must have large positive coefficients in the objective function. In addition, to determine the incoming variable, we have to pick the variable associated with the largest positive coefficient located in the top row of the first simplex tableau. In other words, as long as the top row of the simplex tableau has positive elements, there is no optimal feasible solution and hence the solution can be improved by performing the required iterations. Furthermore, the outgoing variable is determined by the minimum ratio rule, which was discussed in the section on maximization problems.

Now the above program can be put in a standard form as follows:

Minimize $Z = 2X_1 + 3X_2 + 100X_4 + 100X_6$

Subject to

$$4X_1 - 2X_2 - X_3 + X_4 = 3$$

$$20X_1 + X_2 - X_5 + X_6 = 10$$

where (X_3), (X_5), (X_4), and (X_6) are the surplus and the artificial variables, respectively. After transferring the right-hand side of (Z) to the left-hand side, the program becomes

$$Z - 2X_1 - 3X_2 - 100X_4 - 100X_6 = 0$$

$$4X_1 - 2X_2 - X_3 + X_4 = 3$$

$$20X_1 + X_2 - X_5 + X_6 = 10.$$

Putting the coefficients in the required pre-simplex table7.1e yields

The Pre-Simplex Table 7.1e

	Z	X_1	X_2	X_3	X_4	X_5	X_6	RHS
Z	1	-2	-3	0	-100	0	-100	0
X_4	0	4	-2	-1	1	0	0	3
X_6	0	20	1	0	0	-1	1	10

As before, we have to remove the (-100s) from the columns headed by (X_4) and (X_6), the artificial variables. To do so, we multiply the second row of the pre-simplex Table 7.1e by (100) and add the results to the first row, and also multiply the third row by (100) and add the results to the first row; we thus obtain the simplex Tableau Ie:

Tableau Ie

	Z	X_1	X_2	X_3	X_4	X_5	X_6	RHS	
Z	1	2398	-103	-100	0	-100	0	1300	
X_4	0	4	-2	-1	1	0	0	3	3/4 = 0.75
X_6	0	20	1	0	0	-1	1	10	10/20 = 0.5

As can be seen from Tableau Ie, the largest positive element is (2398); hence, the incoming variable is (X_1), and the outgoing variable is (X_6), whose ratio is the minimum, (0.5). Also, our pivotal element is (20), and our pivotal row is the third row. To make the pivotal element (1), we multiply the third row by (1/20) and report the outcome in Tableau IIe.

Tableau IIe

	Z	X_1	X_2	X_3	X_4	X_5	X_6	RHS
Z	1	0	-2229/10	-100	0	199/10	-1199/10	101
X_4	0	0	-11/5	-1	1	1/5	-1/5	1
X_1	0	1	1/20	0	0	-1/20	1/20	1/2

As there is a positive element in the top row of Tableau IIe, the optimal solution has not been reached. Thus, the incoming variable is (X_5), and the outgoing variable is (X_4). The pivotal element is (1), and the second row of Tableau IIe is the pivotal row. Multiply the second row of Tableau IIe by (5) and report the outcome in the second row of Tableau IIIe.

Tableau IIIe

	Z	X_1	X_2	X_3	X_4	X_5	X_6	RHS
Z	1	0	-4	-1/2	-995/10	0	-100	3/2
X_5	0	0	-11	-5	5	1	-1	5
X_1	0	1	-1/2	-1/4	1/4	0	0	3/4

Thus, the optimal solution ($Z = 3/2$, $X_1 = 3/4$, and $X_2 = 0$) has been obtained, as there is no positive element in the top row of Tableau IIIe.

Example 6: Minimize the program

$$160X_1 + 240X_2$$

Subject to

$$4X_1 + 4X_2 \geq 48$$

$$2X_1 + 4X_2 \geq 32$$

$$X_1 \geq 0 \text{ and } X_2 \geq 0.$$

Solution: After adding a surplus and an artificial variable to the first and second restriction, and attaching large positive coefficients to the artificial variables in the objective function, the program can be rewritten as

$$Z - 160X_1 - 240X_2 - 100X_4 - 100X_6 = 0$$

$$4X_1 + 4X_2 - X_3 + X_4 = 48$$

$$2X_1 + 4X_2 - X_5 + X_6 = 32$$

and the pre-simplex table 7.1f becomes

The Pre-Simplex Table 1f

	Z	X_1	X_2	X_3	X_4	X_5	X_6	RHS
Z	1	-160	-240	0	-100	0	-100	0
X_4	0	4	4	-1	1	0	0	48
X_6	0	2	4	0	0	-1	1	32

After removing the (-100s), we obtain the simplex Tableau If:

Tableau If

	Z	X_1	X_2	X_3	X_4	X_5	X_6	RHS
Z	1	440	560	-100	0	-100	0	8000
X_4	0	4	4	-1	1	0	0	48
X_6	0	2	4	0	0	-1	1	32

Hence, the incoming variable is (X_2); the outgoing variable is (X_6); and the pivotal row is the third row. Next, do the following operations to obtain the complete elements of Tableau IIf: Multiply the third row by (1/4) and report the outcome in the third row of Tableau IIf; multiply the third row of Tableau IIf by (-4) and add the outcome to the second row of Tableau If, finally; multiply the pivotal row by (-560) and add the outcome to the first row of Tableau If.

Tableau IIf

	Z	X_1	X_2	X_3	X_4	X_5	X_6	RHS
Z	1	160	0	-100	0	40	-140	3520
X_4	0	2	0	-1	1	1	-1	16
X_2	0	1/2	1	0	0	-1/4	1/4	8

Tableau IIf indicates that (X_1) is the incoming variable, and (X_4) is the outgoing variable. Thus, the second row of Tableau IIf is the pivotal row. Next, do the following operations to obtain the complete elements of Tableau IIIf: Multiply the second row by (1/2) and report the outcome in the second row of Table IIIf; multiply the pivotal row by (-160) and add the outcome to the first row of Tableau IIf; then multiply the pivotal row by (-1/2) and add the outcome to the third row of Tableau IIf.

Tableau IIIf

	Z	X_1	X_2	X_3	X_4	X_5	X_6	RHS
Z	1	0	0	-20	0	-40	-60	2240
X_1	0	1	0	-1/2	1/2	1/2	-1/2	8
X_2	0	0	1	1/4	-1/4	-1/2	1/2	4

Because there is no positive element in the top row of Tableau IIIf, the optimal solution ($Z = 2240$, $X_1 = 8$, and $X_2 = 4$) has been reached.

As a final remark, a minimization (maximization) problem can be converted to a maximization (minimization) problem by multiplying the objective function by (-1).

Problems in the Simplex Method

There are several problems to face in solving a linear programming problem by the simplex algorithm. These problems are explained below.

Degeneracy

This problem is usually manifested by a tie in the minimum ratio rule. When the tie occurs, one of the basic variables will have a zero value in the optimal feasible solution. The mathematical reason behind the occurrence of this problem lies in the situation where one of the restrictions is redundant, or when two restrictions emanate from the same point (Taha 1987). For example, take the following program:

Maximize $6X_1 + 8X_2$

Subject to

$$3X_1 + 12X_2 \leq 16$$

$$3X_1 + 6X_2 \leq 8$$

$$X_1 \geq 0 \text{ and } X_2 \geq 0.$$

Before applying the simplex method, the program is plotted in Figure 7.3.

Figure 7.3. **Degenerate Linear Program**

Figure 7.3 indicates that the two restrictions meet in point ($X_1 = 0$, $X_2 = 4/3$), which is the basic cause of the degeneracy problem. Applying the simplex method to the program, the complete solution is shown in Tableaux Ig, IIg, and IIIg.

Tableau Ig

Z	X_1	X_2	X_3	X_4	RHS	
Z	1	-6	-8	0	0	0	
X_3	0	3	12	1	0	16	$16/12 = 4/3$
X_4	0	3	6	0	1	8	$8/6 = 4/3$

As can be seen from Tableau Ig, there is a tie in the minimum ratio. Arbitrarily, we have selected (X_3) to be the outgoing variable and (X_2) to be the incoming variable. The first and second iterations generate Tableaux IIg and IIIg.

Tableau IIg

	Z	X_1	X_2	X_3	X_4	RHS
Z	1	-4	0	8/12	0	32/3
X_2	0	1/4	1	1/12	0	4/3
X_4	0	3/2	0	-1/2	1	0

Tableau IIIg

	Z	X_1	X_2	X_3	X_4	RHS
Z	1	0	0	7/12	8/3	32/3
X_2	0	0	1	1/6	-1/6	4/3
X_1	0	1	0	-1/3	2/3	0

Tableaux IIg and IIIg indicate that no improvement on the degenerate optimal solution ($Z = 32/3$, $X_2 = 4/3$, and $X_1 = 0$) has been accomplished, and there is a problem of cycling.

To avoid the degeneracy problem, the mathematical formulation of the model must be corrected in that one of the restrictions must be dropped. If the second restriction is dropped, the complete solution is shown in Tableaux Ih, IIh, and IIIh.

Tableau Ih

	Z	X_1	X_2	X_3	RHS
Z	1	-6	-8	0	0
X_3	0	3	12	1	16

Tableau IIh

	Z	X_1	X_2	X_3	RHS
Z	1	-4	0	1/2	32/3
X_2	0	1/4	1	1/12	4/3

Tableau IIIh

	Z	X_1	X_2	X_3	RHS
Z	1	0	16	4/3	96/3
X_1	0	1	4	1/3	16/3

If the first restriction is dropped, the complete solution is shown in Tableaus Ii, IIi, and IIIi.

Tableau Ii

	Z	X_1	X_2	X_3	RHS
Z	1	-6	-8	0	0
X_3	0	3	6	1	8

Tableau IIi

	Z	X_1	X_2	X_3	RHS
Z	1	-2	0	8/6	32/3
X_2	0	1/2	1	1/6	4/3

Tableau IIIi

	Z	X_1	X_2	X_3	RHS
Z	1	0	4	2	16
X_1	0	1	2	1/3	8/3

One should note that dropping the second constraint generates a higher value for the objective function.

Multiple Solutions

This problem indicates that a mathematical program may have several solutions for the basic (decision) variables, although the value of the objective function is the same. The basic reason behind this problem is that the slope of the objective function and the slope of one of the constraints are equal. For example, the program

Maximize $2X_1 + 2X_2$

Subject to

$$X_1 + X_2 \leq 10$$

$$(1/2)X_1 + 3X_2 \leq 6$$

$$X_1 \geq 0 \text{ and } X_2 \geq 0.$$

has no unique solution. As can be seen in Figure 7.4, the slopes of the objective function and the first constraint are equal.

Figure 7.4. **Linear Program With Multiple Solutions**

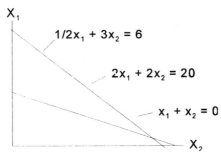

By solving the program by the simplex method, noting that (X_2) in Tableau IIj is considered the incoming variable, we obtain:

Tableau Ij

	Z	X_1	X_2	X_3	X_4	RHS
Z	1	-2	-2	0	0	0
X_3	0	1	1	1	0	10
X_4	0	1/2	3	0	1	6

Tableau IIj

	Z	X_1	X_2	X_3	X_4	RHS
Z	1	0	0	2	0	20
X_1	0	1	1	1	0	10
X_4	0	0	5/2	-1/2	1	1

Tableau IIIj

	Z	X_1	X_2	X_3	X_4	RHS
Z	1	0	0	2	0	20
X_1	0	1	0	6/5	-2/5	96/10
X_2	0	0	1	-1/5	2/5	2/5

Tableaux IIj and IIIj indicate clearly that the program has multiple solutions, because the basic variables have different solutions but the objective function has the same value, 20.

An Unbounded Solution

For example, take the mathematical program

Maximize $2X_1 + 3X_2$

Subject to

$$-2X_1 + 3X_2 \leq 12$$

$$X_2 \leq 5$$

$$X_1 \geq 0 \text{ and } X_2 \geq 0.$$

Figure 7.5 indicates that the program has no solution, because the feasible region is unbounded.

Figure 7.5. **Unbounded Linear Program**

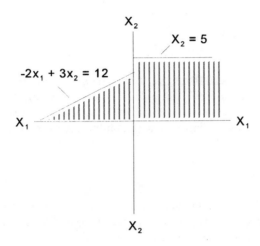

If the mathematical program is solved by the simplex method, the simplex procedure will be terminated because the outgoing variable cannot be determined. The simplex tableaux are shown below.

Tableau Ik

	Z	X_1	X_2	X_3	X_4	RHS
Z	1	-2	-3	0	0	0
X_3	0	-2	3	1	0	12
X_4	0	0	1	0	1	5

Tableau IIk

	Z	X_1	X_2	X_3	X_4	RHS
Z	1	-4	6	1	0	12
X_2	0	-2/3	1	1/3	0	4
X_4	0	2/3	0	-1/3	1	1

Tableau IIIk

	Z	X_1	X_2	X_3	X_4	RHS
Z	1	0	0	-2	6	18
X_2	0	0	1	0	1	5
X_1	0	1	0	-1/2	3/2	3/2

As can be seen from Tableau IIIk, there is no optimal solution because there is a negative element in the top row. In addition, the simplex algorithm has been terminated since the minimum ratio rule cannot be utilized—division by zero or a negative is not allowed—leading to an impossibility in determining the outgoing variable.

An Infeasible Solution

An infeasible solution can be found if the constraints are mutually exclusive. In other words, some of the restrictions of the mathematical program are not overlapping. For example, the mathematical program

Maximize $20X_1 + 16X_2$

Subject to

$$X_1 + X_2 \le 3$$

$$X_1 + 4X_2 \ge 15$$

$$X_1 \ge 0 \text{ and } X_2 \ge 0.$$

is plotted in Figure 7.6. The figure shows the infeasibility of the program.

Figure 7.6. **Infeasible Linear Program**

Solving the program by the simplex algorithm gives the pre-simplex Table 7.11 and the other simplex tableaux as follows:

The Pre-Simplex Table 7.11

	Z	X_1	X_2	X_3	X_4	X_5	RHS
Z	1	-20	-16	0	0	100	0
X_3	0	1	1	1	0	0	3
X_5	0	1	4	0	-1	1	15

Tableau II

	Z	X_1	X_2	X_3	X_4	X_5	RHS
Z	1	-120	-416	0	100	0	-1500
X_3	0	1	1	1	0	0	3
X_5	0	1	4	0	-1	1	15

Tableau III

	Z	X_1	X_2	X_3	X_4	X_5	RHS
Z	1	296	0	416	100	0	-252
X_2	0	1	1	1	0	0	3
X_5	0	-3	0	-4	-1	1	3

The solution is infeasible because it violates the second constraint.

Problems

1.   Solve the following problems graphically and by the simplex method:

(a) Maximize $Z = 4x_1 + 6x_2$

Subject to

$4x_1 + 8x_2 \leq 80$

$10x_1 + 2x_2 \leq 50$

$x_1 \geq 0$ and $x_2 \geq 0$.

(b) Maximize $Z = 5x_1 + 12x_2$

Subject to

$3x_1 + 5x_2 \leq 15$

$3x_1 + x_2 \leq 9$

$2x_1 + 8x_2 \leq 16$

$x_1 \geq 0, x_2 \geq 0,$ and $x_3 \geq 0$.

(c) Maximize $Z = 2x_1 + 5x_2$

Subject to

$8x_1 + 4x_2 \leq 40$

$6x_1 + 10x_2 \leq 60$

$x_1 \geq 0$ and $x_2 \geq 0$.

2.   Solve the following problems garphically and by the simplex method:

(a) Maximize $Z = 2x_1 + 3x_2$

   Subject to

   $4x_1 + 6x_2 \le 36$

   $3x_1 + 2x_2 \le 12$

   $x_1 \ge 0$ and $x_2 \ge 0$.

(b) Maximize $Z = 2x_1 + 3x_2$

   Subject to

   $2x_1 + 3x_2 \le 36$

   $2x_2 + 3x_2 \le 14$

   $x_1 \ge 0$ and $x_2 \ge 0$.

(c) Maximize $Z = 2x_1 + 4x_2$

   Subject to

   $x_2 \le 5$

   $2x_1 + x_2 \ge 10$

   $x_1 \ge 0$ and $x_2 \ge 0$.

3.   Solve the following linear mathematical programs by the simplex method:

Maximize $Z = 2x_1 + 4x_2$

   Subject to

   $x_2 \le 5$

   $2x_1 + x_2 \ge 10$

   $x_1 + x_2 \le 7$

   $x_1 \ge 0$ and $x_2 \ge 0$.

4.   Minimize the following linear programming problems:

(a) $Z = 2x_1 + 4x_2$

Subject to

$6x_1 + 10x_2 \leq 60$

$2x_1 + x_2 \geq 10$

$2x_1 + 3x_2 = 18$

$x_1 \geq 0, x_2 \geq 0, \text{ and } x_3 \geq 0.$

(b) $Z = x_1 + x_2$

Subject to

$x_1 + 2x_2 \geq 10$

$2x_1 + x_2 \geq 10$

$x_1 \geq 0 \text{ and } x_2 \geq 0.$

CHAPTER EIGHT

Linear Programming II: Sensitivity Analysis, Duality, and Integer Programming

In this chapter three objectives will be accomplished. The first objective is to understand the impact analysis in a linear mathematical programing model. This can be studied when the coefficients of the objective function (c_j) are allowed to vary or change individually by one unit, and the effect of this unit change, if it exists, on the objective function is measured. In other words, we are interested in determining what is called in the language of calculus dZ/dc_j, the derivative of Z with respect c_j, Similarly, the effect of a unit change in the capacity of the economic resources (b_i) on the objective function, dZ/db_i can be determined. By the same token, the impact of a unit change in the rate of resource utilization (a_{ij}) on the objective function, da_{ij}/dZ, can be quantified.

As a matter of fact, these effects indicate whether or not a mathematical linear programming model is sensitive to the changes in its coefficients and constants; and this is the core of what is called *sensitivity analysis*. Along with the sensitivity analysis, we are also interested in finding the range over which the coefficients and constants can be varied without changing the marginal contribution of that resource to the objective function, a task that is usually called *range analysis*.

The second objective of this chapter is to study the dual of a linear mathematical programing model. Duality is very useful in solving directly for the marginal cost, marginal revenue product of a factor of production, and the marginal physical products of the economic resources if the primal program is formulated in a specific way. In addition, solving the dual of a primal problem may take less time than solving the primal problem itself.

The third goal of this chapter is to obtain an integer, rather than a fractional, solution to a mathematical linear programming model. Finding an integer solution is a task achieved by *integer linear programming*.

Sensitivity Analysis
To explain sensitivity analysis properly, let us take the mathematical program

Maximize $Z = 6X_1 + 8X_2$

Subject to

$$2X_1 + 2X_2 \leq 20$$

$$2X_1 + 4X_2 \leq 24$$

$$X_1 \geq 0 \text{ and } X_2 \geq 0$$

whose solution is $Z = 64$, $X_1 = 8$, and $X_2 = 2$, where Z represents total profit. We are interested in changing the coefficients and constants of the program individually by one unit in order to determine the impact of that particular unit change on the objective function and optimal solution (Thompson 1971).

Sensitivity of the Program to Changes in c_j

In our program $c_1 = 6$ and $c_2 = 8$. If c_1 takes a range of values between 4 and 8, assuming c_2 is being held constant at 8, the optimal solutions of the program for each new value of c_1 are shown in Table 8.1.

Table 8.1. **Varying the c_1 Coefficient of the Objective Function**

c_1	c_2	Solution	Z	Change in Z (dZ)
4	8	(0, 6)	48	---
5	8	(8, 2)	56	8
6	8	(8, 2)	64	8
7	8	(8, 2)	72	8
8	8	(10, 0)	80	8

Now, hold the c_1 coefficient fixed at 6 and vary c_2. If c_2 changes by a unit within a range between 6 and 12, the optimal solutions of the program are shown in Table 8.2.

Table 8.2. **Varying the c_2 Coefficient of the Objective Function**

c_1	c_2	(X_1, X_2)	Z	Change in Z (dZ)
6	6	(10, 0)	60	---
6	7	(8, 2)	62	2
6	8	(8, 2)	64	2
6	9	(8, 2)	66	2
6	10	(8, 2)	68	2
6	11	(8, 2)	70	2
6	12	(0, 6)	72	2
6	13	(0, 6)	78	6

In fact, the range of the coefficients of the objective function can be obtained from the final simplex tableau. With respect to the mathematical program, the final simplex tableau is

	Z	X_1	X_2	X_3	X_4	RHS
Z	1	0	0	2	1	64
X_1	0	1	0	1	-1/2	8
X_2	0	0	1	-1/2	1/2	2

To obtain the range of c_1, we go to the top row (the Z values) under the columns headed by X_3 (the first slack variable) and X_4 (the second slack variable), and divide the values of the top row by the elements located in the second and the third row. Using the elements of the second row, the row of X_1, to obtain $(2/1) = 2$ and $1/(-1/2) = -2$. These outcomes suggest the following: The lower increment of c_1 is 2, and the upper increment is 2. Similarly, using the elements of the third row, the X_3's row, to obtain $2/(-1/2) = -4$ and $1/(1/2) = 2$ suggests that the lower increment of c_2 is 2, and the upper increment is 4. In other words, the negative outcomes indicate the range by which the c_j coefficients increase from its original value, and the positive outcomes indicate the range by which the c_j coefficients decrease from its original value. Table 8.3 shows these results.

Table 8.3. **Lower and Upper Limits for c_1 and c_2**

	Lower Limit	Original Value	Upper Limit
X_1	6 - 2 = 4	6	6 + 2 = 8
X_2	8 - 2 = 6	8	8 + 4 = 12

Usually, Table 8.3 is written in the format shown in Table 8.4.

Table 8.4. **Lower and Upper Limits for c_1 and c_2**

	Lower Limit	Original Value	Upper Limit
X_1	4	6	8
X_2	6	8	12

In general, as long as the coefficients of the objective function stay within the range indicated by Table 8.4 (ignoring the end points: 4 and 8), the optimal solution will not change nor will dZ/dc_j. For example, if c_1 is reduced from 6 to 5, the optimal solution is the same as before, that is, $X_1 = 8$ and $X_2 = 2$, although the value of the objective function is different. But if c_1 is reduced to 4 (the lowest end point) the solution will be changed to ($X_1 = 0$ and $X_2 = 6$). In other words, by using sensitivity analysis, producers will know whether or not the optimal solution will change.

Example 1: For the program,

$$\text{Maximize } Z = 300X_1 + 160X_2$$

Subject to

$$2X_1 + 2X_2 \le 1200$$

$$6X_1 + 4X_2 \le 4000$$

$$X_1 \ge 0 \text{ and } X_2 \ge 0,$$

the final simplex tableau is

	Z	X_1	X_2	X_3	X_4	RHS
Z	1	0	0	10	35	152000
X_2	0	0	1	1	-1/4	200
X_1	0	1	0	-1/2	1	400

Find the lower and upper limits for c_1 and c_2.
Solution: The lower increment of c_1 is $35/1 = 35$, and the upper increase is $10/(-1/2) = -20$. For c_2, the lower increment is $10/1 = 10$, and the upper increase is $35/(-1/4) = -140$. The lower and upper limits for c_1 and c_2 are shown in Table 8.5.

Table 8.5. **Lower and Upper Limits for c_1 and c_2 for Example 1**

	Lower Limit	Original Value	Upper Limit
X_1	300 - 35	300	300 + 20
X_2	300 - 10	160	300 +140

Example 2: For the program,

Maximize $2X_1 + 4X_2$

Subject to

$$2X_1 + 2X_2 \le 8$$

$$2X_1 \quad \ge 2$$

$$X_1 \ge 0 \text{ and } X_2 \ge 0,$$

the final simplex tableau is

	Z	X_1	X_2	X_3	X_4	X_5	RHS
Z	1	0	0	2	1	99	14
X_2	0	0	1	1/2	1/2	-1/2	3
X_1	0	1	0	0	-1/2	1/2	1

Find the lower and upper limits for c_1 and c_2.
Solution: This program has a surplus variable (X_4), and the column headed by the surplus variable must be multiplied by (-1). Having done so, follow the previous procedure for finding the lower and upper increments. For c_1, the upper increment is -1/(1/2) = -2, and the lower increment is 2/0 which is not defined—that is, the lower increment does not exist (no lower limit). For c_2, the lower increment is 2/(1/2) = 4 and -1/-1/2 = 2. In this situation the lowest increment in absolute value must be taken (i.e., 2). In this program, there is no upper increment for c_2 and hence no upper limit can be found. Table 8.6 shows the required limits.

Table 8.6. **Lower and Upper Limits for c_1 and c_2 for Example 2**

	Lower limit	Original Value	Upper Limit
X_1	No Limit	2	2 + 2
X_2	4 - 2	4	No Limit

Example 3: For the program

Maximize $18X_1 + 12X_2$

Subject to

$$5X_1 + 6X_2 \leq 36$$

$$X_1 + 3X_2 = 9$$

$$X_1 \geq 0 \text{ and } X_2 \geq 0,$$

the final simplex tableau is

	Z	X_1	X_2	X_3	X_4	RHS
Z	1	0	0	14/3	284/3	120
X_1	0	1	0	1/3	-2/3	6
X_2	0	0	1	-1/9	5/9	1

Find the lower and upper limits for c_1 and c_2.
Solution: In this program X_4 is the artificial variable, and the value located in the top row under the column headed by X_4 cannot be used for finding any increment. Hence, the only column that must be used to find the increments is the column headed by X_3, the slack variable. Consequently, for c_1 the lower increment is $14/3/1/3 = 14$, and there is no upper increment. For c_2, the upper increment is $14/3/-1/9 = -42$, and there is no lower increment. These results are reported in Table 8.7.

Table 8.7. **Lower and Upper Limits for c_1 and c_2 for Example 3**

	Lower Limit	Original Value	Upper Limit
X_1	18 - 14	18	No Limit
X_2	No Limit	12	12 + 42

Example 4: For the program

$$\text{Maximize } Z = 2X_1 + 3X_2$$

Subject to

$$X_1 + 2X_2 = 6$$

$$4X_1 + X_2 \geq 8$$

$$3X_1 + 2X_2 \leq 12$$

$$X_1 \geq 0 \text{ and } X_2 \geq 0.$$

the final simplex tableau is

	Z	X_1	X_2	X_3	X_4	X_5	X_6	RHS
Z	1	0	0	101	0	100	1/3	10
X_2	0	0	1	1	0	0	-1/3	2
X_1	0	1	0	-1	0	0	2/3	2
X_4	0	0	0	-3	1	-1	7/3	2

Find the lower and upper limits for c_1 and c_2.

Solution: First of all, one should note that X_3 and X_5 are the artificial variables, and X_4 is the surplus variable. As just indicated, the values in the top row that are located under the artificial variables should not be used in finding the increments for c_1 and c_2. In addition, because X_4 is the surplus variable, which is in the basis with a value of 2, the value in the top row that is associated with the column headed by X_4 should not be used for finding the limits for c_1 and c_2. It follows that the only value in the top row that can be used to calculate the limits is the value associated with the slack variable, X_6. Using the same procedure, the lower increment of c_1 is $1/3 \, / \, 2/3 = 0.5$, and there is no upper increment. For c_2, the upper increment is $1/3 \, / \, {-1/3} = -1$, and there is no lower increment. Table 8.8 shows the required results.

Table 8.8. **Lower and Upper Limits for c_1 and c_2 for Example 4**

	Lower Limit	Original Value	Upper Limit
X_1	2 - 0.5	2	No Limit
X_2	No Limit	3	3 + 1

Sensitivity of the Program to Changes in b_i

In this case the original form of the mathematical program is kept as it is except the capacity of the economic resource, b_i, is allowed to change within a certain range. And for each new value of the right-hand side, the program is solved by the simplex method in order to determine the impact of this unit change on the optimal solution and the objective function. Let us vary the right-hand side of the first constraint within a range between 12 and 24, holding b_2 fixed at 24, and solve the program. Table 8.9 shows all the optimal solutions.

Table 8.9. **Varying b_1, the Capacity of the First Resource**

b_1	b_2	(X_1, X_2)	Z	Change in Z
12	24	(0, 6)	48	----
13	24	(1, 5.5)	50	2
14	24	(2, 5)	52	2
15	24	(3, 4.5)	54	2
16	24	(4, 4)	56	2
17	24	(5, 3.5)	58	2
18	24	(6, 3)	60	2
19	24	(7, 2.5)	62	2
20	24	(8, 2)	64	2
21	24	(9, 1.5)	66	2
22	24	(10, 1)	68	2
23	24	(11, 0.5)	70	2
24	24	(12, 0)	72	2

Table 8.9 suggests that within the specified range, dZ/db_1 (the change in the value of the objective function resulting from a unit increase in the right-hand side, or the shadow price of the first resource) remains fixed at a value of 2—no diminishing returns.

Now, let us vary the right-hand side of the second constraint (resource), b_2, within a range between 20 and 40, holding b_1 constant at 20, and solve the program. Table 8.10 shows all the optimal solutions.

Table 8.10. **Varying b_2, the Capacity of the Second Resource**

b_1	b_2	(X_1, X_2)	Z	Change in Z
20	20	(10, 0)	60	----
20	21	(9.5, 0.5)	61	1
20	22	(9, 1)	62	1
20	23	(8.5, 1.5)	63	1
20	24	(8, 2)	64	1
20	25	(7.5, 2.5)	65	1
20	26	(7, 3)	66	1
20	27	(6.5, 3.5)	67	1
20	28	(6, 4)	68	1
20	29	(5.5, 4.5)	69	1
20	30	(5, 5)	70	1
20	31	(4.5, 5.5)	71	1
20	32	(4, 6)	72	1
20	33	(3.5, 6.5)	73	1
20	34	(3, 7)	74	1
20	35	(2.5, 7.5)	75	1
20	36	(2, 8)	76	1
20	37	(1.5, 8.5)	77	1
20	38	(1, 9)	78	1
20	39	(0.5, 9.5)	79	1
20	40	(0, 10)	80	1

Also, Table 8.10 indicates that within the given range the shadow price remains unchanged. One should note that if b_2's marginal contribution to profit decreases, the implication is that the law of diminishing returns is working.

As a matter of fact, the range of b_1 can be obtained from the final simplex tableau. For the mathematical linear program, the final simplex tableau is

	Z	X_1	X_2	X_3	X_4	RHS
Z	1	0	0	2	1	64
X_1	0	1	0	1	-1/2	8
X_2	0	0	1	-1/2	1/2	2

To find the range of the resource capacity, the right-hand side values of X_1 and X_2 must be divided by the elements of the columns headed by the slack variables X_3 and X_4, which are associated with the first and second constraints. For the first resource, we divide $8/1 = 8$, which gives the lower increment by which the first resource will decrease, and $2/-1/2 = -4$, which indicates the upper increment by which the first resource increases. For the second resource, we divide $8/(-1/2) = -16$, which gives the upper increment by which the second resource increases, and $2/(1/2) = 4$, which indicates the lower increment by which this resource decreases. The results are shown in Table 8.11.

Table 8.11. **Lower and Upper Limits for b_1 and b_2**

	Lower Limit	Original Capacity	Upper Limit
Resource 1: b_1	20 - 8	20	20 + 4
Resource 2: b_2	24 - 4	24	24 + 16

Example 1: Find the range of b_1 and b_2 for the program introduced in example 2. Solution: Use the final simplex tableau and keep in mind that the second restriction has the inequality (>); and the column headed by X_4, the surplus variable, must be multiplied by -1 before it is used in finding the range for b_1. In addition, the column headed by X_5, the artificial variable, cannot be used for finding the range. For the first restriction we use the values of the column headed by X_3, the slack variable associated with that restriction. That is, $3/1/2 = 6$, which indicates the lower increment, and $1/0$ (not defined), which suggeses that there is no upper increment and consequently no upper limit for the first resource. For the second resource, we use the negative of the elements under the surplus variable (i.e. $3/-1/2 = -6$) to obtain the upper increment for the first resource, and $1/1/2 = 2$, which indicates the lower increment for the second resource. Table 8.12 shows all the required results.

Table 8.12. **Lower and Upper Limits for b_1 and b_2 for example 1**

	Lower Limit	Original Value	Upper Limit
b_1	8 - 6	8	No Limit
b_2	2 - 2	2	2 + 6

Example 2: Find the range of b_1 and b_2 for the program introduced in example 3 on page 210. Solution: In this program the first constraint has an inequality sign ($\leq$), and the second constraint has an equality sign (=). Hence, we have to use the elements headed by X_3, the slack variable associated with the first restriction, and the elements headed by X_4, the artificial variable associated with the second restriction. For the first resource (b_1), $6/1/3 = 18$, which indicates the lower increment, and $1/-1/9 = -9$, which indicates the upper increment. For the second resource (b_2), $6/-2/3 = -9$ indicates the upper increment, and $1/5/9 = 1.8$ indicates the lower

increment. Table 8.13 shows all the required results.

Table 8.13. **Upper and Lower Limits for b_1 and b_2 for Example 2**

	Lower Limit	Original Capacity	Upper Limit
b_1	36 - 18	36	36 + 9
b_2	9 - 1.8	9	9 + 9

Example 3: Find the range of the three resources for the program introduced on page 211.
Solution: This program has three restrictions. The first restriction has an equality sign, and the column headed by the artificial variable must be used in finding the range for the first resource; the second restriction has the inequality sign ($\geq$) and the negative of the column headed by the surplus variable must be used in finding the range for the second resource; the third restriction has the inequality sign ($\leq$), and the column headed by the slack variable must be used to find the range for the third resource.

It follows that for the first resource, $2/1 = 2$, $2/-1 = -2$, and $2/-3 = -2/3$. These results suggest that the upper increment for this resource is $2/3$ (the lowest in absolute value), and the lower increment is 2. For the second resource, $2/-1 = -2$, indicating that the upper increment and the lower increment cannot be found. For the third resource, we obtain $2/-1/3 = -6$, indicating the upper increment, and the lower increment is the minimum of ($2/2/3 = 3$ and $2/7/3 = 6/7$), which is $6/7$. Table 8.14 shows the required results.

Table 8.14. **Upper and Lower Limits for b_1 and b_2**

	Lower Limit	Original Capacity	Upper Limit
b_1	6 - 2	6	6 + 2/3
b_2	No Limit	8	8 + 2
b_3	12 - 6/7	12	12 + 6

Sensitivity of the Program to Changes in a_{ij}

Now, let us change individually a_{ij}, the rates of resource utilization by, a unit and find the impact of each new coefficient of aij on the optimal solution and the objective function. We will use the program

$$\text{Maximize } Z = 6X_1 + 8X_2$$

Subject to

$$2X_1 + 2X_2 \leq 20$$

$$2X_1 + 4X_2 \leq 24$$

$$X_1 \geq 0 \text{ and } X_2 \geq 0.$$

If a_{11}, which is equal to 2, varies within a range of 1 to 3, holding the other a_{ij} coefficients fixed, the optimal solutions of the program are shown in Table 8.15.

Table 8.15. **Varying a_{11} Coefficient**

a_{11}	(X_1, X_2)	Z	Change in Z (dZ)
1	(12, 0)	72	----
2	(8, 2)	64	-8
3	(4, 4)	56	-8

If a_{12}, which is equal to 2, changes between a range of 1 to 3, holding the other a_{ij} coefficients fixed, the optimal solutions of the program are shown in Table 8.16.

Table 8.16. **Varying a_{12} Coefficient**

a_{12}	(X_1, X_2)	Z	Change in Z
1	(9.33, 1.33)	66.667	----
2	(8, 2)	64	-2.667
3	(10, 0)	60	-4.00

If a_{21}, which is equal to 2, changes between a range of 1 to 3, the optimal solutions of the program are shown in Table 8.17.

Table 8.17. **Varying a_{21} Coefficient**

a_{21}	(X_1, X_2)	Z	Change in Z
1	(5.33, 4.667)	69.33	----
2	(8, 2)	64	-5.33
3	(0, 6)	48	-16.00

If a_{22}, which is equal to 4, changes within a range of 3 to 4, the optimal solutions are shown in Table 8.18.

Table 8.18. **Varying a_{22} Coefficient**

a_{22}	(X_1, X_2)	Z	Change in Z
3	(6, 4)	68	----
4	(8, 2)	64	-4.00
5	(8.667, 1.333)	62.667	-1.333

As can be seen from Tables 8.15 through 8.18, if the rates of resource utilization decrease by a unit, the value of the objective function will increase because the decreased rate of resource utilization implies higher resource productivities and better technology associated with a more skilled labor force. In addition, it may indicate efficient organization and management. In contrast, if the rates of resource utilization increase, the value of the objective function declines, implying a slowdown in productivity.

Duality

Each primal linear mathematical program has a linear dual program. The mathematical solution of the dual program gives the shadow prices directly (the marginal contribution of economic resources to the objective function) of each economic resource. In addition, the value of the objective function of the dual is the same as the value of the objective function of the primal. Before explaining what has just been said, let us show how the dual of each primal mathematical program can be obtained.

In general, if the primal program takes the form

Maximize C^tX

Subject to

$$AX \le B$$

$$X \ge 0.$$

where C^t is a row vector containing the coefficients of the objective function, B is a column vector containing the values of the right-hand side, A is a matrix containing a_{ij} coefficients, and X is a column vector containing the decision variables, the dual program is

Minimize B^tW

Subject to

$$A^t W \geq C$$

$$W \geq 0,$$

where W is a column vector containing the dual variables. These programs, the primal and dual, are called *symmetric* in that both involve nonnegative variables and inequality constraints.

If the primal program is

Maximize $C^t X$

Subject to

$$AX = B$$

$$X \geq 0,$$

the dual becomes

Minimize $B^t W$

Subject to

$$A^t W \geq C$$

$$W \geq 0.$$

If the primal program is

Minimize $C^t X$

Subject to

$$AX \geq B$$

$$X \geq 0,$$

the dual becomes

Maximize $B^t W$

Subject to

$$\mathbf{A^tW} \le \mathbf{C}$$

$$\mathbf{W} \ge \mathbf{0}.$$

Finally, if the primal program is

Minimize $\mathbf{C^tX}$

Subject to

$$\mathbf{AX} = \mathbf{B}$$

$$\mathbf{X} \ge \mathbf{0},$$

the dual becomes

Maximize $\mathbf{B^tW}$

Subject to

$$\mathbf{A^tW} \le \mathbf{C}$$

$$\mathbf{W} \ge \mathbf{0}.$$

Example 1: Find the dual solution for the linear mathematical program

Maximize $Z = 6X_1 + 8X_2$

Subject to

$$2X_1 + 2X_2 \le 20$$

$$2X_1 + 4X_2 \le 24$$

$$X_1 \ge 0 \text{ and } X_2 \ge 0.$$

where Z represents total profit.

Solution: The final simplex tableau of this program is

	Z	X_1	X_2	X_3	X_4	RHS
Z	1	0	0	2	1	64
X_1	0	1	0	1	-1/2	8
X_2	0	0	1	-1/2	1/2	2

The dual of the program is formed as

Minimize $20W_1 + 24W_2$

Subject to

$$2W_1 + 2W_2 \geq 6$$

$$2W_1 + 4W_2 \geq 8$$

$$W_1 \geq 0 \text{ and } W_2 \geq 0$$

whose solution is shown below.

The Pre-Simplex Table 1a

	Z	W_1	W_2	W_3	W_4	W_5	W_6	RHS
Z	1	-20	-24	0	-100	0	-100	0
W_4	0	2	2	-1	1	0	0	6
W_6	0	2	4	0	0	-1	1	8

The Pre-Simplex Table 2a

	Z	W_1	W_2	W_3	W_4	W_5	W_6	RHS
Z	1	180	176	-100	0	0	-100	600
W_4	0	2	2	-1	1	0	0	6
W_6	0	2	4	0	0	-1	1	8

Tableau Ia

	Z	W_1	W_2	W_3	W_4	W_5	W_6	RHS
Z	1	380	576	-100	0	-100	0	1400
W_4	0	2	2	-1	1	0	0	6
W_6	0	2	4	0	0	-1	1	8

Tableau IIa

	Z	W_1	W_2	W_3	W_4	W_5	W_6	RHS
Z	1	92	0	-100	0	44	-144	248
W_4	0	1	0	-1	1	1/2	-1/2	2
W_2	0	1/2	1	0	0	-1/4	1/4	2

Tableau IIIa

	Z	W_1	W_2	W_3	W_4	W_5	W_6	RHS
Z	1	0	0	-8	-92	-2	-98	64
W_1	0	1	0	-1	1	1/2	-1/2	2
W_2	0	0	1	1/2	-1/2	-1/2	1/2	1

The final simplex tableau of the dual indicates the following points:

1. The negative of the top row values of the columns headed by W_3 and W_5, the surplus variables associated with the first and second constraints of the dual program, give the solutions of X_1 and X_2 for the primal program.

2. The dual solution, W_1 and W_2, shows directly the shadow prices of the two economic resources—dZ/db_1 and dZ/db_2. In other words, the dual solution (W_1 and W_2) gives the marginal contribution of the two resources to profit (Z). These values are also listed in the top row of the final simplex tableau of the primal under the columns headed by X_3 and X_4, the slack variables associated with the two constraints of the primal program.

3. The value of the objective function of the dual is $Z = 64$, which is the same as the value of the objective function of the primal.

To sum up, one can obtain the dual solution directly from the final simplex tableau of the primal program. This solution (the shadow prices) is given by the values located in the top row of the columns headed by the slack variables associated with the constraints of the program.

Example 2: Find the dual solution for the program

Maximize $300X_1 + 160X_2$

Subject to

$$2X_1 + 2X_2 \leq 1200$$

$$6X_1 + 4X_2 \leq 4000$$

$$X_1 \geq 0 \text{ and } X_2 \geq 0$$

whose final simplex tableau is introduced (see also page 183) as

	Z	X_1	X_2	X_3	X_4	RHS
Z	1	0	0	10	35	152000
X_2	0	0	1	1	-1/4	200
X_1	0	1	0	-1/2	1	400

From this tableau one should be able to find the dual solution. It is found in the top row of the tableau under the columns headed by X_3 and X_4, the slack variables associated with the two constraints. Thus, $W_1 = 35$ and $W_2 = 10$. These values, which are the shadow prices of the two economic resources, can be obtained from the dual program as well. To do so, the dual of the primal program is formulated as

Minimize $1200W_1 + 4000W_2$

Subject to

$$2W_1 + 8W_2 \geq 300$$

$$2W_1 + 4W_2 \geq 160$$

$$W_1 \geq 0 \text{ and } W_2 \geq 0.$$

To solve this program by the simplex method, the large positive coefficients of the artificial variables must be 1000, rather than 100, because the coefficients of the objective function are larger than the coefficients of the constraints. Keeping this in mind, the complete solution of the dual program is shown below.

The Pre-Simplex Table 8.1b

	Z	W_1	W_2	W_3	W_4	W_5	W_6	RHS
Z	1	-1200	-4000	0	-1000	0	-1000	0
W_4	0	2	8	-1	1	0	0	300
W_6	0	2	4	0	0	-1	1	160

The Pre-Simplex Table 8.2b

	Z	W_1	W_2	W_3	W_4	W_5	W_6	RHS
Z	1	800	4000	-1000	0	0	-1000	300000
W_4	0	2	8	-1	1	0	0	300
W_6	0	2	4	0	0	-1	1	160

Tableau Ib

	Z	W_1	W_2	W_3	W_4	W_5	W_6	RHS
Z	1	2800	8000	-1000	0	-1000	0	460000
W_4	0	2	8	-1	1	0	0	300
W_6	0	2	4	0	0	-1	1	160

Tableau IIb

	Z	W_1	W_2	W_3	W_4	W_5	W_6	RHS
Z	1	800	0	0	-1000	-1000	0	160000
W_2	0	1/4	1	-1/8	1/8	0	0	300/8
W_6	0	1	0	1/2	-1/2	-1	1	10

Tableau IIIb

	Z	W_1	W_2	W_3	W_4	W_5	W_6	RHS
Z	1	0	0	-400	-600	-200	-800	152000
W_2	0	0	1	-1/4	1/4	1/4	-1/4	35
W_1	0	1	0	1/2	-1/2	-1	1	10

One should note that the solution of the primal is the negative of -400 and -200. Also, if Z represents total output, the dual solution gives the marginal physical products of the two resources. In this case, the marginal physical product of the first resource is $10, and the marginal physical product of the second resource if $35 is. the price of the product is determined by the competitive market at $2.00, the producer should pay $20.00 and $70.00 as compensations for using the first and second resource, respectively.

Example 3: Find the dual solution for the program

Maximize $2X_1 + 4X_2$

Subject to

$$2X_1 + 2X_2 \leq 8$$

$$2X_1 \geq 2$$

$$X_1 \geq 0 \text{ and } X_2 \geq 0.$$

This program was also introduced before, and its final simplex tableau was:

	Z	X_1	X_2	X_3	X_4	X_5	RHS
Z	1	0	0	2	1	99	14
X_2	0	0	1	1/2	1/2	-1/2	3
X_1	0	1	0	0	-1/2	1/2	1

Solution: The dual solution can be obtained from the above tableau (i.e. $W_1 = 2$ and $W_2 = 1$). Also, the solution can be obtained by taking the dual of the primal program. To do so, the primal program is rewritten as

Maximize $2X_1 + 4X_2$

Subject to

$$2X_1 + 2X_2 \leq 8$$

$$-2X_1 \leq -2$$

$$X_1 \geq 0 \text{ and } X_2 \geq 0$$

and the dual becomes

Minimize $8W_1 - 2W_2$

Subject to

$$2W_1 - 2W_2 \geq 2$$

$$2W_1 \geq 4$$

$$W_1 \geq 0 \text{ and } W_2 \geq 0$$

whose solution is shown below.

The Pre-Simplex Table 8.1c

	Z	W_1	W_2	W_3	W_4	W_5	W_6	RHS
Z	1	-8	2	0	-100	0	-100	0
W_4	0	2	-2	-1	1	0	0	2
W_6	0	2	0	0	0	-1	1	4

The Pre-simplex Table 2c

	Z	W_1	W_2	W_3	W_4	W_5	W_6	RHS
Z	1	192	-198	-100	0	0	-100	200
W_4	0	2	-2	-1	1	0	0	2
W_6	0	2	0	0	0	-1	1	4

Tableau Ic

	Z	W_1	W_2	W_3	W_4	W_5	W_6	RHS
Z	1	392	-198	-100	0	-100	0	600
W_4	0	2	-2	-1	1	0	0	2
W_6	0	2	0	0	0	-1	1	4

Tableau IIc

	Z	W_1	W_2	W_3	W_4	W_5	W_6	RHS
Z	1	0	194	96	-196	-100	0	208
W_1	0	1	-1	-1/2	1/2	0	0	1
W_6	0	0	2	1	-1	-1	1	2

Tableau IIIc

	Z	W_1	W_2	W_3	W_4	W_5	W_6	RHS
Z	1	0	0	-1	-99	-3	-97	14
W_1	0	1	0	0	0	-1/2	1/2	2
W_2	0	0	1	1/2	-1/2	-1/2	1/2	1

We note, if Z represents total revenue, the dual solution gives the marginal-revenue product for the first and second resource. In this case, the marginal-revenue products for the first and second resource are $1 and $2, respectively; and resource compensations should not exceed these values.

Example 4: Find the primal and the dual solution for the program

Maximize $18X_1 + 12X_2$

Subject to

$$5X_1 + 6X_2 \leq 36$$

$$X_1 + 3X_2 = 9$$

$$X_1 \geq 0 \text{ and } X_2 \geq 0.$$

Solution: Before obtaining the dual solution, the primal program is rewritten as,

Maximize $18X_1 + 12X_2$

Subject to

$$5X_1 + 6X_2 \leq 36$$

$$X_1 + 3X_2 \leq 9$$

$$X_1 + 3X_2 \geq 9$$

$$X_1 \geq 0 \text{ and } X_2 \geq 0$$

whose final simplex tableau is (also see page 187)

	Z	X_1	X_2	X_3	X_4	X_5	X_6	RHS
Z	1	0	0	14/3	0	16/3	284/3	120
X_1	0	1	0	1/3	0	2/3	-2/3	6
X_4	0	0	0	0	1	1	-1	0
X_2	0	0	1	-1/9	0	-5/9	5/9	1

where (X_5) and (X_6) are the surplus and artificial variables associated with the third constraint. It should be noted that for the above primal program, the equality constraint $(X_1 + 3X_2 = 9)$ is replaced by the two constraints

$$X_1 + 3X_2 \le 9$$

$$X_1 + 3X_2 \ge 9.$$

Now, multiply the constraint $(X_1 + 3X_2 > 9)$ by (-1) to obtain

$$-X_1 - 3X_2 \le -9.$$

Therefore, the primal program becomes

Maximize $18X_1 + 12X_2$

Subject to

$$5X_1 + 6X_2 \le 36$$

$$X_1 + 3X_2 \le 9$$

$$-X_1 - 3X_2 \le -9$$

$$X_1 \ge 0 \text{ and } X_2 \ge 0$$

and the dual form becomes

Minimize $36W_1 + 9W_2 - 9W_3$

Subject to

$$5W_1 + W_2 - W_3 \ge 18$$

$$6W_1 + 3W_2 - 3W_3 \geq 12$$

$$W_1 \geq 0, W_2 \geq 0, \text{ and } W_3 \geq 0$$

whose final simplex tableau is

	Z	W_1	W_2	W_3	W_4	W_5	W_6	W_7	RHS
Z	1	0	0	0	-282/3	-6	-767/3	-1	120
W_3	0	0	-1	1	2/3	-2/3	-5/9	5/9	16/3
W_1	0	1	0	0	1/3	-1/3	-1/9	1/9	14/3

Integer Programming

In most real world problems, integer solutions (Gomory 1963; Balinski 1965) are required, because indivisibility of some products cannot be accepted. For example, a production level of 100.91 car is not accepted by the general manager of a GM plant. In this case an integer solution is needed, because rounding the fractional solution to 101 or 100 may not be feasible.

To find an integer solution, Ralph E. Gomory (1963) developed a solution procedure. The main idea of this procedure is to find a new constraint from the final simplex tableau, a constraint that will shrink the feasible region and will be capable of finding an integer solution. To explain Gomory's procedure (see also Thompson 1971 for an excellent explanation), the following program is employed

$$\text{Maximize } Z = 4X_1 + 3X_2$$

Subject to

$$3X_1 + 2X_2 \leq 9$$

$$X_1 \geq 0 \text{ and } X_2 \geq 0 \text{ and integers.}$$

First, the program must be solved by the simplex method. The final simplex tableau is

	Z	X_1	X_2	X_3	RHS
Z	1	1/2	0	3/2	27/2
X_2	0	3/2	1	1/2	9/2

As can be readily seen, the basic variable X_2 does not have an integer solution. In this situation, we form an equation from the last row of the final simplex tableau (or from a row whose fractional right-hand side is the largest) as follows:

$$(3/2)X_1 + X_2 + (1/2)X_3 = 9/2 = 4 + 1/2.$$

Second, each coefficient of the above equation must be rewritten as a sum of integer and noninteger coefficients, that is,

$$(1 + 1/2)X_1 + (1 + 0)X_2 + (0 + 1/2)X_3 > 1/2 + \text{an integer.}$$

After transferring the integer coefficients along with their variables, the above equation can be rewritten as

$$(1/2)X_1 + (1/2)X_3 \geq 1/2 + \text{an integer.}$$

This constraint, which is called the Gomory constraint, must be put in a standard form by subtracting a surplus variable and adding an artificial variable. That is,

$$(1/2)X_1 + (1/2)X_3 - X_4 + X_5 = 1/2.$$

Third, we incorporate this constraint in the final simplex tableau and make sure to add an artificial variable with a large negative coefficient to the objective function. Therefore, the first simplex tableau becomes

	Z	X_1	X_2	X_3	X_4	X_5	RHS
Z	1	1/2	0	3/2	0	100	27/2
X_2	0	3/2	1	1/2	0	0	9/2
X_5	0	1/2	0	1/2	-1	1	1/2

and the 100 located in the column headed by X_5 must be driven out by multiplying the last row of the table by -100 and adding the results to the top row. The above tableau becomes

	Z	X_1	X_2	X_3	X_4	X_5	RHS
Z	1	-99/2	0	-97/2	100	0	-73/2
X_2	0	3/2	1	1/2	0	0	9/2
X_5	0	1/2	0	1/2	-1	1	1/2

After the simplex procedure, the final tableau gives an integer solution as shown below.

	Z	X_1	X_2	X_3	X_4	X_5	RHS
Z	1	0	0	1	1	99	13
X_2	0	0	1	-1	3	-3	3
X_1	0	1	0	1	-2	2	1

Example 1: Find the optimal solution for the program

Maximize $X_1 + X_2$

Subject to

$$2X_1 + X_2 \leq 8$$

$$X_1 + 2X_2 \leq 8$$

$$X_1 \geq 0 \text{ and } X_2 \geq 0 \text{ and integers.}$$

Solution: The final tableau of the simplex method is

	Z	X_1	X_2	X_3	X_4	RHS
Z	1	0	0	1/3	1/3	16/3
X_1	0	1	0	2/3	-1/3	8/3
X_2	0	0	1	-1/3	2/3	8/3

and the solution is optimal but noninteger. Convert the second row to an equation of the form

$$X_1 + (2/3)X_3 - (1/3)X_4 = 2 + 2/3,$$

which can be rewritten as

$$(1 + 0)X_1 + (2/3 + 0)X_3 + (-1 + 2/3)X_4 \geq 2/3 + \text{an integer.}$$

Transferring the integer coefficients to the right-hand side yields

$$(2/3)X_3 + (2/3)X_4 \geq 2/3 + \text{an integer,}$$

which can be put in a standard form by subtracting a surplus variable ($-X_5$) and adding an artificial variable (X_6), that is,

$$(2/3)X_3 + (2/3)X_4 - X_5 + X_6 = 2/3.$$

Augmenting this constraint in the final simplex tableau and adding an artificial variable with a large negative coefficient to the objective function, we obtain

	Z	X_1	X_2	X_3	X_4	X_5	X_6	RHS
Z	1	0	0	1/3	1/3	0	100	16/3
X_1	0	1	0	2/3	-1/3	0	0	8/3
X_2	0	0	1	-1/3	2/3	0	0	8/3
X_6	0	0	0	2/3	2/3	-1	1	2/3

Eliminating the 100 in the top row yields

	Z	X_1	X_2	X_3	X_4	X_5	X_6	RHS
Z	1	0	0	-199/3	-199/3	100	0	-184/3
X_1	0	1	0	2/3	-1/3	0	0	8/3
X_2	0	0	1	-1/3	2/3	0	0	8/3
X_6	0	0	0	2/3	2/3	-1	1	2/3

As X_4 is the incoming variable and X_6 is the outgoing variable, the integer optimal solution is obtained as shown below:

	Z	X_1	X_2	X_3	X_4	X_5	X_6	RHS
Z	1	0	0	0	0	1/2	199/2	5
X_1	0	1	0	1	0	-1/2	1/2	2
X_2	0	0	1	-1	0	1	-1	3
X_3	0	0	0	1	1	-3/2	3/2	1

Appendix

This appendix is designed to cover some topics that were not explained in chapters 7 and 8.

Unrestricted Variables

If the nonnegativity assumption is ignored in that some decision variables are allowed to be free, there is a way that can be used to deal with these unrestricted (free) variables (Taha 1987). For example, suppose the following program is to be maximized:

$$Z = 6X_1 + 8X_2$$

Subject to

$$2X_1 + 2X_2 \leq 20$$

$$2X_1 + 4X_2 \leq 24$$

$$X_1 \text{ free and } X_2 \geq 0.$$

Before applying the simplex method, we replace the free variable(s) by the difference of two new variables (e.g., $X_1 = X_3 - X_4$). After substituting this equation in the program, we obtain

Maximize $6(X_3 - X_4) + 8X_2$

Subject to

$$2(X_3 - X_4) + 2X_2 \leq 20$$

$$2(X_3 - X_4) + 4X_2 \leq 24$$

$$X_2 \geq 0, X_3 \geq 0, \text{ and } X_4 \geq 0.$$

After some simplifications the program becomes

Maximize $6X_3 - 6X_4 + 8X_2$

Subject to

$$2X_3 - 2X_4 + 2X_2 \leq 20$$

$$2X_3 - 2X_4 + 4X_2 \leq 24$$

$$X_1 \geq 0, X_2 \geq 0, X_3 \geq 0, \text{ and } X_4 \geq 0.$$

Now, we can apply the simplex method, and the final simplex tableau is:

	Z	X_3	X_4	X_2	X_5	X_6	RHS
Z	1	0	2	0	2	1	64
X_3	0	1	0	0	1	-1/2	8
X_2	0	0	-1/2	1	-1/2	1/2	2

Since $X_1 = X_3 - X_4$, therefore $X_1 = 8 - 0 = 8$.

The Two-Phase Method

Instead of using the large coefficient M (such as 100 or 1000) method in finding the dual (or the primal) solution for a linear programming problem when the artificial variables exist, the two-phase method is used. It is called two-phase because in the first phase the artificial variables are driven out by minimizing the objective function consisting of the sum of the artificial variables, and in the second phase the complete solution is obtained. We will explain this method by using the dual mathematical program

Minimize $20W_1 + 24W_2$

Subject to

$$2W_1 + 2W_2 \geq 6$$

$$2W_1 + 4W_2 \geq 8$$

$$W_1 \geq 0 \text{ and } W_2 \geq 0.$$

The first step is to put the restrictions in a standard form by subtracting two surplus variables (W_3 and W_4) and adding two artificial variables (A_1 and A_2), which yields

$$2W_1 + 2W_2 - W_3 + A_1 = 6$$

$$2W_1 + 4W_2 - W_4 + A_2 = 8 \tag{1}$$

The second step is to solve for A_1 and A_2 from system 1, which yields

$$A_1 = -2W_1 - 2W_2 + W_3 + 6$$

$$A_2 = -2W_1 - 4W_2 + W_4 + 8 \tag{1'}$$

since in phase I the objective function is to

$$\text{Minimize } Z = A_1 + A_2 \tag{2}$$

Therefore, this objective function, after substituting for A_1 and A_2 from system 1' in system 2, becomes

$$\text{Minimize } Z = -4W_1 - 6W_2 + W_3 + W_4 + 14. \tag{3}$$

The third step is to combine equation (3) and system 1 (which is already in a standard form), yielding

$$\text{Minimize } Z = -4W_1 - 6W_2 + W_3 + W_4 + 14$$

Subject to

$$2W_1 + 2W_2 - W_3 + A_1 = 6$$

$$2W_1 + 4W_2 - W_4 + A_2 = 8.$$

After transferring the variables of the objective function to the left-hand side, the first simplex tableau becomes

Tableau Id

	Z	W_1	W_2	W_3	W_4	A_1	A_2	RHS
Z	1	4	6	-1	-1	0	0	14
A_1	0	2	2	-1	0	1	0	6
A_2	0	2	4	0	-1	0	1	8

and the complete solution is shown below.

Tableau IId

	Z	W_1	W_2	W_3	W_4	A_1	A_2	RHS
Z	1	1	0	-1	1/2	0	-3/2	2
A_1	0	1	0	-1	1/2	1	-1/2	2
W_2	0	1/2	1	0	-1/4	0	1/4	2

Tableau IIId

	Z	W_1	W_2	W_3	W_4	A_1	A_2	RHS
Z	1	0	0	0	0	-1	-1	0
W_1	0	1	0	-1	1/2	1	-1/2	2
W_2	0	0	1	1/2	-1/2	-1/2	1/2	1

Thus, $Z = 0$, $A_1 = 0$, and $A_2 = 0$. In other words, the artificial variables are driven out, and we are ready to use phase II.

Phase II starts by converting the first and second row of the final simplex tableau, ignoring the columns headed by A_1 and A_2, into the following two equations:

$$W_1 - W_3 + (1/2)W_4 = 2$$

$$W_2 + (1/2)W_3 - (1/2)W_4 = 1 \tag{4}$$

Solving system 4 for W_1 and W_2 yields

$$W_1 = W_3 - (1/2)W_4 + 2$$

$$W_2 = (-1/2)W_3 + (1/2)W_4 + 1. \tag{5}$$

Now, using system 5 in the original objective function yields

$$\text{Minimize } Z = 20[W_3 - (1/2)W_4 + 2] + 24[(-1/2)W_3 + (1/2)W_4 + 1]$$

or

$$\text{Minimize } Z = 8W_3 + 2W_4 + 64. \tag{6}$$

After combining equation (6) and system 4 (which is the last two rows of the final simplex tableau of phase I), we obtain the program

Minimize $Z = 8W_3 + 2W_4 + 64$

Subject to

$$W_1 - W_3 + (1/2)W_4 = 2$$

$$W_1 + (1/2)W_3 - (1/2)W_4 = 1$$

$$W_1 \geq 0, W_2 \geq 0, W_3 \geq 0, \text{ and } W_4 \geq 0$$

whose simplex tableau is

	Z	W_1	W_2	W_3	W_4	RHS
Z	1	0	0	-8	-2	64
W_1	0	1	0	-1	1/2	2
W_2	0	0	1	1/2	-1/2	1

As there is no positive element in the top row, the optimal solution $Z = 64$, $W_1 = 2$, and $W_2 = 1$ has been obtained; otherwise, the simplex algorithm will be used as usual.

The Dual-Simplex Method

This method is used to find a solution to a mathematical program requiring artificial variables (Hillier and Lieberman 1980). The dual of the previous program was

Minimize $20W_1 + 24W_2$

Subject to

$$2W_1 + 2W_2 \geq 6$$

$$2W_1 + 4W_2 \geq 8$$

$$W_1 \geq 0 \text{ and } W_2 \geq 0.$$

Multiplying the constraints by -1 yields

Minimize $20W_1 + 24W_2$

Subject to

$$-2W_1 - 2W_2 \le -6$$

$$-2W_1 - 4W_2 \le -8$$

$$W_1 \ge 0 \text{ and } W_2 \ge 0.$$

This program can be solved by the dual-simplex method. The method works as follows. First, put the program in a standard form; thus, the first simplex tableau becomes

	Z	W_1	W_2	W_3	W_4	RHS
Z	1	-20	-24	0	0	0
W_3	0	-2	-2	1	0	-6
W_4	0	-2	-4	0	1	-8

As there are negative elements in the column of the RHS, there is no optimal solution. Second, determine the most negative element in the RHS column; it is -8. Third, divide the top row of the tableau by the elements in the third row to determine the minimum ratio; the minimum ratio is -24/-4 = 6. Fourth, follow the same procedure of the simplex method. Hence, W_2 is the incoming variable and W_4 is the outgoing variable. The second simplex tableau becomes

	Z	W_1	W_2	W_3	W_4	RHS
Z	1	-8	0	0	-6	48
W_3	0	-1	0	1	-1/2	-2
W_2	0	1/2	1	0	-1/4	2

Finally, the optimal solution has not been found as there is a negative element in the RHS column. Divide the top row elements of the above tableau by the second row; ignoring the division by zero (or using the zero as numerator), the minimum ratio is -8/-1 = 8; hence, W_3 is the outgoing variable and W_1 is the incoming variable. The final simplex tableau becomes

	Z	W_1	W_2	W_3	W_4	RHS
Z	1	0	0	-8	-2	64
W_1	0	1	0	-1	1/2	2
W_2	0	0	1	1/2	-1/2	1

As can be seen, the solution is optimal; it is the same solution as the one obtained by using the two-phase and the large cofficient methods.

Multiple Objective Functions

In some cases, a producer (firm) has more than one goal (objective) to achieve (Thompson 1971). Suppose the producer has two goals. The first goal is to maximize profit (P), and the second goal is to maximize total sale revenues (R). These two goals are formulated as follows:

$$\text{Maximize } P = 5X_1 + 4X_2 \tag{7}$$

and

$$\text{Maximize } R = 13X_1 + 6X_2 . \tag{8}$$

These two objectives are restricted by three resources as follows:

$$X_1 + 3X_2 \le 35$$

$$X_2 \le 10 \tag{9}$$

$$2X_1 \le 28.$$

The firm can achieve its goals by maximizing equation (7) subject to system 9. That is,

$$\text{Maximize } P = 5X_1 + 4X_2$$

Subject to

$$X_1 + 3X_2 \le 35$$

$$X_2 \le 10$$

$$2X_1 \le 28$$

$$X_1 \geq 0 \text{ and } X_2 \geq 0.$$

Using the simplex method, the solution of this program is $X_1 = 14$, $X_2 = 7$, and $P = 98$.

Also, the firm has to maximize its revenue; equation (8), subject to system 9. That is,

Maximize $R = 13X_1 + 6X_2$

Subject to

$$X_1 + 3X_2 \leq 35$$

$$X_2 \leq 10$$

$$2X_1 \leq 28$$

$$X_1 \geq 0 \text{ and } X_2 \geq 0.$$

The solution of this program is $X_1 = 14$, $X_2 = 7$, and $R = 224$.

Finally, the firm maximizes its revenue R subject to system 9 and to a profit minimum. Let us say that the acceptable minimum profit is assumed to be 90; hence, the mathematical linear program becomes

Maximize $R = 13X_1 + 6X_2$

Subject to

$$X_1 + 3X_2 \leq 35$$

$$X_2 \leq 10$$

$$2X_1 \leq 28$$

$$5X_1 + 4X_2 \geq 90$$

$$X_1 \geq 0 \text{ and } X_2 \geq 0.$$

The solution of this program is $X_1 = 14$, $X_2 = 7$, $X_3 = 3$, $X_4 = 8$, and $R = 224$. It should be noted that one can vary the profit minimum by a unit—from 90 to 91—to find the impact on the optimal solution. In this case, the solution will stay the same.

Problems

1.   Find the dual solution for the following problems:

(a) Maximize $Z = 4x_1 + 6x_2$ (b) Maximize $Z = 5x_1 + 12x_2$

Subject to   Subject to

$4x_1 + 8x_2 \le 80$ $3x_1 + 5x_2 \le 15$

$10x_1 + 2x_2 \le 50$ $3x_1 + x_2 \le 9$

$x_1 \ge 0$ and $x_2 \ge 0$. $2x_1 + 8x_2 \le 16$

$x_1 \ge 0, x_2 \ge 0$, and $x_3 \ge 0$.

(c) Maximize $Z = 2x_1 + 5x_2$

Subject to

$8x_1 + 4x_2 \le 40$

$6x_1 + 10x_2 \le 60$

$x_1 \ge 0$ and $x_2 \ge 0$.

2.   Find the dual solution for the following linear mathematical programs:

Maximize $Z = 2x_1 + 4x_2$

Subject to

$x_2 \le 5$

$2x_1 + x_2 \ge 10$

$x_1 + x_2 \le 7$

$x_1 \ge 0$ and $x_2 \ge 0$.

3.   Find the range of c_j and b_i for problem 1.

4.   Find the dual solution for

(a) $Z = 2x_1 + 4x_2$

Subject to

$6x_1 + 10x_2 \leq 60$

$2x_1 + x_2 \geq 10$

$2x_1 + 3x_2 = 18$

$x_1 \geq 0, x_2 \geq 0,$ and $x_3 \geq 0.$

Also, find the range of c_j and b_i.

(b) $Z = x_1 + x_2$

Subject to

$x_1 + 2x_2 \geq 10$

$2x_1 + x_2 \geq 10$

$x_1 \geq 0$ and $x_2 \geq 0.$

CHAPTER NINE

Decision Analysis

In the real world, economists, managers, and other individuals confront many problems that force them to make decisions. For example, an individual with $1000 must decide whether to invest this money in government bonds or in shares issued by IBM. Another individual may have to decide whether to go to graduate school or to find a job. Given these problems, a decision maker also wishes to know the conditions under which one must make a decision. Is the situation under condition of risk, uncertainty, certainty, or conflict? Knowing the type of condition is important, because there are criteria that decision makers use in these particular circumstances.

In this chapter we shall discuss various decision criteria under several conditions, except under condition of conflicts, which will be discussed in chapter 10: Game Theory. Before discussing these criteria, students should know the difference between a risky and an uncertain condition. A *risky condition* indicates that a decision maker is able to know the probability distribution of events prevailing under this condition. An *uncertain condition* reflects a situation in which the probability distribution and hence the probability of event(s) cannot be obtained. In other words, the decision maker just does not know.

Formulation of Decision Problems

To formulate a decision problem, three components must be specified. First, the decision maker should list all the alternative courses of action of which one decision or strategy (course of action) will be selected. For example, a producer may have to decide whether to come out with a new product, say a car, or to continue manufacturing a truck—the producer does not face any other decision. These two decisions emanating from a decision (a choice) node can be called D_1 and D_2, respectively; Figure 9.1 shows these decisions on a decision tree (Thompson 1976).

Figure 9.1. **The Decision Problem: A Car or a Truck**

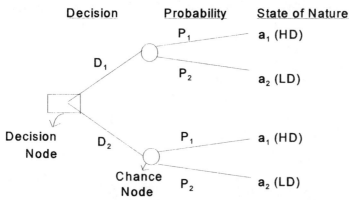

Second, the decision maker must have an exhaustive list of all future possible events associated with decisions D_1 and D_2. These possible events are mutually exclusive (one of them will occur) and are called the *states of nature*. For our example, the decision maker may be faced with only two possible events (states of nature) associated with D_1 and D_2; these states of nature may be the existence of high demand (a_1) or low demand (a_2). These possible events, whose probabilities of occurrence are (P_1) and (P_2), respectively, are graphed in Figure 9.1 after each chance node.

Third, a payoff table must be constructed. The decision maker must assign a monetary outcome to each combination of decision i and particular state of nature a_j. These monetary outcomes, which may be specified in terms of profit, losses, costs, and revenues, are called *payoffs*. As a matter of fact, the outcomes (payoffs) need not be in terms of money—they may be specified in terms of utility. For the decision problem, the payoff table is shown in Table 9.1.

Table 9.1. **Decisions, States of Nature, and Payoffs**

	High Demand	Low Demand
	(a_1)	(a_2)
D_1	300,000	-40,000
D_2	250,000	20,000
Probability	0.6	0.4

Using the decision tree, the complete decision problem is graphed in Figure 9.2.

Figure 9.2. **The Complete Decision Problem**

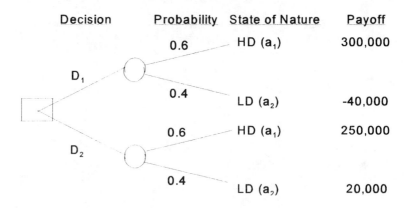

Figure 9.2 indicates that if decision D_1 is selected, there are two possible events (a_1) and (a_2) associated with this decision, whose payoffs are $300,000 (profit) and -$40,000 (loss or negative profit), respectively. If D_2 is selected, there are two possible states of nature (a_1) and (a_2) with two payoffs of $250,000 and $20,000, respectively. In addition, the prior probabilities of the two events are reported on the branches of the decision tree (Bierman et al. 1977; Anderson et al. 1978).

Decision Making Under Various Conditions

Decision makers face decision problems under various conditions; hence, they should understand how to select the best course of action given such circumstances. In decision science, several conditions in which a decision must be made are specified. These conditions are explained below.

First: Decision Making Under Certainty

In this situation the decision makers know with certainty (for sure) that a particular state of nature will occur. In other words, the decision makers know that the probability of a state of nature to take place is 1. Indeed, this suggests that the decision makers have perfect information. For our decision problem, let us assume that the producer knows for sure (with a probability of 1) that the state of high demand (a_1) will occur. Accordingly, the decision tree and the states of nature with their corresponding probabilities are shown in Figure 9.3.

Figure 9.3. **Decision Problem Under Certainty**

Decision	Probability	State of Nature	Payoff
		HD(a₁)	300,000
	300,000 1		
D₁	0	LD(a₂)	-40,000
300,000			
D₂	250,000 1	HD(a₁)	250,000
	0	LD(a₂)	20,000

This suggests that the expected monetary values (or the mean values) for the two decisions are

$$\text{EMV}(D_i) = P(a_j)\, PO(D_i, a_j), \quad i = 1 \text{ and } 2 \tag{1}$$

where D_i is decision i; $P(a_j)$ is the probability of state of nature j, (j = 1,2); and $PO(D_i, a_j)$ is the payoff associated with decision (strategy) i and state (possible event) j. For our example, we can obtain

$$\text{EMV}(D_1) = (300,000)(1) + (-40,000)(0) = 300,000, \quad \text{for } i = 1$$

$$\text{EMV}(D_2) = 250,000(1) + (20,000)(0) = 250,000, \quad \text{for } i = 2$$

and the best course of action is to select D_1 because EMV (D_1) is higher than EMV (D_2). (Note: These calculations are actually a movement from right to left on the decision tree of Figure 9.3. D_2 was cut because it was not selected.)

Second: Decision Making Under Uncertainty

In this situation the decision makers do not know the probabilities of the states of nature. For such a situation there are five criteria that can be used to help decision makers select the best course of action; these criteria are discussed below.

1. The Maximax Criterion. This criterion reflects optimism, because the decision maker selects the maximum payoff associated with the states of nature of each decision. After this selection, the decision maker will select the maximum out of these maximum payoffs, and this maximum will determine the best decision (course of action). For our example, the criterion works as shown in Table 9.2.

Table 9.2. **The Maximax Criterion**

	a_1	a_2	Maximum Payoff	Maximax
D_1	300,000	-40,000	300,000	300,000
D_2	250,000	20,000	250,000	

That is, the decision maker selects the maximum payoff of each row (300,000 and 250,000) and then selects the maximum of these maximum payoffs, 300,000 (Holloway 1979; Bunn 1984; Winkler and Hayes 1975). Hence, the best decision under uncertainty is D_1.

2. The Maximin Criterion. This criterion reflects pessimism. The decision maker in this situation selects the minimum payoff associated with the states of nature of each decision, and then selects the maximum out of these minimum payoffs. This maximum payoff will be used to select the best course of action (decision). For our decision problem, this criterion works as shown in Table 9.3.

Table 9.3. **The Maximin Criterion**

	a_1	a_2	Minimum Payoff	Maximin
D_1	300,000	-40,000	-40,000	
D_2	250,000	20,000	20,000	20,000

That is, the decision maker selects the minimum payoff of each row (-40,000 and 20,000), and then selects the maximum out of those minimum payoffs, 20,000. Thus, D_2 is the best course of action.

3. Realism Criterion. This criterion is actually a combination of the first two criteria. In other words, it is a compromise between optimism and pessimism. According to this criterion the decision maker selects a coefficient, say (a), where $(0 < a < 1)$, to reflect the degree of optimism. If $a = 0$, the decision maker is perfectly pessimist; if $a = 1$, the decision maker is perfectly optimist. Once the value of (a) is determined, $(1 - a)$ would measure the degree of pessimism.

Having determined (a), the decision maker first selects the minimum and maximum payoffs for the states of nature associated with the courses of action, D_i, and then must find the weighted value, $WV(D_i)$, for each decision from equation

(2) below:

WV (D_i) = (a) (maximum payoff) + (1- a)(minimum payoff), i = 1, ..., n   (2)

It follows that the decision maker will select the best course of action according to the highest value of WV(D_i). For our decision problem, if a = 0.7, the criterion works as shown in Table 9.4. The decision maker selects the maximum and minimum payoff for the states of nature associated with D_1. These values are 300,000 and -40,000, respectively. Using the same procedure, the maximum and minimum values are determined for D_2; and they are 250,000 and 20,000, respectively.

Table 9.4. **Maximum and Minimum Payoffs**

	a_1	a_2	Maximum Payoff	Minimum Payoff
D_1	300,000	-40,000	300,000	-40,000
D_2	250,000	20,000	250,000	20,000

Having determined these values and (a), one can use equation (2) to obtain

WV(D_1) = 0.7 (300,000) + 0.3 (-40,000) = 210,000 - 12,000 = 198,000

WV(D_2) = 0.7 (250,000) + 0.3 (20,000) = 175,000 + 6,000 = 181,000

Accordingly, the decision maker must select D_1.

4. Equally Likely Criterion. Because the probability of any possible future event is unknown, each state of nature (possible event) can be assigned the same probability of occurrence. In other words, each possible event is assumed to be equally likely to take place. After assigning equal probabilities, the expected monetary value of each act [EMV (D_i)] can be determined, and the best act (decision) can be selected according to the highest expected value; see equation (1).

For our decision problem, there are two states of nature, and hence each one has a probability of occurrence of (0.5). Figure 9.4 shows the payoffs and the probability of each state of nature.

Figure 9.4. **Payoffs and Probabilities**

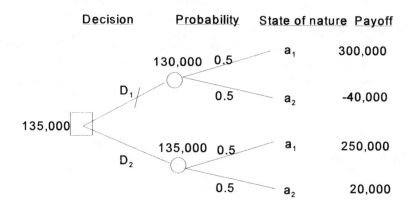

| Decision | Probability | State of nature | Payoff |

Using equation (1), the expected monetary value for each act is

$$EMV(D_1) = 300,000\ (0.5) + (-40,000)(0.5) = 13,000$$

$$EMV(D_2) = 250,000(0.5) + (20,000)(0.5) = 135,000.$$

Hence, D_2 must be selected because it has the highest expected monetary value.

5. The Minimax Criterion. This criterion is based upon the concept of opportunity cost, the cost of not taking the best course of action. To use this criterion, the payoff table must be constructed in terms of opportunity cost, which is calculated by

$$R(D_i, a_j) = BP(a_j) - PO(D_i, a_j) \qquad (3)$$

where $R(D_i, a_j)$ is the opportunity loss associated with the combination of decision D_i and state of nature a_j; $BP(a_j)$ is the best payoff associated with the state of nature a_j; and $PO(D_i, a_j)$ is the payoff associated with decision D_i and state of nature a_j. Given the opportunity cost, the maximum opportunity costs of the states of nature associated with decision D_i can be found, and the minimum of the maximum opportunity loss can be determined. This minimum will be used to select the best course of action (Chernoff and Moses 1959).

For our decision problem, the opportunity losses, calculated by equation (3), associated with state 1 and decisions D_1 and D_2 are

$$R(D_1, a_1) = 300,000 - 300,000 = 0$$

$$R(D_2, a_1) = 300,000 - 250,000 = 50,000$$

and the opportunity losses associated with state 2 and decisions D_1 and D_2 are

$$R(D_1, a_2) = 20,000 - (- 40,000) = 60,000$$

$$R(D_2, a_2) = 20,000 - 20,000 = 0.$$

Now, the maximum opportunity loss for each decision can be obtained as shown in Table 9.5. Given the maximum opportunity losses, the minimum cost is easily obtained.

Table 9.5. **The Minimax Criterion**

	a_1	a_2	Maximum Opportunity Loss	Minimum
D_1	0	60,000	60,000	
D_2	50,000	0	50,000	50,000

Hence, D_2 is selected because it has the minimum (loss) of the maximum opportunity losses.

Third: Decision Making Under Conflict

Under this condition two or more decision makers have objectives for which they are competing. Accordingly, they have to consider courses of action of their competitors. Decision making under conflict is best described by the game theory, which will be discussed in chapter 10.

Fourth: Decision Making Under Risk

Under this condition the decision maker can estimate the probabilities of various states of nature. Decisions under this condition are classified as decision making under prior (existing) information and decision making after obtaining additional information—Bayesian decisions (Thompson 1976; Schlaifer 1969; Sasaki 1969). These decisions are explained below.

1. Decision Making Under Prior Information

For our decision problem, the expected monetary value (EMV) is used to select the decision whether to produce a car or to continue producing a truck. The EMV of decision D_i is calculated by equation (1). For our example, the EMVs for decisions D_i, i = 1 and 2, given $P(a_1) = 0.6$ and $P(a_2) = 0.4$, are

$$EMV (D_1) = P(a_1) PO(D_1, a_1) + P(a_2)PO(D_1, a_2)$$

$$= (0.6)(300,000) + (0.4)(-40,000) = 164,000$$

and

$$EMV (D_2) = P(a_1)PO(D_2, a_1) + P(a_2)PO(D_2, a_2)$$

$$= (0.6)(250,000) + (0.4)(20,000) = 158,000.$$

Accordingly, the decision to produce a car is worthwhile because its EMV is higher than that of D_2. Figure 9.5 shows the EMV of each decision.

Figure 9.5. **EMVs for Decisions 1 and 2**

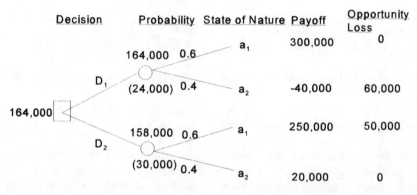

The second way to determine the best decision is to minimize the opportunity loss associated with not selecting the best strategy. This has been done by using the regret function formula (equation 3). Given these opportunity costs, the expected opportunity loss (EOL) for each decision can be found. For decision D_i, the EOL is

$$EOL(D_i) = P(a_j)R(D_i, a_j) \qquad (4)$$

and hence

$$EOL(D_1) = P(a_1)R(D_1, a_1) + P(a_2)R(D_1, a_2)$$

$$= (0.6)(0) + (0.4)(60,000) = 24,000$$

and for decision D_2,

$$EOL(D_2) = P(a_1)R(D_2, a_1) + P(a_2)R(D_2, a_2)$$

$$= (0.6)(50,000) + (0.4)(0) = 30,000.$$

The same calculation can be done by using the decision tree. The EOLs are reported in parentheses under each decision in Figure 9.5. Under this criterion, the best decision is associated with the minimum opportunity loss; it is D_1, a decision whose EMV is also the best.

The Expected Value of Perfect Information (EVPI)

It is called *perfect information* because it will change a decision situation from one of risk to one of certainty. The EVPI is calculated by using two methods. The first method is to use the regret function. That is,

$$EVPI = \quad P(a_j)R(D^*_i, a_j), \quad 1 = 1, ..., n \tag{5}$$

where $R(D^*_i, a_j)$ is the opportunity loss associated with the best decision D_i and the state of nature a_j. For our car-truck decision problem, the best decision is D_1. Thus, after applying equation (5), the EVPI (see Figure 9.5) is

$$EVPI = P(a_1)R(D^*_1, a_1) + P(a_2)R(D^*_1, a_2)$$

$$= (0.6)(0) + (0.4)(60,000) = 24,000,$$

which is equal to the minimum EOL. The EVPI indicates that a producer who obtains perfect information will reduce EOL by 24,000. It follows that our producer should not pay more than 24,000 for obtaining that information. In other words, the optimal expected cost of information is 24,000.

The second method for obtaining the EVPI is to subtract the expected monetary value without perfect information (which is the EMV of the best decision) from the expected monetary value with perfect information (EMVWPI). For our decision problem, we know the EMV of the best decision, (EMV_{ba}), which is 164,000; and the expected monetary value with perfect information (EMVWPI) can be calculated by

$$EMVWPI = \quad [Po_b(a_j)]P(a_j) \tag{6}$$

where $PO_b(a_j)$ is the best payoff associated with each state of nature a_j. Now, selecting the best payoff associated with each state of nature a_j, $j = 1$ and 2, equation (6) becomes

$$EMVWPI = PO_b(a_1)P(a_1) + PO_b(a_2)P(a_2)$$

$$= (300,000)(0.6) + (20,000)(0.4) = 188,000.$$

Since

$$EVPI = EMVWPI - EMV_{ba} \qquad (7)$$

therefore,

$$EVPI = 188,000 - 164,000 = 24,000$$

which is equal to EOL.

2. Decision Making After Obtaining Additional Information

The decision tree of Figure 9.5 reflects a decision making under prior information.The decision maker always tries to obtain additional information. Suppose that our producer obtains some conditional probabilities, which reflect new information, for new events associated with the states of nature (a_1) and (a_2). For example, let us assume that the new events (NE) are good market condition (G) given the states of high demand (a_1) and low demand (a_2), and bad market condition (B) given high demand (a_1) and low demand (a_2). These events have conditional probabilities shown in Table 9.6.

Table 9.6. **New Events and Conditional Probabilities**

NE	State of Nature	
	a_1	a_2
G	$P(G|a_1) = 0.7$	$P(G|a_2) = 0.5$
B	$P(B|a_1) = 0.3$	$P(B|a_2) = 0.5$

Table 9.6. can be interpreted as follows: 0.7 is the conditional probability of good market condition (G) given high demand (a_1); 0.3 is the conditional probability of bad market condition (B) given high demand (a_1); 0.5 is the conditional probability of good market condition (G) given low demand (a_2); and 0.5 is the conditional probability of bad market condition (B) given low demand (a_2).These conditional probabilities, along with the prior probabilities, are shown on the probability tree of Figure 9.6.

Figure 9.6. **Prior, Conditional, and Joint Probabilities**

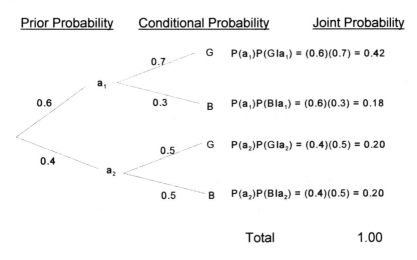

| Prior Probability | Conditional Probability | Joint Probability |

$P(a_1)P(G|a_1) = (0.6)(0.7) = 0.42$

$P(a_1)P(B|a_1) = (0.6)(0.3) = 0.18$

$P(a_2)P(G|a_2) = (0.4)(0.5) = 0.20$

$P(a_2)P(B|a_2) = (0.4)(0.5) = 0.20$

Total   1.00

If the probabilities on each branch of the tree are multiplied throughout, one can obtain the joint probabilities, which are shown on the right side of the probability tree of Figure 9.6–the multiplication rule–and reported in Table 9.7. And the sum of each row in this table gives the marginal (total) probabilities for the new events G and B (Thompson 1976).

Table 9.7.**Joint and Marginal Probabilities**

NE	States of Nature		Marginal Probability
	a_1	a_2	
G	0.42	0.20	0.62
B	0.18	0.20	0.38
		Total	1.00

Given the marginal probabilities of the new events G and B, one can find the Bayesian (posterior) probabilities for the following events. First, the probability of high demand given a good market condition $P(a_1|G)$ is

$$P(a_1|G) = P(a_1)P(G|a_1) / [P(a_1)P(G|a_1) + P(a_2)P(B|a_2)]$$

$$= 0.42 / [0.42 + 0.20] = 0.677.$$

Second, the probability of low demand given a good market condition is

$$P(a_2|G) = P(a_2)P(G|a_2) / [P(a_1)P(G|a_1) + P(a_2)P(B|a_2)]$$

$$= 0.20 / [0.42 + 0.20] = 0.323.$$

Third, the probability of high demand given a bad market condition is

$$P(a_1|B) = P(a_1)P(B|a_1) / [P(a_1)P(B|a_1) + P(a_2)P(B|a_2)]$$

$$= 0.18/[0.18 + 0.20] = 0.47.$$

Fourth, the probability of low demand given a bad market condition is

$$P(a_2|B) = P(a_2)P(B|a_2)/P(a_1)P(B|a_1) + P(a_2)P(B|a_2)]$$

$$= 0.20 / [0.18 + 0.20] = 0.53.$$

One should note that the posterior probabilities can be found by reversing the initial probability tree as well. The initial probability tree is shown in Figure 9.7.

Figure 9.7. **The Initial Probability Tree**

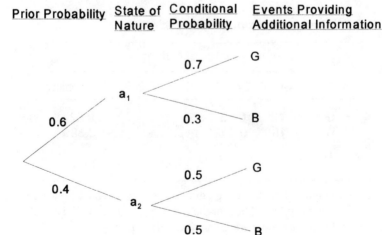

and the joint probability table is shown in Table 9.7. The Bayesian probabilities are shown in Figure 9.8 (the reverse probability tree).

Figure 9.8. **The Bayesian Probabilities (The Reverse Probability Tree)**

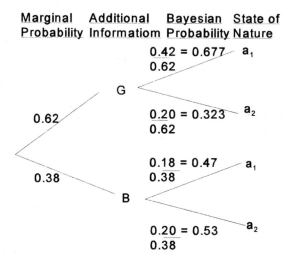

Marginal   Additional   Bayesian   State of
Probability Informatiom Probability Nature

0.42 = 0.677 a₁
0.62

G

0.62

0.20 = 0.323 a₂
0.62

0.18 = 0.47 a₁
0.38   0.38

B

0.38

0.20 = 0.53 a₂
0.38

Having found the posterior probabilities, the expected profits using additional and prior information are shown on the decision tree of Figure 9.9.

Figure 9.9. **Expected Profits Using Prior and Additional Information**

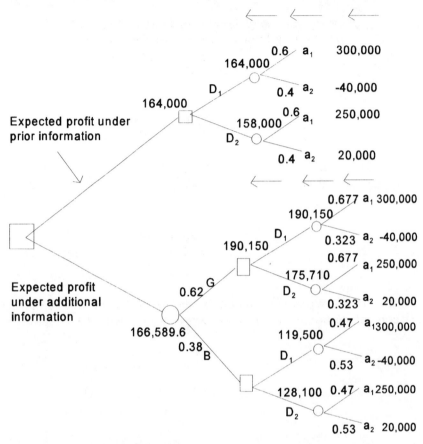

The expected profit using additional information is obtained through several steps. The first step is to find EMV (D_i) by multiplying the payoffs by the corresponding Bayesian probabilities. That is,

EMV(D_1) given G = (300,000)(0.677) + (-40,000)(0.323) = 190,180

EMV(D_2) given G = (250,000)(0.677) + (20,000)(0.323) = 175,710

EMV(D_1) given B = (300,000)(0.47) + (-40,000)(0.53) = 119,800

EMV(D_2) given B = (250,000)(0.47) + (20,000)(0.53) = 128,100.

Then the best expected monetary values [EMV(D₁)IG] and [EMV(D₂)IB] are multiplied by their marginal probabilities to obtain the expected profit using additional information (EVAI). That is,

$$EVAI = (190,180)(0.62) + (128,100)(0.38) = 166,589.60$$

From Figure 9.9, one can obtain the expected value of sample information EVSI by using

EVSI = expected profit using additional information (EVAI) - expected profit under prior information (EVPRI)

$$(8)$$

For our example,

$$EVSI = 166,589.60 - 164,000 = 2589.60,$$

which is equal to the expected value of additional information. This suggests that the firm can pay up to 2589.60 to obtain additional information. Also, one can find the expected value of perfect information EVPI, which is equal to expected profit using perfect information minus the expected profit using additional information (see equation [9]). The expected profit using perfect information (see equation [6]) is actually the best profit outcome of each state multiplied by the probability of that state. For our example, the EVPI is

$$EVPI = EMVWPI - EVAI \qquad (9)$$

$$EVPI = [(300,000)(0.6) + (20,000)(0.4)] - 166,589.60$$

$$= [180,000 + 8,000] - 166,589.6 = 21,410.40.$$

Example 1: A firm must decide whether to invest (D₁) or not (D₂). The decision maker believes that market may be good or poor with prior probabilities of 0.8 and 0.2, respectively. If the firm invests and the market is good, a profit of $2500 will be obtained. If the firm invests and the market is poor, the company will lose $5000. If the firm does not invest, it will be at a breakeven point—no profit—regardless of the market conditions.

The marketing analyst of the firm obtains a sample of three people from the good market (G) and poor market (P), and finds that the proportions of buying in good and poor markets are 0.9 and 0.10, respectively. From this information, the marketing analyst must calculate various conditional probabilities for the following events: P(ZIG), P(ZIP), P(OIG), P(OIP), P(TIG), P(TIP), P(HIG), and P(HIP), where Z is the event that no one buys; O is the event that one person out of three buys; T is the event that two out of three people buy; and H is the event that three out of three people buy. All these new events (NE) are expected to occur in both markets. Find the expected profit using prior and additional information.

Solution: The profits (payoffs) of the two decisions and two states of nature along with their corresponding probabilities are shown in Table 9.8.

Table 9.8. **Payoffs, Decisions, and Market Conditions**

	G	P
D_1	2500	-5000
D_2	0	0
Prior Probability	0.8	0.2

Consequently, the expected profit under prior information is

$$\text{EMV } (D_1) = 2500\ (0.8) + (-5000)(0.2) = \$1000$$

$$\text{EMV } (D_2) = 0(0.8) + (0)(0.2) = \$0.$$

Hence, the firm must invest; Figure 9.10 shows the decision tree for this problem.

Figure 9.10. **The Decision Tree for the Investment Problem**

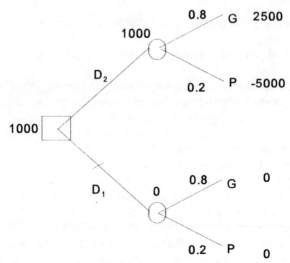

To find the expected monetary value using additional information, various conditional and Bayesian probabilities must be computed.The conditional probabilities are computed as follows: For the good market, we know the proportion of buying (B) is 0.9; hence, the proportion of no buying (N) is 1 - 0.9 = 0.10. The probability tree for the three sampled people is shown in Figure 9.11.

Figure 9.11. **The Probability Tree for Three Sampled Persons Given Good Market, G**

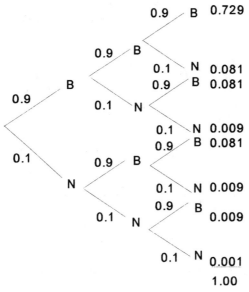

It follows that the conditional probabilities for the various events given a good market (G) are

$$P(ZIG) = P(NNN) = 0.001$$

$$P(OIG) = P(NBN) + P(NNB) + P(BNN) = 0.009 + 0.009 + 0.009 = 0.027$$

$$P(TIG) = P(BBN) + P(BNB) + P(NBB) = 0.081 + 0.081 + 0.081 = 0.243$$

$$P(HIG) = P(BBB) = 0.729.$$

For the poor market, the proportion of buying (B) is 0.10 and hence the proportion of no buying (N) is 1 - 0.10 = 0.90. The probability tree for the three sampled persons is shown in Figure 9.12.

Figure 9.12. **The Probability Tree for Three Sampled Persons Given Poor Market**

This suggests that the conditional probabilities for the various events given a poor market (P) are

$$P(ZIP) = P(NNN) = 0.729$$

$$P(OIP) = P(BNN) + P(NBN) + P(NNB) = 0.081 + 0.081 + 0.081 = 0.243$$

$$P(TIP) = P(BBN) + P(BNB) + P(NBB) = 0.009 + 0.009 + 0.009 = 0.027$$

$$P(HIP) = P(BBB) = 0.001.$$

Because we know the prior and conditional probabilities, we can find the joint probabilities as shown in Figure 9.13 and Table 9.9.

Figure 9.13. **The Initial Probability Tree (Prior, Conditional, and Marginal Probabilities)**

Table 9.9. **Joint and Marginal Probabilities**

NE	G	P	Marginal Probability
Z	0.0008	0.1458	0.1466
O	0.0216	0.0486	0.0702
T	0.1944	0.0054	0.1998
H	0.5832	0.0002	0.5834
		Total	1.0000

From Table 9.9 one can find the Bayesian, posterior, probabilities. This can be done by reversing the initial probability tree. Figure 9.14. shows the reverse probability tree and the posterior probabilities.

Figure 9.14. **The Reverse Probability Tree**

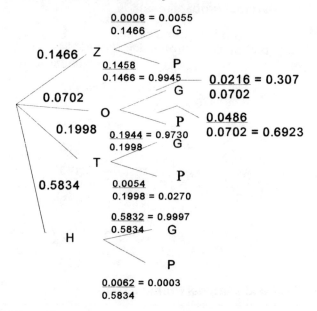

The posterior probabilities are

P(GIZ) = 0.0055   P(GIT) = 0.9730

P(PIZ) = 0.9945   P(PIT) = 0.0270

P(GIO) = 0.3077   P(GIH) = 0.9997

P(PIO) = 0.6923   P(PIH) = 0.0003.

Now we are ready to find the expected profits using additional information. The decision tree consists of three series of branches. The first branches reflect the new events (Z, O, T, and H) along with their marginal probabilities. From each branch of a new event, two branches emanate, each of which reflects the original decisions, D_1 and D_2. And from each decision two branches are shown to reflect the two states of nature, G and P. The decision tree is graphed in Figure 9.15.

Figure 9.15. **Expected Profit Using Additional Information**

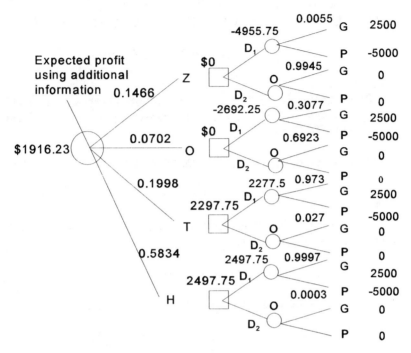

The expected profit is calculated by multiplying the payoffs by the posterior (Bayesian) probabilities as follows:

$$\text{EMV } (D_1) \text{ given } Z = 2500(0.0055) + (-5000)(0.9945) = -\$4958.75$$

$$\text{EMV } (D_2) \text{ given } Z = 0(0) + 0(0) = 0$$

and the best decision is D_2.

$$\text{EMV } (D_1) \text{ given } O = (2500)(0.3077) + (-5000)(0.6923) = -\$2692.25$$

$$\text{EMV } (D_2) \text{ given } O = (0)(0) + (0)(0) = \$0.0$$

and the best decision is D_2.

$$\text{EMV } (D_1) \text{ given } T = (2500)(0.9730) + (-5000)(0.0270) = \$2297.5$$

$$\text{EMV } (D_2) \text{ given } T = (0)(0) + (0)(0) = \$0.0$$

and the best decision is D_1.

$$EMV (D_1) \text{ given } H = (2500)(0.9997) + (-5500)(0.0003) = 2497.75$$

$$EMV (D_2) \text{ given } H = (0)(0) + (0)(0) = 0.00$$

and the best decision is D_1.

Now, the best EMVs given Z, O, T, and H are multiplied by their corresponding marginal probabilities in order to obtain the expected profit using additional information (EVAI). That is,

$$EVAI = (0)(0.1466) + (0)(0.0702) + (2297.5)(0.1998) + (2497.75)(0.5834)$$

$$= 1916.23.$$

Because we know EVAI and the expected value under prior information (EVPRI), EVSI (see equation [8]) is equal to

$$1916.23 - 1000 = 916.23.$$

In addition, the expected value of perfect information (EVPI) is

$$EVPI = [(2500)(0.8) + (0)(0.2)] - 1916.23 = 83.77.$$

Example 2: Zin oil company must decide whether to drill an oil field in Iraq. Zin's decision maker believes that the area may be dried up (y_1), may have 10,000 barrels of heavy oil (y_2), or may have 20,000 barrels of sweet oil (y_3) with probabilities of 0.05, 0.35, and 0.60, respectively. If the area has no oil, Zin will lose $30,000. If the 10,000 barrels are found they will be sold at $18 per barrel; if the 20,000 barrels are found they will be sold at $18 per barrel. In any case, the cost of drilling a barrel of oil is $5.00.

Zin can obtain information from its Department of Geology about the oil area. The department will be able to provide the company with information about whether there is no structure (x_1), open structure (x_2), or closed structure (x_3). Past experience has indicated the following conditional probabilities:

$$P(x_1|y_1) = 0.20 \quad P(x_1|y_2) = 0.10 \quad P(x_1|y_3) = 0.20$$

$$P(x_2|y_1) = 0.30 \quad P(x_2|y_2) = 0.30 \quad P(x_2|y_3) = 0.30$$

$$P(x_3|y_1) = 0.50 \quad P(x_3|y_2) = 0.60 \quad P(x_3|y_3) = 0.50.$$

Find the expected profits using prior and additional information.

Solution: The payoff table is constructed in Table 9.10.

Table 9.10. **Decisions, States of Nature, and Payoffs**

	y_1	y_2	y_3
D_1	-30,000	130,000	260,000
D_2	0	0	0
Prior Probability	0.05	0.35	0.60

The expected profit under prior information is

$$\text{EMV}(D_1) = -30,000(0.05) + 130,000(0.35) + 260,000(0.60) = \$159,050$$

$$\text{EMV}(D_2) = 0.$$

It follows that the best act is to drill, D_1.

To find the expected profit using additional information, the posterior probabilities must be found. To find these probabilities one must find the joint and marginal probabilities as well as the reverse probability tree. The joint probabilities, reported in Table 9.11, are obtained by using the multiplication rule as shown in Figure 9.16 (which also shows the initial probability tree).

Figure 9.16. **Conditional and Joint Probabilities (The Initial Probability Tree)**

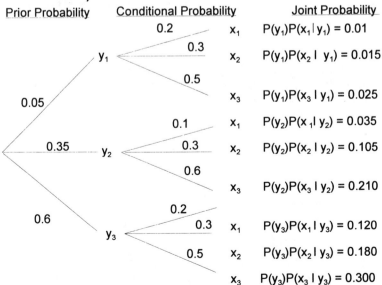

Prior Probability	Conditional Probability	Joint Probability

0.2 x_1 $P(y_1)P(x_1|y_1) = 0.01$

y_1 0.3 x_2 $P(y_1)P(x_2|y_1) = 0.015$

0.5 x_3 $P(y_1)P(x_3|y_1) = 0.025$

0.05

0.1 x_1 $P(y_2)P(x_1|y_2) = 0.035$

0.35 y_2 0.3 x_2 $P(y_2)P(x_2|y_2) = 0.105$

0.6 x_3 $P(y_2)P(x_3|y_2) = 0.210$

0.2 x_1 $P(y_3)P(x_1|y_3) = 0.120$

0.6 y_3 0.3 x_1

0.5 x_2 $P(y_3)P(x_2|y_3) = 0.180$

x_3 $P(y_3)P(x_3|y_3) = 0.300$

Table 9.11. **Joint and Marginal Probabilities**

	y_1	y_2	y_3	Marginal Probability
x_1	0.01	0.035	0.120	0.165
x_2	0.015	0.105	0.180	0.300
x_3	0.025	0.210	0.300	0.535
			Total	1.000

The Bayesian probabilities, obtained by dividing the elements of each row of the joint probability table by their corresponding marginal probability, and the reverse probability tree are shown in Figure 9.17.

Figure 9.17. **The Reverse Probability Tree**

Now we are ready to use the posterior (Bayesian) probabilities to find the expected profit using additional information by moving back through the branches of the decision tree of Figure 9.18.

Figure 9.18. **Expected Profit Using Additional Information**

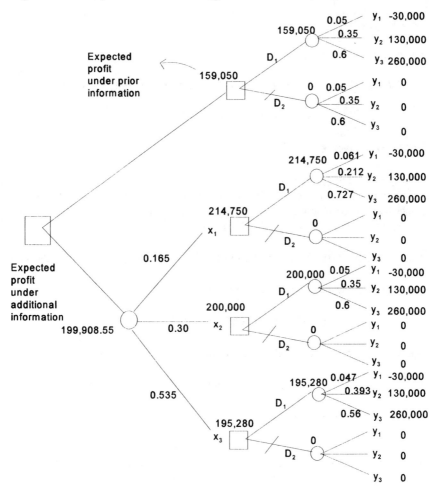

EMV (D_1) given $x_1 = (-30,000)(0.061) + (130,000)(0.212) + (260,000)(0.727)$

$$= \$214,750$$

EMV (D_2) given $x_1 = 0$

so the best act is D_1.

EMV (D_1) given $x_2 = (-30,000)(0.05) + (130,000)(0.35) + (260,000)(0.60)$

$$= 200,000$$

EMV (D_2) given $x_2 = 0$;

hence, the best act is D_1.

EMV (D_1) given $x_3 = (-300,00)(0.047) + (130,000)(0.393) + (260,000)(0.556)$

$$= 195,280$$

EMV (D_2) given $x_3 = 0$

consequently, the best act is D_1.

Having obtained these expected values, we multiply the best expected monetary values by their corresponding marginal probabilities to obtain the expected profit using additional information, EVAI. That is,

EVAI $= (214,750)(0.165) + (200,000)(0.30) + (195,280)(0.535) = 199,908.55$

The expected value of sample information is

EVSI $= 199,908.55 - 159,050 = 40,858.55$

and the expected value of perfect information is

EVPI $= [0 + 45,500 + 156,000] - 199,908.55 = 1591.45.$

Utility and Decision Making

Most individuals do not always select the best decision according to the criterion of maximum expected monetary value (EMV). Von Neumann and Morgenstern provided an alternative criterion for decision selection (Thompson 1976; Bierman et al. 1977). They argued that decisions were made according to the criterion of maximum expected utility. In other words, if there are two decisions D_1 and D_2 and a decision maker prefers D_1 to D_2, this suggests that the expected utility of D_1 is higher than that of D_2.

Various assumptions about the utility theory have to be explained. The first assumption is that with any two acts D_1 and D_2 the decision maker can decide whether he or she is indifferent to them or prefers one over the other. The second assumption is that if D_1 is preferred to D_2, and D_2 is preferred to D_3, then D_1 is preferred to D_3. Also, if D_1 equals D_2 and D_2 equals D_3, then D_1 equals D_3—the transitivity assumption. The third assumption is that if an individual is indifferent to two decisions, the utility values of the two decisions are equal. The fourth assumption suggests that if two decisions have the same two possible outcomes whose probabilities are not the same, the decision whose possible outcomes have the higher probability is the preferred decision. The fifth assumption suggests that if there are two decisions D_1 and D_2, and D_1 has two possible outcomes A_1 and A_3, but D_2 has a certain (for sure) outcome, say A_2, provided that A_1 is preferred to A_2 and A_2 is preferred to A_3, then one can write the following:

$$A_2 = A_1(P) + A_3(1 - p); \tag{10}$$

For example, if $A_1 = 2000$ with a probability of P, $A_2 = 900$, and $A_3 = 0$ with a probability of $(1 - P)$, the question becomes: What is the value of P that will make the decision maker indifferent to the two acts? If there is such a probability, then A_2 is called *certainty equivalent*. The probability (P) can be determined by asking whether the individual is indifferent between D_1 and D_2 at that probability.

The sixth assumption is that if A_1 is preferred to A_2, and there is another alternative A_3, then any combination of A_1 plus A_3 (given that the probability of A_3 is less than one) is preferred to a combination of A_2 plus A_3. That is,

$$A_1(P) + A_3(1 - P) \text{ is preferred to } A_2(P) + A_3(1 - P).$$

For example, if $A_1 = 2000$, $A_2 = 800$, and $A_3 = 400$, assuming $P = 0.6$, then

$$2000(0.6) + 400(0.4) \text{ is preferred to } 800(0.6) + 400(0.4).$$

The last assumption is that the utility of a decision is defined to be equal to the expected utility of its components. That is, the expected utility of D_1, $U(D_1)$, assuming D_1 has two possible outcomes A_1 (with probability P_1) and A_2 (with probability P_2), is equal to

$$(D_1) = P_1U(A_1) + P_2U(A_2) \tag{11}$$

where $U(A_1)$ and $U(A_2)$ are the utilities of the outcomes A_1 and A_2, respectively. Also, if D_1 has a probability of r and D_2 has a probability of $(1 - r)$, the expected utility of the two decisions, $U(D)$, is equal to

$$U(D) = rU(D_1) + (1 - r)U(D_2) \tag{12}$$

where $U(D_i)$ is calculated from equation (11).

Derivation of the Utility Function

To derive the utility of money associated with decisions (Thompson 1976), the following steps must be used, assuming there are two decisions and two possible outcomes whose payoffs are shown in Table 9.12.

Table 9.12. **Decisions With Two Possible Outcomes**

	A_1	A_2
D_1	450,000	-40,000
D_2	250,000	20,000

Step 1: Arrange the payoffs from the lowest to the highest value, and assign a utility of one to the highest payoff and a utility of zero to the lowest payoff. The payoff values along with their utilities are shown in Table 9.13.

Table 9.13. **Payoffs and Utilities**

Payoff	Utility
-40,000	0
20,000	0.25
100,000	0.50
250,000	0.75
450,000	1.00

(Note: The 100,000 is introduced arbitrarily.)

Step 2: Create a decision problem of two acts D_1 and D_2. The first act is a risky one with two possible outcomes (-40,000) and (450,000)--their utilities are known-- each of which has a probability of 0.5. The second act is a certain act D_2 in that the individual will receive for sure a sum of money of 10,000 (set arbitrarily). This decision problem is shown in Figure 9.19.

Figure 9.19. **Creation of a Decision Problem**

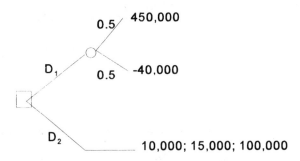

450,000

-40,000

10,000; 15,000; 100,000

Now, ask whether the person is indifferent between D_1 and D_2. If the person prefers D_1 to D_2, increase the certain payoff of D_2 from 10,000 to, say, 15,000 and ask the individual whether he or she is indifferent between D_1 and D_2. If the person still prefers D1 to D2, increase the payoff from 15,000 to, say, 100,000 and ask whether he or she is indifferent. If the person is now indifferent between D_1 and D_2, the utility of D_1 must equal to the expected utility of D_2. That is,

$$U(100,000) = 0.5U(-40,000) + 0.5U(450,000). \qquad (11^*)$$

As we know the utilities of the -40,000 and 450,000 to be equal to zero and one respectively, equation (11*) becomes

$$U(100,000) = 0.5\,(0) + 0.5\,(1) = 0.5$$

and we can put this utility in Table 9.13.
Step 3: Once again, create two acts D_1 (risky) and D_2 (certain). D_1 has two possible outcomes, -40,000 and 100,000, each of which has a probability of 0.5. Let D_2 generate 10,000 for sure to our individual. Figure 9.20 shows the decision problem.

Figure 9.20. **Creation of a Decison Problem**

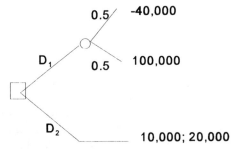

-40,000

100,000

10,000; 20,000

Now, ask whether the individual is indifferent between D_1 and D_2. If the person prefers D_1 over D_2 increase the certain payoff from 10,000 to 20,000 and ask again. If the person is now indifferent, the utility of 20,000 becomes

$$U(20,000) = 0.5U(-40,000) + 0.5U(100,000)$$

$$= 0.5(0) + 0.5(0.5) = 0.25$$

and we can put this utility in Table 9.13.

By using the same procedure, the utility of 250,000 is found to be 0.75. That is

$$U(250,000) = 0.5U(100,000) + 0.5U(450,000)$$

$$= 0.5 (0.5) + 0.5 (1) = 0.75.$$

As we know the utilities of all possible outcomes (money), we can find the marginal utility of each outcome—the marginal utility of money. Both the total and marginal utility curves are shown in Figure 9.21.

Figure 9.21. **Total and Marginal Utilities**

One should note that the marginal utility is diminishing, a result consistent with the utility theory. Also, from the total utility curve one can find the utility of any payoff within the range of -40,000 and 450,000 by locating the payoff on the horizontal line and going up until the utility curve is reached. The height of the utility will determine the utility of that payoff.

Example 1: Suppose our individual has a decision problem constructed as follows:

	A_1	A_2
D_1	300,000	-40,000
D_2	250,000	40,000
Probability	0.6	0.4

Select the best decision.

Solution: The utility values are obtained from Figure 9.21. If the decision maker uses the criterion of the expected monetary value (EMV), D_1 must be selected because its EMV is 164,000 (see Figure 9.22). However, if the decision maker uses the criterion of the expected utility (EU), D_2 must be selected because its expected utility is 0.55 [(0.75)(0.6) + (0.25)(0.4)] (see Figure 9.22).

Figure 9.22. **Expected Utility**

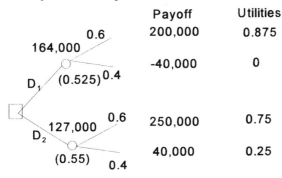

Payoff	Utilities
200,000	0.875
-40,000	0
250,000	0.75
40,000	0.25

Example 2: Suppose a decision problem is constructed as follows:

	A_1	A_2
D_1	0	500
D_2	100	300
Probability	0.4	0.6

Select the best decision by using the EMV and EU.

Solution: Arrange the payoff form the lowest to the highest payoff, and assign a zero utility to the former and a utility value of one to the latter. This arrangement is shown in Table 9.14.

Table 9.14. **Money and Utility**

Money	Utility
0	0.00
100	0.40
200	0.76
300	0.90
400	0.96
500	1.00

To derive other utility values, create a decision problem of two acts, D_1 and D_2. D_1 is a risky act with two possible outcomes, 0 and 500, whose probabilities are assumed to be 0.4 and 0.6 (other probabilities can be chosen as well). The second act is a certain one whose payoff is assumed to be 50. Figure 9.23 shows this decision problem.

Figure 9.23. **Creation of a Decision Problem**

Having done so, ask whether the individual prefers D_1 to D_2. If the person prefers D_1 to D_2, increase the certain payoff from 50 to 100, and ask whether he or she still prefers D_1 to D_2. If the person is now indifferent, the expected utility of 100 is

$$U(100) = 0.4U(0) + 0.6U(500)$$

$$= 0.4(0) + 0.6(1) = 0.4.$$

To derive the utility value for the 200, create a decision problem of two acts D_1 and D_2. D_1 is a risky act whose payoffs are 100 and 500 with probabilities of 0.4 and 0.6, respectively. The second act, D_2, is a certain one whose payoff is 150. This problem is shown in Figure 9.24.

Figure 9.24. **Creation of a Decision Problem**

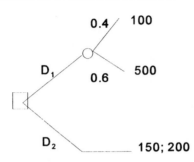

Now, ask whether the individual is indifferent between D_1 and D_2. If the person is not indifferent, increase the payoff of the certain act to 200 and ask whether the individual is indifferent between D_1 and D_2. If the answer is yes, the utility of 200 is

$$U(200) = 0.4U(100) + 0.6U(500)$$

$$= 0.4(0.4) + 0.6(1) = 0.76.$$

Using the same procedure, one can find the utility of 300, which is

$$U(300) = 0.4U(200) + 0.6U(500)$$

$$= 0.4(0.76) + 0.6(1) = 0.90$$

and the utility of 400 is

$$U(400) = 0.4U(300) + 0.6U(500)$$

$$= 0.4(0.90) + 0.6(1) = 0.96.$$

The graph of the total utility is shown in Figure 9.25.

Figure 9.25. **The Utility Function**

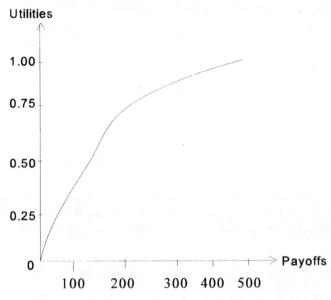

From this graph, one can obtain the utility values of the dollar amount within the range of 0 to 500. To select the best decision, a decision tree is shown in Figure 9.26.

Figure 9.26. **Expected Utility and the Best Decision**

	Payoff	Utilities
	0	0
	500	1
	100	0.4
	300	0.9

According to the EMV, we have

$$\text{EMV}(D_1) = 0(0.4) + 500(0.6) = 300$$

$$EMV(D_2) = 0.4(100) + 0.6(300) = 220.$$

Thus, the best decision is D_1.

If the decision maker uses the EU criterion, the best decision is selected by using

$$EU(D_1) = 0(0.4) + 1(0.6) = 0.60$$

$$EU(D_2) = 0.4(0.4) + 0.9(0.6) = 0.70.$$

Hence, D_2 is the best act.

Problems

1.   Given the following two decisions along with their payoffs:

	A_1	A_2
D_1	25	-5
D_2	20	4
Probability	0.7	0.3

Graph the decision tree and determine the best decision according to the expected value criterion. Also, select the best decision according to the criteria of maximax, maximin, and minimax. Can you pick the best decision under certainty?

2.   A student faces two decisions. The first is to go to college to earn a master's degree in economics (E), and the second decision is to study for a master's degree in Management Information System (MIS). The two decisions, payoffs, and their probabilities are

	Good Economy (A_1)	Bad Economy (A_2)
E	80,000	55,000
MIS	90,000	40,000
Probability	0.8	0.2

Also, some other information is obtained to help the student make a decision. The conditional probability a goverment tax cut given that the economy is good is 0.3, and the conditional probability of increased government spending given that the economy is bad is 0.1. Determine the best decision under prior information and after obtaining additional information. What is the value of the additional information?

3.   A producer faces two decisions: to invest and not to invest in producing more computers. If the producer invests and there is an expansionary economic condition, the producer will make profits of $15 million with a probability of 0.80; otherwise, the producer will lose $2 million with a probability of 0.2 if there is a recessionary economic condition. If the producer decides not to invest and there is a recessionary economic condition, the producer will make $1 million with a probability of 0.2. If the producer decides not to invest and there is an expansionary economic condition, there will be a loss of $3 million with a probability of 0.8. If we know that the conditional probability of having high demand given an expansionary economic condition is 0.6, and the conditional probability of having low demand given a recessionary economic condition is 0.7, determine the best decision under prior and additional information. Also, find the value of the additional information.

4.   Consider the following two decisions and payoffs:

	A_1	A_2
D_1	380,000	-30,000
D_2	210,000	350,000
Probability	0.8	0.2

Use the utility function of Table 9.13 to derive utilities associated with the given payoffs. Find the best decision according to the criterion of expected utility.

5.   Use the payoffs of problem 3 to derive the utility function. Find the best decision under the criterion of expected utility.

6.   Consider the following three decisions along with their payoffs:

	A_1	A_2	A_3
D_1	380,000	-30,000	50,000
D_2	210,000	350,000	25,000
D_3	160,000	50,000	-40,000
Probability	0.50	0.30	0.20

Use the utility function of Table 9.13 to derive utilities associated with the given payoffs. Find the best decision according to the criteria of expected value and expected utility. If you obtain the following conditional probabilities, $P(S_1IA_1) = 0.20$, $P(S_2IA_1) = 0.70$, $P(S_1IA_2) = 0.50$, $P(S_3IA_2) = 0.30$, $P(S_2IA_3) = 0.60$, and $P(S_3IA_3) = 0.20$, find the best decision under prior information and after obtaining additional information.

CHAPTER TEN

Game Theory

Games are classified into *finite* and *infinite* games. A game is said to be *finite* if either player has a finite number of strategies. If either player has an infinite number of strategies, the game is called an *infinite game*. In this chapter finite games will be discussed. A game is called a *zero-sum game* if player I gains what player II loses. That is, the total sum of the gain and loss is zero; if the total sum is not equal to zero, the game is called a *nonzero-sum game*.

In this chapter various methods for solving zero-sum games will be explained. Some of these games are solved by the dominance and minimax methods, and other games are solved by matrix methods and the simplex method. Similarly, nonzero sum games are discussed in this chapter, and some methods of solution are also furnished.

Concepts and Problem Formulation

The main objective of game theory is to provide a recommendation for a decision maker to select the optimal strategy in situations of conflict. Before providing the basic concepts that will be used in this chapter, let us show how a game model is formulated. Suppose there are two firms (or players) called *firm I* and *firm II* producing a similar product. Firm (player) I wants to capture 60 percent of the market share. Firm (player) I has two strategies, A and B. Firm II also has two strategies, A and B. The game is a zero-sum game whose payoff matrix is as follows:

		Firm II	
		A	B
Firm I	A	2	-3
	B	-2	5

This game can be interpreted in this way. If firm (player) I plays strategy A, firm II can play either strategy A or B. If firm II plays strategy A, firm I will gain \$2 million; if firm II plays strategy B, firm I will lose $3 million (or firm II will gain $3 million). Accordingly, if firm I plays strategy A, firm II must play strategy B—firm I will lose $3 million. In addition, if firm I plays strategy B, firm II will play either strategy A or B (but B is the best). If firm II plays strategy A, it will gain $2 million (or firm I will lose $2 million) should firm I play strategy B. If firm II plays strategy B, firm I will gain $5 million (or firm II will lose $5 million) if it plays strategy B.The question is how do firm I and firm II select their optimal strategies? The answer to these questions is provided by game theory.

If the previous game is not a zero-sum game, the payoff matrix may take the following form (Zagare 1984):

		Firm II	
		A	B
Firm I	A	(2,3)	(4,-3)
	B	(-2,4)	(6,7)

The payoff matrix can be interpreted as follows: If firm I plays strategy A, firm II can play either strategy A or B. If firm II plays strategy A, firm I will gain 2 and firm II will gain 3; if firm II plays strategy B, firm I will gain 4 and firm II will lose 3. If firm I plays strategy B, firm II can play either strategy A or B. If firm II plays strategy A, firm I will lose 2 and firm II will gain 4; if firm II plays strategy B, firm I will gain 6 and firm II will gain 7. This interpretation suggests that the first element in each cell reflects gain (or loss) to the row player, and the second element of that cell reflects gain (or loss) to the column player. At any rate, the basic task is to find the optimal strategies played by the two firms (or players), a task accomplished by game theory.

Solving Zero-Sum Games

There are several methods for solving a zero-sum game (Luce and Raiffa 1957). These methods will be used for solving several game models.

Dominance

In this situation some strategies are said to dominate others; the dominated strategies must be eliminated. Strategy A is said to dominate strategy B if each element of strategy A is equal to or greater than each element of strategy B. From Player II's viewpoint, strategy A is said to dominate strategy B if each element of strategy A is equal to or less than each element of strategy B. By convention the row player is the one who wins if the payoff is positive; the column player is the one who loses if the payoff is positive. In contrast, the row player is the one who loses if the payoff is negative; the column player is the one who gains if the payoff is negative.

Example 1: Suppose the following payoff is given:

Firm II

		A	B
	A	4	5
Firm I			
	B	2	3

Find the optimal strategy played by both players.

Solution: After a careful check of the payoff matrix, one can find that each element of strategy A, taken from firm I's viewpoint, dominates the corresponding elements of strategy B. Hence, there is no rationale for firm I to play strategy B; this suggests that strategy A dominates strategy B, or strategy B is dominated by strategy A. With respect to firm II, it seems rational that firm II should not play strategy B at all. This is because if firm II plays strategy B, firm I will gain 5 if it plays strategy A and gain 3 if it plays strategy B. This suggests that firm II should play strategy A only in order to minimize its loss. In other words, strategy B is dominated by strategy A.

In sum, if the dominated strategy is eliminated, the equilibrium value of the game is 4. Therefore, both firms should use strategy A, which suggests that firm I will gain 4 and firm II will lose 4. And the sum of the gain and loss is zero.

Example 2: Suppose the following payoff matrix exists:

Firm II

		A	B	C
	A	100	80	90
Firm I	B	120	81	95
	C	120	70	93

Find the optimal strategies for firms I and II.

Solution: For firm I, strategies A and C are dominated by strategy B, suggesting that firm I will never use strategies A and C. Hence, strategies A and C are eliminated. For firm II, strategies A and C are dominated by strategy B, suggesting that firm II will not utilize these strategies—these strategies are eliminated. Recall that if firm II plays strategy A or C it will lose $120 or $95 to firm I. In contrast, if firm II plays strategy B, it will lose $81 to firm I. It follows that firm I will use strategy B and gain $81, and firm II will employ the same strategy and lose $81.

Minimax and Maximin

Suppose there are two firms whose payoff matrix is as follows:

Firm II

		B_1	B_2	B_3 ...	B_n	
	A_1	a_{11}	a_{12}	a_{13} ...	a_{1n}	min $a_{1j} = g_1$
Firm I	A_2	a_{21}	a_{22}	a_{23} ...	a_{2n}	min $a_{2j} = g_2$
	A_1	a_{31}	a_{32}	a_{33} ...	a_{3n}	min $a_{3j} = g_3$ max min a_{ij}
	A_m	a_{m1}	a_{m2}	a_{m3} ...	a_{mn}	min $a_{mj} = g_m$

max a_{i1} =   max a_{i2} =   max a_{i3} = ...max a_{in}

| l_j | l_1 | l_2 | l_3 ... | l_n |

min max a_{ij}

If firm I plays A_1, firm II can respond by playing strategies B_1, B_2, B_3, and B_n for which firm I's gain is minimal--the smallest of a_{ij} in the *ith* row over column j, j = 1, 2, 3, ..., n. Let this smallest gain be g_i (i = 1,2,3,..., m) where

$$g_i = \min a_{ij} \qquad j = 1,2,3,..., n, \qquad (1)$$

which are shown in the last column of the above payoff matrix (Von Neumann and Morgenstern 1944; Shubik 1987).This suggests that firm I will not gain more than g_i. Hence, firm I must decide on strategy A_i for which g_i is maximal—select the maximum of g_i. If this maximal value is g, then

$$g = \max g_i \qquad (2)$$

and using equation (1) in equation (2) yields

$$g = \max \min a_{ij} \qquad (3)$$

where g is called the *maximin*.

Firm II is interested in minimizing firm I's gain. Thus, it must select a value, call it l, such that

$$l_j = \max a_{ij}, \qquad i = 1, 2, 3, ..., m \qquad (4)$$

and the minimum value of l_j, say it is l, must be found. That is,

$$l = \min l_j \qquad (5)$$

which, after using equation (4) in equation (5), yields

$$l = \min \max a_{ij} \tag{6}$$

where l is called the *minimax*.

One should note that if $l = g$, or equation (6) is equal to equation (3), the equilibrium value of the game is found, or the game is said to have a saddle point. Once this value is found, the optimal pure strategies for the two firms are determined. However, not all game problems have this saddle point. If the saddle point does not exist, games do not have pure strategy (i.e., the games have mixed strategies).

Example 3: Solve the game introduced in example 2 by the minimax method.

		Firm II			
		A	B	C	
	A	100	80	90	80
Firm I	B	120	81	95	81
	C	120	70	93	70
		120	81	95	

Solution: Find the minimum of each row and write it on the right-hand side of the above payoff matrix. Then find the maximum value of these minimums (the maximin), which is 81. Find the maximum value of each column of the payoff matrix and write it at the bottom of the payoff matrix as shown above. Then find the minimum value of these maximums (minimax), which is 81. As can be seen, the minimax is equal to the maximin at an equilibrium value of 81. Hence, the value of the game is 81, suggesting that firm I will gain 81 and firm II will lose 81. Also, the saddle point of 81 suggests that the best strategy for firm I is to play strategy B, and the best strategy for firm II is to use strategy B.

Example 4: For the following payoff matrix, find the optimal strategies for players I and II.

		Player II				
		A	B	C	D	
	A	10	-7	-3	9	-7
Player I	B	-2	-5	7	11	-5
	C	13	-12	7	-34	-34
	D	-34	-5	5	7	-34
		10	-5	7	11	

Solution: According to the minimax criterion, the optimal strategy that must be used by the two players is strategy B. This strategy is obtained at the point where the maximin (-5) is equal to the minimax (-5); this (-5) is the saddle point. Strategy B makes player I lose $5 and makes player II gain $5.

Example 5: For the following payoff matrix, find the optimal strategy that must be used by firms I and II.

		Firm II		
		A	B	
Firm I	A	3	12	3
	B	6	-6	-6
		6	12	

Solution: According to the criterion of maximin, the above payoff matrix has no saddle point--there is no equilibrium value. This is because the maximum of the minimum values is 3, whereas the minimum of the maximum values is 6. This game can be solved by other methods, which will be discussed below. That is, this model does not have a pure strategy, but it does have a mixed strategy.

The Algebraic Solution

Suppose there is a game whose payoff matrix is as follows:

		Player II	
		A	B
Player I	A	a_{11}	a_{12}
	B	a_{21}	a_{22}

Also, let us assume that this game has no saddle point and hence the players cannot find a pure strategy. In this situation, the game is called a *mixed strategy game* that can be solved as follows: For player I, the expected gain (EG), given that player II plays strategy A, is

$$p_1 a_{11} + p_2 a_{21} = EG, \qquad (7)$$

where p_1 and p_2 are the probabilities of playing strategies A and B, respectively. If player II plays strategy B, the expected gain for player I is

$$p_1 a_{12} + p_2 a_{22} = EG. \qquad (8)$$

After equating the two equations, one can obtain

$$p_1 a_{11} + p_2 a_{21} = p_1 a_{12} + p_2 a_{22} \qquad (9)$$

but $p_2 = 1 - p_1$; therefore, equation (9) becomes

$$p_1 a_{11} + (1 - p_1)a_{21} = p_1 a_{12} + (1 - p_1)a_{22}$$

and one can solve for p_1, that is,

$$p_1 = [-a_{21} + a_{22}] / [a_{11} - a_{21} - a_{12} + a_{22}]. \qquad (10)$$

Once p_1 is found, p_2 can be obtained as follows:

$$p_2 = 1 - p_1 = [a_{11} - a_{12}] / [a_{11} - a_{21} - a_{12} + a_{22}]. \qquad (11)$$

Given p_1 and p_2, one can find the EG for player I.

Similarly, for player II the expected loss (EL) (negative expected gain) can be found as follows. If player I plays strategy A, player II's expected loss is

$$EL = q_1 a_{11} + q_2 a_{12} \qquad (12)$$

where q_1 and q_2 are the probabilities of using strategies A and B, respectively. If player I plays strategy B, player II's EL is

$$EL = q_1 a_{21} + q_2 a_{22}. \qquad (13)$$

Equating the expected loss and solving for q_1 and q_2 yields

$$q_1 = [-a_{12} + a_{22}] / [a_{11} - a_{12} - a_{21} + a_{22}] \qquad (14)$$

$$q_2 = [a_{11} - a_{21}] / [a_{11} - a_{12} - a_{21} + a_{22}]. \qquad (15)$$

Example 6: For the payoff matrix of example 5, find the optimal mixed strategies for players I and II.

		Firm II	
		A	B
Firm I	A	3	12
	B	6	-6

Solution: For firm I, the expected gain is

$$3p_1 + 6p_2 = EG$$

$$12p_1 + (-6)p_2 = EG.$$

Equating the two equations yields

$$3p_1 + 6p_2 = 12p_1 - 6p_2$$

$$-9p_1 = -12p_2$$

$$= -12(1 - p_1)$$

$$= -12 + 12p_1$$

$$-12p_1 = -12$$

$$p_1 = 12/21 = 4/7.$$

This suggests that player I will play strategy A with a probability of 4/7. Also, p_2 = 1 - 4/7 = 3/7, suggesting that the player will use strategy B with a probability of 3/7. (Equations [10] and [11] can be used to find p_1 and p_2. Equation [10] gives p_1 = 4/7 and equation [11] gives p_2 = 3/7.)

For player II, the expected loss (EL) is

$$EL = 3q_1 + 12q_2$$

$$EL = 6q_1 - 6q_2.$$

Equating these two equations yields

$$3q_1 + 12(1 - q_1) = 6q_1 - 6(1 - q_1)$$

$$3q_1 + 12 - 12q_1 = 6q_1 - 6 + 6q_1$$

$$3q_1 - 12q_1 - 6q_1 - 6q_1 = -6 - 12 - 21q_1 = -18$$

$$q_1 = 18/21 = 6/7,$$

which suggests that player II should play strategy A with a probability of 6/7. Also, q_2 = 1/7, suggesting that player II plays strategy B with a probability of 1/7 (q_1 and q_2 can be found by using equations [14] and [15]).

Therefore, the expected gain and expected loss to players I and II are

$$EG = 3(4/7) + 6(3/7) = 12/7 + 18/7 = 30/7$$

$$EL = 6(6/7) - 6(1/7) = 36/7 - 6/7 = 30/7.$$

Example 7: Solve the game presented in example 6 by using the matrix method.
Solution: The game has the following payoff matrix:

		Firm II	
		A	B
Firm I	A	3	12
	B	6	-6

For firm I, the EG is

$$3p_1 + 6p_2 = EG$$

$$12p_1 - 6p_2 = EG$$

but

$$p_1 + p_2 = 1$$

Accordingly, there are three simultaneous equations, which can be rewritten as

$$3p_1 + 6p_2 - EG = 0$$

$$12p_1 - 6p_2 - EG = 0$$

$$p_1 + p_2 + 0EG = 1$$

and this system can be solved for the three unknowns, p_1, p_2, and EG.
Using Cramer's rule, the solution is

$$p_1 = \frac{\begin{vmatrix} 0 & 6 & -1 \\ 0 & -6 & -1 \\ 1 & 1 & 0 \end{vmatrix}}{\begin{vmatrix} 3 & 6 & -1 \\ 12 & -6 & -1 \\ 1 & 1 & 0 \end{vmatrix}} = 4/7, \quad p_2 = \frac{\begin{vmatrix} 3 & 0 & -1 \\ 12 & 0 & -1 \\ 1 & 1 & 0 \end{vmatrix}}{\begin{vmatrix} 3 & 6 & -1 \\ 12 & -6 & -1 \\ 1 & 1 & 0 \end{vmatrix}} = 3/7, \quad EG = \frac{\begin{vmatrix} 3 & 6 & 0 \\ 12 & -6 & 0 \\ 1 & 1 & 1 \end{vmatrix}}{\begin{vmatrix} 3 & 6 & -1 \\ 12 & -6 & -1 \\ 1 & 1 & 0 \end{vmatrix}} = 30/7.$$

For firm II, the above system becomes

$$3q_1 + 12q_2 = EL$$

$$6q_1 - 6q_2 = EL$$

$$q_1 + q_2 = 1$$

This system can be rewritten as

$$3q_1 + 12q_2 - EL = 0$$

$$6q_1 - 6q_2 - EL = 0$$

$$q_1 + q_2 + 0EL = 1$$

Solving the system by Cramer's rule, one can obtain

$$\begin{vmatrix} 3 & 12 & -1 \\ 6 & -6 & -1 \\ 1 & 1 & 0 \end{vmatrix} = -21, \quad \begin{vmatrix} 0 & 12 & -1 \\ 0 & -6 & -1 \\ 1 & 1 & 0 \end{vmatrix} = -18, \quad \begin{vmatrix} 3 & 0 & -1 \\ 6 & 0 & -1 \\ 1 & 1 & 0 \end{vmatrix} = -3, \quad \begin{vmatrix} 3 & 12 & 0 \\ 6 & -6 & 0 \\ 1 & 1 & 1 \end{vmatrix} = -90.$$

Thus,

$$q_1 = 6/7, \quad q_2 = 1/7, \quad \text{and} \quad EL = 30/7.$$

It should be mentioned that the above system can be solved by either the inverse method or the Gauss-Jordan method. For example, using the inverse method, the solution for firm II's probabilities and expected loss becomes:

$$\begin{bmatrix} q_1 \\ q_2 \\ EL \end{bmatrix} = \begin{bmatrix} -0.04761 & 0.047619 & 0.857142 \\ 0.047619 & -0.04761 & 0.142857 \\ -0.57142 & -0.42857 & 4.285714 \end{bmatrix} \begin{bmatrix} 0 \\ 0 \\ 1 \end{bmatrix} = \begin{bmatrix} 6/7 \\ 1/7 \\ 30/7 \end{bmatrix}$$

where

$$A = \begin{bmatrix} 3 & 12 & -1 \\ 6 & -6 & -1 \\ 1 & 1 & 0 \end{bmatrix} \text{ and } A^{-1} = \begin{bmatrix} -0.04761 & 0.047619 & 0.857142 \\ 0.047619 & -0.04761 & 0.142857 \\ -0.57142 & -0.42857 & 4.285714 \end{bmatrix}.$$

Example 7a: Assume that the administration and labor union of a university have the following payoff (average salary increases) matrix reflecting two strategies: A (hard- line strategy) and B (moderate strategy):

		Union strategy	
		A	B
Administration	A	1500	700
strategy	B	800	1100

If the administration uses strategy A, the best bet for the union is to play strategy A, because the union will gain an average salary increase of 1500. If the administration has decided to use strategy B, the union will employ strategy B and obtain an increase of 1100. As there is no dominant strategy, the union and the administration will use a mixture of strategies for determining the best solution. Following the procedure of example 7, the administration's expected salary increase to the union workers given that the union uses strategy A is

$$EG = 1500\, p_1 + 800\, (1 - p_1)$$

and the administration's expected salary increase to the union workers given that the union uses strategy B is

$$EG = 700\, p_1 + 1100\, (1 - p_1).$$

Equating the two equations and solving for p_1 and p_2 yields $p_1 = 3/11$ and $p_2 = 8/11$, and the value of the game is $10,900/11$, where p_1 and p_2 are the probabilities that the administration uses strategies A and B, respectively.

Using the decision tree, the value of the game, given that the administration moves first, is shown in Figure 10.1.

Figure 10.1. **The Value of the Game**

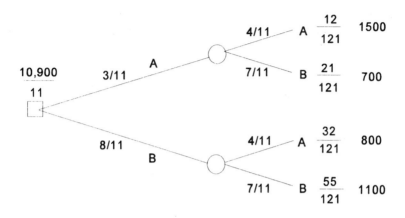

From the union's viewpoint, the algebraic solution is

$$1500 q_1 + 700 (1 - q_1)$$

and

$$800 q_1 + 1100 (1 - q_1).$$

After equating the two equations, we obtain $q_1 = 4/11$, $q_2 = 7/11$, and the value of the game is $10,900/11$ (the union's expected salary increase). If the decision tree is used, the value of the game is shown in Figure 10.2.

Figure 10.2. **The Value of the Game**

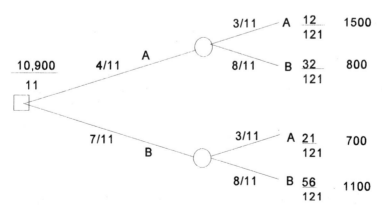

The Matrix Solution

The best strategies and the equilibrium value of a game that does not have a saddle point can be found by the matrix method as well. For example, for the game

$$
\begin{array}{ccc}
 & \text{Player II} & \\
 & A & B \\
\text{Player I } A & a_{11} & a_{12} \\
B & a_{21} & a_{22}
\end{array}
$$

player I's best strategies are found by

$$
[p_1 \quad p_2] = \frac{i\,(\text{adj } A)}{i\,(\text{adj } A)i^t}
$$

where A is the payoff matrix, (i) is a row vector of ones, and (adj) is the adjoint matrix of A.

For firm II, the optimum strategies are found by

$$
(q_1, \quad q_2) = \frac{i\,(\text{adj } A)^t}{i\,(\text{adj } A)\,i^t}
$$

and the equilibrium value of the game (EV) is

$$
EV = [p_1 \quad p_2]
\begin{bmatrix}
a_{11} & a_{12} \\
a_{21} & a_{22}
\end{bmatrix}
\begin{bmatrix}
q_1 \\
q_2
\end{bmatrix}.
$$

Example 8: Find the optimum strategies for firms I and II and the value of the following nonstrictly determined game—it does not have a saddle point:

$$
\begin{array}{ccc}
 & \text{Firm II} & \\
 & A & B \\
\text{Firm I } A & 3 & 12 \\
B & 6 & -6
\end{array}
$$

Solution: The adjoint matrix of the payoff matrix, A, is obtained as follows:

$IM_{11}I = -6$, $IM_{12}I = 6$, $IM_{21}I = 12$, and $IM_{22}I = 3$. The cofactors are found by $IC_{ij}I = (-1)^{i+j} IM_{ij}I$. Thus, $IC_{11}I = -6$, $IC_{12}I = -6$, $IC_{21}I = -12$, and $IC_{22}I = 3$. This suggests that the cofactor matrix (**C**) is

$$\mathbf{C} = \begin{bmatrix} -6 & -6 \\ -12 & 3 \end{bmatrix}, \text{ and the adjoint is } \mathbf{C}^t = \begin{bmatrix} -6 & -12 \\ -6 & 3 \end{bmatrix}.$$

Now, $i \, (\text{adj } \mathbf{A}) = \begin{bmatrix} 1 & 1 \end{bmatrix} \begin{bmatrix} -6 & -12 \\ -6 & 3 \end{bmatrix} = \begin{bmatrix} -12 & -9 \end{bmatrix}.$

Now, $i \, (\text{adj } \mathbf{A}) i^t$ is equal to

$$\begin{bmatrix} 1 & 1 \end{bmatrix} \begin{bmatrix} -6 & -12 \\ -6 & 3 \end{bmatrix} \begin{bmatrix} 1 \\ 1 \end{bmatrix} = \begin{bmatrix} -12 & -9 \end{bmatrix} \begin{bmatrix} 1 \\ 1 \end{bmatrix} = [-12 - 9] = -2.1.$$

Therefore,

$$\begin{bmatrix} p_1 & p_2 \end{bmatrix} = (1/-21) \begin{bmatrix} -12 & -9 \end{bmatrix} = \begin{bmatrix} -12/-21 & -9/-21 \end{bmatrix} = \begin{bmatrix} 4/7 & 3/7 \end{bmatrix}.$$

For player II, the solution can be found as follows: $i \, (\text{adj } \mathbf{A})^t$ is equal to

$$\begin{bmatrix} 1 & 1 \end{bmatrix} \begin{bmatrix} -6 & -6 \\ -12 & 3 \end{bmatrix} = \begin{bmatrix} -18 & -3 \end{bmatrix}$$

and $i \, (\text{adj } \mathbf{A}) i^t$ is equal to -21.
Therefore,

$$\begin{bmatrix} q_1 & q_2 \end{bmatrix} = \begin{bmatrix} -18 & -3 \end{bmatrix} / -21 = \begin{bmatrix} -18/-21 & -3/-21 \end{bmatrix} = \begin{bmatrix} 6/7 & 1/7 \end{bmatrix}$$

and the value of the game is

$$EV = \begin{bmatrix} 4/7 & 3/7 \end{bmatrix} \begin{bmatrix} 3 & -12 \\ 6 & -6 \end{bmatrix} \begin{bmatrix} 6/7 \\ 1/7 \end{bmatrix} = \begin{bmatrix} 30/7 & 30/7 \end{bmatrix} \begin{bmatrix} 6/7 \\ 1/7 \end{bmatrix} = 210/49 = 30/7.$$

The Linear Programming Solution

This method is actually a general technique for solving a game problem (Dorfman et al. 1958). As was shown before, for two firms I and II the payoff matrix can be stated as follows:

		Firm II			
		B_1	B_2	B_3 ...	B_n
	A_1	a_{11}	a_{12}	a_{13} ...	a_{1n}
Firm I	A_2	a_{21}	a_{22}	a_{23} ...	a_{2n}
	A_3	a_{31}	a_{32}	a_{33} ...	a_{3n}
	A_m	a_{m1}	a_{m2}	a_{m3} ...	a_{mn}

Also, it was indicated that firm I is interested in maximizing the expected gain (EG) and firm II wants to minimize its expected loss (EL). Because the game is a zero-sum game, EG = EL = V, where V is the expected value of the game. Accordingly, firm I's maximization program becomes

Maximize V

Subject to

$$a_{11}P_1 + a_{21}P_2 + a_{31}P_3 + ... + a_{m1}P_m \geq V$$

$$a_{12}P_1 + a_{22}P_2 + a_{32}P_3 + ... + a_{m2}P_m \geq V$$

$$.....................................$$

$$a_{1n}P_1 + a_{2n}P_2 + a_{3n}P_3 + ... + a_{mn}P_m \geq V$$

$$P_1 + P_2 + P_3 + ... + P_m = 1$$

$$P_1 \geq 0, P_2 \geq 0, P_3 \geq 0, ..., P_m \geq 0, \text{ and } V \geq 0$$

Because we can make every element of the payoff matrix positive, we can assume that V is greater than zero. Also, divide all the constraints by V and let $Y_i = P_i/V$. The last equation suggests that

$$Y_1 + Y_2 + Y_3 + ... + Y_m = 1/V\ [P_1 + P_2 + P_3 + ... + P_m] = 1/V.$$

It follows that V is maximized if the sum of Y_i is minimized.) In sum, the linear programming problem can be rewritten as

Minimize $Z = Y_1 + Y_2 + Y_3 + ... + Y_m$

Subject to

$$a_{11}Y_1 + a_{21}Y_1 + ... + a_{m1}Y_1 \geq 1$$

$$a_{12}Y_1 + a_{22}Y_2 + ... + a_{m2}Y_2 \geq 1$$

....

$$a_{1n}Y_1 + a_{2n}Y_2 + ... + a_{mn}Y_m \geq 1$$

$$Y_1 \geq 0,\ Y_2 \geq 0,\ ...,\ Y_m \geq 0.$$

This suggests that the probability of using each strategy by firm I, P_i, will be obtained from $P_i = Y_i V$.

For firm II, we can find the probabilities of its mixed strategies and its expected loss by finding the dual of the previous linear mathematical program. That is,

Maximize $Z = S_1 + S_2 + S_3 + ... + S_n$

Subject to

$$a_{11}S_1 + a_{12}S_2 + a_{13}S_3 + ... + a_{1n}S_n \leq 1$$

$$a_{21}S_1 + a_{22}S_2 + a_{23}S_3 + ... + a_{2n}S_n \leq 1$$

....

$$a_{m1}S_1 + a_{m2}S_2 + a_{m3}S_3 + ... + a_{mn}S_n \leq 1$$

$$S_1 \geq 0,\ S_2 \geq 0,\ S_3 \geq 0,\ ...,\ S_n \geq 0$$

We should note that $S_i = q_i/V$, where $S_1 + S_2 + S_3 + ... + S_n = 1/V$, and q_i is the probability of firm II's mixed strategies. It follows that after finding S_i, we must use the equation $q_i = S_iV$ to find q_i. Also, solving the dual is easier than solving the primal in this case, because the dual does not require artificial variables.

Example 9: Solve the game model introduced in example 5 by the linear programming technique.
Solution: The payoff matrix was as follows:

		Firm II	
		A	B
Firm I	A	3	12
	B	6	-6

By adding 7 to each element of the payoff matrix to make it positive, the matrix becomes

		Firm II	
		A	B
Firm I	A	10	19
	B	13	1

Using the procedure just described, firm II's linear programming problem becomes

Maximize $Z = S_1 + S_2$

Subject to

$$10S_1 + 19S_2 \le 1$$

$$13S_1 + 1S_2 \le 1$$

$$S_1 \ge 0 \text{ and } S_2 \ge 0.$$

Introducing slack variables S_3 and S_4 to the two constraints, the program becomes

Maximize $Z = S_1 + S_2$

Subject to

$$10S_1 + 19S_2 + S_3 = 1$$

$$13S_1 + 1S_2 + S_4 = 1$$

$$S_1 \geq 0 \text{ and } S_2 \geq 0.$$

The standard form becomes

$$Z - S_1 - S_2 = 0$$

$$10S_1 + 19S_2 + S_3 = 1$$

$$13S_1 + 1S_2 + S_4 = 1$$

and the solution is shown below.

Tableau I

	Z	S_1	S_2	S_3	S_4	RHS
Z	1	-1	-1	0	0	0
S_3	0	10	19	1	0	1
S_4	0	13	1	0	1	1

Tableau II

	Z	S_1	S_2	S_3	S_4	RHS
Z	1	0	-12/13	0	1/13	1/13
S_3	0	0	237/13	1	-10/13	3/13
S_1	0	1	1/13	0	1/13	1/13

Tableau III

	Z	S_1	S_2	S_3	S_4	RHS
Z	1	0	0	12/237	117/3081	273/3081
S_2	0	0	1	13/237	-10/237	39/3081
S_1	0	1	0	-1/237	247/3081	234/3081

Because the maximum of V is 273/3081, the minimum is 3081/273 = 79/7. Hence, $q_1 = S_1V = (234/3081)(79/7) = 6/7$; $q_2 = S_2V = (39/3081)(79/7) = 1/7$. The actual value of the game is 79/7 - 7/1 = 30/7. (Do not forget that we added 7 to each element of the payoff matrix to make it positive.)

For firm I's mixed strategies, the primal solution is

$$P_1 = Y_1 V = (12/237)(79/7) = 948/1659 = 4/7$$

and

$$P_2 = Y_2 V = (117/3081)(79/7) = 3/7$$

where the values of Y_1 and Y_2 are obtained from the top row of Tableau III, the tableau of the optimal solution.

Example 10: Find the mixed strategies for the two players by using the linear programming technique if the payoff matrix is as follows:

		Player II		
		A	B	C
	A	3	4	1
Player I	B	4	1	5

Solution: For player II's mixed strategy, the linear programming problem becomes:

Maximize $Z = S_1 + S_2 + S_3$

Subject to

$$3S_1 + 4S_2 + S_3 \leq 1$$

$$4S_1 + 1S_2 + 5S_3 \leq 1$$

$$S_1 \geq 0, S_2 \geq 0, \text{ and } S_3 \geq 0.$$

After adding two slack variables, the standard form becomes

$$Z - S_1 - S_2 - S_3 = 0$$

$$3S_1 + 4S_2 + S_3 + S_4 = 1$$

$$4S_1 + 1S_2 + 5S_3 + S_5 = 1$$

and the complete solution is

Tableau Ia

	Z	S_1	S_2	S_3	S_4	S_5	RHS
Z	1	-1	-1	-1	0	0	0
S_4	0	3	4	1	1	0	1
S_5	0	4	1	5	0	1	1

Tableau IIa

	Z	S_1	S_2	S_3	S_4	S_5	RHS
Z	1	-1/5	-4/5	0	0	1/5	1/5
S_4	0	11/5	19/5	0	1	-1/5	4/5
S_3	0	4/5	1/5	1	0	1/5	1/5

Tableau IIIa

	Z	S_1	S_2	S_3	S_4	S_5	RHS
Z	1	43/5	0	0	4/19	3/19	7/19
S_2	0	11/19	1	0	5/19	-1/19	4/19
S_3	0	-13/19	0	1	-5/95	4/19	3/19

As 7/19 is the maximum, then 19/7 is the minimum. Hence, $q_1 = S_1V = 0$, $q_2 = S_2V$ = 4/19 (19/7) = 4/7, and $q_3 = S_3V = (3/19)(19/7) = 3/7$. The optimal solution for player I's problem (the primal) is found as follows: $Y_1 = 4/19$ and $Y_2 = 3/19$; therefore, $P_1 = Y_1V = (4/19)(19/7) = 4/7$ and $P_2 = Y_2V = (3/19)(7/19) = 3/7$.

Nonzero-Sum Games

In nonzero sum games, the gain of player I does not equal the loss of player II (Luce and Raiffa 1957; Friedman 1990; McDonald 1975; Rapoport 1960). For example, the game shown below is a nonzero-sum game:

		Player II	
		A	B
	A	(3, -2)	(4, 3)
Player I			
	B	(5, 7)	(6, 11)

There are various methods for solving nonzero-sum games, and these methods depend on the structure of the given game. These methods are explained below.

Dominance

The concept of dominance has already been introduced earlier. In a nutshell, each player will select the best strategy for making money. For example, the payoff matrix just introduced can be solved by the method of dominance. The method works as follows: For player I, strategy B is the best because player I can gain 5 and 6, given that player II uses strategy A and strategy B, respectively. That is, strategy B of player I dominates strategy A. For player II, the best strategy is B, because player II can gain 3 and 11, given that player I uses strategy A and strategy B, respectively. As can be seen, for both players strategy B is the dominant (pure) strategy. Therefore, if the above game is played, players I and II will have to use strategy B and gain 6 and 11, respectively.

Example 11: For the following game, determine the optimal strategy for firm I and firm II.

$$
\begin{array}{cccc}
& & \text{Firm II} & \\
& A & B & C \\
A & (2, 5) & (-2, -3) & (4, 7) \\
\text{Firm I} & & & \\
B & (5, 7) & (3, 2) & (11, 13) \\
C & (-2, -4) & (2, 3) & (1, 6)
\end{array}
$$

Solution: For firm I, the dominant strategy is B, because the firm will gain 5, 3, and 11, respectively, relative to strategies A and C. Thus, firm I will not play strategies A and C at all. For firm II, the best strategy is C because the firm will gain 7, 13, and 6 relative to strategies A and B. It follows that strategy C will be dominant when firm II plays the above game. Eventually, firms I and II will gain 11 and 13, respectively, by playing strategy B (for firm I) and strategy C (for firm II).

Example 12: Find the best strategy for the following game:

$$
\begin{array}{ccc}
& & \text{Firm II} \\
& A & B \\
A & (2, 2) & (6, -2) \\
\text{Firm I} & & \\
B & (-2, 6) & (4, 4)
\end{array}
$$

Solution: For firm I, A is the dominant strategy because the payoffs 2 and 6 are larger than the payoffs -2 and 4 obtained if strategy B was employed. Similarly, for firm II, strategy A is the dominant strategy because firm II would gain 2 and 6 if this strategy was used; these gains are larger than -2 and 4 of strategy B. Thus, both firms will use strategy A, and the solution (2, 2) is obtained because there is no cooperation between the players. If there is cooperation between the two firms, these firms can use strategy B, which makes both firms better off. In other words, (4, 4) represents Pareto optimality, because both firms will be worse off if they change their B strategy.

Nash Equilibrium Solution

Nash's solution (Bierman and Fernandez 1993; Gardner 1995) is used if there is no dominant strategy in given games. For example, the following game has no dominant strategy:

		Firm II	
		A	B
	A	(4, 2)	(0.5, 0)
Firm I			
	B	(0, 0)	(1, 4)

However, the game has an equilibrium point, called *Nash equilibrium*, which represents firm I's optimal choice given firm II's optimal choice. For this game, if firm I plays strtegy A, the optimal choice for firm II is to play strategy A, because firm II will gain 2. If firm II plays strategy A, the best bet for firm I is to play strategy A, because firm I will gain 4. Hence, strategy A for both firms is the Nash equilibrium point, which is the solution for the game. Similarly, if firm I plays strategy B, the best for firm II is to play B; if firm II plays B, the best for firm I is to play B. Hence, strategy B for firms I and II gives another Nash equilibrium point (solution).

Example 13: Does the following game have a Nash equilibrium?

		Firm II	
		A	B
	A	(3, 5)	(2, 7)
Firm I			
	B	(5, 6)	(1, 3)

Solution: If firm I plays strategy A, the best for firm II is to play B; if firm II plays B, the best for firm I is to play A. Thus, (2, 7) is a Nash equilibrium. If firm I plays B, the best for firm II is to play A because it will gain 6; if firm II plays A, the best for firm I is to play B because it will gain 5. Hence, there is another Nash equilibrium point, (5, 6), which represents another solution.

Example 14: Does the following game have a Nash equilibrium?

Firm II

		A	B
	A	(4, 2)	(2, 0)
Firm I			
	B	(0, 0)	(1, 3)

Solution: If firm I uses strategy A, firm II must play strategy A; if firm II uses strategy A, firm I must play A. Hence, (4, 2) is a Nash equilibrium point. Now, if firm I uses strategy B, firm II uses strategy B; if firm II uses B, firm I uses strategy A. Hence, (1, 3) is not a Nash equilibrium point. It follows that the above game has one solution: (4, 2). (Note that the solution reflects a dominant strategy.)
Example 15: Does the following game have a Nash equilibrium point?

Firm II

		A	B
	A	(2, 2)	(2, 1)
Firm I			
	B	(3, 2)	(1, 3)

Solution: If firm I plays A, the best for firm II is to play A; if firm II plays A, the best for firm I is to play B; thus, there is no Nash equilibrium point. If firm I plays B, the best for firm II is to play B; if firm II plays B, the best for firm I is to play A—no Nash equilibrium point. This game has no dominant strategy nor does it have a Nash equilibrium point. However, the game can be solved by using the mixed strategy procedure. For example, the game can be represented by a probability tree as shown in Figure 10.3.

Figure 10.3 **Probability Tree for the Game Problem**

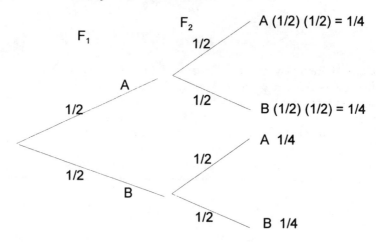

Let us assume that a probability assignment of 0.5 is used for both strategies that are employed by these two firms. Having done so, we can obtain the average gain for each firm as follows: If firm II plays strategy A, the average (expected) gain for firm I is

$$2(0.25) + 3(0.25) = 5/4.$$

If firm II plays strategy B, the average (expected) gain for firm I is

$$2(0.25) + 1(0.25) = 3/4.$$

Thus, the total average gain for firm I if firm II uses strategy A and B is

$$5/4 + 3/4 = 2.$$

Similarly, one can find the average gain for firm II by using the decision tree, and students are encouraged to do it. If firm I uses strategy A, the average gain for firm II is

$$2(0.25) + 1(0.25) = 3/4.$$

If firm I uses strategy B, the average gain for firm II is

$$2(0.25) + 3(0.25) = 5/4.$$

Thus, the total gain for player II is $3/4 + 5/4 = 2$. Because the average gain is equal for both players, the game is said to be fair.

The Prisoner's Dilemma

This type of game requires that $F > S > D > G$ for a 2 x 2 game such as the one shown below.

		Firm II	
		A	B
	A	(D, D)	(F, G)
Firm I			
	B	(G, F)	(S, S)

This game suggests that if firm II plays B, firm I must play A; if firm II plays A, firm I plays A. Thus, the best for firm I is to play A whatever firm II plays. Also, if firm I plays A, firm II must play A; if firm I plays B, firm II must play A. Hence, firm II plays A whatever firm I does, suggesting that both firms must use strategy A, which is actually a Nash equilibrium.

This game is called the *prisoner's dilemma* because it describes a situation where two prisoners are questioned separately. For example, let the two strategies A and B of the above example reflect *confess* and *deny*, respectively. Also, let the payoff matrix be

		Prisoner II	
		Confess	Deny
	Confess	(-9,-9)	(0,-12)
Prisoner I			
	Deny	(-12,0)	(-7,-7)

This suggests that if both prisoners confess they will serve nine years in prison; if prisoner I confesses but prisoner II denies the crime, prisoner I will be free and prisoner II will serve 12 years in prison; if prisoner I denies the crime but prisoner II confesses, prisoner I will serve 12 years in prison and prisoner II will go free; and if both prisoners deny the crime they will serve 7 years in prison. [One should note the following: $0(F) > -7(S) > -9 (D) > -12(G)$.]

Example 16: Find the cooperative and noncooperative solutions for the following game:

		Firm II	
		A	B
	A	(4, 4)	(5, 3)
Firm I			
	B	(3, 5)	(4.5, 4.5)

Solution: If firm II plays B, firm I plays A; if firm II plays A, firm I plays A. Or if firm I plays A, firm II plays A; if firm II plays A, firm I plays A. Thus, the best strategy for firm I is to play A—a Nash equilibrium—whatever firm II does. Also, if firm I plays B, firm II plays A; if firm II plays B, firm I plays A—no Nash equilibrium point. But one should note that if firm I plays A, firm II must play A; if firm I plays B, firm II plays A. Hence, firm II plays A whatever firm I does. This suggests that both firms play strategy A—Nash equilibrium point—which provides the solution for the above game.

But if there is cooperation between these two firms, the firms may reach a different solution for the above game. Under cooperation, the two firms can play B-B strategy by which they gain 4.5 each, a solution that is better than the solution obtained under no cooperation (Nash solution). The better solution (4.5, 4.5) does represent Pareto optimality: Both firms are better off, and if they are forced out of this equilibrium one of them at least will be worse off.

Problems

1.   Two firms have the following payoff matrix, reflecting two strategies. Strategy I shows a gain (loss) if the price increases by 10 percent (A). Strategy II shows a gain (loss) if the price decreases by 5 percent (B). Find the best strategy by using the dominance and minimax methods.

		Firm II	
		A	B
Firm I	A	5	4
	B	3	2

2.   A firm has unionized workers. When the workers obtain information that the firm has made a large profit, they want to receive salary increases. If the workers use the strategy of making 10 percent increase in salary and management uses the same strategy, the workers gain $2 million; if they use the strategy of making 10 percent and management uses the strategy of paying 8 percent increase in salary, the workers gain $1.5 million. If the workers use the strategy of making 8 percent and management uses the strategy of paying 10 percent, the workers will gain $1.8 million. If both workers and management employ the strategy of making an 8 percent increase in salary, workers will gain $3 million. Formulate the payoff matrix and find its value by using the matrix and linear programming methods.

3.   Solve the following game and determine the best strategy for each player:

		Player II	
		A	B
	A	(10, 12)	(6, 8)
Player I	B	(9, 12)	(3, -3)

4.   Solve the following game by the minimax method:

		Firm II		
		A	B	C
	A	1000	1320	1100
Firm I	B	950	1200	1000
	C	1250	1400	1220

5.   For the following game

		Firm II	
		A	B
	A	(4, 4)	(5, -3)
Firm I	B	(-3,5)	(8, 8)

determine the best strategy for firms I and II under cooperative and noncooperative situations.

6.   For the following game

		Firm II	
		A	B
	A	(4, 3)	(1, 0)
Firm I	B	(0, 0)	(2, 8)

determine the best strategy for firms I and II. Is there a Nash equilibrium point?

7.   Determine the best strategy for the two players of the following game:

		Player II	
		A	B
	A	(4, 4)	(11, 0)
Player I	B	(0, 11)	(5, 5)

CHAPTER ELEVEN

Markov Chains

The Markov model is based on the transitional probability describing a situation that changes between two stages. The first stage occurs at time $t - 1$, and the second stage takes place at time t. In other words, the current probability of a certain state depends on the probability of the immediate preceding state only (Thompson 1976).

The Markov model has various applications in business and economics. For example, it can be applied to a model where customers are buying products from two different stores and where managers are interested in knowing how these customers change stores or continue buying from the same store over the long run. Also, the Markov model can be applied to a situation where people migrate from region to region between time $t - 1$ and time t. Also the long-run transitional probability of people among different regions can be found.

In this chapter the transitional probabilities, stages, and states are explained. Also, a regular transition matrix is described, and the limiting steady-state transition matrix is outlined with examples. In addition, absorbing and nonabsorbing states are analyzed.

States, Stages, and Transitional Probabilities

Imagine the following table of probabilities:

		State at the End of Stage t				
		1	2	3	4	... n
	1	P_{11}	P_{12}	P_{13}	P_{14}	... P_{1n}
	2	P_{21}	P_{22}	P_{23}	P_{24}	... P_{2n}
State at the End of Stage t-1	3	P_{31}	P_{32}	P_{33}	P_{34}	... P_{3n}
		. . . .				
	n	P_{n1}	P_{n2}	P_{n3}	P_{n4}	... P_{nn}

The table reveals some technical concepts. The first concept is the *state* concept such as state 1, 2, and so forth, which means that the system is in a certain category or condition (Kemeny and Snell 1960). For example, it is sunny today (stage t-1) and will be cloudy tomorrow (stage t). The second concept is the *stage* concept. The table shows that there are two stages: stage t-1 and stage t. This means that if stage t-1 represents yesterday, stage t represents today (or a future day). Similarly, if stage t-1 represents the month of May, stage t indicates the month of June (or a future month).   The third concept is the *transition* probabilities, P_{ij}. P_{ij}, i = 1, 2, ... n and j = 1,2, ... n, which represent the probabilities that the system will change from state i to state j during stage t. For example, P_{12} reflects the probability that the system will change from state 1 to state 2 during stage t. Similarly, P_{23} reflects the probability that the system will change from state 2 to state 3 during stage t. In fact, this is the reason why the probability matrix **P**, where

$$P = \begin{bmatrix} P_{11} & P_{12} & P_{13} & P_{14} \cdots P_{1n} \\ P_{21} & P_{22} & P_{23} & P_{24} \cdots P_{2n} \\ P_{31} & P_{32} & P_{33} & P_{34} \cdots P_{3n} \\ \cdots\cdots\cdots\cdots\cdots\cdots\cdots \\ P_{n1} & P_{n2} & P_{n3} & P_{n4} \cdots P_{nn} \end{bmatrix} .$$

is called the *transition matrix*. The transition matrix, which is a stochastic matrix, is a square matrix of dimension n x n with the following properties:

(a) All the elements Pij must be between 0 and 1 (i.e., Pij ≥ 0) and

(b) the sum of each row must equal 1.

The fourth technical concept that the table of probabilities provides is the concept of a *system*. In Markov analysis, the system consists of all the states along with their transition probabilities, P_{ij}.

To understand the totality of the foregoing argument, an example is needed. Assume a weather record showing that it will be sunny tomorrow with a probability of 70 percent if it is sunny today; otherwise it will be cloudy tomorrow if it is sunny today. Also, the record shows that the probability that it will be cloudy tomorrow 50 percent of the time if it is cloudy today; otherwise it will be sunny tomorrow if it is cloudy today. The task is to formulate the transition probability matrix, taking into consideration the two states of sunny and cloudy. The transition probability is shown below. The table reveals two stages: today (t-1) and tomorrow (t). The transition probabilities reflect two states: cloudy and sunny.

		Tomorrow	
		Sunny	Cloudy
Today	Sunny	0.70	0.30
	Cloudy	0.50	0.50

As can be seen, each entry of the transition matrix is between zero and one, and each entry can be described as follows. The probability of 0.70 represents the probability that it will be sunny tomorrow if it is sunny today. The probability of 0.30, which is (1 - 0.70), reflects the probability that it will be cloudy tomorrow if it is sunny today. The probability of 0.50 represents the probability that it will be sunny tomorrow if it is cloudy today. The entry, 0.50, represents the probability that it will be cloudy tomorrow if it is cloudy today. Stated differently, these transition probabilities are actually conditional probabilities. If S represents the event sunny, and C represents the event cloudy, then given that the state cloudy has occurred today, the probability of being sunny tomorrow [or P(SIC)] is equal to 0.70; this is called a *conditional probability*. Similarly, P(CIC) is the conditional probability of cloudy tomorrow given it is cloudy today, which is equal to 0.50 (Ross 1983, 1985).

The transition (conditional) probabilities can be described by probability trees (Thompson 1976). Given the state that it is sunny today, the probabilities that it will be sunny or cloudy tomorrow are 0.70 and 0.30, respectively, as shown in Figure 11.1.

Figure 11.1 **A Probability Tree for the Two Events**

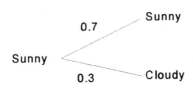

Given the state that it is cloudy today, the probabilities that it will be sunny or cloudy tomorrow are 0.50 and 0.50, respectively; and this is shown in Figure 11.2.

Figure 11.2. **A Probability Tree for the Two Events**

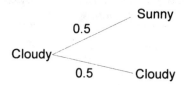

Graphically, the transition probabilities for the above problem are shown in Figure 11.3 in a diagram called the *transition diagram*.

Figure 11.3. **The Transition Diagram**

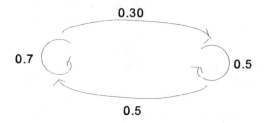

Example 1: *Market share.* A marketing record shows that 80 percent of the time consumers will purchase their groceries from Jewel in June if they purchase them there in May, and 20 percent of the time they will be buying from National in June if they buy from Jewell in May. Also, the record shows that 30 percent of the time the customers will buy from Jewell in June if they purchase their groceries from National in May, and 70 percent of the time they will be purchasing from National in June given that they purchase their groceries from National in May. Formulate the transition probability table.

Solution: The transition probabilities are shown below. The states are Jewell and National, respectively; and the stages are May, which is t-1, and June, which is stage t. As mentioned, these probabilities are conditional probabilities. For example, if we let J and N stand for Jewell and National, respectively; then P(NIJ) is the conditional probability of shopping from National in June given the state that the customers buy groceries from Jewell in May; this probability is 0.20.

		June (stage t)	
		Jewell	National
	Jewell	0.80	0.20
May (stage t-1)			
	National	0.30	0.70

The transitional probabilities can be described by probability trees. The first tree (Figure 11.4) is related to the condition that, given the customers buy from Jewell in May, the probabilities that they will be buying from Jewell and National are 0.80 and 0.20, respectively.

Figure 11.4. **Probability Tree for the Two States**

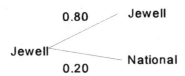

The second tree (Figure 11.5) is related to the condition that, given the customers purchase from National in May, the probabilities that they will be buying from Jewell and National in June are 0.30 and 0.70, respectively.

Figure 11.5. **Probability Tree for the Two States**

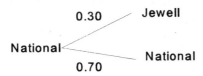

In addition, a researcher may be interested in knowing, for example, the probability that the customers will be buying from National two months from now (that is, in July) given they purchase from Jewell now (that is, May). To answer this question, one has to perform a very simple operation: Multiply the transition matrix, **P**, by itself to obtain $PP = P^2$. That is,

$$\mathbf{p}^2 = \mathbf{PP} = \begin{bmatrix} 0.80 & 0.20 \\ 0.30 & 0.70 \end{bmatrix} \begin{bmatrix} 0.80 & 0.20 \\ 0.30 & 0.70 \end{bmatrix} = \begin{bmatrix} 0.70 & 0.30 \\ 0.45 & 0.55 \end{bmatrix}.$$

The required probability is 0.30. Also, 0.70 reflects the probability that the customers will be buying from Jewell in July, given that they purchase groceries from Jewell in May. One should indicate that P^2 is called the *two-step transition probability matrix*. The conditional probabilities of the P^2 matrix are shown in Figure 11.6.

Figure 11.6. **Probability Trees for P²**

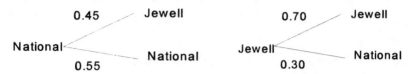

If the researcher knows the number of customers buying from Jewell and National in May, which is a row vector, say $\mathbf{A}$, consisting of two elements, the researcher can obtain the number of customers buying their groceries in June by finding $\mathbf{A_1}$ = $\mathbf{AP}$. For example, if $\mathbf{A}$ = [500   450], Jewell's and National's customers who shop in June are

$$\mathbf{A_1} = \mathbf{AP} = [500 \quad 450] \begin{bmatrix} 0.80 & 0.20 \\ 0.30 & 0.70 \end{bmatrix} = [535 \quad 415].$$

For the month of July, the number of customers buying from Jewell and National can be obtained by finding $\mathbf{A_2}$ = $\mathbf{AP^2}$, which is

$$[500 \quad 450] \begin{bmatrix} 0.70 & 0.30 \\ 0.45 & 0.55 \end{bmatrix} = [552 \quad 398].$$

One can find the percentage of customers buying from Jewell and National in June if the initial percentage of customers, say $\mathbf{A_i}$, is known. This can be done by replacing $\mathbf{A}$ by $\mathbf{A_i}$, and $\mathbf{AP}$ becomes $\mathbf{A_iP}$. If $\mathbf{A_i}$ = [0.53   0.47], then

$$\mathbf{A_iP} = [0.53 \quad 0.47] \begin{bmatrix} 0.80 & 0.20 \\ 0.30 & 0.70 \end{bmatrix} = [0.565 \quad 0.435].$$

This suggests that in June about 56.5 percent of the customers will buy from Jewell and 43.5 percent will purchase from National. If the total numbers of customers is 950, the numbers of customers buying from Jewell and National are

$$(950)\mathbf{A_iP} = 950 \, [0.565 \quad 0.435] = [537 \quad 413].$$

If the researcher is interested in finding the probabilities that the customers will be buying from Jewell in August (three months from May), given that they buy from National in May, P^3 must be found: *the three-step transition probability matrix.* The researcher can extend that to P^4, P^5, and P^n. In general, P^n represents the n-step (month) transition probability matrix, and (A_n) represents the distribution vector after n years, where

$$A_n = AP^n \qquad (1)$$

(In terms of shares or percentages, equation [1] can be written as $A_n = A_iP^n$.)

Example 2: *Migration among three regions.* Individuals migrate among three regions in the United States: Eastern (E), Midwest (MW), and Western region (W). A record shows that the Midwest region is expected to retain 30 percent of its population and lose 50 percent to the Western region and 20 percent to the Eastern region. The Eastern region is expected to lose 5 percent of its population to the Midwest region and 25 percent to the Western region. The Western region is expected to lose 7 percent to the Midwest region and 15 percent to the Eastern region. If the initial distribution of the population in each region is 50 percent in the Eastern region, 10 percent in the Midwest, and 40 percent in the Western region, find the population share (percentage) in each region after one and two years. Also, graph the transition probabilities.
Solution: The graph of the transition probabilities is shown in Figure 11.7.

Figure 11.7. **Transition Diagram**

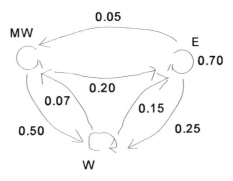

The transition matrix **P** for this problem is

	E	MW	W
E	0.70	0.05	0.25
MW	0.20	0.30	0.50
W	0.15	0.07	0.78

and the initial percentage distribution of the population A_i is

$$[0.50 \quad 0.10 \quad 0.40].$$

Accordingly, the population shares after one year, A_iP, are

$$[0.50 \quad 0.10 \quad 0.40] \begin{bmatrix} 0.70 & 0.05 & 0.25 \\ 0.20 & 0.30 & 0.50 \\ 0.15 & 0.07 & 0.78 \end{bmatrix} = [0.43 \quad 0.083 \quad 0.487].$$

The population shares (percentages) of each region after two years, A_iP^2, are

$$[0.50 \quad 0.10 \quad 0.40] \begin{bmatrix} 0.70 & 0.05 & 0.25 \\ 0.20 & 0.30 & 0.50 \\ 0.15 & 0.07 & 0.78 \end{bmatrix} \begin{bmatrix} 0.70 & 0.05 & 0.25 \\ 0.20 & 0.30 & 0.50 \\ 0.15 & 0.07 & 0.78 \end{bmatrix} =$$

$$[0.39065 \quad 0.08049 \quad 0.52886]$$

Example 3: *Student mobility.* A college of business has four departments: Business Administration (BA), Economics (E), Accounting (A), and Management (M). A record shows that 20 percent of the junior students initially selected (A), 50 percent (M), 20 percent (BA), and 10 percent (E). These initial percentages can be grouped in a vector termed the *initial percentage distribution vector*, A_i. Find the current percentage of students in each discipline assuming that the following transition matrix (which reflects the percentage of students who have changed their disciplines) exits and is shown below. Also, find the same percentage after two years (and after n years), and graph the two-year transition probabilities.

	BA	E	A	M
BA	0.85	0.05	0.09	0.01
E	0.20	0.70	0.02	0.08
A	0.10	0.02	0.87	0.01
M	0.01	0.15	0.01	0.83

We know the initial distribution vector A_i, which is equal to

$$A_i = [0.20 \quad 0.10 \quad 0.20 \quad 0.50].$$

Therefore, $A_1 = A_i P$ is

$$A_1 = [0.20 \quad 0.10 \quad 0.20 \quad 0.50] \begin{bmatrix} 0.85 & 0.05 & 0.09 & 0.01 \\ 0.20 & 0.70 & 0.02 & 0.08 \\ 0.10 & 0.02 & 0.87 & 0.01 \\ 0.01 & 0.15 & 0.01 & 0.83 \end{bmatrix}$$

$$= [0.215 \quad 0.159 \quad 0.199 \quad 0.427].$$

The transition matrix after two years is $PP = P^2$, which is

$$P^2 = \begin{bmatrix} 0.7416 & 0.0808 & 0.1559 & 0.0217 \\ 0.3128 & 0.5124 & 0.0502 & 0.1246 \\ 0.1761 & 0.0379 & 0.7664 & 0.0196 \\ 0.0478 & 0.2302 & 0.0209 & 0.7011 \end{bmatrix}$$

and the probability trees are shown in Figures 11.8 to 11.11.

Figure 11.8. **Probability Tree for Two-Step Matrix Given BA**

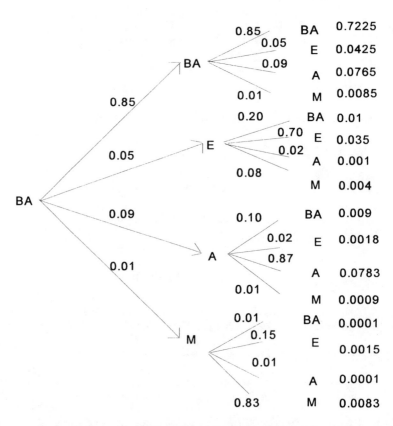

If the probabilities of BA are summed (0.7225 + 0.01 + 0.009 + 0.0001 = 0.7416), the first element of $\mathbf{P}^2$ is obtained. Similarly, if the probabilities of E are summed (0.0425 + 0.035 + 0.0018 + 0.0015 = 0.0808), the second element of $\mathbf{P}^2$ is obtained. And other elements can be obtained in the same way.

Figure 11.9. **Probability Tree for Two-Step Matrix Given E**

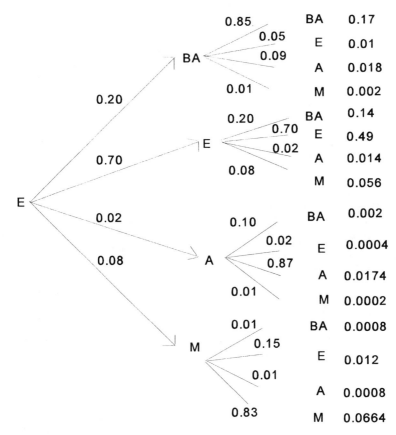

If the probabilities of BA are summed $(0.17 + 0.14 + 0.002 + 0.0008 = 0.312)$, the first element of the second row of $\mathbf{P}^2$ is obtained. Similarly, other elements can be obtained in the same way.

Figure 11.10. **Probability Tree for Two-Step Matrix Given A**

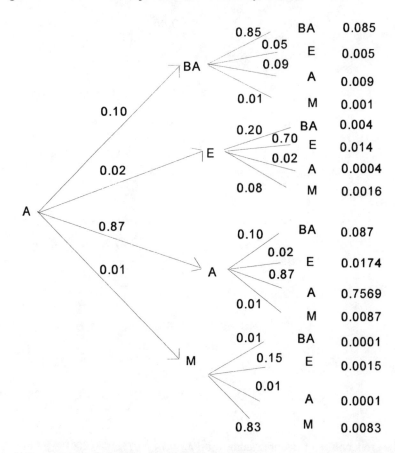

If the probabilities of BA are summed (0.085 + 0.004 + 0.087 + 0.0001 = 0.1761), the first element of the third row of $\mathbf{P}^2$ is obtained. Similarly, the other elements of the same row can be obtained.

Figure 11.11. **Probability Tree for Two-Step Matrix Given M**

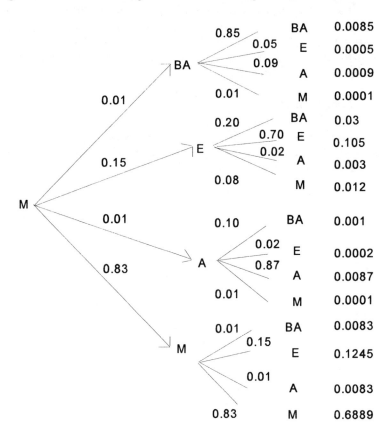

BA	0.0085	
E	0.0005	
A	0.0009	
M	0.0001	
BA	0.03	
E	0.105	
A	0.003	
M	0.012	
BA	0.001	
E	0.0002	
A	0.0087	
M	0.0001	
BA	0.0083	
E	0.1245	
A	0.0083	
M	0.6889	

If the probabilities of BA are summed, one can obtain the elements of the fourth row of $\mathbf{P}^2$.

The percentages of students after two years are found from $\mathbf{A_2} = \mathbf{A_i}\mathbf{P}^2$, which is equal to

$$[0.23872 \quad 0.19008 \quad 0.19993 \quad 0.37127],$$

and the percentages of students after n years can be obtained from $\mathbf{A_n} = \mathbf{A_i}\mathbf{P}^n$.

The preceding analysis implies that Markov chains are based on three assumptions. The first assumption is the Markovian property suggesting that the probability of state 1 in stage t depends on the probability of state 1 in stage t-1. For example, the probability that a customer will be shopping at Jewell in June depends only on the probability that the customer purchases from Jewell in May. The second assumption is that the transition probability matrix is time- independent, that is, stationary. This means that the transition matrix, **P**, for different time periods is essentially the same. The third assumption is that the number of states is finite, not infinite. (However, it should be noted that if the third assumption is replaced by the assumption that the number of states is infinite, then the Markov chain is called the *Markov process*.)

A Regular Transition Matrix

A transition matrix, **P**, is said to be a regular transition matrix if all entries of **P** are nonnegative, that is, having entries of zero and positive values, but $\mathbf{P}^n$, say for $n = 2$, has entries that are all positive in values (Taha 1987). For example,

$$\mathbf{P} = \begin{bmatrix} 1/4 & 4/5 \\ 0 & 0 \end{bmatrix}$$

but

$$\mathbf{P}^2 = \begin{bmatrix} 1/4 & 4/5 \\ 0 & 0 \end{bmatrix} \begin{bmatrix} 1/4 & 4/5 \\ 0 & 0 \end{bmatrix} = \begin{bmatrix} 1/16 & 1/5 \\ 0 & 0 \end{bmatrix}.$$

Therefore, **P** is not a regular transition matrix, because there are entries in $\mathbf{P}^2$ that are not positive. But if

$$\mathbf{P} = \begin{bmatrix} 0 & 1 \\ 1/4 & 3/4 \end{bmatrix},$$

then $\mathbf{P}^2$ is

$$
\begin{bmatrix} 0 & 1 \\ 1/4 & 3/4 \end{bmatrix} \begin{bmatrix} 0 & 1 \\ 1/4 & 3/4 \end{bmatrix} = \begin{bmatrix} 1/4 & 3/4 \\ 3/16 & 13/16 \end{bmatrix}.
$$

Thus, the **P** is a regular transition matrix, because all entries in $\mathbf{P}^2$ are positive. This matrix represents a very important condition that makes the transition probability matrix converge to a matrix called *steady-state* (or the *limiting steady-state* or the *long-run*) *transition matrix* as (n) approaches infinity (Anderson et al. 1985).

The Limiting Steady-State Transition Matrix

Given a regular transition probability matrix, $\mathbf{P}^n$, as (n) approaches infinity such as $n = 20$, $n = 21$, and so forth, the transition matrix will stay the same no matter how large n may be. In other words, each column (or row) of the transition matrix will have the same values. For example, if the regular transition matrix is $\mathbf{P}^n$, then for $n = 1$, we obtain

$$
\mathbf{P}_1 = \begin{bmatrix} 0 & 1 \\ 1/4 & 3/4 \end{bmatrix}
$$

and for $n = 10, 11$, and 12, the matrix becomes

$$
\mathbf{P}^{10} = \begin{bmatrix} 0.20 & 0.8 \\ 0.20 & 0.8 \end{bmatrix}, \quad \mathbf{P}^{11} = \begin{bmatrix} 0.20 & 0.8 \\ 0.20 & 0.8 \end{bmatrix} \quad \text{and} \quad \mathbf{P}^{12} = \begin{bmatrix} 0.20 & 0.8 \\ 0.20 & 0.8 \end{bmatrix}.
$$

Mathematically, the transition probability matrix $\mathbf{P}^n$ will converge to a finite matrix **S** as n approaches infinity; the **S** matrix is called the *limiting steady-state* (or the *long-run*) *transition matrix*. That is, **S** for the above example is

$$
\mathbf{S} = \begin{bmatrix} S_1 & S_2 \\ S_1 & S_2 \end{bmatrix}.
$$

In reality it is very difficult to find the steady-state transition matrix by multiplying the **P** matrix by itself many times. The alternative approach for finding the **S** matrix is to do the following:
Let

$$S = SP.$$

For the **S** matrix of two states only, we have

$$\begin{bmatrix} S_1 & S_2 \\ S_1 & S_2 \end{bmatrix} = \begin{bmatrix} S_1 & S_2 \\ s_1 & s_2 \end{bmatrix} \begin{bmatrix} P_{11} & P_{12} \\ P_{21} & P_{22} \end{bmatrix}.$$

For the market share example, **P** becomes

$$P = \begin{bmatrix} 0.80 & 0.20 \\ 0.30 & 0.70 \end{bmatrix},$$

which is the market share transition matrix. Because the **S** matrix has identical two rows, we can pick one row only, giving

$$[S_1 \quad S_2] = [S_1 \quad S_2] \begin{bmatrix} 0.80 & 0.20 \\ 0.30 & 0.70 \end{bmatrix}.$$

After performing the required multiplication, we obtain

$$S_1 = 0.80S_1 + 0.30S_2$$

$$S_2 = 0.20S_1 + 0.70S_2.$$

As each row of matrix S sums to one, one has to add the condition that $S_1 + S_2 = 1$ to the above two equations (Taha 1987; Anderson et al. 1985). The new system of equations becomes

$$S_1 = 0.80S_1 + 0.30S_2$$

$$S_2 = 0.20S_1 + 0.70S_2$$

$$S_1 + S_2 = 1.$$

After arranging the above system, we obtain

$$0.20S_1 - 0.30S_2 = 0$$

$$-0.20S_1 + 0.30S_2 = 0$$

$$S_1 + S_2 = 1.$$

This is a system of three equations but two unknowns. As the first two equations are linearly dependent (det $|A| = 0$), one of the equations has to be dropped. Assuming the first equation is dropped, the system becomes

$$-0.20S_1 + 0.30S_2 = 0$$

$$S_1 + S_2 = 1,$$

which can be rewritten in matrix form as follows:

$$A = \begin{bmatrix} -0.20 & 0.30 \\ 1 & 1 \end{bmatrix} \quad \text{and} \quad b = \begin{bmatrix} 0 \\ 1 \end{bmatrix}$$

whose solution is

$$S = A^{-1}b.$$

That is,

$$\begin{bmatrix} S_1 \\ S_2 \end{bmatrix} = \begin{bmatrix} -2 & 0.6 \\ 2 & 0.4 \end{bmatrix} \begin{bmatrix} 0 \\ 1 \end{bmatrix} = \begin{bmatrix} 0.6 \\ 0.4 \end{bmatrix}.$$

Hence, the steady-state matrix becomes

$$S = \begin{bmatrix} 0.6 & 0.4 \\ 0.6 & 0.4 \end{bmatrix}.$$

The S matrix can be obtained by multiplying **P** by itself 20 times. That is,

$$P^{20} = \begin{bmatrix} 0.60 & 0.40 \\ 0.60 & 0.40 \end{bmatrix}$$

and

$$P^{21} = \begin{bmatrix} 0.60 & 0.40 \\ 0.60 & 0.40 \end{bmatrix}.$$

Similarly, for the migration example the transition matrix was

$$\begin{bmatrix} 0.70 & 0.05 & 0.25 \\ 0.20 & 0.30 & 0.50 \\ 0.15 & 0.07 & 0.78 \end{bmatrix}.$$

To find the population share in the long run, we have to follow the same procedure used in the above example. That is,

$$S_1 = 0.70S_1 + 0.20S_2 + 0.15S_3$$

$$S_2 = 0.05S_1 + 0.30S_2 + 0.07S_3$$

$$S_3 = 0.25S_1 + 0.50S_2 + 0.78S_3.$$

After arranging the system of equations, we obtain

$$0.30S_1 - 0.20S_2 - 0.15S_3 = 0$$

$$-0.05S_1 + 0.37S_2 - 0.07S_3 = 0$$

$$-0.25S_1 - 0.50S_2 + 0.22S_3 = 0.$$

Dropping the first equation and adding the condition that the sum of S_i is equal to one, we have

$$-0.05S_1 + 0.37S_2 - 0.07S_3 = 0$$

$$-0.25S_1 - 0.50S_2 + 0.22S_3 = 0$$

$$S_1 + S_2 + S_3 = 1$$

and the solution is obtained

$$
A = \begin{bmatrix} -0.25 & 0.37 & -0.07 \\ -0.25 & -0.50 & 0.22 \\ 1 & 1 & 1 \end{bmatrix}, \ B = \begin{bmatrix} 0 \\ 0 \\ 1 \end{bmatrix}.
$$

And $S = A^{-1}b$. That is,

$$
\begin{bmatrix} -3.74220 & -2.2869 & 0.241164 \\ 2.442827 & 0.10395 & 0.148128 \\ 1.299376 & 2,182952 & 0.610706 \end{bmatrix} \begin{bmatrix} 0 \\ 0 \\ 1 \end{bmatrix},
$$

which gives the solution

$$
S = \begin{bmatrix} 0.241164 \\ 0.148128 \\ 0.610706 \end{bmatrix}
$$

and the steady-state matrix becomes

$$S = \begin{bmatrix} 0.241164 & 0.148128 & 0.610706 \\ 0.241164 & 0.148128 & 0.610706 \\ 0.241164 & 0.148128 & 0.610706 \end{bmatrix} \cdot$$

Using the initial distribution of the population A_i and the steady-state matrix, the population shares in the long run are

$$[0.241164 \quad 0.148128 \quad 0.610706],$$

which is the same as the first row of the steady-state matrix.

Absorbing and Nonabsorbing States

In some cases the transition matrix is not regular. The absorbing probabilistic matrix is a transition matrix in which at least one state has a probability of one. These matrices are not regular. Also, an absorbing matrix has two properties. The first is that there is at least one absorbing state, and the second is that there is a likelihood that there will be a transition from the nonabsorbing state to the absorbing one. To put the argument differently, in the case of having absorbing states, we do not compute steady-state probabilities but rather probabilities of moving from nonabsorbing states to absorbing ones. For example, assume we have the following absorbing matrix:

		States			
		1	2	3	4
	1	0	0	0	0
States	2	0	1	0	0
	3	0.2	0.4	0.2	0.2
	4	0.2	0.3	0.2	0.3

States 1 and 2 are *absorbing states* in that once the object makes a transition to these states it will not leave them—the probability of leaving state 1 and 2 is zero. States 3 and 4 are called *nonabsorbing states*, and an object has a possibility to move to these absorbing states. In fact, an object in state 3 can make a transition to state 1 with a probability of 0.2, and make a transition to state 2 with a probability of 0.4. Similarly, an object in state 4 can move to state 1 with a probability of 0.2, and can make a transition to state 2 with a probability of 0.3. It follows that the above matrix is indeed an absorbing matrix.

In this situation, one can compute the probabilities that an object will move from the nonabsorbing states, 3 and 4, to the absorbing states, 1 and 2, and these probabilities do represent the long-run probabilities. To do so, we need to obtain the steady-state matrix of **B**, where **B** is arranged as follows:

$$\mathbf{B} = \begin{array}{c} \text{Absorbing States} \\ \text{Nonabsorbing States} \end{array} \left[\begin{array}{c|c} \mathbf{I} & \mathbf{O} \\ \hline \mathbf{R} & \mathbf{Q} \end{array} \right]$$

where **I** is the identity matrix whose order depends on the number of the absorbing states: 2 x 2 for the above example; **O** is a zero matrix whose order is the same as the identity matrix; **R** and **Q** are submatrices related to the nonabsorbing states. The steady-state matrix of **B**, which is matrix **S** is defined as

$$\mathbf{S} = \left[\begin{array}{c|c} \mathbf{I} & \mathbf{O} \\ \hline \mathbf{K} = (\mathbf{I} - \mathbf{Q})^{-1} & \mathbf{O} \end{array} \right].$$

And the probability of moving from the nonabsorbing states to the absorbing states can be found from $\mathbf{KR} = (\mathbf{I} - \mathbf{Q})^{-1}$.

Example 4: *Student mobility.* The example of student mobility (with a minor difference) has the transition matrix **B**, which is

	BA	A	E	M
BA	1	0	0	0
A	0	1	0	0
E	0.2	0.4	0.2	0.2
M	0.2	0.3	0.2	0.3

The task is to find the long-term probabilities of moving from the nonabsorbing states E and M, Economics and Management, to the absorbing states BA and A, Business Administration and Accounting.

The **B** matrix is

$$B = \begin{bmatrix} 1 & 0 & | & 0 & 0 \\ 0 & 1 & | & 0 & 0 \\ ---&---&+&---&--- \\ 0.2 & 0.4 & | & 0.2 & 0.2 \\ 0.2 & 0.3 & | & 0.2 & 0.3 \end{bmatrix} = \begin{bmatrix} I & | & O \\ --&+&-- \\ R & | & Q \end{bmatrix}.$$

It follows that

$$I - Q = \begin{bmatrix} 1 & 0 \\ 0 & 1 \end{bmatrix} - \begin{bmatrix} 0.2 & 0.2 \\ 0.2 & 0.3 \end{bmatrix} = \begin{bmatrix} 0.8 & -0.2 \\ -0.2 & 0.7 \end{bmatrix}.$$

Therefore,

$$K = (I - Q)^{-1}$$

is

$$K = \begin{bmatrix} 1.34615 & 0.384615 \\ 0.384615 & 1.538461 \end{bmatrix}.$$

K is also called the *fundamental matrix*. The required steady-state matrix S is

$$S = \begin{bmatrix} 1 & 0 & \vdots & 0 & 0 \\ 0 & 1 & \vdots & 0 & 0 \\ \cdots & \cdots & \vdots & \cdots & \cdots \\ 1.346153 & 0.384615 & \vdots & 0 & 0 \\ 0.384615 & 1.538461 & \vdots & 0 & 0 \end{bmatrix}.$$

To find the probabilities that students will move from Economics (the third nonabsorbing state) and Management (the fourth nonabsorbing state) to Business Administration (the first absorbing state) and Accounting (the second absorbing state), we have to find **KR**. That is,

$$\mathbf{KR} = \begin{bmatrix} 1.346153 & 0.384615 \\ 0.384615 & 1.538461 \end{bmatrix} \begin{bmatrix} 0.2 & 0.4 \\ 0.2 & 0.3 \end{bmatrix}.$$

Thus, the probability that an economics student will eventually move to Business Administration is 0.346; the probability that an economics student will eventually be in Accounting is 0.653; the probability that a management student will eventually be in Business Administration is 0.385; and the probability that a management student will eventually be in Accounting is 0.615. If the initial vector of total students in Economics and Management is [50   400], then

$$[50 \quad 400]\mathbf{KR} = [50 \quad 400] \begin{matrix} & \overset{\text{BA} \qquad \text{A}}{\begin{bmatrix} 0.346153 & 0.653846 \\ 0.384615 & 0.615384 \end{bmatrix}} \\ \begin{matrix} E \\ \\ M \end{matrix} & \end{matrix} \simeq [171 \quad 279].$$

and the resulting vector will provide us with the long-run number of Economics and Management students who will eventually be in Business Administration and Accounting.

Problems

1.   Consider the following information. The probability of being sunny on
        Monday given that it is cloudy on Sunday is 0.60, and the probability of
        being cloudy on Monday given that it is cloudy on Sunday is 0.40. Also,
        the probability of being sunny on Monday given that it is sunny on
        Sunday is 0.50, and the probability of being cloudy on Monday given it
        is sunny on Sunday is 0.50. Formulate the transition probability matrix
        and find the two-step transition matrix. Also, use the probability tree to
        find the two-step transition matrix.

2.   A record indicates that 60 percent of the time consumers purchase
        groceries from Jewell in May if they purchase their groceries there in
        April, and 40 percent of the time they purchase from National in May if
        they purchase the groceries from Jewell in April. The record shows that
        50 percent of the time the customers will buy from Jewell in May if they
        purchase their groceries from National in April, and 50 percent of the time
        they will purchase from National in May given that they purchase the
        groceries from National in April. Find the transition probability matrix
        and the long run probabilities. If Jewell's and National's customers are
        800 and 1000, respectively, how many customers will shop from Jewell
        and National in the long run?

3.   A business college has three departments: Economics, Accountancy, and
        Finance, with the following transition probabilities:

	Economics	Accountancy	Finance
Economics	0.30	0.30	0.40
Accountancy	0.01	0.89	0.10
Finance	0.25	0.20	0.55

        Interpret the above probabilities. If the initial distributions of students are
        [200   500   600], find the distribution after two years. Find the long-
        run probabilities   for each department and the long-run distribution of
        students.

4.   Assume the following absorbing matrix

		States		
	1	2	3	4
States 1	1	0	0	0
2	0	1	0	0
3	0.3	0.1	0.4	0.2
4	0.4	0.2	0.2	0.2

Determine the absorbing and nonabsorbing states. Find the steady-state matrix and the probabilities of moving from the nonabsorbing to the absorbing states.

5.   Consider the following probability transition matrix over a period of time, which describes mobility among three social classes: poor (P), middle class (MC), and rich (R):

	P	MC	R
P	0.50	0.40	0.10
MC	0.20	0.50	0.30
R	0.01	0.49	0.50

Find the steady-state probabilities of these three classes. If the vector of the current population is [1000   10000   2300], find the size of each class currently and in the long run.

6.   Assume the following absorbing matrix describing four social classes: poor (P), middle class (MC), Rich (R), Very Rich (VR):

		States		
	P	MC	R	VR
P	1	0	0	0
States MC	0	1	0	0
R	0.01	0.19	0.60	0.20
VR	0.00	0.40	0.45	0.15

Determine the absorbing and nonabsorbing states. Find the steady-state matrix and the probabilities of moving from the nonabsorbing to the absorbing states.

CHAPTER TWELVE

The General Linear Model

The *general linear model* is designed to estimate the impacts of independent variables, one at a time, on the dependent variable. This model has been utilized by economists to test economic propositions and their predictive power. Once this testing is successful, a hypothesis becomes a theory. In addition, there are numerous usages of the general linear model in economics and business to measure and quantify economic impacts and business relations, and economists have used this model effectively in these situations.

In this chapter the assumptions of the general linear model are outlined, and the estimation procedure is explained. Hypothesis testing as a central part of statistical inference will be illustrated as well as the coefficient of determination, R^2, and the analysis of variance (ANOVA). The utilization of the general linear model in economic forecasting is described, and some economic applications of the general linear model are provided.

The General Linear Model

Let us assume that there are k independent variables, X_1, X_2, X_3, ..., X_k, that have an influence on the dependent variable Y_i. The stochastic specification of the general linear model can be presented as

$$Y_i = B_0 + B_1X_{i1} + B_2X_{i2} + B_3X_{i3} + ... + B_kX_{ik} + U_i \qquad (1)$$

for i = 1, 2, 3, ..., n observations. For this equation, Y_i is a set of observations on the dependent variable Y; X_{ik} represents sets of observations on the k independent variables; B_0 is an intercept measuring the influence of the omitted independent variables from equation (1); U is a random disturbance; and B_k is a set of k coefficients to be estimated, coefficients that measure the impact of each X on Y. Also, it should be indicated that if U does not exist, equation (1) will reflect a deterministic, exact relation. But in the real world, nothing is exact; accordingly,

U is introduced to make equation (1) a probabilistic (stochastic) equation.

If there are n observations on each variable in equation (1), equation (1) will take the following form:

$$Y_1 = B_o + B_1 X_{11} + B_2 X_{12} + B_3 X_{13} +...+ B_k X_{1k} + U_1$$

$$Y_2 = B_o + B_1 X_{21} + B_2 X_{22} + B_3 X_{23} +...+ B_k X_{2k} + U_2$$

$$...$$ (1')

$$Y_n = B_o + B_1 X_{n1} + B_2 X_{n2} + B_3 X_{n3} +...+ B_k X_{nk} + U_n$$

The above form can be written in matrix notations (bold face letters) as

$$Y = XB + U$$ (2)

where

$$
Y = \begin{bmatrix} Y_1 \\ Y_2 \\ Y_3 \\ Y_4 \\ . \\ . \\ . \\ . \\ Y_n \end{bmatrix}, \quad
X = \begin{bmatrix}
1 & X_{11} & X_{12}...X_{1k} \\
1 & X_{21} & X_{22}...X_{2k} \\
1 & X_{31} & X_{32}...X_{3k} \\
1 & X_{41} & X_{42}...X_{4k} \\
. & . & . \\
. & . & . \\
. & . & . \\
1 & X_{n1} & ...X_{nk}
\end{bmatrix}, \quad
B = \begin{bmatrix} B_o \\ B_1 \\ B_2 \\ B_3 \\ . \\ . \\ . \\ B_k \end{bmatrix}, \text{ and } U = \begin{bmatrix} U_1 \\ U_2 \\ U_3 \\ U_4 \\ . \\ . \\ . \\ U_n \end{bmatrix}.
$$

The column vector of ones in matrix **X** reflect the intercept, and the column vectors of **B** and **U** are unknown and must be estimated.

To estimate the column vector of **B**, and usually the estimated coefficients are written as **B^**, several assumptions are made. The first assumption is that

$$E(U) = E \begin{bmatrix} U_1 \\ U_2 \\ U_3 \\ U_4 \\ \cdot \\ \cdot \\ U_n \end{bmatrix} = \begin{bmatrix} E(U_1) \\ E(U_2) \\ E(U_3) \\ E(U_4) \\ \cdot \\ \cdot \\ E(U_5) \end{bmatrix} = \begin{bmatrix} 0 \\ 0 \\ 0 \\ 0 \\ \cdot \\ \cdot \\ 0 \end{bmatrix} = \mathbf{0}.$$

indicating that the mean (the expected value) of the stochastic disturbance term is zero. (See the Appendix for the rules of expectations.)

The second and third assumptions can be explained after obtaining $E(UU')$. This term is equal to

$$E(UU') = E \begin{bmatrix} U_1 \\ U_2 \\ U_3 \\ U_4 \\ \cdot \\ \cdot \\ \cdot \\ U_n \end{bmatrix} \begin{bmatrix} U_1 & U_2 & U_3 & U_4 & \cdot & \cdot & \cdot & U_n \end{bmatrix}$$

or

$$= E \begin{bmatrix} U^2_1 & U_1U_2 & U_1U_3 & U_1U_4 & \ldots & U_1U_n \\ U_2U_1 & U^2_2 & U_2U_3 & U_2U_4 & \ldots & U_2U_n \\ U_3U_1 & U_3U_2 & U^2_3 & U_3U_4 & \ldots & U_3U_n \\ U_4U_1 & U_4U_2 & U_4U_3 & U^2_4 & \ldots & U_4U_n \\ \ldots & \ldots & \ldots & \ldots & \ldots & \ldots \\ U_nU_1 & U_nU_2 & U_nU_3 & U_nU_4 & \ldots & U^2_n \end{bmatrix},$$

which is equal to

$$\begin{bmatrix} Var(U_1) & Cov(U_1,U_2) & Cov(U_1,U_3) & \ldots Cov(U_1,U_2) \\ Cov(U_1,U_2) & Var(U_2) & Cov(U_2,U_3) & \ldots Cov(U_2,U_n) \\ Cov(U_1,U_3) & Cov(U_2,U_3) & Var(U_3) & \ldots Cov(U_3,U_n) \\ \ldots & \ldots & \ldots & \ldots \\ Cov(U_1,U_n) & Cov(U_2,U_n) & Cov(U_3,U_n) & \ldots & Var(U_n) \end{bmatrix}.$$

As can be seen, the variances [$Var(U_i)$] are on the main diagonal, obtained from

$$Var(U_i) = E[U_i - E(U_i)]^2 = E(U^2_i) = \sigma^2 \qquad (3)$$

for $i = 1, 2, ..., n$. This result implies that the disturbance terms are assumed to have an identical and a constant variance for all observations (i.e., $Var(U_i)$, $i = 1, 2, ...,$ n, are equal). In other words, the variance is homoscedastic, and this is the second assumption of the general linear model. Also, if it is assumed that $Cov(U_iU_j) = 0$, then $E(UU^t)$ is equal to

$$\begin{bmatrix} \sigma^2 & 0 & 0 & 0 & \ldots & 0 \\ 0 & \sigma^2 & 0 & 0 & \ldots & 0 \\ 0 & 0 & \sigma^2 & 0 & \ldots & 0 \\ 0 & 0 & 0 & \sigma^2 & \ldots & 0 \\ & & & & & \\ 0 & 0 & 0 & 0 & \ldots & \sigma^2 \end{bmatrix}$$

or

$$E(UU^t) = \sigma^2 I \qquad (4)$$

where **I** is an identity matrix of dimension n x n, and S^2 is the variance of the disturbance term, which can be found from equation (25), as we shall see later in the chapter.

The third assumption can be expressed in this way. $Cov(U_i, U_j)$ is equal to zero, because

$$Cov(U_i U_j) = E[(U_i - E(U_i)(U_j - E(U_j)] = E(U_i U_j) = 0; \ i, j = 1, 2, \ldots, n \ \text{and} \ i \neq j.$$

Consequently, the error terms corresponding to different observations are not serially correlated (i.e., autocorrelation does not exist). If homoscedasticity exists and autocorrelation does not exist, the variance-covariance matrix is the same as in equation (4).

The fourth assumption suggests that the disturbance term U_i is a normally distributed random variable with a mean of zero and variance of σ^2, that is, $U_i \sim N(0, \sigma^2)$. One should note that U_i is indeed a random variable because it may take (according to chance) negative, positive, or zero values.

The fifth assumption demonstrates that the independent variables, **X**, are fixed (nonstochastic), while the dependent variable Y varies as a result of various random impacts. Because the independent variables are fixed, the disturbance term U_i is assumed to be independent of these variables. In other words,

$$E(UX) = XE(U) = 0$$

or

$$Cov(XU) = E\{[X - E(X)][U - E(U)]\} = XE(U) = 0.$$

Other assumptions can be cited as well. First, there is no error of measurements in the independent variables; second, there is no multicollinearity or strong correlations among the independent variables; and third there is no specification error in the model.

The OLS Method of Statistical Estimation

One method, which is used in this chapter, for estimating the true coefficients **B** is the ordinary least squares (OLS). This method works as follows. Suppose the general linear model is estimated and written as

$$Y = XB^\wedge + e \tag{5}$$

where the hat ($\wedge$) indicates estimated values for the true coefficients **B**, and **e** represents the residual vector. The OLS aims to minimize the sum of the squares of residuals **e'e**. Using equation (5) for the sum of the squares (Gujarati 1995), we obtain

$$e'e = (Y - XB^\wedge)'(Y - XB^\wedge), \tag{6}$$

which is actually the sum of the squares of the differences between the actual Y_i and the estimated Y_i (or $Y^\wedge_i$). Figure 12.1 shows the difference between $Y^\wedge_i$ and Y_i for a simple regression model, and what the OLS does is to minimize this distance: **e'e**.

Figure 12.1. **Estimated Regression Line**

Using the property of the transpose, equation (6) can be rewritten as

$$e^te = (Y^t - B^{\wedge t}X^t)(Y - XB^{\wedge})$$

$$= (Y^t - B^{\wedge t}X^t)(Y) - (Y^t - B^{\wedge t}X^t)(XB^{\wedge})$$

$$= Y^tY - B^{\wedge t}X^tY - Y^tXB^{\wedge} + B^{\wedge t}X^tXB^{\wedge} \tag{7}$$

but $B^{\wedge t}X^tY$ is a scalar (a number such as 50) whose transpose is equal to $Y^tXB^{\wedge}$. Therefore,

$$e^te = Y^tY - 2B^{\wedge t}X^tY + B^{\wedge t}X^tXB^{\wedge}. \tag{8}$$

To minimize equation (8), the equation must be differentiated partially with respect to B, and setting the outcome equal to zero yields

$$2X^tXB^{\wedge} - 2X^tY = 0$$

or

$$X^tXB^{\wedge} = X^tY. \tag{9}$$

After multiplying equation (9) by $(X^tX)^{-1}$, we obtain

$$B^{\wedge} = (X^tX)^{-1}X^tY, \tag{10}$$

which is the estimator that must be used to find the column vector of the estimated coefficients $B^{\wedge}$—the estimates.

To simplify the computations, one can find $B^{\wedge}$ by using the deviational form of variables. That is, instead of using Y one can employ the deviation

$$y = Y - Y^-,$$

where Y^- is the mean of Y. Similarly, the deviation of X from its mean is

$$x = X - X^-,$$

where X^- is the mean of X. If the deviational form is used, equation (10) becomes

$$B^{\wedge} = (x^tx)^{-1}x^ty, \tag{11}$$

where x is a matrix that does not have the column vector of ones, and $B^{\wedge}$ does not include the intercept $B^\wedge_o$, which is obtained from the following equation:

$$B^\wedge_o = Y^- - B^\wedge_1 X^-_1 - B^\wedge_2 X^-_2 - ... - B^\wedge_k X^-_k. \tag{12}$$

Having outlined the estimation technique, it is appropriate to indicate that the OLS estimator has several properties for small samples (Koutsoyiannis 1977), and these properties are explained below.

1. It is an unbiased estimator. That is,

$$E(\mathbf{B}^\wedge) - \mathbf{B} = \text{Bias} = \mathbf{0}.$$

In other words, the expected value of the estimated **B** is equal to the true **B**. This property is shown in Figure 12.2.

Figure 12. 2. **Biased and Unbiased Estimators**

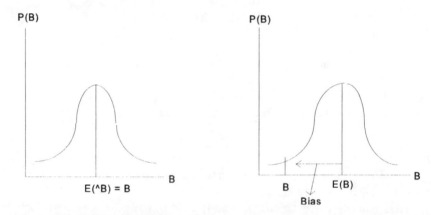

2. It is the best estimator. A best estimator has a minimum variance relative to all other estimators obtained by using other methods of statistical estimation (see Figure 12.3). Mathematically,

$$\text{Var}(\mathbf{B}^\wedge) < \text{Var}(\mathbf{B}\sim)$$

where **B**~ is another estimator for the true **B**, and **B**^ is the best estimator.

Figure 12.3. **Property of Best Estimators**

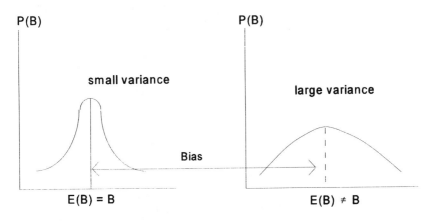

3. It is an efficient estimator. This property contains the previous two properties. An estimator is said to be efficient if it is unbiased and has a minimum variance within the class of all unbiased estimators.

4. It is a linear estimator. It can be shown that the OLS estimator is a linear function of Y_i.

In sum, these properties indicate that $B^\wedge$ is BLUE: *B*est, *L*inear, *U*nbiased *E*stimator.

Example 1: The consumption function is written as

$$Y = B_o + B_1 X_1 + B_2 X_2 + U,$$

where Y is consumption; X_1 is disposable income; X_2 is one year lagged consumption (Y_{t-1}); B_o is an intercept; B_1 is the marginal propensity to consume; and B_2 measures the impact of past consumption on current consumption. Suppose that we are interested in estimating B_o, B_1, and B_2 by using equation (10) given the following time series data on X and Y (in the United States of America) for the period 1980 to 1989:

Time	1980	1981	1982	1983	1984	1985	1986	1987	1988	1989
Consumption $(Y)	2.00	2.02	2.05	2.15	2.25	2.35	2.45	2.52	2.61	2.66
Income $(X_1)	2.21	2.25	2.26	2.33	2.47	2.54	2.64	2.67	2.80	2.87
Past consumption $(X_2)	2.00	2.00	2.02	2.05	2.15	2.25	2.35	2.45	2.52	2.61

Solution: The column vector **Y** and matrix **X** take the forms

$$
\mathbf{Y} = \begin{bmatrix} 2.00 \\ 2.02 \\ 2.05 \\ 2.15 \\ 2.25 \\ 2.35 \\ 2.45 \\ 2.52 \\ 2.61 \\ 2.66 \end{bmatrix}, \mathbf{X} = \begin{bmatrix} 1 & 2.21 & 2.00 \\ 1 & 2.25 & 2.00 \\ 1 & 2.26 & 2.02 \\ 1 & 2.33 & 2.05 \\ 1 & 2.47 & 2.15 \\ 1 & 2.54 & 2.25 \\ 1 & 2.64 & 2.35 \\ 1 & 2.67 & 2.45 \\ 1 & 2.80 & 2.52 \\ 1 & 2.87 & 2.61 \end{bmatrix}.
$$

Therefore,

$$
\mathbf{X'X} = \begin{bmatrix} 1 & 1 & 1 & 1 & 1 & 1 & 1 & 1 & 1 & 1 \\ 2.21 & 2.25 & 2.26 & 2.33 & 2.47 & 2.54 & 2.64 & 2.67 & 2.80 & 2.87 \\ 2.00 & 2.00 & 2.02 & 2.05 & 2.15 & 2.25 & 2.35 & 2.45 & 2.52 & 2.61 \end{bmatrix} \begin{bmatrix} 1 & 2.21 & 2.00 \\ 1 & 2.25 & 2.00 \\ 1 & 2.26 & 2.02 \\ 1 & 2.33 & 2.05 \\ 1 & 2.47 & 2.15 \\ 1 & 2.54 & 2.25 \\ 1 & 2.64 & 2.35 \\ 1 & 2.67 & 2.45 \\ 1 & 2.80 & 2.52 \\ 1 & 2.87 & 2.61 \end{bmatrix}
$$

$$
= \begin{bmatrix} 10 & 25.04 & 22.4 \\ 25.04 & 63.211 & 56.5494 \\ 22.4 & 56.5794 & 50.6554 \end{bmatrix}
$$

$$\text{and } (\mathbf{X^t X})^{-1} = \begin{bmatrix} 15.02176 & -20.6834 & 16.45969 \\ -20.6834 & 96.02103 & -98.1040 \\ 16.45969 & -98.1040 & 102.3182 \end{bmatrix}.$$

$$\mathbf{X'Y} = \begin{bmatrix} 1 & 1 & 1 & 1 & 1 & 1 & 1 & 1 & 1 & 1 \\ 2.21 & 2.25 & 2.26 & 2.33 & 2.47 & 2.54 & 2.64 & 2.67 & 2.80 & 2.87 \\ 2.00 & 2.00 & 2.02 & 2.05 & 2.15 & 2.25 & 2.35 & 2.45 & 2.52 & 2.61 \end{bmatrix} \begin{bmatrix} 2.00 \\ 2.02 \\ 2.05 \\ 2.15 \\ 2.25 \\ 2.35 \\ 2.45 \\ 2.52 \\ 2.61 \\ 2.66 \end{bmatrix} =$$

$$\begin{bmatrix} 23.0600 \\ 58.2726 \\ 52.1648 \end{bmatrix}$$

and

$$\mathbf{B^{\wedge}} = (\mathbf{X'X})^{-1}\mathbf{X'Y} = \begin{bmatrix} 15.02176 & -20.6834 & 16.45969 \\ -20.6834 & 96.02103 & -98.1040 \\ 16.45969 & -98.1040 & 102.3182 \end{bmatrix} \begin{bmatrix} 23.0600 \\ 58.2726 \\ 52.1648 \end{bmatrix} = \begin{bmatrix} -0.26267 \\ 0.853386 \\ 0.192764 \end{bmatrix}.$$

Accordingly, the estimated regression model is reported as

$$Y^{\wedge} = -0.26267 + 0.853386 X_1 + 0.19 X_2$$

and the derivative of $Y^{\wedge}$ with respect to X_1 is 0.853386, which means that if income increases by \$1 million, consumption will increase by \$853,386.

Example 2: Estimate the previous model by using the deviational form of the variables, that is, equation (11).

Solution: The means of Y, X_1, and X_2 are 2.306, 2.504, and 2.24, respectively. Because $y = Y - Y^-$, $x_1 = X_1 - X^-_1$, and $x_2 = X_2 - X^-_2$, the observations of example 1 become

$$
y = \begin{bmatrix} -0.306 \\ -0.286 \\ -0.256 \\ -0.156 \\ -0.056 \\ -0.044 \\ -0.144 \\ -0.214 \\ -0.304 \\ -0.354 \end{bmatrix}, x_1 = \begin{bmatrix} -0.294 \\ -0.254 \\ -0.244 \\ -0.174 \\ -0.034 \\ 0.036 \\ 0.136 \\ 0.166 \\ 0.296 \\ 0.366 \end{bmatrix}, \text{ and } x_2 = \begin{bmatrix} -0.24 \\ -0.24 \\ -0.22 \\ -0.19 \\ -0.09 \\ 0.01 \\ 0.11 \\ 0.21 \\ 0.28 \\ 0.37 \end{bmatrix}
$$

$$
x^t x = \begin{bmatrix} 0.51084 & 0.4898 \\ 0.4898 & 0.4794 \end{bmatrix}, \quad (x^t x)^{-1} = \begin{bmatrix} 96.02103 & -98.1040 \\ -98.1040 & 102.3182 \end{bmatrix}
$$

$$
\text{and } x^t y = \begin{bmatrix} 0.53036 \\ 0.5104 \end{bmatrix}. \quad \text{Thus, } \mathbf{B}^\wedge = (x^t x)^{-1} x^t y = \begin{bmatrix} 0.853386 \\ 0.192764 \end{bmatrix} = \begin{bmatrix} B^\wedge_1 \\ B^\wedge_2 \end{bmatrix}.
$$

To find the intercept, equation (12) is used, and the result is

$$B^\wedge_o = Y^- - B^\wedge_1 X^-_1 - B^\wedge_2 X^-_2 = 2.306 - 0.853386(2.504) - 0.192764(2.24) = -0.26267.$$

Example 3: Estimate the model $Y_t = B_o + B_1 X_{1t} + U_t$ using the same observations on consumption and income only. Also, find the Durbin-Watson statistic $\mathbf{d}^*$, used for detecting whether or not observations are autocorrelated, which can be found from equation (13)

$$\mathbf{d}^* = 2(1 - p),$$ (13)

where p is the autocorrelation coefficient.

Solution: This model is called a *simple regression model* because it contains two variables: the dependent variable Y and one independent variableX. Vector **Y** and matrix **X** take the forms:

$$
\mathbf{Y} =
\begin{bmatrix}
2.0 \\
2.02 \\
2.05 \\
2.15 \\
2.25 \\
2.35 \\
2.45 \\
2.52 \\
2.61 \\
2.66
\end{bmatrix},
\quad
\mathbf{X} =
\begin{bmatrix}
1 & 2.21 \\
1 & 2.25 \\
1 & 2.26 \\
1 & 2.33 \\
1 & 2.47 \\
1 & 2.54 \\
1 & 2.64 \\
1 & 2.67 \\
1 & 2.80 \\
1 & 2.87
\end{bmatrix}
$$

and

$$
\mathbf{X'X} =
\begin{bmatrix}
10 & 25.04 \\
25.04 & 63.211
\end{bmatrix},
\quad
\mathbf{X'Y} =
\begin{bmatrix}
23.0600 \\
58.2726
\end{bmatrix}
$$

$$
(\mathbf{X'X})^{-1} =
\begin{bmatrix}
12.37393 & -4.90173 \\
-4.90173 & 1.95756
\end{bmatrix};
\text{ hence, }
\mathbf{B}^{\wedge} =
\begin{bmatrix}
-0.29368 \\
1.038211
\end{bmatrix}
=
\begin{bmatrix}
B^{\wedge}_{o} \\
B^{\wedge}_{1}
\end{bmatrix}.
$$

Accordingly, the estimated regression model is reported as

$$Y^{\wedge}_t = -0.29368 + 1.038X_{1t}.$$

One should note that the column vector $\mathbf{B}^{\wedge}$ can be obtained by using equation (9), which can be rewritten as

$$\begin{bmatrix} 10 & 25.40 \\ 25.40 & 63.71 \end{bmatrix} \begin{bmatrix} B^{\wedge}_o \\ B^{\wedge}_1 \end{bmatrix} = \begin{bmatrix} 23.06 \\ 58.2726 \end{bmatrix}.$$

As can be seen, this is a system of two equations

$$10B^{\wedge}_o + 25.4\ B^{\wedge}_1 = 23.06$$

$$25.4\ B^{\wedge}_o + 63.71\ B^{\wedge}_1 = 58.2726$$

whose solutions are $B^{\wedge}_o = -0.29368$ and $B^{\wedge}_1 = 1.038211$.

With respect to Durbin-Watson statistic $\mathbf{d}^*$, it can also be obtained from

$$\mathbf{d}^* = \Sigma\ (e_t - e_{t-1})^2\ /\ \Sigma\ e^2_t. \tag{14}$$

(This equation can also be written as $\mathbf{d}^* = 2(1 - p)$, which is equation (13), and p is as before the autocorrelation coefficient, which is equal to $\Sigma\ e_t e_{t-1} / \Sigma\ e^2_{t-1}$.) In matrix notations we know that $e_t = \mathbf{Y} - \mathbf{Y}^{\wedge}$ and $\mathbf{Y}^{\wedge} = \mathbf{XB}^{\wedge}$, thus suggesting that $e_t = \mathbf{Y} - \mathbf{XB}^{\wedge}$. Using these matrix equations one can find the necessary components for finding the statistic $\mathbf{d}^*$.

Initially, vector e_t is

$$
e_t = Y - Y^\wedge =
\begin{bmatrix}
2.00 \\
2.02 \\
2.05 \\
2.15 \\
2.25 \\
2.35 \\
2.45 \\
2.52 \\
2.61 \\
2.66
\end{bmatrix}
-
\begin{bmatrix}
2.000765 \\
2.042294 \\
2.052676 \\
2.125351 \\
2.27070 \\
2.343375 \\
2.447196 \\
2.478343 \\
2.61331 \\
2.685985
\end{bmatrix}
=
\begin{bmatrix}
-0.000765 \\
-0.022294 \\
-0.002676 \\
0.024649 \\
-0.02070 \\
0.006625 \\
0.002804 \\
0.041657 \\
-0.00331 \\
-0.025985
\end{bmatrix}
; \text{ and } e_{t-1} =
\begin{bmatrix}
--- \\
-0.000765 \\
-0.022294 \\
-0.002676 \\
0.024649 \\
-0.0207 \\
0.006625 \\
0.002804 \\
0.041657 \\
-0.00331
\end{bmatrix}
$$

Therefore, the column vector $(e_t - e_{t-1})$ (after losing the first observation) becomes

$$
\begin{bmatrix}
-0.021529 \\
0.019618 \\
0.027325 \\
-0.045349 \\
0.027325 \\
-0.00382 \\
0.038853 \\
-0.044967 \\
-0.022675
\end{bmatrix}
$$

and $\Sigma (e_t - e_{t-1})^2 = 0.00846$. In matrix notations, $\Sigma (e_t - e_{t-1})^2 = (e_t - e_{t-1})^t (e_t - e_{t-1})$ and $\Sigma e^2_t = e^t e$. Using these equations one should obtain $\Sigma (e_t - e_{t-1})^2 = (e_t - e_{t-1})^t (e_t - e_{t-1}) = 0.00846$ and $\Sigma e^2_t = e^t e = 0.004107$. Hence, the calculated Durbin-Watson statistic is

$$\mathbf{d}^* = 0.00846 / 0.004107 = 2.05.$$

And $\mathbf{d}^*$ must be compared to the tabulated $\mathbf{d}$ (a table containing upper and lower values for $\mathbf{d}$, which can be found in any econometrics text such as Gujarati [1995, pp. 818–821] in order to find whether the observations are autocorrelated. If $\mathbf{d}^* < \mathbf{d_L}$ there is autocorrelation, where $\mathbf{d_L}$ is the lower limit for $\mathbf{d}^*$, obtained from the table; if $\mathbf{d}^* > 4 - \mathbf{d_L}$, there is negative autocorrelation; if $\mathbf{d_U} < \mathbf{d}^* < 4 - \mathbf{d_L}$ there is no autocorrelation, where $\mathbf{d_U}$ is the upper limit of $\mathbf{d}^*$, obtained from the table; and if $\mathbf{d_L} < \mathbf{d}^* < \mathbf{d_U}$ there is an inconclusive result (Koutsoyiannis 1977). For our example, there is no autocorrelation as $\mathbf{d}^*$ is very close to 2.

It should be mentioned that $\mathbf{d}^*$ is based on some assumptions. The first assumption is that the regression model should have an intercept and have no missing data. The second assumption suggests that the disturbance term U_t is generated according to a first- autoregressive process, that is, $U_t = pU_{t-1} + e_t$. And the third assumption is that the regression model should not include a lagged dependent variable as an independent variable.

Example 4: For a simple regression model one can develop the following normal equations to find $B^\wedge_0$ and $B^\wedge_1$ without using matrix algebra (Salvatori 1982; Koutsoyiannis 1977). The population regression equation is

$$Y_i = B_0 + B_1 X_{1i} + U_i, \tag{15}$$

which can be rewritten as

$$U_i = Y_i - B_0 - B_1 X_{1i}.$$

We can minimize the sum of the squares

$$Z = \Sigma(Y_i - B_0 - B_1 X_{1i})^2 \tag{16}$$

by differentiating equation (16) partially with respect to B_0 and B_1; thus we obtain

$$\partial Z / \partial B_0 = 2 \,\Sigma(Y_i - B^\wedge_0 - B^\wedge_1 X_{1i})(-1) = 0$$

$$\partial Z / \partial B_1 = \Sigma(Y_i - B^\wedge_0 - B^\wedge_1 X_{1i}) = 0 \tag{17}$$

and

$$= 2 \,\Sigma(Y_i - B^\wedge_0 - B^\wedge_1 X_{1i})(-X_1) = 0$$

$$= \Sigma(Y_i - B^\wedge_0 - B^\wedge_1 X_{1i})(-X_1) = 0. \tag{18}$$

Equations (17) and (18) can be rewritten, respectively, as

$$\Sigma\, Y_i - B\hat{}_1\, \Sigma X_{1i} = NB\hat{}_0 \qquad (17^*)$$

$$\Sigma\, Y_iX_{1i} - B\hat{}_0\, \Sigma\, X_{1i} - B\hat{}_1\, \Sigma\, X^2_{1i}. \qquad (18^*)$$

After arranging equations (17*) and (18*) we obtain

$$\Sigma\, Y_i = NB\hat{}_0 + B\hat{}_1\, \Sigma\, X_{1i}$$

$$\Sigma\, Y_iX_1 = B\hat{}_0\, \Sigma\, X_{1i} + B\hat{}_1\, \Sigma X^2_{1i}.$$

Solving for $B\hat{}_0$ and $B\hat{}_1$ by Cramer's rule, we obtain

$$\begin{vmatrix} N & \Sigma x_{1i} \\ \\ \displaystyle\sum_i x_{1i} & \displaystyle\sum_i x^2_{1i} \end{vmatrix} = N \sum_i x^2_{1i} - (\sum_i x_{1i})^2$$

$$\begin{vmatrix} \displaystyle\sum_i Y_i & \displaystyle\sum_i X_{1i} \\ \\ \displaystyle\sum_i Y_1x_1 & \displaystyle\sum_i X^2_{1i} \end{vmatrix} = \sum_i Y \sum_i x^2_{1i} - \sum_i Y_iX_{1i} \sum_i x_{1i}$$

$$\begin{vmatrix} N & \displaystyle\sum_i Y_i \\ \\ \displaystyle\sum_i X_{1i} & \displaystyle\sum_i Y_iX_{1i} \end{vmatrix} = N \sum_i Y_iX_{1i} - \sum_i X_{1i} \sum_i Y_i$$

and, $B\hat{}_0$ and $B\hat{}_1$ are

$$B\hat{}_0 = [\, \Sigma Y_i\, \Sigma X^2_{1i} - \Sigma Y_iX_{1i}\, \Sigma X_{1i}\,] \,/\, [N\, \Sigma X^2_{1i} - (\, \Sigma X_{1i})^2] \qquad (19)$$

$$B\hat{}_1 = [N\, \Sigma Y_iX_{1i} - \Sigma X_{1i}\, \Sigma Y_i] \,/\, [N\, \Sigma X^2_{1i} - (\, \Sigma X_{1i})^2] \qquad (20)$$

$$= [\, \Sigma(X_{1i} - X\bar{})(Y_i - Y\bar{})] \,/\, [\, \Sigma(X_{1i} - X\bar{})^2].$$

Note that

$$N \Sigma(X_{1i} - X^-)^2 = N \Sigma X^2_{1i} - (\Sigma X_{1i})^2.$$

In any event, equations (19) and (20) can be used to estimate the regression model of example 3; the basic results are

Y_i	X_{1i}	$X_{1i}Y_i$	X^2_{1i}
2.00	2.21	4.42	4.8841
2.02	2.25	4.545	5.0625
2.05	2.26	4.633	5.1076
2.15	2.33	5.0095	5.4289
2.25	2.47	5.5575	6.1009
2.35	2.54	5.969	6.4516
2.45	2.64	6.468	6.9696
2.52	2.67	6.7284	7.1289
2.61	2.80	7.308	7.84
2.66	2.87	7.6342	8.2369

$\Sigma Y_i = 23.06$ $\Sigma X_{1i} = 25.04$ $\Sigma X_{1i}Y_i = 58.2726$ $\Sigma X^2_{1i} = 63.211$

Also, we know that $N = 10$, $(\Sigma X_{1i})^2 = (25.04)^2 = 627.0016$; therefore,

$B^\wedge_o = [(23.06)(63.211) - (48.2726)(25.04)] / [(10)(63.211) - 627.0016] = -0.2936$

and

$B^\wedge_1 = [(10)(58.2726) - (23.06)(25.04)] / [(10)(63.211) - 627.0016] = 1.0382.$

It should be noted that a regression model may not have an intercept. If this is the case, equation (16) becomes

$$Z = \Sigma (Y_i - B_1X_{1i})^2$$

and upon minimizing, the estimator becomes

$$B^\wedge_1 = \Sigma X_{1i}Y_i / \Sigma X^2_{1i}. \qquad (20^*)$$

If the same observations are used, the result is

$$B^\wedge_1 = 58.2726/63.211 = 0.92$$

and the estimated regression line becomes

$$Y^\wedge_i = 0.92X_{1i,}$$

which emanates from the origin; that is, if X_1 is equal to zero, $Y^\wedge_i$ is also equal to zero.

Testing of Statistical Hypotheses

To test statistical hypotheses in the general linear model, the variance-covariance matrix of $B^\wedge$ has to be determined (Pindyck and Rubinfield 1991; Gujarati 1995). As we have obtained equation (10)

$$B^\wedge = (X^tX)^{-1}X^tY$$

and we know from equation (2) that

$$Y = XB + U$$

we can use equation (2) in equation (10) to obtain

$$B^\wedge = (X^tX)^{-1}X^t(XB + U)$$

$$= (X^tX)^{-1}X^tXB + (X^tX)^{-1}X^tU$$

$$= IB + (X^tX)^{-1}X^tU$$

$$= B + (X^tX)^{-1}X^tU$$

or

$$B^\wedge - B = (X^tX)^{-1}X^tU. \tag{21}$$

By definition, the variance-covariance of $B^\wedge$, var-cov($B^\wedge$), is equal to

$$\text{var-cov}(B^\wedge) = E[(B^\wedge - B)(B^\wedge - B)^t]. \tag{22}$$

Using equation (21) in equation (22), we obtain

$$\text{var-cov}(B^\wedge) = E\{[(X^tX)^{-1}X^tU][(X^tX)^{-1}X^tU]^t\}. \tag{23}$$

But the transpose of $(X^tX)^{-1}$ is equal to $(X^tX)^{-1}$ because these matrices are symmetrical; therefore, equation (23) becomes

$$= E[(X^tX)^{-1}X^tUU^tX(X^tX)^{-1}]$$

$$= (X^tX)^{-1}X^tE(UU^t)X(X^tX)^{-1}$$

$$= (X^tX)^{-1}X^t\sigma^2X(X^tX)^{-1}$$

$$= \sigma^2(X^tX)^{-1} \tag{24}$$

where

$$\sigma^2 = e^te / (N - K) \tag{25}$$

and N-K is the degrees of freedom. (K is the number of estimated coefficients.) Also, note that $e^te = Y^tY - B^{\wedge t}X^tY$, where (e^te) is called the *residual sum of squares*; (Y^tY) is the total sum of squares; and the last term is the *error sum of squares*. In addition, the diagonal elements of the variance-covariance matrix are the variances of the estimated coefficients, and the elements off the diagonal represent the covariances of the estimated coefficients.

Example 5: Find the variance-covariance matrix for the model introduced in example 1.
Solution: To obtain the variance-covariance matrix, we need to find S^2. To do so, we have to determine Y^tY and $B^{\wedge t}X^tY$.

$$Y^tY = [2.00 \quad 2.02 \quad 2.05 \quad 2.15 \quad 2.25 \quad 2.35 \quad 2.45 \quad 2.52 \quad 2.61 \quad 2.66] \begin{bmatrix} 2.00 \\ 2.02 \\ 2.05 \\ 2.15 \\ 2.25 \\ 2.35 \\ 2.45 \\ 2.52 \\ 2.61 \\ 2.66 \end{bmatrix} = 53.731.$$

and

$$B^{\wedge t}X^tY = [-0.26267 \quad 0.853386 \quad 0.1922764] \begin{bmatrix} 23.0600 \\ 58.2726 \\ 52.1648 \end{bmatrix} = 53.72734.$$

Thus, $\mathbf{e'e} = 53.731 - 53.72734 = 0.00366$, and $\mathbf{S^2} = 0.00366/(10-3) = 0.00052$. It follows that

$$\mathbf{S^2(X'X)^{-1}} = [0.00052] \begin{bmatrix} 15.02176 & -20.6834 & 16.45969 \\ -20.6834 & 96.02103 & -98.1040 \\ 16.45969 & -98.1040 & 102.3182 \end{bmatrix} =$$

$$\begin{bmatrix} 0.00781 & -0.0108 & 0.00856 \\ -0.0108 & 0.0499 & -0.0510 \\ 0.00856 & -0.0510 & 0.0532 \end{bmatrix} .$$

And this matrix shows not only the variances of the estimated coefficients but also their covariances. That is, $\mathbf{S^2(X'X)^{-1}}$ gives

$$\begin{bmatrix} \text{cov } (\mathbf{B_o,B_o}) = \mathrm{Var}(b_o) & \text{cov } (\mathbf{B_o,B_1}) & \text{cov } (\mathbf{B_o,B_2}) \\ \text{cov } (\mathbf{B_1,B_o}) & \text{cov } (\mathbf{B_1,B_2}) = \mathrm{Var}(\mathbf{B_1}) & \text{cov } (\mathbf{B_1,B_2}) \\ \text{cov}(\mathbf{B_2,B_o}) & \text{cov } (\mathbf{B_2,B_1}) & \text{cov } (\mathbf{B_2,B_2}) = \mathrm{Var}(\mathbf{B_2}) \end{bmatrix} .$$

For example, cov $(\mathbf{B_2,B_o}) = 0.00856$, which gives the linear association between the estimated coefficients $B^{\wedge}_2$ and $B^{\wedge}_o$.

Example 6: Find the variance-covariance matrix for the deviational-form model of example 2.
Solution: Calculate

$\mathbf{y'y} = 0.55464$, $\mathbf{B^{\wedge t}X'y} = 0.550989$, $\mathbf{e'e} = 0.55464 - 0.550989 = 0.003651$, $\mathbf{S^2} = 0.003651 / (10-3) = 0.00052$,

and

$$S^2 (x^t x)^{-1} = \begin{bmatrix} 0.0499 & -0.510 \\ -0.0510 & 0.0532 \end{bmatrix}.$$

Having found $S^2(X^tX)^{-1}$, hypotheses that are related to the estimated coefficients can be tested by using the t distribution, or as it is called the *t-ratio*. Before doing so, it should be stated that there are several forms of hypotheses testing (Yamane 1964), of which two forms will be employed here. One form is

$$\text{Ho: } B_i = 0$$

$$\text{Ha: } B_i \neq 0$$

or

$$\text{Ho: } B_i = 1$$

$$\text{Ha: } B_i \neq 1$$

where Ho is the null hypothesis, Ha is the alternative hypothesis, and the zero and one are the hypothesized values for the *ith* coefficient. The above form indicates that the test is conducted on both sides of the t distribution, as shown in Figure 12.4.

Figure 12.4. **Acceptance and Rejection Regions**

$$\alpha = 0.05$$
$$\alpha/2 = 0.025$$
$$t_{0.025, 8} = 2\cdot306$$

Acceptance Region

Rejection Region

-2·306   0   2·306

The second form is to test the hypothesis so that

$$\text{Ho: } B_i = 0$$

$$Ha: B_i > 0$$

or

$$Ho: B_i = 0$$

$$Ha: B_i < 0.$$

This form conducts the test on one side of the t distribution. $Ha: B_i > 0$ indicates that the test is conducted on the right side of the t distribution, whereas $Ha: B_i < 0$ indicates the test is conducted on the left side of the distribution. Figure 12.5 shows how these forms are used.

Figure 12.5. **Rejection Regions In Other Testing Forms**

In either form, a tabulated value of the t-ratio (with a certain level of significance and degrees of freedom) is obtained from the t table, which can be found in Gujarati (1995). Then for each $B^{\wedge}_i$ of the column vector of **B**$^{\wedge}$, a t-ratio with (N-K) degrees of freedom should be calculated from

$$t^* = (B^{\wedge}_i - B_i) / se(B^{\wedge}_i), \tag{26}$$

where $B^{\wedge}_i$, an element of the estimated **B**, is the *ith* estimated coefficient; B_i is the hypothesized value of the *ith* B$^{\wedge}$; and $se(B^{\wedge}_i)$ is the *ith* standard error of estimate of the *ith* B$^{\wedge}$, obtained by taking the square root of the ith variance from the variance-covariance matrix. For example 5, $Se(B^{\wedge}_0) = 0.08837$, $Se(B^{\wedge}_1) = 0.22338$, and $Se(B^{\wedge}_2) = 0.23065$. And for the deviational-form model (example 6), the standard errors of the estimates are $Se(B^{\wedge}_1) = 0.22338$ and $Se(B^{\wedge}_2) = 0.23066$. A hypothesis is rejected at a certain level of significance, for example, ($\alpha = 0.05$), if the tabulated t-ratio (obtained from the table) is less than the calculated t-ratio (obtained from equation [26]).

Example 7: Use example 1 to test the hypotheses that $Ho = B_1 = B_2 = 0$ against $Ha: Bi \neq 0$ (i = 1 and 2) at $\alpha = 0.05$.
Solution: As the standard errors of the estimates are just found, the t-ratios for the

estimated coefficients can be obtained by using equation (26).The required results are

$$t^*_{B0} = -0.26267/0.08837 = -2.97$$

$$t^*_{B1} = 0.853386/0.22338 = 3.82$$

$$t^*_{B2} = 0.192764/0.23065 = 0.84.$$

Hence, the hypothesis $B_2 = 0$ is accepted, because 0.84 is within the acceptance region.That is, the tabulated t-value of $t_{0.05(2,\ 7)}$ is greater than 0.84. But the hypotheses $B_0 = 0$ and $B_1 = 0$ are rejected because their calculated t-ratios are greater than the tabulated t-values. Figure 12.6 shows these results.

Figure 12.6. **Rejection Regions**

Example 8: Find a 95 percent confidence interval for the three population coefficients of example 1.
Solution: As long as we know the standard error of each estimated coefficient, we can find a confidence interval for each of the population (true) coefficients. For example, a 95 percent confidence interval for B_1 is equal to

$$B^{\wedge}_1 \pm t_{a/2,\ n-k}\ se(B^{\wedge}_1). \tag{27}$$

As we know the value of each term in equation (27), the required interval becomes

$$0.853386 \pm t_{0.05(2,\ 10-3)}\ (0.22338)$$

$$0.853368 \pm (2.365)(0.22338)$$

$$0.3251 < B_1 < 1.3816.$$

This interval indicates that 95 percent of the time the true (population) regression coefficient (B_1) is less than 1.3816 and greater than 0.3251.The intervals for B_0 and B_2—or any B_i—can be found by generalizing equation (27). That is,

$$B^{\wedge}_i \pm t_{a/2,\ n-k}\ se(B^{\wedge}_i) \tag{27'}$$

for i = o, 1, ..., k estimated coefficients.

The Coefficient of Determination (R^2)

The sample coefficient of determination, R^2, is determined by

$$R^2 = ESS / TSS, \tag{28}$$

where ESS and TSS are the *error sum of squares* and the *total sum of squares*, respectively; or it can be found from

$$R^2 = B^{\wedge t}X^tY / Y^tY. \tag{29}$$

After subtracting the correction factor for means, which is NY^{-2}, the coefficient of determination becomes

$$R^2 = [B^{\wedge t}X^tY - NY^{-2}] / [Y^tY - NY^{-2}]. \tag{30}$$

This coefficient is used to measure the percentage of the total variation in the dependent variable explained (or accounted for) by the independent variables. The closer R^2 is to one, the better the model fits the data--*goodness of fit.*

Example 9: For example 1, find the coefficient of determination, R^2.
Solution: $Y^- = 2.306$, $N = 10$, $Y^tY = 53.731$, $B^{\wedge t}X^tY = 53.72734$, and $NY^{-2}= 10(2.306)^2 = 53.2$; therefore,

$$R^2 = (53.72734 - 53.2)/(53.731 - 53.2) = 0.993.$$

This value indicates that the model fits the data very well because about 99 percent of the variation in the dependent variable is accounted for by the independent variables (or the regression model).

Example 10: Find the coefficient of determination for the deviational-form model of example 2.
Solution: Using equation (29) yields

$$R^2 = b^{\wedge t}x^ty/y^ty = 0.550989/0.55464 = 0.993.$$

The Adjusted R^2

The adjusted R^2, written as R^{-2}, is obtained from

$$R^{-2} = [1 - (1 - R^2)](N-1/N-k). \tag{31}$$

This coefficient measures the percentage of the total variation in the dependent variable accounted for by the independent variables (the model) after adjusting the regression model to the number of independent variables. In other words, if there is a model with four independent variables, and there is another model with two independent variables, then R^2 of the former model is larger than R^2 of the latter model. It follows that the effect of the additional variables has to be eliminated. To do so, the adjusted R^2 is used rather than R^2.

Example 11: Find the adjusted R^2 for the regression model of example 1 (or example 9).
Solution: Using equation (31), the result is

$$R^{-2} = [1 - (1 - 0.993)](9/7) = 1 - [0.009] = 0.991.$$

Analysis of Variance

Analysis of variance (ANOVA) studies the components of the sum of squares (TSS): ESS and RSS, where the latter means the residual sum of squares, (Pindyck and Rubinfield 1991).These components are shown below in a table usually called the *analysis of variance table*.

Table 12.1. **Analysis of Variance**

Source of Variation	SS*	df	MSS**
Due to regression (ESS)	$B^{\wedge t}X^tY - NY^{-2}$ (ESS)	K-1	$[B^{\wedge t}X^tY - NY^{-2}]/[K-1]$
Due to residual (RSS)	$Y^tY - B^{\wedge t}X^tY$ (RSS)	N-K	$[Y^tY - B^{\wedge t}X^tY]/[N-K]$
Total (TSS)	$Y^tY - NY^{-2}$	N-1	

*Sum of squares. **Mean square error.

From this table one can calculate the **F** statistic, which is required to test the overall significance (or the joint hypothesis) of the general linear model. This statistic is obtained from

$$F^* = [B^{\wedge t}X^tY - NY^{-2}]/(K-1) \ / \ [Y^tY - B^{\wedge t}X^tY]/(N-K) \qquad (32)$$

$$= ESS/(k-1)/RSS/(N-k).$$

This calculated value of F can be compared to the tabulated (critical) value of $F_{a,k-1,n-k}$ at the level of significance of (α) to decide whether the null joint hypothesis (Ho: $B_1 = B_2 = ... = B_k = 0$) can be rejected or accepted. Note that (K-1) represents the numerator degrees of freedom in the F table (Gujarati 1995, pp. 810–815), and (N-K) represents the denominator degrees of freedom in the same table. In sum, if F^* is greater than $F_{a(k-1,N-k)}$, the null hypothesis is rejected. It should be stated that the statistic F^* can also be obtained from

$$F^* = R^2/(k - 1) / (1 - R^2)/(N - K).$$ (33)

Example 12: Find the F^* statistic and test the null joint hypothesis at $\alpha = 0.05$ for the general linear model of example 1.
Solution: Use equation (33) to obtain

$$F^* = 0.993/2 / 0.007/7 = 496.5.$$

The critical value of $F_{0.05\ (2,\ 7)}$ is 4.74, a value obtained from the F table. As the calculated F^* exceeds the critical (tabulated) value of F, the null hypothesis is rejected, suggesting that the independent variables (the model) do have significant impact on the dependent variable.

Prediction From the General Linear Model

The general linear model can be used to forecast a single value of the dependent variable Y, which is $Y^\wedge_f$, given new values for the independent variables. The predicted value can be obtained from

$$Y^\wedge_f = RB^\wedge,$$ (34)

where $B^\wedge$ is the estimated coefficients and R is a row vector containing the given values of the independent variables along with a value of one for X_0 (to keep the same value of the intercept).

Example 13: Use example 3 and assume that the new X value is 3. Predict the Y value (the predicted value of the forecast period) using equation (34).

$$\text{Solution: } Y^\wedge_f = RB^\wedge = \begin{bmatrix} 1 & 3 \end{bmatrix} \begin{bmatrix} -0.29368 \\ 1.038211 \end{bmatrix} = 2.821.$$

The Forecast Error e_f

The actual value of the forecast period is

$$Y_f = RB + U_f \tag{35}$$

and the forecast error is defined by

$$e_f = Y_f - Y^\wedge_f. \tag{36}$$

Using equations (34) and (35) in equation (36), we obtain

$$e_f = RB + U_f - RB^\wedge = -R(B^\wedge - B) + U_f. \tag{37}$$

Thus, the variance of e_f will be

$$var(e_f) = E\{[-R(B^\wedge - B) + U_f][-R(B^\wedge - B) + U_f]^t\}. \tag{38}$$

After simplification, equation (38) becomes

$$Var\,(e_f) = E\{[-R(B^\wedge - B) + U_f][(B^\wedge - B)^t(-R)^t + U^t_f]\}$$

$$= \sigma^2 R(X^tX)^{-1}R^t + \sigma^2$$

$$= \sigma^2[R(X^tX)^{-1}R^t + 1] \tag{39}$$

where σ^2 can be estimated by $S^{\wedge 2}$, whose value has already been found from equation (25). It follows that the 95 percent confidence interval for Y_f (the predicted, individual value of Y) is

$$Y^\wedge_f \pm t_{a/2(n-k)}\, S/[1 + R(X^tX)^{-1}R^t]. \tag{40}$$

Example 14: Find a 95 percent confidence interval for Y_f using the results of examples 3 and 13.
Solution: We need to find $S^{\wedge 2}$. We know that $Y^tY = 53.731$,

$$X^tY = \begin{bmatrix} 23.0600 \\ \\ 58.2726 \end{bmatrix}, \quad B^\wedge X^tY = 53.729, \quad e^te = 0.002;$$

hence, $S^{\wedge 2} = 0.002/(10 - 2) = 0.00025$, and

$$\mathbf{R(X^tX)^{-1}R^t} = \begin{bmatrix} 1 & 3 \end{bmatrix} \begin{bmatrix} 12.37393 & -4.90173 \\ -4.90173 & 1.95756 \end{bmatrix} \begin{bmatrix} 1 \\ 3 \end{bmatrix} = 0.58159.$$

Consequently, equation (40) becomes

$$2.821 \pm 2.306 \, (0.0158)/[1 + 0.58159]$$

and the confidence interval for Y_f is

$$2.7753 \; < \; Y_f \; < \; 2.8667.$$

Example 15: Find the confidence interval for $E(Y_f)$, the predicted mean value of Y.

Solution: To find the confidence interval for $E(Y_f)$, the variance of e_f must be determined. This variance can be obtained as follows. As

$$\mathbf{Y_f = RB + U_f}$$

$$\mathbf{E(Y_f) = RB}$$

because $E(\mathbf{U_f}) = \mathbf{0}$. After using equation (36) one can obtain

$$\mathbf{e_f = E(Y_f) - Y^\wedge_f = RB - RB^\wedge} \tag{41}$$

and

$$\mathbf{var(e_f) = E\{[-R(B^\wedge - B)][-R(B^\wedge - B)]^t\}} \tag{42}$$

And equation (42) can be simplified into

$$\mathbf{var\,(e_f) = E\{[-R(B^\wedge - B)][(B^\wedge - B)^t(-R)^t]\}}$$

$$\mathbf{= E[-R(B^\wedge - B)(B^\wedge - B)^t R^t]}$$

$$\mathbf{= RE[(B^\wedge - B)(B^\wedge - B)^t]R^t.}$$

Hence,

$$\text{var}(e_f) = R\sigma^2 (X^tX)^{-1}R^t$$

or

$$\text{var}(e_f) = \sigma^2 R(X^tX)^{-1} R^t. \tag{43}$$

Thus, the 95 percent confidence interval for $E(Y_f)$ becomes

$$Y^\wedge_f -^+ t_{a/2\,(n-k)} S/[R(X^tX)^{-1}R^t]. \tag{44}$$

Example 16: Find a 95 percent confidence interval for $E(Y_f)$ using the results of examples 13 and 14.

Solution: We know that $Y^\wedge_f = 2.821$, $t_{0.05(2,\,8)} = 2.306$, $S = 0.0158$, and $R(X^tX)^{-1}R = 0.58159$; hence, the confidence interval for the predicted mean value, $E(Y_f)$, becomes

$$2.821 \pm (2.306)(0.0158)/(0.58159)$$

or

$$2.793 < E(Y_f) < 2.849.$$

Some Economic Applications

Numerous economists have utilized the general linear model in testing economic propositions. In this section, a very short list of applications will be introduced.

Demand Function

Pindyck and Rubinfeld (1991) developed a model for demand for housing. The *demand function* was specified as

$$Q = B_1 P^{B2} Y^{B3} U,$$

where Q is the number of houses consumed by a family (of a total of 3,120 families) per year, P is the price of one house in that area, Y is the family income, and B2 and B3 are coefficients to be estimated. For the purpose of statistical estimation, the demand function can be rewritten as

$$Log\ Q = Log\ B_1 + B2\ Log\ P + B3\ Log\ Y + Log\ U.$$

The estimated regression equation was

$$\text{Log}^\wedge Q = 4.17 - 0.247 \text{ Log } P + 0.96 \text{ Log } Y \qquad R^2 = 0.371$$

$$(0.11)\ (0.017) \qquad (0.026)$$

$$(t = 14.53)\ \ (t = 36.9).$$

The coefficients were statistically significant at $\alpha = 0.05$, because the calculated t-ratios $[(-0.247/0.017) = -14.53$ and $(0.96/0.026) = 36.9]$ are greater than the tabulated $t_{0.05,\ 3117} = 1.96$. To obtain the price elasticity of demand, we differentiate the estimated equation with respect to P to obtain

$$\partial(\text{Log}^\wedge Q)/\partial P = (1/Q)(\partial Q/\partial P) = -0.247\ (1/P).$$

After multiplying the above result by P, the elasticity is determined as $e_p = -0.247$. Similarly, the income elasticity of demand is found by differentiating the estimated equation with respect to Y:

$$\partial(\text{Log}^\wedge Q)/\partial Y = (1/Q)(\partial Q/\partial Y) = 0.96\ (1/Y)$$

and multiplying the outcome by Y, the elasticity is $e_y = 0.96$.

Production Function

The *production function* shows the relationship between input and output. This function is usually written as

$$Y = AL^a K^b U,$$

where Y is the gross domestic product; A is a constant showing the technological progress; K is capital; L is labor; and a and b are coefficients to be estimated. In some cases the production function can be specified as

$$Y = A_o e^{mt} L^a K^b U,$$

where t is time and m is the rate of disembodied technical change reflecting the shift in the production function--growth of output through efficiency, not through the growth of labor and capital. Intriligator (1978) estimated the above production function for Norway for the period 1900 to 1955 (excluding 1940 to 1945), and the statistical result was

$$\text{Ln}^\wedge Y = 2.62 + 0.76 \text{ Ln } L + 0.20 \text{ Ln } K + 0.018\ t$$

$$(0.10)\quad (0.19)\quad (0.003).$$

From the estimated equation, one can obtain the elasticity of output with respect to L and K. The elasticities were

$$e_L = \partial Ln\ Y/\ \partial Ln\ L = [(1/Y)(dY/dL)] / [1/L] = 0.76$$

and

$$e_K = \partial Ln\ Y/\ \partial Ln\ K = [(1/K)(dY/dK)] / [1/K] = 0.20.$$

In addition, the rate of disembodied technical change, m, was 1.8 percent annually. This rate suggests that if the two resources, labor and capital, do not increase, the output will increase by 1.8 percent a year.

Inflation

The monetarist school argues that the inflation rate is related positively to the growth rate of the money supply. Accordingly, the following equation was specified for the United States over the period 1880 to 1986:

$$CPI = bo + b_1 MG_{t-2} + U,$$

where the CPI and MG_{t-2} indicate the growth rates of price level (the consumer price index) and the quantity of money, respectively. The estimated equation turned out to be

$$CPI^{\wedge} = 2.856 - 0.044 MG_{t-1} \qquad R^2 = 0.422$$

$$(-0.85).$$

The statistical result does not support the monetarist position, because the coefficient (-0.044) does not have the right sign nor is it significantly different from zero.

International Competition

It is argued that net exports (NE)--exports minus imports--are negatively related to labor cost per unit of output (LC). To measure this relation, the following estimated equation is obtained for the American economy over the period 1965 to 1988:

$$NE^{\wedge} = 73.07 - 1.03\ LC \qquad R^2 = 0.77$$

$$(-8.58)$$

This suggests that if labor cost per unit of output (which is the ratio of labor compensation to productivity) increases by 1 percent, net exports will decline by 1.03 percent.

Cost Function

Wilson (1981) employed the regression analysis to estimate the *cost function* of the savings and loan (S&L) associations. The specification of this cost was

$$AOE = Bo + B_2TA + B_3TA^2 + B_4NB/TA,$$

where AOE is the average operating expense, which is the measure of the long run average cost, defined as the ratio of total operating expense to total assets; TA is the total assets, which measures the output of the S&L associations; and NB is the number of branches from which NB/TA was used to measure the effect of branching on AOE.

Complete observations were obtained for 86 savings and loan associations, and the estimated cost for 1975 was

$$A\hat{}OE = 0.0238 - 6.153(10^{-5})TA + 5.3359(10^{-8})TA^2 + 0.192NB/TA \qquad R^2 = 0.6$$

$$(2.84) \quad (2.37) \qquad\qquad (2.63) \qquad\qquad (2.69)$$

where the value of the t-statistic is reported below each coefficient, indicating significant coefficients. If NB/TA is assumed to be zero (no branch case), and the cost is minimized by differentiating the estimated equation with respect to output (TA), the minimum total asset of each S&L association should equal $574 million. Any level of TA that is less than this minimum value will indicate an inefficiency in that particular S&L association.

Appendix : Rules of Expectations

Some of the important rules of expectations (Newbold 1995; Koutsoyiannis 1977) are outlined in this appendix. These rules consist of the following:

1. $E(X) = \Sigma\ p_i X_i$, where p_i is the probability of X_i, $\Sigma\ p_i = 1$, and E is the expectations operator. Actually, the expected value of X is the mean value of the random variable X.

2. $E(k) = k$, that is, the expected value of the constant k is the same constant.
    For $Y = aX + b$, where Y is a random variable, X is a fixed variable, and a and b are constants, the expected value is

$$E(Y) = E(aX) + E(b) = a\ E(X) + b.$$

3. If X and Y are two random variables, then

$$E(X + Y) = E(X) + E(Y).$$

4. The variance of a random variable X is

$$\text{var}\ (X) = E[X - E(X)]^2.$$

For $Y = aX + b$, the variance of Y is

$$\text{var}\ (Y) = E[aX + b - aE(X) - b]^2$$

$$= a^2\ E[X - E(X)]^2$$

$$= a^2\ \text{var}(X).$$

Problems

1.   For the following annual data on Y and X

$$\mathbf{Y} = [12 \quad 14 \quad 16 \quad 15 \quad 13 \quad 17 \quad 18 \quad 20 \quad 25 \quad 31]$$
$$\mathbf{X} = [2 \quad 3 \quad 4 \quad 6 \quad 8 \quad 7 \quad 10 \quad 11 \quad 13 \quad 17]$$

find the impact of X on Y. Test the hypothesis that $B_o = 0$ against $B_o \neq 0$ at $\alpha = 0.05$. Find R^2 and R^{-2}. Predict Y if X = 20, and find a 95 percent confidence interval for the slope of the function. (Solve the problem by using the matrix and nonmatrix approach.)

2.   For the following annual data on Y, X_1 and X_2

$$Y = [12 \quad 14 \quad 16 \quad 13 \quad 17 \quad 18 \quad 20 \quad 25 \quad 31 \quad 33]$$
$$X_1 = [2 \quad 3 \quad 4 \quad 6 \quad 8 \quad 7 \quad 10 \quad 11 \quad 13 \quad 17]$$
$$X_2 = [15 \quad 14 \quad 13 \quad 11 \quad 9 \quad 8 \quad 6 \quad 5 \quad 3 \quad 2]$$

Find the impacts of X_1 and X_2 on Y. Test the estimated coefficients and find R^2 and R^2. Report the regression results. Find the 95 percent confidence interval for the estimated coefficients. Predict Y if $X_1 = 18$ and $X_2 = 1$.

3.   Use the *Economic Report of the President* as a source of data and test the validity of the Keynesian import function where imports depend on gross domestic product.

4.   Use the *Economic Report of the President* as a source of data and test the validity of the Keynesian consumption function, where consumption (C) depends on gross domestic product (Y). Also, find the MPC and the multiplier. Extend this specification by including Y_{t-1} as a second independent variable. Do the same by including C_{t-1} as a second independent variable.

5.   Using the data of problem 1, find the two normal equations to quantify the estimated coefficients.

6.   Using the data of problem 2, estimate the coefficients by using the deviation from the mean data.

7.   Use the data of problem 2 to find d^*.

References

Aitken, A.C. 1948. *Determinants and Matrices*. Edinburgh: Oliver and Boyd.

Allen, R.G.D. 1938. *Mathematical Analysis for Economists*. New York: St. Martin's Press.

————.1956. *Mathematical Economics*. London: Macmillan.

Anderson, David R., Dennis J. Sweeney, and Thomas A. Williams. 1978. *Essentials of Management Science: Applications to Decision Making*. St. Paul, MN: West Publishing.

————. 1985. *An Introduction to Management Science: Quantitative Approaches to Decision Making*. 4th ed. St. Paul, MN: West Publishing.

Balinski, M. L. 1965. "Integer Programming: Methods, Uses, Computation." *Management Science* 12 (November):253-313.

Baumol, W. J.. 1952. "The Transaction Demand for Cash: An Inventory Theoretic Approach," *Quarterly Journal of Economics* 24, 3 (November): 545-56.

————. 1977. *Economic Theory and Operations Analysis*. 4th ed. Englewood Cliffs, NJ: Prentice-Hall.

Bierman, Harold, Jr., Charles P. Bonini, and Warren H. Hausman. 1977. *Quantitative Analysis for Business Decisions*. 5th ed. Homewood, IL: Richard D. Irwin.

Bierman, Scott, H., and Luis Fernandez. 1993. *Game Theory with Economic Applications*. New York: Addison-Wesley.

Binger, Brian R., and Elizabeth Hoffman. 1988. *Microeconomics with Calculus*. Glenview, IL: Scott, Foresman.

Boulding, Kenneth, and W. Allen Spivey. 1960. *Linear Programming and the Theory of the Firm*. New York: Macmillan.

Bressler, Barry. 1975. *A Unified Introduction to Mathematical Economics*. New York: Harper & Row.

Brown, R.G. 1967. *Decision Rules for Inventory Management*. New York: Holt, Rinehart, & Winston.

Bunn, Derek W. 1984. *Applied Decision Analysis*. New York: McGraw-Hill.

Chenery, Hollis B., and Paul G. Clark. 1959. *Interindustry Economics*. New York: Wiley.

Chernoff, H., and L. Moses. 1959. *Elementary Decision Theory*. New York: Wiley.

Chiang, Alpha C. 1984. *Fundamental Methods of Mathematical Economics*. 3d ed. New York: McGraw-Hill.

Dantzig, George B. 1963. *Linear Programming and Extensions*. Princeton, NJ: Princeton University Press.

Domar, E. 1946. "Capital Expansion, Rate of Growth and Employment." *Econometrica* 14: 137-47.

Dorfman, Robert. 1953. "Mathematical, or 'Linear,' Programming: A Non-mathematical Exposition." *American Economic Review* 43 (December): 797-825.

Dorfman, Robert , Paul Samuelson, and Robert M. Solow. 1958. *Linear Programming and*

Economic Analysis. New York: McGraw-Hill.

Dowling, Edward T. 1980. *Mathematics for Economics.* New York: McGraw-Hill.

Draper, Jean E., and Jane S. Klingman. 1972. *Mathematical Analysis: Business and Economic Applications.* 2d ed. New York: Harper & Row.

Emerson, Jarvin M., and F. Charles Lampheer. 1975. *Urban and Regional Economics: Structure and Change.* Boston: Allyn & Bacon.

Friedman, J. 1990. *Game Theory With Applications to Economics.* 2d ed. New York: Oxford University Press.

Gardner, Roy. 1995. *Games for Business and Economics.* New York: Wiley.

Gass, Saul I. 1985. *Linear Programming: Methods and Applications.* 5th ed. New York: McGraw-Hill.

Glaister, Stephen. 1984. *Mathematical Methods for Economists.* 3d ed. New York: Basil Blackwell.

Goldberg, S. 1971. *Introduction to Difference Equations.* New York: Wiley.

Gomory, Ralph E. 1963. "An Algorithm for Integer Solutions to Linear Programs." In *Recent Advances in Mathematical Programming,* ed. Robert Graves and Philip Wolfe. New York: McGraw-Hill.

Gondolfo, Giancarlo. 1971. *Mathematical Methods and Models in Economic Dynamics.* New York: North Holland.

Gujarati, D.N. 1995. *Basic Econometrics.* 3d ed. New York: McGraw-Hill.

Hadley, G. 1962. *Linear Programming.* Reading, MA: Addison-Wesley.

————.1973. *Linear Algebra.* Reading, MA: Addison-Wesley.

Hadley, G. and T.M. Whitin. 1963. *Analysis of Inventory Systems.* Englewood Cliffs, NJ: Prentice-Hall.

Henderson, James M., and Richard E. Quandt. 1980. *Microeconomic Theory: A Mathematical Approach.* 3d ed. New York: McGraw-Hill.

Hillier, F.S., and G.J. Lieberman. 1980. *Introduction to Operation Research.* 3d ed. San Francisco: Holden-Day.

Holloway, Charles A.1979. *Decision Making Under Uncertainty: Models and Choices.* Englewoods Cliffs, NJ: Prentice-Hall.

Intriligator, M.D. 1978. *Econometric Models, Techniques, and Applications.* Englewood Cliffs, NJ: Prentice Hall.

Kamien, Morton I., and Nancy L Schwartz. 1981. *Dynamic Optimization: The Calculus of Variations and Optimal Control in Economics and Management.* New York: North Holland.

Kantorovich, L. 1960. "Mathematical Methods of Organization and Planning Production." *Management Science* 6: 366–422. (Originally published by the Publication House of the Leningrad State University, 1939).

————.1965. *Essays in Optimal Planning.* White Plains, New York: International Arts and Sciences Press.

Kemeny, John J., and J. Laurie Snell. 1960. *Finite Markov Chains.* New York: Van Nostrand.

Kolman, Bernard. 1980. *Introductory Linear Algebra With Applications.* 2d ed. New York: Macmillan.

Koopmans, Tjalling C. 1951. *Activity Analysis of Production and Allocation,* ed. T.C. Koopmans. New York: Wiley.

Koutsoyiannis, A. 1977. *Theory of Econometrics.* 2d ed. Totowa, NJ: Barnes & Noble.

Lambert, Peter J. 1985. *Advanced Mathematics for Economists: Static and Dynamic*

Optimization. London: Basil Blackwell.

Lapin, Lawrence L. 1991. *Quantitative Methods for Business Decisions.* 5th ed. New York: Harcourt Brace Jovanovich.

Leontief, Wessily. 1986. *Input-Output Economics.* 2d ed. Oxford: Oxford University Press.

Lipschutz, Seymour. 1968. *Linear Algebra.* New York: McGraw-Hill.

Luce, Duncan R., and Howard Raiffa. 1957. *Games and Decisions: Introduction and Critical Survey.* New York: Wiley.

McDonald, J. 1975. *The Game of Business.* New York: Doubleday.

McGuigan, James R., and R. Charles Moyer. 1986. *Managerial Economics*, 4th ed. St. Paul, MN: West Publishing.

Miernyk, William H. 1965. *Elements of Input-Output Analysis.* New York: Random House.

————. 1967. *Impact of the Space Program on a Local Economy.* Morgantown, WV: McClain Printing.

Miller, Ronald E., and Peter D. Blair. 1985. *Input-Output Analysis: Foundations and Extension..* Englewood Cliffs, NJ: Prentice-Hall.

Newbold, Paul. 1995. *Statistics for Business and Economics.* 4th ed. Engelwood Cliffs, NJ: Prentice Hall.

Ostrosky, Anthony L. Jr., and James V. Koch. 1986. *Introduction to Mathematical Economics.* Prospect Heights, IL: Waveland Press.

Perlis, S. 1952. *Theory of Matrices.* Reading, MA: Addison-Wesley.

Pindyck, Robert S., and Daniel L. Rubinfield. 1991. *Econometric Models and Economic Forecasting.* 3d ed. New York: McGraw-Hill.

Pleeter, Saul. 1980. *Economic Impact Analysis: Methodology and Applications*, ed. Saul Pleeter. Boston: Martinus Nijhoff Publishing.

Rapoport, A. 1960. *Fights, Games and Debates.* Ann Arbor: University of Michigan Press.

Richardson, Harry W. 1972. *Input-Output and Regional Economics.* London: Weidenfeld and Nicolson.

————. 1979. *Regional Economics.* Urbana: University of Illinois Press.

Robbins, L. 1932. *An Essay on the Nature and Significance of Economic Science.* London: Macmillan.

Ross, Sheldon M. 1983. *Stochastic Processes.* New York: Wiley.

————. 1985. *Introduction to Probability Models.* 3d ed. New York: Academic Press.

Salvatori, D. 1982. *Statistics and Econometrics.* New York: McGraw-Hill.

Samuelson, P. 1939. "Interactions between the Multiplier Analysis and the Principle of Acceleration." *Review of Economics and Statistics* 21: 75-78.

Sasaki, Kyohei. 1969. *Statistics for Modern Business Decision Making.* Belmont, CA: Wadsworth.

Schlaifer, Robert. 1969. *Analysis of Decisions Under Uncertainty.* New York: McGraw-Hill.

Shubik. M. 1987. *Game Theory in the Social Sciences: Concepts and Solutions.* Cambridge, MA: The MIT Press.

Silberberg, Eugene. 1990. *The Structure of Economics: A Mathematical Analysis.* 2d ed. New York: McGraw-Hill.

Taha, Hamdy A. 1987. *Operations Research: An Introduction.* 4th ed. New York: Macmillan.

Thompson, Gerald E. 1971. *Linear Programming: An Elementary Introduction.* New York: Macmillan.

————. 1976. *Management Science: An Introduction to Modern Quantitative Analysis and Decision Making.* New York: McGraw-Hill.

Tintner, Gerhard, and Charles B. Millham. 1970. *Mathematics and Statistics for Economists.* 2d ed. New York: Holt, Rinehart & Winston.

Varian, Hal R.1996. *Microeconomic Analysis,* 4th ed. New York: W. W. Norton.

Von Neuman, J., and O. Morgenstern. 1944. *Theory of Games and Economic Behavior.* Princeton, NJ: Princeton University Press.

Wilson J.H. 1981. "A Note on Scale Economies in the Savings and Loan Industry." *Business Economics* (January): 45–49.

Winkler, Robert L., and William L. Hayes. 1975. *Statistics: Probability, Inference, and Decision.* 2d ed. New York: Holt, Rinehart & Winston.

Winston, Wayne L. 1987. *Operations Research: Applications and Algorithms.* Boston, MA: Duxbury Press.

Yamane, T. 1964. *Statistics, An Introductory Analysis.* New York: Harper & Row.

Zagare, F. 1984. *Game Theory: Concepts and Applications.* Beverly Hills, CA: Sage.

Index

About the Author

Adil H. Mouhammed, associate professor of economics, has taught at the University of Illinois at Springfield since 1988. Dr. Mouhammed received his M.A. and Ph.D. degrees in economics from the University of Nebraska, Lincoln, and his B.A. degree in economics from Al-Mustansyriah University; Baghdad, Iraq, in 1975. His articles have appeared in various journals, including the *Review of Radical Political Economics*, the *Canadian Journal of Development Studies*, the *Journal of Economics*, the *Scandinavian Journal of Development Alternatives*, the *International Social Science Review*, and the *Social Science Quarterly*.

When Dr. Mouhammed is not teaching economics, he spends his time with his wife, Majda, his two boys, Mouhammed and Hayder, and his daughter, Shayma, traveling the breadth of the United States and enjoying its natural beauty.